PLANT POWER

PLANT POWER

TRANSFORM YOUR KITCHEN, PLATE, *and* LIFE
with MORE THAN 150 FRESH *and* FLAVORFUL
VEGAN RECIPES

NAVA ATLAS

PHOTOGRAPHS BY HANNAH KAMINSKY

HarperOne
An Imprint of HarperCollins*Publishers*

HarperOne

FIRST EDITION

Designed by Campana Design
Photographs by Hannah Kaminsky used by permission.

Library of Congress Cataloging-in-Publication Data

Atlas, Nava.
    Plant power : transform your kitchen, plate, and life with more than 150 fresh and flavorful vegan recipes / by Nava Atlas ; photographs by Hannah Kaminsky. — First edition.
        pages cm
    Includes index.
    ISBN 978–0–06–227329–1   1.   Vegan cooking. 2.   Cooking (Vegetables) 3.   Kitchens—Management.
4. Veganism—Health aspects. 5.   Nutrition. 6.   Veganism—Moral and ethical aspects. I. Title.
    TX837.A846 2014
    641.5'636—dc23   2013043023

14 15 16 17 18   RRD(C)   10 9 8 7 6 5 4 3 2 1

CONTENTS

PART ONE: PLANT-POWERED LIVING 1

My Personal Journey **4**

The Benefits of a Plant-Powered Life **6**

The Top Myths About Plant-Based Diets **10**

Plant-Based Nutrition Basics **12**

Setting Up Your Plant-Powered Pantry **17**

Produce: Stocking Up and Storing **35**

Non-Produce Staples for the Refrigerator **39**

Kitchen Tools **44**

Meal Planning Basics and Strategies **45**

Top Ten Make-Aheads to Get You Through the Week **51**

Plant-Powered Food Shopping Savvy **52**

Organic Produce **57**

Five Easy Ways to Eat More Leafy Greens **60**

Plant-Powered Families, Couples, and Singles **62**

PART TWO: PLANT-POWERED RECIPES AND MENUS 70

1: Plant-Powered Protein **76**

2: Bountiful Bowlfuls: Main Dish Soups and Stews **118**

3: Plant-Powered Pasta and Pizza **152**

4: Asian Express **190**

5: Tortilla Specialties **224**

6: Wraps, Sandwiches, and Burgers **252**

7: More Veggie Love: Salad and Vegetable Entrées and Sides **284**

8: Breakfast, Lunch, Snacks, and Healthful Sweets **332**

Acknowledgments **357**

Universal Conversion Chart **359**

Recipe Index **361**

Subject Index **373**

PART ONE

PLANT-POWERED LIVING

Interest in plant-based diets and lifestyles has grown exponentially in the past decade. And with it there has been a proliferation of books, websites, publications, and other media promoting plant-based eating. Want to know more about the health benefits of eating plant foods? The information is easy to find. Ethical considerations? Check. Recipes, plain and fancy? They're out there in droves. Vegan cupcakes and other treats free of animal products? They're showing up everywhere.

Whether you call it vegan, plant-based, plant-strong, or plant-powered, it's in the air, but all the information floating around can be overwhelming—and confusing. What this book aims to give you is one neat volume on how to put the edible elements of the plant-powered lifestyle into practice—easily, practically, and joyfully, every day. In *Plant Power,* you'll find not just a collection of accessible, adaptable recipes but also a slew of helpful tips and ideas. Whether you're looking to transition to a fully vegan lifestyle or just want to explore a more plant-based diet, you'll find plenty of inspiration and encouragement in these pages.

Going beyond *why* you should adopt this way of life, this guide will focus on *how* to do it, from setting up a whole-foods, plant-based pantry and refrigerator and planning practical menus to choosing the best seasonal fresh foods and streamlining daily meal preparation. And what are whole foods? They're simply foods that are as close to the state they're in when harvested—unprocessed and natural, like brown rice, beans, carrots, and apples, for instance.

This book is also a celebration. A switch to a plant-based diet doesn't mean sacrifice or missing out; we get to revel in and enjoy the most flavorful, colorful, life-enhancing foods available. Depending on how consistently you practice it, you may find that adopting this way of life confers numerous benefits, including the expected ones—increased energy, fewer digestive issues, less frequent and shorter colds, and maybe even weight loss. And though many who've gone plant-based have reported such perks and more, this book isn't a health and weight-loss guide. Rather, it shows us how to have more fun in the kitchen, become more intuitive and creative with whole foods, and gain an appreciation for how downright delicious foods in their most elemental, unprocessed form can be! What I'd like you to take away from these pages is a message of ease, abundance, and pleasure. Cooking with the most healthful (not the most exotic or expensive) ingredients nature has to offer is a joy, not a chore!

Many people transitioning to a plant-based diet go vegetarian first. It's a logical step, and many have gone the route of giving up red meat, then poultry, and finally fish. And similarly, those deciding to go from vegetarian to vegan give up dairy first, then eggs—or vice versa. But I know plenty of people who, having experienced a major health event (such as a heart attack or cancer), go plant-based all at once. In other cases, it's not illness but ethics that inspires a cold-turkey (so to speak) conversion. Suddenly what we didn't know—or didn't want to know—becomes too compelling to deny or ignore.

This book's aim is not to convince you to go vegan. Ultimately that's a decision you need to make with your heart as much as with your head. With recipes, menus, and strategies (along with Hannah Kaminsky's mouthwatering photographs), this book aims to take you on an enjoyable visual journey, demonstrating how gratifying and delicious a plant-powered life can be. If a daily habit of meat, dairy, and/or junk food falls away or at least diminishes, so much the better for your health, the planet, and the cause of compassion. Any steps taken are to be applauded; going vegan need not be an all-or-nothing proposition.

Whether your decision to adopt a more plant-based way of life is driven by health or ethical concerns, you still need to eat every day. This guide will take you through the practical steps in the kitchen and tempt you with many delectable and doable meals.

To that end, I won't plunge you into a world of unfamiliar and expensive foods. That's not what a whole-foods, plant-based diet is about. On the contrary: unless meat is at the center of your plate at each meal each day, you'll find lots of common ingredients and preparations, including pastas, pizzas, sandwiches and wraps, soups, stews, stir-fries, and salads—the kinds of meals you're already familiar with. I'm going to show you how easy it is to make more healthful, plant-powered versions of the kinds of meals you already like.

That said, you won't find highly processed meat substitutes in this book, either. That's not what plant-based eating is about. Meat substitutes are helpful for many who are making the transition. But in general, they're salty, expensive, and often contain questionable ingredients such as "isolated soy protein." Enjoy them as a treat occasionally if you must, but you don't need a cookbook to tell you how to use them.

Classic Veggie Chili (page 140) with Corn-Kernel Cornbread (page 144)

What about ingredients for all these plant-based meals? I do my grocery shopping in a town where there are two major supermarkets and a couple of small but well-stocked natural foods stores. There are plenty of CSA (community-supported agriculture) farms and farm markets, though these are seasonal. We have no Whole Foods, no Trader Joe's, and no ethnic groceries. While these might be fun to have close at hand, they're not at all necessary for enjoyment of plant-based living.

Many supermarkets now have natural foods aisles that bear a striking resemblance to natural foods superstores—only without the fancy prices. In addition, ethnic foods aisles in regular supermarkets now offer items that were once arcane, like chipotle peppers in adobo sauce and hoisin marinade. My favorite supermarket meets almost all of my basic organic produce needs, perfect for those months when no farm markets are open. From what I've seen during my travels, it seems this trend is spreading. So if I can fulfill my family's plant-based needs where I live, chances are you can, too.

The food writer Michael Pollan summed up the goal for a sound and healthy way of life when he popularized the succinct phrase "Eat food. Not too much. Mostly plants." It sounds so simple, but for many it's an elusive goal. This book's aim is to help you get there in a way that's easier and more delectable than you ever thought possible.

My Personal Journey

By training, I'm a visual artist, illustrator, and graphic designer. I've never been a chef or caterer. I've never even worked in a restaurant, unless you count the summer I was sixteen, when I was a very confused and slow waitress. It was at just about that age that I went vegetarian, and in that era, the word "vegetarian" was not yet casually bandied about. I was a pioneer within my family (in which I was the youngest by far), though it was more an act of rebellion than conviction. I never liked meat and couldn't bear to look at it on my plate; it often made me want to cry, and sometimes I shed actual tears.

My announcement that I was giving up all meat was met with chagrin by my parents; my mom told me I would have to cook for myself, as she wasn't about to prepare two different meals. This response is quite typical, as I've learned from my many years of corresponding with kids and teens who wonder how to get their parents on board. What I did was to start preparing my own meals—concoctions centered on brown rice, lentils, barley, wheat berries, and all the brown foods prevalent in that hippie-vegetarian era. As meals go, they were nothing special, but to me they were heavenly. They must not have been half bad, since my family wanted to try my meals, and I was happy to share. Soon even my skeptical mom was making meals that I could eat, an improvement over the bland, meaty Eastern European Jewish fare I'd grown up with.

Fast-forward past my college days—once armed with my bachelor of fine arts degree from the University of Michigan, I fulfilled my dream of moving to New York City to become a freelance illustrator and graphic designer. In short order, I married a fellow starving artist who was an aspiring vegetarian but no cook himself. He was delighted by the meals I created on our modest budget. He urged me to write down the recipes I concocted so that I could repeat them.

Before long I found myself with a collection of scrawled recipes and an idea for an unusual cookbook that would combine my illustration and design skills with my recipes and even my love of literature. The result was *Vegetariana.* Since there were still relatively few vegetarian cookbooks out at the time, it reached a wide audience and was the springboard for my new, unexpected career as cookbook author.

Though I still enjoyed making art and writing other forms of nonfiction, producing cookbooks was my primary occupation as we raised our two kids. By then we'd moved out of New York City to the Hudson Valley, where we still make our home. We raised our children as vegetarians from the start. Had information about animal products been as available back then as it is today, I'm sure we would have all gone vegan much earlier. Just before the kids hit adolescence, the Internet burst forth, and the funky facts about dairy appeared on my radar. Interestingly, my son, then ten years old, was first to declare himself vegan. History had repeated itself—as the youngest in my family, I was the first to go vegetarian; years later, the youngest child in my husband's and my family paved the way for the rest of us, who followed suit quickly. Later in this section, I'll discuss more of the mealtime strategies I used as my kids grew up (see pages 62–65).

To sum up, I wanted our meals to be easygoing and fun, not anxiety-producing, as my childhood meals were. When my husband and I ate with our children, I tried to ensure that our meals were built around pleasant associations and were devoid of power struggles. As a result, my kids have grown up to prefer healthful food. It comes back to joy, pleasure, and, above all, gratitude. Why should those of us fortunate enough to have enough to eat every day (unlike so many people around the world and even around this country) turn mealtime into a battleground and a chore? By savoring and being grateful for the abundance of whole foods we have at our disposal, a powerful message is conveyed: this is what we choose to eat; this is sustainable. And best of all, eating this way makes the world a better and more compassionate place.

The Benefits of a Plant-Powered Life

Call it what you will. But for simplicity's sake, let's go with the term "vegan." Vegans avoid all animal products, including eggs, dairy, and even honey. Vegetarians, on the other hand, avoid only meat, fowl, and seafood. But for most vegans, ethical considerations weigh as heavily as, if not more heavily than, health and environmental considerations in their lifestyle decision. Concern for animal welfare and the embracing of a more compassionate lifestyle also mean that ethical vegans won't wear leather, fur, or wool. In general, any products that are animal-derived or that contain animal by-products are avoided.

Many people would love to adopt a lifestyle that includes more fresh and whole foods and is better for their health. The goal of this book is to provide a template for you to do just that. Many vegan cookbooks, as well as other books about plant-based diets, assume that the reader is transitioning toward becoming vegan or is there already. This one doesn't—it's for anyone who wants a more plant-strong diet, whether that diet is going to be followed full-time or not. No matter where you are on the path, a bit of motivation is always helpful, so I'd like to present you with some benefits of this way of life.

HEALTH

Research has shown that populations who eat primarily plant-based diets suffer from a fraction of the ailments that meat eaters suffer from. These ailments include heart disease, certain forms of cancer, and adult-onset (type 2) diabetes. When it comes to cancer, studies of vegetarians and vegans have shown lower cancer rates compared to the general population. Here are a few more benefits:

- Fiber-rich plant-based diets may reduce the risk of cancers of the digestive organs and may protect against heart disease. Health experts agree that eating foods high in fiber and complex carbohydrates can help reduce the risk of heart disease. In addition, plant-based proteins are more likely to reduce cholesterol levels, whereas animal protein raises them.

- Vegetarians, and especially vegans, tend to have lower overall rates of obesity, not a small point to make at a time when 60 percent of American adults are overweight.

Some three hundred thousand yearly deaths occur from obesity-related diseases, including not only those listed above but also hypertension and kidney disease. Obesity-related diseases also include osteoporosis and arthritis. A well-planned diet that centers on whole grains, legumes, vegetables, and fruits provides a feeling of fullness that keeps the body fueled and satisfied for hours.

Sizzling Tempeh or Tofu Fajitas (page 230)

Thai-Style Pineapple-Coconut Rice (page 210)

- Those who eat plant-based diets are less likely to contract virulent food-borne illnesses caused by *E. coli, Salmonella,* and *Listeria.* Children are especially vulnerable where food-borne illness is concerned, as their immune systems may not be developed enough to withstand the dangers of contaminated meat products.

- If you're intrigued by the promise of longevity, studies conducted on Seventh-day Adventists (who advocate a plant-based diet) have shown that they typically live an average of seven to fifteen years longer than meat eaters.

- Finally, farmed animals are fed a steady diet of antibiotics and often hormones that have no place in their system, let alone yours. There have been many well-researched articles on how this practice can lead to antibiotic resistance in humans, and it is rather alarming.

ETHICS

For ethical vegans, the driving motivation is about compassion toward all sentient beings. Those who have chosen to go vegan appreciate knowing that their food choices can be not only tasty and healthful but compassionate and humane as well. Animal agriculture is unimaginably cruel. Each year, tens of billions of animals are confined, overcrowded, and disfigured. Their demise in the slaughterhouse (which, by the way, is no picnic for its human workers—slaughterhouse jobs are among the most hazardous) is almost a mercy compared to the way in which they are compelled to live their short lives.

What about dairy cows? Isn't using dairy all right, since the animal doesn't have to die? Suffice it to say that after my family visited an "ethical" dairy farm some years ago, my ten-year-old couldn't go vegan fast enough. And consider—humans are the only animals who drink the milk of another species and the only animals who drink milk after being weaned. I don't want to beat you over the head with this kind of information, but any discussion of a plant-based life needs to at least broach the subject. If you do want to learn more, films like *Peaceable Kingdom, Earthlings,* and *Vegucated* are eye-openers and sometimes life-changers.

ENVIRONMENT

Getting most or all of your nutrition needs from plant-based foods means that you're "eating low on the food chain." This practice is not only good for your health, but by "voting" with your fork you're potentially reducing the demand for animal products, which will in turn reduce the demand for animal feed, which will in turn reduce the use of the pesticides and antibiotics needed to grow it. Consider the following:

- The raising of livestock depletes enormous land and water resources and contributes to the loss of millions of tons of irreplaceable topsoil each year. It takes twenty-five gallons of water to produce a pound of wheat, but it takes 390 gallons of water to produce a pound of beef.

- And I don't want to be gross here, because we're about to talk about recipes, so I'll say this as simply as possible: animal waste is a major pollutant of soil, water, and air.

- From the practical standpoint of food security (having access to sufficient and nutritious food at the local level), animal agribusiness cements a system that feeds those who already have enough to eat. Vast land resources are given over to grow the grain used for feeding animals (most of it not organic, so there are pesticide and genetically modified organism [GMO] issues as well)—land that could be used to grow food for direct human consumption.

- Animal agriculture is a major contributor to the greenhouse gases that lead to climate change. According to a 2006 report by the Food and Agriculture Organization (FAO) of the United Nations, the global animal agriculture sector emits 18 percent of human-induced greenhouse gas emissions, and, according to the report, "mapping has shown a strong relationship between excessive nitrogen in the atmosphere and the location of intensive farm animal production areas." Furthermore, deforestation for farm animal production carries devastating repercussions for the environment as well.

If you're at all interested in the impact of animal agriculture on climate change, this concise, one-page report based on the FAO's findings, available at the website of the Humane Society of the United States, can change your worldview: tinyurl.com/3hsh46c. So while you're eating the yummy meals in the pages ahead, you can also feel good knowing that your food choices can help mitigate the climate crisis.

The Top Myths About Plant-Based Diets

You'll never get enough protein on a plant-based diet. While longtime vegans regard the "Where do you get your protein" question as an annoyance, I look at it as an opportunity to enlighten the curious. It truly isn't difficult to get sufficient good-quality protein on a whole-foods plant-based diet. This topic is covered on pages 14–17 ahead.

It's easy to get weak and sickly on a plant-based diet. Weak and sickly? Tell that to the growing number of elite athletes who are fueling their feats on entirely plant-based regimens. In *Becoming Vegan,* authors Brenda Davis, RD, and Vesanto Melina, MS, RD, write, "The vast majority of studies assessing the dietary intake and nutritional status of vegans reassure us that well-planned vegan diets can supply adequate nutrition . . . It is important to recognize, however, that as with non-vegetarian or lacto-ovo vegetarian diets, vegan diets can be both adequate and inadequate."

It might be convenient to argue that unless some planning is done, a plant-based diet can leave its practitioner feeling less than optimal. But the same can be true of any regimen, including the standard American diet. Just look at the statistics, and the damage done to our collective health is obvious and alarming.

Plant-based diets are by definition more healthful than other diets. Some "junk-food vegans" and "carboholics" believe that simply by eliminating animal products they're automatically healthier. Not true. A diet based on baked goods and snacks, even if they're vegan, won't promote good health in the long run.

You'll always be hungry, as the food isn't filling enough. I hear this one a lot, but, oddly, I hear it only from people who don't actually eat a plant-based diet. They're anticipating hypothetical hunger rather than reporting actual results. If you're an active, athletic person, a salad for lunch might not sustain you until dinnertime. But many plant-based staples are made up of complex carbohydrates that the body digests slowly and steadily, fueling you for hours at a time. I defy anyone to have a hefty (yet low-calorie) bowl of Classic Veggie Chili (page 140) for lunch or dinner and feel hungry anytime soon after! Yet this kind of filling fare doesn't result in an unpleasant, overly stuffed feeling.

Many people who adopt plant-based diets report feeling lighter and cleaner. Animal foods are harder to digest than plants and might indeed leave you feeling full, but it's a kind of heaviness that's not fueling. Your body adjusts to a new level of satiety.

Plant-based diets are centered on soy products, and soy is bad for you. Admittedly, there are many people who have soy allergies and sensitivities, and this is a legitimate concern. As with any food to which one is allergic or sensitive, one should avoid it if these conditions exist. Otherwise, soy is a fine addition to plant-based diets, so long as you consume it in its most basic forms. Fermented soy foods, which include miso and tempeh, are considered the best ways to use soy, followed by tofu, edamame (fresh green soybeans), and soy milk.

There's so much contradictory information—and disinformation—available concerning soy products. But according to the Physicians Committee for Responsible Medicine, "Evidence to date indicates that soy products may reduce the risk of breast cancer and breast cancer recurrence. They do not appear to have adverse effects on the thyroid gland, but may reduce the absorption of thyroid medications. The benefits of soy products appear to relate to traditional soy products, not to concentrated soy proteins."

Note that even soy proponents such as PCRM warn against overuse of soy protein isolate, the form of soy found in meat substitutes and protein shakes. Any form of concentrated protein, no matter what the source, can have adverse effects. If you're concerned about soy, read the well-researched article by PCRM on their website at www.pcrm.org/health/health-topics/soy-and-your-health.

Plant-based diets are boring and restrictive. If this book can dispel but one myth, I would want it to be this one! Before going vegan more than a decade ago, I worried that family meals might be terribly restrictive, but making the transition to vegan home cooking was surprisingly easy. With a wide variety of nondairy cheeses and milks so readily available, we were still able to enjoy favorite recipes, including the easy comfort foods to which our kids gravitated.

The bottom line, though, is that plant-based diets aren't just about substituting. The optimal plant-based diet abounds with fresh vegetables and fruits—organic whenever possible—plus whole grains, beans and other legumes, nuts, seeds, and minimally processed soy foods such as tofu and tempeh. Everyone I know who has adopted a plant-based diet claims that their culinary horizons have expanded. When you realize that there are new grains to discover, more veggies to love, and ethnic cuisines to explore, you'll see that this way of life is about addition, not subtraction. Even if you have no intention of going fully vegan, anyone can benefit from incorporating more plant-based meals into his or her repertoire. You'll be pleasantly surprised at how hearty and satisfying plant-powered meals can be.

Plant-Based Nutrition Basics

As mentioned, there's a lot of solid information out there on plant-based diets from a nutritional angle—and many thorough and informative books on the subject. If you want to delve more deeply into plant-based or vegan nutrition, I recommend the following books:

> *Forks Over Knives*, edited by Gene Stone
> *Vegan for Life* by Jack Norris, RD, and Virginia Messina, MPH, RD
> *The China Study* by T. Colin Campbell, PhD, with Thomas M. Campbell II
> *The Complete Idiot's Guide to Plant-Based Nutrition* by Julieanna Hever, MS, RD, CPT
> *The New Becoming Vegetarian* by Vesanto Melina, MS, RD, and Brenda Davis, RD
> *Becoming Vegan* by Brenda Davis, RD, and Vesanto Melina, MS, RD

In addition, a good reference is *Main Street Vegan* by Victoria Moran with Adair Moran—a friendly tome about committing fully to being vegan in the world. The books in the list above show you how the engine works, so to speak, while *Main Street Vegan* teaches you how to drive the car. But enough of flimsy metaphors: to prevent stepping into territory that has been amply covered by people who are qualified to do so—that is, plant-based dietitians—let's cover the big topics briefly.

Center your diet on a variety of vegetables (including a generous amount of dark leafy greens), fruits, whole grains, legumes, nuts and seeds, and minimally processed soy foods, and you can count on taking in a wide range of vitamins, minerals, and micronutrients. Eat this way and you'll be enjoying the benefit of a high-fiber diet as well. Other nutritional needs you'll want to be aware of include the following:

CALCIUM

The dairy industry and the advertising industry have succeeded in equating calcium with milk and cheese. But other sources have questioned whether dairy is a reliable source of absorbable calcium. Some studies have shown that countries with the highest consumption of dairy products have the highest incidence of osteoporosis. Some researchers hypothesize that animal protein may actually leach calcium from bones.

Controversies aside, calcium is crucial for the formation and maintenance of bones and teeth, in addition to other functions. It's best absorbed in conjunction with adequate amounts of vitamin D. But dairy products aren't the only way to get calcium. Some good plant-based sources are tofu (if prepared with calcium sulfate—check the package nutrition label), tempeh, tahini, quinoa, sesame seeds, almonds, and dark green leafy vegetables (especially collard greens and spinach). Some of the best sources of large doses of calcium are enriched foods such as fruit juices and nondairy milks.

VITAMIN B_{12}

Essential for general growth and for the functions of the blood cells and nervous system, vitamin B_{12} looms large in discussions of plant-based diets. Tempeh and some sea vegetables contain naturally occurring B_{12}, though they're not considered reliable sources. In general, B_{12} isn't found in plant sources, and so anyone going completely vegan needs to take a B_{12} supplement as well as look for foods fortified with it, which include nondairy milks and some breakfast cereals.

Vegan multivitamin supplements usually contain an adequate amount of B_{12}; there are also tiny vitamin B tablets that can be taken sublingually. Nutritional yeast is another excellent source of B_{12}. With its slightly cheesy flavor, it has become a standard in many plant-based kitchens, where it's valued as a condiment as well as a supplement. Vitamin B_{12} is essential for good health, and only a small amount is required—2.4 micrograms per day for adults.

IRON

Iron deficiency is commonplace, no matter what one's dietary preference is. Iron is more easily and completely absorbed by the body when it's contained in food rather than dietary supplements, which can wreak havoc on the digestive system. Fortunately, many plant foods are rich in iron. These include spinach, chard, and other leafy greens as well as broccoli, cabbages, and dried fruits. Absorption of iron is aided by foods containing vitamin C, including oranges and their juice, bell peppers, grapefruit, and orange-fleshed veggies such as winter squashes and pumpkin.

VITAMIN D

Vitamin D is needed for optimal calcium and phosphorus absorption, which in turn are crucial to the health of bones and teeth. Like calcium, vitamin D is often associated with milk, but it isn't a component of dairy products at all. Nondairy milk is enriched with it the same way dairy milk is. It's widely accepted that the best way to get enough vitamin D is from brief (about fifteen minutes) daily exposure to sunlight. This isn't always possible, especially in the cold months. If your diet is sparse in foods containing vitamin D, and you don't have access to a few minutes of direct sun, make sure to take a supplement. Vitamin D is an ingredient in many standard multivitamins. If you're planning to go fully vegan, be aware that vitamin D_3 is often derived from animal sources; D_2 is from nonanimal sources, such as yeast.

PROTEIN

The body can manufacture all but nine of the twenty-two amino acids that make up proteins. These nine amino acids are referred to as essential amino acids and must be derived from food. That is why getting sufficient good-quality protein is crucial. The operative word here is "sufficient"—this isn't a case where more is necessarily better. Many Americans eat twice as much protein as they need. Excess protein can't be stored, and its elimination puts a strain on the kidneys and liver. Too-high protein consumption is linked to kidney disease, cancers of the colon, breast, prostate, and pancreas, and even osteoporosis.

The amount of protein a person needs is based on a simple calculation. The recommended daily allowance (RDA), established by the National Academy of Sciences, states that an adult in good health needs 0.36 grams of protein per pound of body weight. Thus a 160-pound man needs about fifty-eight grams of protein a day, and a 120-pound woman needs about forty-three grams.

There are exceptions to the RDA guidelines. Pregnant and lactating woman need considerably more protein—add at least twenty-five grams of protein per day—as do those recovering from surgery and other physical trauma. Infants and children need more total protein per body pound than adults, and the protein must be of high quality and rich in amino acids. For toddlers age one through three years, calculate 0.5 grams per pound of body weight; children four through thirteen years, 0.43 grams per pound; and teenagers, 0.39 grams per pound.

"How do you get your protein?" is a question that just won't go away. It's often dismissed as unimportant, but it is possible to become protein-deficient on any sort of poorly planned regimen.

The myth that vegan diets can't and don't provide adequate protein is tenacious. However, there's plenty of evidence that a varied, whole-foods diet that provides sufficient calories has little chance of falling short in protein. As more people cut back on their intake of meat and dairy products, incorporating alternative protein sources into the diet is of paramount interest. With the exception of sugars and oils, most foods have at least some protein. Whole grains, legumes, minimally processed soy foods, and nuts and seeds all offer high-quality protein. Many common vegetables also contain protein. The bottom line is that a vegan diet when properly varied will, like any other diet, provide ample protein.

The following is by no means an exhaustive list of plant-based protein-rich foods, but it's a pretty thorough rundown of the most common sources—the ones you're likely to use most:

BEANS AND LEGUMES

The quantities of protein listed here are all based on a half-cup serving of cooked beans and legumes. But beans and legumes are so blessedly low in calories and fat that if you need more protein, a one-cup serving isn't unreasonable—so you can double the protein count listed below.

Black beans= 8 grams
Chickpeas = 7 grams
Lentils, brown = 6 to 8 grams
Lentils, red = 13 grams
Pinto beans = 6 grams
Split peas (green or yellow) = 8 to 10 grams

TOFU, TEMPEH, AND SEITAN

Though tempeh is a terrific source of protein, it has an intense flavor and texture, and in some dishes, 2 ounces is a more than adequate serving size.

Seitan (2 ounces) = 14 grams
Tempeh (4 ounces) = 20 to 21 grams
Tofu, firm (4 ounces) = 10 grams
Tofu, extra firm (4 ounces) = 8 grams
Tofu, baked (SoyBoy brand, 2 ounces) = 10 grams

NUTS

The protein counts below are all based on quarter-cup servings.

Almonds = 8 grams

Cashews = 5 grams

Peanuts = 7 grams

Pistachios = 6 grams

Walnuts = 4 grams

NUT BUTTERS

The protein counts below are all based on 2-tablespoon servings.

Almond butter = 8 grams

Cashew butter = 6 grams

Peanut butter = 8 grams

SEEDS

Chia seeds (2 tablespoons) = 4 grams

Flaxseeds (2 tablespoons) = 3.8 grams

Hemp seeds, also known as hemp hearts (2 tablespoons) = 6 grams

Pumpkin seeds (¼ cup) = 8 grams

Sunflower seeds (2 tablespoons) = 3.5 grams

GRAINS

The protein counts below are based on half-cup servings of cooked grains. But, like legumes, whole grains are low in fat and high in fiber. If you need a higher-than-average quantity of protein, you could eat a one-cup serving for double the protein listed below.

Barley = 8 grams

Brown rice = 3 grams

Millet = 3 grams

Oatmeal (old-fashioned, not instant) = 3 grams

Oats, steel-cut = 5 grams

Quinoa = 4 to 4.5 grams

PASTAS

The protein counts below (except for soba noodles) are based on a one-cup serving of cooked pasta.

Durum wheat pasta = 7 grams

Quinoa pasta = 4 grams

Soba noodles (2-ounce serving) = 7 to 8 grams

Spelt pasta = 12 grams

Whole-wheat pasta = 7 grams

VEGETABLES

Asparagus (1 cup cooked) = 4 grams
Broccoli (1 cup cooked florets) = 2 to 3 grams
Brussels sprouts (1 cup cooked) = 4 grams
Kale (1 cup wilted, packed) = 2 grams
Spinach (1/2 cup wilted, packed) = 3 grams
Sweet potato (1 medium, baked) = 2.25 grams

MORE...

Other vegetables and fruits, including butternut squash, green peas, blueberries, and Medjool dates, have between 1 and 2 grams of protein per serving. So it does all add up! Even ordinary foods such as bread (whole grain, of course) add to your day's total protein intake. A slice of whole-grain bread has between 2.5 and 4 grams of protein, so a two-slice sandwich gives you 5 to 8 grams before you even add the filling. So a simple peanut-butter-and-banana sandwich on whole-grain bread provides nearly a third of the daily protein requirement of an average-size woman. Then there's nutritional yeast (Red Star brand). It's not only a great source of protein but also of vitamin B_{12}—you can get 130 percent of your daily dose from a mere 1 1/2 tablespoons (which equals 8 grams).

Setting Up Your Plant-Powered Pantry

One of the biggest obstacles to eating well every day is having no clue what to make, let alone having the ingredients on hand to make an appealing (or, on some days, merely edible) meal. How many times have you stood in your kitchen at 6:30 or 7:00 in the evening, one hand reaching for the drawer that holds the take-out menu?

A well-stocked pantry is the first step to carrying out easy meal plans. The thorough (but, I hope, not overwhelming) list presented here serves as a guideline for stocking up on key ingredients. Few, if any, of the foods on this list are exotic or arcane. Most can be obtained at a well-stocked supermarket, and the vast majority offer economy as well as nutrition. Transitioning to a more plant-based kitchen is a process, so don't feel that you need to purchase everything at once or make this transition over the course of one weekend. If you're starting at the base of the learning curve, try approaching one group of foods at a time. For example, during one month you can learn about and stock up on several varieties of beans—sampling them, trying a few recipes—to see which are your favorites. The next month you can explore grains, or leafy greens, and so on.

Remember, this doesn't have to be an all-or-nothing approach. Certain foods will work for you, and some won't. Go at your own pace. You'll be most successful if you focus on foods that you already like and use them in dishes that appeal to you most.

So many commonly available foods are good for you. No one could possibly eat them all every day or even every week. Get to know and incorporate these healthful foods (most of which have the added bonus of being delicious) in a way that suits your schedule and taste. The aim is to make this transitional process a joy and not just another tedious task on your already too-long-to-do list!

CONVENIENT FOODS VERSUS CONVENIENCE FOODS

With most everyone living such overfilled lives, it's often unrealistic to think that we can cook a from-scratch meal each and every night. I love to cook, and do so a lot. (Duh! Thirteen or so cookbooks!) But occasionally even I find myself in the kitchen at seven P.M., wasted from the day, and wanting a full, delicious, and healthful meal to magically appear.

As a hugely busy person who, despite being a cookbook author, has little time to spend in the kitchen, I've always had much empathy for the time-crunched cook. And that's why I'm totally on board with natural, good-quality, convenient foods. Let's make a distinction between convenience foods and convenient foods. The former are completely prepared foods, such as frozen dinners and canned soups—things that, for the most part, just require being heated and served. We need not delve into those: after all, this is a cookbook, and I'm not that far gone.

Convenient foods, on the other hand, are fresh or whole foods that are precut or in some way partially prepared and lend a hand to the weary cook. On days when an entire meal needs to be on the table in less than an hour (and sometimes less than half an hour), shortcuts are a necessity. Using natural, convenient products such as salsa, salad dressings, marinara sauce, canned beans or lentils, flavored baked tofu, and the like smooth the way when time is short.

The availability of high-quality natural convenient foods allows you to strike a balance when time is an issue. For example, when I make a meal centered on pizza, I prefer to start with store-bought natural marinara sauce and ready-made pizza crust so that I can allocate my time to prepping fresh veggie toppings for the pizza and making a big salad to accompany it. Sometimes the choice rests on seasonal availability; when tomatoes are at their peak, I prefer to make my own salsa. Otherwise, I let Paul Newman, may he rest in peace, or other worthy salsa creators, make it for me. All this being said, homemade versions of many of these kinds of meal helpers, including marinara sauce, pizza crust, salsa, and lots more, are presented in the recipe chapters—the choice is always there and always yours!

Buy convenient products in the natural foods aisle of your supermarket or your natural foods store. Read labels. You'll see that many natural brands of staples such as canned beans and prepared sauces are low in sodium and have no added sugar, unlike their supermarket counterparts.

A top pantry staple, canned beans play a role in a variety of easy-to-prepare meals. And just tossing a half cup per serving into some part of the meal (such as a salad) is a great way to add quality protein. Look for beans without additives. Canned beans do have a lot of sodium, but some of that can be taken out by draining and rinsing them. Organic canned beans are a better choice than supermarket brands, as they're packed with far less sodium, and you can even find cans that are free of BPA (bisphenol A), the controversial chemical that's part of the standard canning process. See more information on BPA in chapter 1, page 91.

Canned beans are an economical form of protein, and buying them dried, in bulk, is even more economical. If you're inclined to cook dried beans from scratch, so much the better! There seems to be a bit of a revival of that practice in the plant-based culinary community. If you have a pressure cooker or a slow cooker, you might want to explore this possibility. These tools are at opposite ends of the spectrum—pressure cookers get the job done fast, while slow cookers . . . well, you can figure that one out. But the set-it-and-forget-it mode on your slow cooker does bring out the flavor of beans in a most appealing way. Look for tips on cooking beans from scratch in chapter 1, pages 89–90.

Beans are sturdy and versatile across so many categories of cooking. They're as welcome in soups and salads as they are in hearty stews and chilis. They team well with pasta and whole grains. If you're a big fan of beans, keep all kinds on hand—you'll use them up fast, and if you don't, they keep for a long time, whether canned or dried. If you're only an occasional user of beans and legumes, just keep a modest amount of your favorites on hand. Here's a list of common varieties:

- Black beans
- Black-eyed peas
- Cannellini
- Chickpeas (garbanzo beans)
- Great northern beans
- Kidney beans
- Navy beans
- Pink beans
- Pinto beans
- Red beans

There are lots of other varieties, including heirlooms, and you can delve into them if you develop a passion for beans.

LENTILS AND SPLIT PEAS

Even though common lentils (sometimes called brown or green lentils) don't take as long to cook as dried beans do, canned lentils have become more common as cooks have gotten ever more time-crunched. When you want to put dinner on the table quickly, even the relatively fast thirty minutes or so that lentils take to cook can be a bit much. Organic canned brown lentils taste good and hold their shape nicely. When you have more time and inclination to cook them from scratch, please do so. Cooking tips can be found in chapter 1, page 91.

Tiny red lentils cook up quickly (between fifteen and twenty minutes), and I highly recommend considering them a pantry staple. They cook to a delectably mushy texture that makes a great base for soups and stews. They're good in burgers, too—like the Quinoa and Red Lentil Burgers in chapter 6 (page 274). You'll find red lentils in the bulk section of natural foods stores.

Beluga lentils (a tiny black variety) and French lentils (an even tinier brown variety) are lovely; they're interchangeable with the more common brown and green lentils. They don't taste all that different, but they are small and cute and hold together well when cooked, giving the dishes in which they're used a little more flair.

Green and yellow split peas are easily digestible and high in protein. These two varieties can be used interchangeably, and are best known for their use in thick, hearty soups. You can also add them to winter stews. They're especially compatible with eggplant, potatoes, and hardy greens. For such a tiny legume—which even comes halved, for goodness' sake—they take a surprisingly long time to cook—almost as long as dried beans. Any soup or stew made with split peas is a great choice for those times when you want to make a huge pot of soup that will last for several days and freeze well.

GRAINS

Grains provide the complex carbohydrates and fiber that contribute to a healthy lifestyle. Truthfully, I used to use quick-cooking grains such as couscous and bulgur (both made from wheat) more often before quinoa burst on the scene. As a grain food (though it is, like many grains, technically a seed), quinoa's protein quality and digestibility are hard to beat. If by chance you don't care for quinoa and you aren't gluten-free, bulgur and whole-grain couscous are still good choices.

Apart from adding character to meals, whole grains are good sources of fiber and protein and are low in fat. Because the bran and germ are left intact, they're also fine sources of B vitamins, vitamin E, and an array of minerals.

Whole grains are economical when bought in bulk, but I'm not a huge fan of buying them in large quantities. If you're going to store whole grains at room temperature, don't buy more than what you'll use up in two to three cool months or just one warm month. Grains can and do go rancid. If your kitchen is really warm during the hot summer months, refrigerate the grains. And if you see that they aren't being eaten, freeze them, uncooked, in one-cup or 1½-cup portions.

There are lots of whole grains to discover, though in this book I mainly use quinoa and brown rice. Occasionally you'll encounter whole-grain couscous, bulgur, millet, and wild rice. Try a new whole grain from time to time, and buy as needed. For specifics, see chapter 1, page 112. Following is a basic list of staple grains; stock only what you're most likely to use:

- Barley
- Brown rice (long-grain, medium-grain, basmati)
- Bulgur
- Couscous (preferably whole-grain)
- Millet
- Quinoa
- Wild Rice

My favorite way to store them is in clear jars on open kitchen shelves along with my dried legumes. Not only is this an attractive (and inexpensive) form of kitchen decor, having them on display also serves as a reminder to use them!

NUTS, SEEDS, AND THEIR BUTTERS

Eaten in moderation, nuts and seeds are a great source of concentrated protein in the plant-based diet and are abundant in valuable B vitamins, vitamin E, and a wide range of minerals, including calcium, zinc, and iron. Moderation is key—a cup of nuts every day is way too much of a good thing, as you'll be adding lots of fat and calories to your daily intake. To be exact, nuts contain an average of forty-five grams of fat and 529 calories per cup. But cut that down to a quarter cup or less, and it's within reason. Though nuts and seeds are between 50 and 70 percent fat, these fats are the primarily good-for-you polyunsaturated and monounsaturated varieties. Surprisingly, the type of fat found in nuts has been shown to lower overall blood cholesterol while maintaining "good" cholesterol.

Moderation is key to enjoying nuts—perhaps an ounce or two a day can be a fantastic addition to a healthy diet. Combine them with dried fruits for an out-of-hand snack. And judicious sprinklings add luscious flavor and good fats to grain and noodles dishes, veggie stir-fries, salads, hot and cold breakfast cereals, and desserts.

One downside to nuts and seeds is that some varieties can be pricey. Look for dry-roasted or raw nuts in bulk. If you find good deals, purchase extra—nuts freeze well, as do seeds. Another caveat is that nuts are one of the top food allergens. But if that doesn't apply to anyone in your household, this food group will be a boon to you and yours.

Quart-size or pint-size jars make good storage containers for nuts and seeds bought in bulk. Their high fat content makes them prone to rancidity, so buy only what you'll use within a month or so; if your kitchen stays warm during the summer, it's best to refrigerate or freeze nuts and seeds.

NUTS TO KEEP ON HAND

- Almonds (whole nuts are good for snacking; slivered or sliced almonds work well in recipes)
- Cashews (use dry-roasted cashews for snacking and garnishes; raw cashews for sauces)
- Peanuts
- Pecans
- Pistachios
- Walnuts

FOR OCCASIONAL USE

- Hazelnuts
- Macadamia nuts
- Pine nuts (a rich treat; they're expensive as well as perishable)

MOST USEFUL COMMON SEEDS

- Pumpkin seeds
- Sunflower seeds
- Sesame seeds

A TRIO OF SUPERSEEDS (GET TO KNOW THEM!)

- Hemp seeds
- Chia seeds
- Flaxseeds

As long as nut allergies don't factor in, nut butters, like whole nuts, deserve a prominent place in the plant-based pantry. Just be sure to use natural, organic nut butters with no added fats, salt, sugar, or other potentially unhealthful ingredients.

Though peanut butter is most families' go-to choice because it's so familiar and economical, there are many other kinds of nut and seed butters. Consider cashew butter (creamy and delicious), almond butter, and sunflower butter, both of which are dense, tasty, and nutritious, with a slightly grainy texture. Don't forget tahini, which is basically sesame butter, though it's more commonly referred to as sesame paste.

On average, most nut and seed butters contain about fifteen grams of fat, 180 calories, and six grams of protein per two-tablespoon serving. Nutrient-dense, they're a great choice for growing bodies and a treat for grown-up palates. Used in moderation, nut and seed butters provide healthful fats and a multitude of minerals, B vitamins, and vitamin E.

DRIED FRUITS

Dried fruits are concentrated sources of natural sweetness and nutrition, good sources of dietary fiber, and deserve a more prominent role in the plant-powered pantry. Their natural sweetness enhances hot and cold cereals, trail mixes, and baked goods. Dried fruits are rich in minerals—notably, iron, magnesium, phosphorus, and calcium—as well as vitamins A and C, depending on the fruit.

Many dried fruits available in supermarkets have been treated with sulfur dioxide, which helps them retain their color. This preservative is defined as GRAS (generally recognized as

safe) by the FDA, but it is applied primarily for cosmetic purposes. If you prefer unsulfured dried fruits, purchase them in natural foods stores.

Most of us keep raisins in our pantry, but consider other fruits available in dried form, including dates, prunes, apples, peaches, pears, papayas, mangos, bananas, Turkish and Mission figs, cranberries, cherries, and pineapple. Here are a few ways to enjoy dried fruits on a regular basis:

As a snack: Dried fruits are excellent as a naturally sweet snack eaten out of hand, either on their own or mixed with nuts, for children and adults alike.

In baked goods: Raisins, dates, and currants are commonly used in muffins and quick breads; for a change of pace, try using chopped apricots, peaches, pears, or prunes.

In trail mixes and cereals: Combine whole or chopped dried fruits with nuts and seeds to make high-energy snacks. Go beyond raisins and use other dried fruits, chopped into small bits, to dress up hot and cold cereals.

Liquid sweetener: Cover pitted dates with hot water, let stand for a half hour or so, then blend with any remaining liquid in a food processor or blender to make a naturally sweet substitute for agave nectar, maple syrup, and other plant-based sweeteners.

Embellished fruit and veggie salads: Add any kind of dried fruit (chopped or sliced if large) to fresh fruit salads for variety and texture. Dried cranberries and raisins are delicious in carrot salads and slaws.

Sweet side dishes: Combine dried fruits with sweet vegetables such as carrots, butternut squash, and sweet potatoes. Chopped pitted prunes, Mission figs, cranberries, and raisins are especially good for this purpose.

NATURAL SWEETENERS

While the detrimental effects of simple white sugar and high-fructose corn syrup continue to be debated, there's little doubt that consumers in Western cultures use far too much of both. Yet most of us would be loath to give up sweets altogether, no matter how bad they are for us. While most natural sweeteners aren't nutritional bell ringers, they are generally thought to produce less of a shock to the body's blood sugar level and metabolism than do simple sugars. No matter what kind of sweetener you use, the key is moderation.

Since we won't be delving into baking in this book, I'll save some paper by forgoing a thorough discussion of sweeteners, natural or otherwise. Here's a brief description of the few that are used in the recipes in this book—along with honey, which isn't. Many people embarking on the plant-based path want to consider whether to keep it in their diet or not.

Agave nectar: Agave nectar comes from the same succulent plant from which tequila is derived. The syruplike nectar (which comes in dark and light varieties) is somewhat akin to honey, though not as cloyingly sweet or sticky. For strict vegans who don't use honey, it's a good substitute, and for everyone else, it's a decent all-purpose liquid sweetener. Agave nectar doesn't crystallize, as honey does, and so it has a long shelf life. And it's easier to pour and measure than honey.

Agave nectar can also be used as a substitute for maple syrup, though it does have a milder, less distinct flavor and aroma. Use agave nectar as you would any liquid sweetener in baking (where you can substitute it in a one-to-one ratio with honey or maple syrup), in beverages, and to lend a touch of sweetness to salad dressings (including vinaigrette) and sauces (such as teriyaki).

When agave first gained popularity, it was being touted as the holy grail of sweeteners. It has been praised for having a lower glycemic index than many other liquid and granular sweeteners, causing fewer blood sugar spikes. However, its sugar is mainly in the form of fructose, which some say is even worse for the body than glucose (the main form of sugar in honey, for example). Bottom line: agave nectar is mainly for flavoring and should be used just as sparingly as you'd use any other sweetener.

Honey: Honey isn't customarily used by strict vegans, since it's considered an animal product. Still, many vegans consider it okay to use honey if it's locally sourced and comes from a beekeeper who doesn't smoke out his or her hive boxes. There are numerous articles online arguing for and against the vegan use of honey: search for "vegans and honey" and you'll get both sides of the debate. There's even a term—"beegans"—for vegans who use ethically produced honey.

Natural foods stores offer ways to enjoy this sweetener beyond the common clover variety, from mild alfalfa honey to more complex wildflower honeys to strong, dark buckwheat honey. Since honey is primarily glucose, a simple sugar, it's doubtful whether it's any better for you than granulated sugar. However, it does contain trace amounts of some B vitamins and many minerals. The darker the honey, the more nutrients it contains. More important, honey (especially raw honey) has many antiviral and immune-boosting properties. About half a cup of honey equals the sweetness of one cup of sugar.

Maple syrup: While this well-loved sweetener is mainly sucrose, a simple sugar, it does contain several trace minerals as well as measurable amounts of calcium and iron. Avoid imitation maple syrups; look for those labeled "pure" and graded Grade A or Fancy (Grade A light amber). While you wouldn't want to chug down cupfuls of maple syrup, it remains blessedly uncontroversial and a worthy sweetener to use sparingly.

Molasses: Long prized in southern American cookery, molasses, derived from sugarcane, is arguably the most nutritious of natural sweeteners. Look for organic unsulfured molasses for optimal quality. Molasses is rich in iron and vitamin B_6 and also contains calcium and potassium. Use molasses in sweet potato and root vegetable dishes and to make robust barbecue sauces. Barbados molasses is a close relative of blackstrap molasses; it's somewhat lighter in color and flavor.

Natural granulated sugar: Brand names for natural granulated sugars include Sugar in the Raw, Florida Crystals, and others. You might also enjoy experimenting with coconut sugar. Natural sugar is easy to find in bulk in natural foods stores, where the variations include organic raw sugar (though sugar crystals are not truly raw) and turbinado sugar. Buying this kind of sugar in bulk is the most economical way to purchase it. My personal favorite is organic unbleached sugar. I find it yields excellent results in baking.

DRIED HERBS AND SPICES

Keep a good range of commonly used dried herbs and spices on hand. Depending on the types of dishes or ethnic cuisines you enjoy making most, you'll be inclined toward some seasonings more than others. For example, if you don't care for curries, you won't need to stock up on the blends or individual spices characteristic of Indian cuisine.

One question I get fairly regularly is how to spice plant-based dishes. There's no great difference between spicing plant-based versions of dishes and spicing their meaty counterparts. For example, in a classic marinara sauce, you'd use basil and oregano whether it's meat-based or not. Similarly, Mexican and southwestern-style dishes are seasoned with chilies, cumin, and cilantro. Asian dishes typically use garlic, ginger, and soy sauce. In this department, at least, nothing much changes. Here are a few simple tips for using seasonings to their full advantage:

- When buying dried herbs and spices by weight, buy only what will fit into an average-size spice jar. In other words, don't stock up. Most go a very long way and are at their optimal flavor for up to a year, after which they begin losing their potency.

- Introduce dried herbs and spices into your recipe as early in the cooking process as possible so that they have a chance to develop their flavors. Add fresh herbs toward the middle or even the end of the cooking if you'd like to retain their pronounced flavors.

- Keep dried herbs and spices in a place in your kitchen that is away from heat and moisture.

- Find a way to organize your dried seasonings. It doesn't have to be obsessive or alphabetical, but there should be some way in which you can see what you have and what's running low so that you don't wind up with four jars of cumin, as has sometimes happened in my kitchen. Hannah Kaminsky's kitchen has a nifty pull-out drawer, as shown in the photo on page 30; in another arrangement I admired, a length of narrow molding displayed spices in a long row, which was not only practical but decorative as well. All kinds of ready-made spice racks are useful and can save space.

These common dried herbs and spices are most useful to keep on hand:

Basil
Bay leaves
Black peppercorns
Cayenne pepper
Chili powder
Cinnamon
Cumin (ground)
Curry powder
Dill weed
Nutmeg (ground)
Oregano
Paprika
Red pepper flakes
Rosemary
Thyme

I'm also a big fan of seasoning blends, especially for soups and stews. Particularly useful are a salt-free all-purpose seasoning blend (I discuss my favorite brand, Frontier, in "Seasoning Tips for Plant-Powered Soups and Stews," pages 120–21) and an Italian seasoning blend.

OILS

There's a controversy among experts about whether any oils are necessary at all in a vegan diet. Some say no oil at all; others wish to enjoy a modest amount of oil, especially extra-virgin olive oil, in their diets. Still others say what the heck—I like oil, and I'll keep using as much of it as I want. Honestly, I have no idea who's right, but I fall in the middle. You won't find any dishes in this book that are swimming in oil. Possibly the most oil-rich recipes in this book would be the vinaigrettes.

So far, this practice has not done me or any of my family members any harm as part of a whole-foods, high-fiber diet. But I have no basis to insist that I'm right and that the no-oil people are wrong. Yes, we do need fat in our diets, but there are other ways to get it—nuts, seeds, and my beloved avocados. To that end, I've recommended broth or water as an alternative to oil in all recipes; the choice is ultimately yours.

The most oil you'll find in any recipe, other than those for vinaigrette, will be two tablespoons—which, divided among four or six servings, is a very small amount. To my palate, this small amount adds richness and boosts flavor. The nutritional data following the recipes in this book demonstrate that the difference in calories and fat between the oil and no-oil versions is minimal. Here are a few basic oils to keep on hand and to use in scrupulous moderation:

- **Coconut oil:** Some people swear by coconut oil—it has been suggested that, unlike most fats, it's as easy to digest as a carbohydrate and that it's good for the brain. Some love the slightly sweet coconut flavor. The jury is still out, but if you like coconut oil, use it in moderation. I find it too assertive, but that's my palate's personal view.

- **Dark (or toasted) sesame oil:** Cold-pressed from toasted sesame seeds, this oil lends a nutty, distinctive flavor to Asian preparations. To my mind, it's more of a condiment than a cooking oil; even a little goes a long way.

- **Extra-virgin olive oil:** Extra-virgin olive oil is one of the premier oils that has stood the test of time as both healthful and highly palatable. A primarily monounsaturated oil, EVOO is great for salads, dressings, and low-heat sautéing, especially in Italian, Mexican, and Spanish-style dishes.

- **Safflower, sunflower, peanut, and other high-heat oils:** There are several types of high-heat oils that are good for stir-fries. EVOO isn't for high-heat cooking and doesn't taste right in Asian stir-fried preparations. Use high-heat oils in moderation, of course.

So, whatever happened to canola oil? Much has been said and written, both positive and negative, on the subject. A web search for "canola oil" will result in both favorable and highly unfavorable articles. Proponents claim that it has the best fatty-acid ratio of all oils, including the lowest levels of saturated fat. The opposing viewpoint charges that rape (the plant from which canola oil is derived) is a questionable food source and that nonorganic canola oil is a genetically engineered (GMO) food. If you feel that the pros of canola oil outweigh the cons, consider at least using it in organic form. The canola debate is far from settled, so it seems logical to choose less controversial oils.

PASTAS AND NOODLES

If you're a fan of pasta-centered meals, keep a good supply of different sizes and shapes of pasta in your pantry. Some useful varieties to have on hand include angel hair, thin spaghetti, spirals (rotini), ziti or penne, and linguine. Some short, chunky shapes to consider are cavatappi, gemelli, and farfalle—truly, this is a matter of preference. You'll find a growing array of whole-grain varieties that offer inherent nutritional value beyond pasta's traditional role as a willing receptacle for sauces and vegetables. There are a variety of gluten-free pastas on the market as well; many of these have improved over the years in terms of flavor, texture, and sturdiness.

A few Asian noodles, such as udon, soba, rice vermicelli, and bean threads are available in natural food stores or in the Asian foods aisle and are nice have on hand if you frequently make Asian-style dinners; otherwise, just purchase them as needed. A mini lexicon of Asian noodles appears in chapter 4, page 207.

SILKEN TOFU

This type of tofu is a pantry item, as it comes in 12.3-ounce aseptic packages that can be kept on the pantry shelf indefinitely. Soft and smooth, silken tofu makes good scrambles and, when pureed, is ideal for use as a thickening base for soups, dressings, dips, and sauces. You can even make dessert puddings out of it.

SOY SAUCE

Look for natural brands of soy sauce for best flavor. If sodium is a concern, choose a reduced-sodium variety (which still contains plenty of sodium); gluten-free varieties are also available. Note that mass-produced soy sauces are made with a sped-up fermentation process that does not allow as fine a flavor to develop.

The Japanese-style natural soy sauce (shoyu) that is sold in natural foods stores is naturally fermented and has a full-bodied flavor. It is made of soybeans, roasted wheat, and sea salt. Tamari, also naturally fermented, is a bit stronger and thicker; it also comes in a wheat-free variety. Stored at room temperature, all varieties of soy sauce will keep indefinitely.

CANNED TOMATO PRODUCTS

While it's always nice to use fresh tomatoes, it's difficult to get the juicy, full-bodied variety unless it's July, August, or September. For soups, stews, and sauces, a few canned or jarred tomato products are useful. Ideally, look for organic brands in BPA-free cans.

- Diced, in 14-ounce to 16-ounce cans (fire-roasted or Italian-style offer extra flavor)
- Crushed or pureed, in 14-ounce to 16-ounce as well as 28-ounce cans
- Tomato sauce

VINEGARS

There's no need to go crazy with lots of fancy, expensive vinegars. Two basic vinegars that will get a lot of use in the kitchen are

- Organic apple cider vinegar—an all-purpose vinegar with health benefits
- Red wine or white wine vinegar—this is among the best for salads and vinaigrettes

Optional varieties include the following:

- Balsamic vinegar (dark or white)—also good for vinaigrettes and salads; a modest amount drizzled onto roasted veggies somehow boosts their natural sweetness
- Rice vinegar—this mild white vinegar is useful if you enjoy Asian-style home cooking; it's also a mellow alternative to other white vinegars

ONCE-IN-A-WHILE AND OPTIONAL ITEMS

Depending on what kinds of meals are your favorites, keep the following items on hand if they're frequently used, or buy only as needed:

Barbecue sauce: This familiar tomato-based condiment offers a spiced, sweet-and-salty flavor useful for preparing tofu, tempeh, and seitan in the oven or on the stove top or grill. On the other hand, although I'm not one to shy away from natural condiments, I've yet to find a prepared barbecue sauce that I truly like. Still, if you want to go the prepared route, look for sauces that are made with good-quality sweeteners such as molasses and maple syrup rather than high-fructose corn syrup. As an alternative, make the No-Cook Barbecue Sauce on page 86.

Coconut milk: If you're new to making Thai-style curries and other specialties (including noodle dishes, stews, and sauces), or if these aren't going to be your go-to meals, coconut milk might be an as-needed item. I love those kinds of meals, so I most always keep a small number of cans on hand. Light coconut milk, which contains less fat than the full-fat variety, is preferable. Please note that canned coconut milk is different in flavor and consistency than a coconut milk beverage. You may use an unsweetened coconut milk beverage in place of canned coconut milk in many cases, but not the reverse.

Vegetable broth: For added depth of flavor to soups that aren't long-simmering, like quick Asian-style soups, keep a couple of 32-ounce aseptic cartons of low-sodium (preferably organic) vegetable broth in the pantry. Pacific and Health Valley, especially their organic varieties, are two brands to look for, though there are others. Look for an all-natural ingredients list and a modest amount of sodium.

Lemon or lime juice: By all means, stock fresh lemons and limes if you use them regularly, but for those times when you need one or the other, and you happen to be out, it's handy to keep a bottle of organic lemon and lime juice in the fridge. It's not a big deal to juice a lemon or lime, but when you're out of the fresh fruit, bottled juice is a nifty shortcut. Use it lavishly on salads, as an ingredient in dressings, to make lemonade or limeade, and in other preparations.

Marinara sauce: For quick pizzas and easy pasta dishes, keep a couple of 28-ounce jars of marinara sauce on hand. There are so many flavors available; choose whichever has ingredients that please your palate—garlic, wine, mushrooms, peppers, assorted vegetables, and herbs. Just make sure to choose brands that have no added sugar. Supermarket brands are often loaded with high-fructose corn syrup, and you don't need that at all.

Salsa: Like marinara sauce, salsa comes in numerous varieties and has many uses. Go beyond mild, medium, and hot and choose those with intriguing flavors. Try pineapple or mango salsa, those with added chipotle chilies, or those with a good dose of cilantro. For a change of pace, there's also salsa verde, made of piquant tomatillos.

Thai peanut satay sauce: This sauce, available in the Asian foods aisle of well-stocked supermarkets and natural foods stores, adds a blast of flavor to Asian-style noodle and vegetable dishes.

Produce: Stocking Up and Storing

Stocking up on fresh produce, bolstered by your pantry staples, is a sure route to making nutritious meals, whether you're following a recipe or improvising.

IN THE REFRIGERATOR

Keeping an array of fresh produce in the refrigerator year-round goes a long way toward guaranteeing that you will be able to make healthful and delicious meals on a regular basis. The availability of produce once restricted to a specific season has widened dramatically; still, I prefer to use produce that reflects seasonal availability as much as possible. Here's a basic list of what to keep on hand:

PRODUCE OR CRISPER DRAWERS

Must-have vegetables: Cabbage, lettuce or baby greens, cucumbers, peppers, carrots, celery, hardy greens (kale, collards, chard), leafy greens (baby spinach is my favorite), broccoli, and scallions.

Seasonal and occasional veggies: Depending on how much you use them, these can include cauliflower, eggplant, watercress, broccoli rabe, beets, fresh corn, asparagus, daikon radish, turnips, beets, leeks, brussels sprouts, green beans, yellow summer squash, corn on the cob, jicama, and fennel.

Any spillover that doesn't fit in the drawers, such as large bunches of greens or lots of ears of fresh corn, can go on the shelves.

The fruit drawer: The contents of this drawer vary a bit more than those of the vegetable drawer, as fruit availability still seems to be more seasonal. A few fruits that are always present in my fridge are ripe avocados, lemons, limes, and apples. In the winter, pears and oranges are added to those. In the summer, an array of grapes, cherries, strawberries, blueberries and other berries, stone fruits, and melons should be part of the rotation.

EXTENDING THE LIFE OF YOUR REFRIGERATED PRODUCE

If you're a farm market aficionado, a CSA member, or a simply a produce fan, your produce finds might spill over from the produce drawers onto the shelves. Though not absolutely necessary, food storage containers help extend the life of your fresh foods—not that you want them to linger in your refrigerator, many fruits and veggies will do just that for a week or more.

Ventilated containers are especially useful for highly perishable foods such as lettuces, greens, and berries. Semidisposable food storage containers from the supermarket can come in handy as well. Whether you go for the fancy (though not necessarily expensive) variety or the supereconomical kind, make sure that they're made from BPA-free material.

My friend and fellow author Leslie Cerier, a.k.a. the Organic Gourmet, has a nifty trick. She finds that laying her produce in crisper drawers between slightly damp kitchen towels (rather than in bags or containers) helps extend its life.

PANTRY PRODUCE

Here are a few tips for fresh items that can be stored at room temperature in the pantry. Why the pantry? Because some items need to be stored away from light. But if your kitchen is in an overheated apartment, or if it gets hot during summer months, there's no harm in refrigerating these items for a short time. Better that they should toughen slightly than start sprouting and quickly spoil.

No pantry? No problem—use a drawer. Regardless, though, don't store onions and potatoes too near one another, as onions give off a gas that quickly ripens potatoes.

Garlic: This useful vegetable should be perfectly dry when stored, and, like the following vegetables, it should be placed in a cool, dark place in a ventilated container. I've had a ceramic garlic keeper on my countertop for years; it keeps the garlic aerated and fresh. A mesh or paper bag in the pantry or a cabinet works, too.

Onions: Yellow, red, and white onions can be stored in mesh bags, in open paper bags, or an open basket in the pantry.

Potatoes: All varieties of potatoes can be kept in wicker baskets, ventilated boxes, or open paper bags. It's just as important to keep them dry as it is to keep them cool, so don't rinse them before storing.

Sweet potatoes: It's tempting to refrigerate sweet potatoes, but refrigerating them makes them tougher. Store them as you would regular potatoes, in a dark pantry or drawer.

Tomatoes of any size and variety, including heirloom, cherry, and grape tomatoes, *must* be stored on the countertop (or on the table). For those who may not know, refrigerating tomatoes makes them mealy and affects their flavor. Keep them in a bowl or basket, away from light.

Bananas are a countertop fruit and, like tomatoes, can be kept in a bowl or basket away from light.

Winter squashes keep well on the countertop or on a table; they're not only hardy but also quite decorative. Most varieties—sugar pumpkin, acorn squash, butternut squash, hubbard squash, and others—keep well for several weeks at room temperature.

Non-Produce Staples for the Refrigerator

While you need not have all the following items on hand at all times, see which you use most often—having those items in your refrigerator helps to ensure that ingredients for tasty meals are always around.

ON THE SHELVES

Here's a basic list of what you'll find on my refrigerator shelves:

- Earth Balance or another brand of vegan buttery spread
- Nondairy milks (which should be refrigerated after opening)
- Salsa (which should be refrigerated after opening)
- Bread
- Olives
- Perishable seeds, such as flaxseed, hemp seed, chia seed, and sesame seed
- Roasted coffee beans
- Well-sealed containers of leftovers
- Whole-grain flours, which can be perishable at warm temperatures

Door storage is great for small containers that can get lost in the refrigerator. I use them for

- Mustard
- Vegan mayonnaise
- Sriracha and other hot sauces
- Prepared lemon and lime juice (for those times when we run out of fresh)
- Fruit juices and nectars
- Nutritional yeast
- All-fruit jams and spreads

IN THE DELI DRAWER

Here we keep mainly tofu in tubs, packaged baked tofu, tempeh, and vegan cheese—our current favorite brand is Daiya. Seitan, tempeh bacon, and good-quality vegan sausages

(Tofurky and Field Roast brands, both made without isolated soy protein) are occasional items—mostly for when the kids are home. And because this drawer is wide and flat, it's a handy place to store wraps and tortillas. Below is more detail about the "big three"—tofu, tempeh, and seitan.

TOFU

You need not keep all varieties of tofu in your refrigerator at all times—buy only what you need for the week ahead. The tub variety comes in 14-ounce to 16-ounce containers. You'll learn how to press and prepare tofu in Tofu Prep Basics on page 79. In addition to a few 12.3-ounce aseptic packages of firm and extra-firm silken tofu in your pantry (see page 33), here are the varieties you'll choose from:

Soft and firm tofu: These varieties can be crumbled for use in scrambles, like the one on page 82, or in eggless egg salads, like the one on page 270. When well crumbled, both make a good substitute for ricotta cheese. Like silken tofu, soft and firm tofu can be pureed for use as a soup or sauce base, though the consistency won't be as smooth as that of silken tofu.

Extra-firm tofu: This is available in the usual tubs and also in fresh chunks and cakes. Use this variety when you want the tofu to hold its shape. Extra-firm tofu is ideal for use in stir-fries, stews, and cutlets.

Baked tofu: As of this writing, I've yet to find this tasty, flavored form of very firm tofu in supermarkets. It's good stuff, though, so look for it in natural foods stores. Most often, it comes in 8-ounce packages and is not packed in water, as tub varieties are. Available in several flavor varieties (including Asian, Caribbean, and smoked), it can be sliced, diced, or crumbled for use in stir-fries, sandwiches, salads, and tortilla specialties.

TEMPEH

Because tempeh is a fermented soy food, it's considered more nutritious and digestible than other soy foods—even more so than tofu. Its flavor is somewhat of an acquired taste, but those who love it do so in a big way. I was always a moderate fan of tempeh, and my kids like it, but since my husband isn't a big fan, I don't put it in the rotation that often. But lately I've learned to love it—it's a matter of using the right flavorings to tease the best quality out of it. Tempeh is a fantastically concentrated source of protein.

Tempeh comes in 8-ounce packages and in several varieties: plain or flavored with grains, flax, veggies, and other ingredients. Truth be told, they all taste pretty much the same—the difference is the additional nutritional benefit. Fakin' Bacon, a brand of smoky tempeh strips, is another product I purchase from time to time. Unlike highly processed imitation bacon, it is primarily made up of spiced tempeh. Or you can make your own Smoky Tempeh Strips (page 268).

SEITAN

Seitan—which, like tofu, is an ancient Asian product that has been adopted by the modern Western vegan and vegetarian movements—is pure wheat gluten, so it's not for those with any sort of gluten sensitivity. But otherwise, seitan offers an appealing protein alternative to soy products. Making your own seitan is an economical option; recipes are all over the Web. It's not difficult, but it is a bit of a project. The next best alternative is to find a source for locally made fresh seitan. Sometimes you'll find local seitan in natural foods stores and food co-ops. Otherwise, the widely marketed WhiteWave seitan products, found in natural foods stores (and, increasingly, in supermarkets), are quite good—especially their stir-fry strips.

Vegans don't use dairy milk because of their conscious choice to avoid any animal products; others avoid it because they are allergic to it or lactose intolerant. The notion that no one really needs cow's milk (unless you are a calf) is spreading, and many companies have jumped onto the bandwagon with a growing number of nondairy milk options. Is using nondairy milk a kind of fakery, like eating faux meat? Not really: making milk-like beverages from nuts isn't anything new. Almond milk was a common item in medieval kitchens; before the age of refrigeration, nut milks kept better than animal milks. Nut milks were likely being made long before then, as they're an easy thing to produce and require little equipment. If you'd like to make nut milk, there are lots of easy recipes and video tutorials online; your homemade nut milks will be delicious, though they won't have the generous enrichment provided by commercial brands.

Although nut milks themselves provide a nourishing base (almonds, for example, are rich in calcium, and hemp seeds are a good source of valuable omega fatty acids), manufacturers add extra calcium, vitamin D, and, often, vitamin B_{12}. So there are few reasons to continue drinking cow's milk when the alternatives are plentiful and good-tasting.

One note of caution—many alternative milks are naturally sweet, so opt for unsweetened varieties. Sweetened nondairy milks can be high in sugar. In sum, milks made from nuts, seeds, grains, and soybeans aren't "fake" anything. It's not surprising that humans have an innate penchant for milky, subtly sweet liquid: it's a substance that characterizes one of our earliest sense memories—milk is every infant's first food. Here are a few ways to get it—all of them better than getting it from a cow:

- **Almond milk:** Naturally high in vitamin E and calcium, almond milk has a sweet flavor and a thick, rich consistency that belie the fact that it's amazingly low in calories—just thirty to forty calories per cup. Commercial brands of almond milk are also enriched with vitamins D and B_{12}.

- **Hemp milk:** Like the hemp seeds from which it's made, hemp milk is rich in omega-3 and omega-6 fatty acids, essential amino acids, a multitude of vitamins, and a plethora of minerals, including a generous amount of calcium. Just writing this makes me want to pour a cupful for myself!

- **Rice milk:** As a beverage alone, it's not as palatable as the others because of its thin consistency. But for soups, especially, I prefer to use plain unsweetened rice milk above the others because of its neutral flavor. Rice milk comes in 32-ounce aseptic cartons that keep for a long time in the pantry. It's enriched with vitamins and minerals, but it's not as much of a powerhouse as almond milk and hemp milk.

- **Soy milk:** I'm not a big fan of soy milk, either as a beverage or for cooking (in soups, sauces, and other creamy dishes). Its beany, slightly sweet taste asserts itself in ways I don't enjoy. And since we use tofu and tempeh regularly, I prefer to avoid the regular use of yet another soy product. Still, there is one benefit soy milk has over other nondairy milks: it contains significantly more protein. Soy milk has fewer calories, less fat, and lots more calcium than dairy milk, and it has no cholesterol, so there are plenty of good reasons to use it if you actually like the flavor.

Other, less common, nondairy milks include sunflower, cashew, and coconut milks (the latter being a different beverage from the coconut milk that comes in cans—see page 34).

FREEZER STAPLES

Whole-grain buns or English muffins: I keep these on hand to serve with homemade and prepackaged veggie burgers and soy hot dogs.

Whole-grain pita or panini breads: These are great to have on hand for making mini pizzas. You can also cut them into triangles and serve them with hummus or other dips.

Whole-grain pizza crust: You're welcome to make your own pizza crust from scratch, and there are two basic recipes for it in chapter 4—one for whole-wheat crust and another for gluten-free crust (pages 180 and 181). But with all the good prepared crusts available, I rarely use this recipe, and I won't be insulted if you don't, either.

Frozen vegetables: I always keep green peas in the freezer, as they're useful and taste quite good. When local fresh corn isn't in season, frozen kernels come in handy, too. And since the window for tender fresh green beans is so limited, I occasionally buy frozen whole baby green beans, which are actually pretty decent. Another once-in-a-while frozen item is shelled edamame (green soybeans). As with fresh produce, I prefer organic frozen vegetables.

Frozen fruit: It's just a sad fact of life that organic blueberries, which are one of the most antioxidant-rich foods on the planet, have such a pathetically short season in most areas. Fortunately, they and other berries retain much of their goodness after flash-freezing. Frozen berries aren't nearly as delicious as fresh berries, but they make welcome additions to smoothies year-round. Organic peaches, raspberries, and mangos can also spark up smoothies, muffins, and desserts when the choices in fresh fruits are limited.

Nondairy ice cream: Yummy in and of itself, nondairy ice creams offer a great excuse to eat more fruit. In the summer, my go-to dessert, whether for guests or family, is strawberries and blueberries served over most any flavor of nondairy ice cream; tree-ripened peaches and nectarines taste delicious with the vanilla flavor. Not so long ago, most nondairy frozen desserts were made of soy; they're still available and quite good, but now the choices include coconut-, almond-, and cashew-based creams. And they're all delicious.

Kitchen Tools

The plant-powered kitchen need not be magazine-gorgeous and outfitted with the latest gadgets and appliances. These things would be nice, of course, but they are not required to create delicious meals. Most of the recipes in this book aren't dependent on machines, though an assortment of basic tools can make life in the kitchen easier and, in some cases, more enjoyable. Just as with pantry items, you don't have to run out and buy all these items at once—or at all. These are tools I enjoy having in my kitchen and that you might, too, as you work your way through this book's plant-based meals:

Food processor: A food processor's multiple uses—chopping, grating, and pureeing—make it your best friend among kitchen tools. If you get one of the name brands and take care of it, it may outlive you! I've had the same Cuisinart food processor for at least fifteen years, and it shows little sign of slowing down.

Wire whisk or coated wire whisk: This inexpensive tool helps make sauces, dressings, and gravies, and it helps when cooking fine grains (such as polenta) to lump-free textures. For cake and pancake batters that come out smooth without overbeating, a whisk is a must.

Kitchen shears: Shears, or kitchen scissors, have endless uses in the kitchen—cutting long Asian noodles, thinly slicing scallions and basil leaves, opening packages, even cutting pizza into wedges if you don't have a pizza wheel.

Stir-fry pan: This type of wok-shaped pan will serve you well if you enjoy making stir-fries. It's easier to deal with, in many ways, than a traditional wok—from cleaning to storage. If you plan to make plenty of dishes involving quick-cooked veggies, such as the those in chapter 1, you'll get a lot of use from a stir-fry pan.

Here are a few more items that are quite useful but aren't must haves:

Immersion blender: If you have no room for a full-fledged blender, or don't want to spring for one, an immersion blender can do a lot of the same tricks. My favorite way to use it is for pureeing soups in the same pot in which they cook. With it, there's no need to transfer hot ingredients in and out of a food processor or blender. As a major soup cook, I really appreciate this. Easy to use, even easier to clean, and costing a fraction of what a food processor or blender costs, the immersion blender is also good for making smoothies and velvety sauces.

Pizza pan or pizza stone: A pizza pan is nothing more than a large round pan designed for baking pizzas. And a pizza stone is just that—a smooth round stone used for the same purpose. A stone ensures crisper crusts and is more tolerant of sharp pizza wheels. With veggie-driven pizzas in regular rotation in our home, both these tools have seen much use. If you like to make pizza, they won't break the bank.

Salad spinner: A salad spinner isn't an absolute must have. Even as a huge fan of salads of all kinds, I did without one for a long time. But once I finally got one and started using it, I was sold! I regret all those paper towels I wasted, blotting delicate leaves for salads and wraps and pressing liquid from kale before massaging it or making kale chips. A salad spinner works kind of like the spin cycle in your washing machine, except that it needs no electricity.

Nut chopper or grinder: I enjoy my nut chopper, which grinds a few nuts at a time into a container, making the process easy and neat. While you can definitely live without it, nut enthusiasts will enjoy this item. It's handy for turning nuts into a tasty topping for noodle dishes, grains, salads, and cereals. Mine, made by Progressive International, can be seen in the photo on page 212, with the Veggie Lo Mein.

Tofu press: Despite the fact I've been using and enjoying tofu for ages, this is the most recent addition to my roster of favorite kitchen tools. Tofu presses are simple devices using springs or tightening bolts to extract water from tofu efficiently, without any further weights and using no paper towels whatsoever! I enjoy both the EZ Tofu Press and the TofuXpress, which work a bit differently from each other but are both quite handy. Look for them online.

Meal Planning Basics and Strategies

Now that you know how to stock the pantry and refrigerator with the most essential plant-powered staples, and now that you have the essential tools you need in your kitchen, the next step on the path is becoming comfortable with meal planning and food shopping. Better yet is being able to do these tasks with ease and enjoyment. Meal planning—a practice that can take as little as twenty minutes a week—not only saves time and money but also restores sanity. Last-minute shopping trips, expensive convenience foods, makeshift meals, and take-out dinners become the exception rather than the rule.

If this book accomplishes anything, I want it to help you adopt a new way of thinking about meals—a new paradigm of the plate, if you will. It's not always necessarily about deciding on a main course and one or two sides, or laboring to decide what goes with what. The entire enterprise becomes more pleasurable when you apply the same enthusiasm to it that you bring to eating out:

- Should we do a fajita dinner this week, so that we can all build our own?

- There are a lot of bits of veggies in the crisper; looks like a good time for a big stir-fry over noodles with some premade spring rolls added for fun.

- This week will be cold, and we're all going to be superbusy. A big pot of chili in the fridge would be a good thing to come home to.

- It's Friday, and a pizza-and-movie night sounds fun and relaxing (of course, we're going to start thinking of pizza as a delivery system for veggies, not dairy cheese).

You get the idea. As you become more experienced, you'll be able to build meals according to your and your family's tastes, culinary moods, the season, and availability of ingredients,

Red Pizza with Bell Peppers and Artichokes (page 183)

all in a more intuitive way. Adopting a plant-powered diet is commendable, but without a few basic strategies, frequent eating out, takeout, and make-do will remain a part of your new lifestyle, much as it is for many busy people, whatever their dietary preference.

Back when our kids were growing up and I still was in the midst of the classic juggling act, I was a lot more disciplined about meal planning. I found that it really did buy me time and sanity. For our family of four, I planned three meals per week. If I made ample quantities, I could count on leftovers for three more dinners. And leftovers can always be tweaked so that they're slightly different the next day. For example, today's salad can be tomorrow's wrap; tonight's soup-and-wrap dinner can become tomorrow's soup-and-vegan-quesadilla dinner. And on the seventh day, we rested. That is, we'd go out to eat, order in, have a potluck with friends, or just do something out of the ordinary.

There are all kinds of meal-planning apps available, but no magic bullet. A lot of the impetus has to come from you and what you see as your ideal meal-making style. Decide whether you want to make different meals every night or most nights and rotate them through the season or whether you want to try the three-meals-with-leftovers strategy. If you want to be a seat-of-the-pants cook, more power to you—I like to cook that way, and so does my son. For that kind of spontaneity, you've got to have an especially well-stocked pantry and fridge as well as the imagination to look at a bunch of ingredients and envision what they can become.

If you've picked up this book and gotten to this point, it's safe to assume that your goal is to cook and eat more healthful meals at home, so here are some of my tried-and-true tips for making cooked-from-scratch meals a daily reality, even after the most exhausting days:

Stock your refrigerator, pantry, and freezer with basic ingredients. We've tackled this big task on pages 17–43, but it's so important that it earns its top spot on this list! Not having basic, healthful, and useful ingredients on hand sabotages even the best of intentions. Making sure your pantry and freezer are stocked with the nutritious staples you use most will go a long way toward making meals a whole lot less stressful.

You can bank the time you might have spent on last-minute food-shopping trips (which can be expensive and stressful) toward creating more thoughtful meals. Even when you haven't planned ahead—and we all have those kinds of days—there will be something great to fall back on at home, such as easy pizzas or burritos or a veggie burger accompanied by coleslaw and steamed veggies.

Plan three full meals for each week. From those meals, you can plan two nights of leftovers, which makes life easier—though this is challenging if you have hungry teens or athletes at home. Don't think of leftovers as boring. They can be repurposed in ways that might not make it into the culinary hall of fame, but with a few tweaks they can be as tasty as the original preparation. For instance, leftover chili can become Cincinnati Chili Mac (page 143). Grain pilafs can be stuffed into squashes or made into wraps embellished with leafy lettuces. I'll be talking up the idea of repurposing meals as we travel through the recipe chapters.

Plan meals *before* going shopping. Planning your meals before you go food shopping will ensure that you don't waste time, money, and energy running back and forth to the store all week. A mere twenty to thirty minutes of meal planning per week will simplify your life immeasurably, especially if you have a tight schedule, young children, or both.

At first it might be challenging to get into a regular meal-planning session that includes making a shopping list. If you do your grocery shopping on the weekend, that might mean making your meal plans on Friday night or Saturday morning. That sounds like about as much fun as getting your teeth cleaned or taking your car in for an oil change. But you'll be amazed at how much time is saved by a twenty-minute meal-planning and shopping list–making session. You can create a master list of staples that you can copy or print out each week, checking off items that need replenishing. I did this for a long time, and it worked like a charm. Now my staples needs are pretty much imprinted onto my brain, so I find I don't need such a list any longer.

Plan meals *after* going shopping. What? Didn't I just say to plan meals before going shopping? Sometimes it's good to think outside the box. When farm market or CSA season is in full swing—or during the summer and fall harvest season in general—and you're getting basketloads of fresh produce, it may be wiser to retrofit your meal plans to your fresh food finds. What's the point of getting lots of kale or tons of tomatoes if you're not going to plan your meals around them? I've heard many a guilty tale of perfectly good produce tossed out

for this very reason. So during the seasons of abundance, do take those same twenty minutes and plan your meals around what's already in your refrigerator.

Prepare basics for the week ahead. On whatever day or evening is the most home-centered, prepare a few basics for the days ahead. Sunday afternoons and evenings are ideal as you're looking to the coming week, but do whatever is good for your schedule. Even the simplest things can ease weeknight meal preparation immeasurably. Cook some plain brown rice (or other grains); bake some potatoes, sweet potatoes, or squash. Knowing that you have even one item that's already prepared when you enter the kitchen at six P.M. or later is a fantastic feeling, and the rest of the meal then comes together quickly. For additional ideas, see "Top Ten Make-Aheads to Get You Through the Week," pages 51–52.

At least once a week, prepare a big one-pot or one-pan meal. This kind of meal can stretch to cover at least two nights. Such meals include hearty soups and stews, bean dishes, abundant pastas, and casseroles. You'll find many such recipes later on in this book. Double the quantities if you need to, especially if you have a large family. Then you need little more than salad and fresh whole-grain bread to accompany the meal.

Here's one real-life example of how this strategy gets a busy family through the week: my friend Kevin Fort and his wife have demanding weekday professions, and as the family's main cook, he relies on two soup recipes each week. He makes a giant potful each time, enough for two meals and sometimes a third, for the freezer. The first meal is consumed the evening he makes it, followed by an easy night of quickly reheated soup and fresh bread made by a local grocer. He enjoys the fact that these two hefty soup recipes cover the family's meals for four nights. The fifth night he usually makes a hearty pasta dinner. Weekends are for eating out or making an out-of-the-ordinary meal. These kinds of rituals can and do work, lending comfort and order to our occasionally chaotic lives.

Develop a weekly repertoire. Make slight variations on your standard recipes each week so that meals don't get boring. For example, Friday dinner has long been a pizza and salad meal, but within this basic framework, there are endless variations! As an example, your week could look something like this:

- Sunday is your day to make a big soup or stew that will last at least a couple of nights as well as provide extra portions for lunches and possible freezing.
- On Monday you'll enjoy the fruits of Sunday's labors. Soup can be served with sandwiches, wraps, and/or salads, depending on appetites.
- Tuesday that soup is still looking good, so it's soup and wraps or vegan quesadilla night.
- Wednesday can be spaghetti day, but by "spaghetti" I mean any kind of pasta and any kind of sauce. You'll find all kinds of ideas for easy pasta meals in chapter 3.

Follow the suggestions for simple veggie side dishes and salads to accompany them. If there are any leftovers, you can use them for portable lunches the next day or put them in single-serving containers and freeze for later use.

- Thursday, depending on which style of food you prefer, can be Mexican or Asian night. Or you can alternate: serve one kind of cuisine the first week and the other the following week. Mexican-style tortilla and soft-taco specialties are about putting the right ingredients on the table and letting people assemble their own. But that will be our little secret, okay? And if you've done just a little bit of prep, seasonal Asian-style stir-fries can be on the table in thirty minutes or less; see my suggestions in chapter 4.

- Friday is your night to kick back and watch a movie. The perfect companion is an almost-instant pizza, a lovely blend of shortcut ingredients (namely, a prepared whole-grain crust and marinara sauce) and fresh veggies, piled on so generously that you forget you've used shortcuts. The best accompaniment for pizza is a colorful salad. To balance the slight decadence of the pizza, you might consider a kale salad.

This is but one example of a meal plan. The goal is to make your meal plans work for your lifestyle and center them on the kinds of foods you might enjoy if you were eating out. A dinner of burgers and fries (or, more accurately, vegan burgers and roasted potatoes or sweet potatoes) is also easy to make in good-for-you, plant-powered form. So is a Middle Eastern feast (pages 315–16), which is nothing more than an emergency meal in fancy clothes.

Create a seasonal repertoire. An alternative to a weekly repertoire is a seasonal repertoire, consisting of ten or fifteen basic meals that you like best. These ten tasty meals—one for each weeknight for two weeks—are repeated as needed throughout the season. Weekends can bring a heavenly leftovers buffet. That doesn't sound too daunting, right?

Keep things simple. Let go of the idea that healthful cooking is complicated and time-consuming. It doesn't have to be! The quality of ingredients and the thought put into meals far outweigh any other considerations. Not every component of a meal needs to be a recipe. In fact, I offer loads of recipe-free ways to complete meals in every chapter. Baked sweet potato fries are a fantastic side dish, but if all you can manage are plain baked sweet potatoes, that's fine. They may not be as exciting, but they're just as good.

Do your meal planning and food shopping on a consistent day. This can be once or twice a week, depending on your schedule and the size of your household. When my young adult offspring are home (they're currently in the bouncing-in-and-out stage), we need to shop twice a week, but when it's just me and the hubby, once a week suffices.

Top Ten Make-Aheads to Get You Through the Week

Dinner preparation suffers greatly because it's usually prepared so late in the day. Most of us get into the kitchen at six P.M. or later (sometimes *much* later). We're tired from our workdays, our commutes, our kids' activities, and the general stress of our overstuffed lives. If you're a parent, there's homework that needs to be supervised; if you're a student, there's homework that needs to be done. Household chores still need to be completed before our heads can hit the pillow. No wonder, then, that dinnertime can feel so fraught, that it gets short shrift on so many days.

Here are my top ten make-aheads, in no particular order, that can help streamline weeknight meal preparation. And by "make-ahead," I don't mean freezing your garden greens in August so you can enjoy them in November. I'm talking about taking an hour or two on Sunday, or even on a weekday evening after all is settled and calm, to prepare some basics. Even something as simple as having some cooked quinoa, baked potatoes, sweet potatoes, or kale that's been cleaned and chopped can go a long way toward making evening meal preparation a breeze.

1. Make a hearty soup, stew, or multiserving dish such as lasagna.

2. Bake or microwave potatoes, sweet potatoes, or winter squashes.

3. Cook a few servings of quinoa, brown rice, and/or other grains.

4. Clean, stem, and chop kale, collards, or other sturdy greens; store in an airtight container.

5. Cook dried beans (if you prefer cooking them from scratch).

6. Make hummus or another kind of protein-rich spread.

7. Caramelize two or three onions (or a combination of onions and peppers: see how-to on page 88).

8. Prepare a few sturdy cooking vegetables that keep well—cut broccoli and/or cauliflower into small florets; stem and halve brussels sprouts; prebake winter squashes.

9. Prepare a variety of healthful, easy-to-grab fresh veggies and fruits that keep well when cut, such as peppers and carrots, to use as snacks or toss into salads.

10. Make homemade salad dressings and/or dips.

Plant-Powered Food Shopping Savvy

Ninety percent of all food shopping dollars in the United States are spent on processed foods. Now, there's a sobering statistic! The overall goal in transitioning to a plant-based diet is to purchase and use as many whole foods as possible. Fresh fruits and vegetables, dried beans and lentils, whole grains (such as brown rice and quinoa), nuts, and seeds are about as close to the source as possible. Some minimally processed foods, still close enough to their origins, also have good value—think of nut butters, frozen peas, and organic canned beans. Tempeh is closer to its source (soybeans) than is tofu, though the latter is also not a terribly processed food; both are far better than highly processed fake meats fashioned from isolated soy protein.

The idea here is to do the best you can, not to be perfect. Often it's a matter of degree. Pasta and noodles might be (minimally) processed foods, but a dish of whole-grain Asian noodles, embellished with lots of veggies, is a far sight better than a package of frozen macaroni and cheese. As you take the steps in this journey, you'll learn to trust your instincts on what constitutes real food and what constitutes a pale imitation.

Most of us are aware of the tried-and-true supermarket shopping tips—shop the periphery of the store (because that's where the least-processed foods and fresh produce usually are), don't buy foods just because you have coupons for them, don't shop when you're hungry or without a list, and the like. Following are tips for shopping outside the big box, in venues that those embarking on the plant-powered path might be less familiar with, particularly natural foods stores and farm markets. But no worries—most of the ingredients used in the recipes in this book can be found in well-stocked supermarkets, if that's what is available near where you live.

Shopping at natural foods stores isn't rocket science, but if you're new to the experience, here are some tips:

- If you live in an area that has a small natural foods store that can't stock as many products as the big-box natural foods stores do, know that most stores will special-order items that you don't see on the shelves.

- Many natural foods companies offer coupons online. If there are brands of good-quality packaged items you like, such as vegetable stock, tofu, vegan cheeses, and canned beans, check the company's website.

- Prices can vary significantly from one natural foods store to another. The one in the town in which I live has prices that are about 20 percent lower than the natural foods store about ten miles away.

- Natural foods stores often distribute circulars detailing weekly discounts on various foods. These are often tied into specials offered by their distributors. Pay attention to these, as the savings can be significant. Of course, the key is to use these savings only on items you'll actually consume.

- Bulk-bin buying is truly cost-effective. But just because an item is available in bulk doesn't mean you need to go crazy and buy ten pounds of quinoa or brown rice at once. As a rule of thumb, buy what you'll use within a month or two. Nuts and

seeds, rich in fats, can go rancid if kept too long. Even dried items such as grains and lentils can go rancid.

- When buying in bulk, make sure to patronize a busy store, where regular turnover ensures that what you're buying is fresh.

- Natural foods stores often sell herbs and spices in bulk. If you go through a lot of certain seasonings, this can be a source of savings. Bulk seasonings can also be especially fresh and fragrant if there's good turnover in that area of the store.

- Just because certain food products are sold in natural foods stores doesn't mean they're good for you. "Naturally sweetened" candies, fruit juices high in sugar, and snacks that provide empty calories, even if they have no additives, do nothing for your health or budget.

FARM MARKETS: TIPS FOR SHOPPING AND ENJOYING

The sights and aromas of just-harvested produce and the sheer variety of veggies that you'll rarely find at the supermarket are truly inspiring as you browse the aisles at farm markets. Often there are samples, food demos, and even music to make your shopping trip more of a fun outing than an errand. The experience can be a great one for kids and can help them make the connection between the food (you hope) they eat and the people who grow it. With produce looking so appealing, and without the distraction of the supermarket's sugary treats, they may clamor for peaches and tomatoes instead!

Visiting farm markets is the next best thing to going straight to the farm (which you can do if you patronize pick-your-own venues and farm stands). The closer you can get to the source the better. Just-harvested farm market fare, which hasn't had to be trucked across the country, is at the peak of its flavor and nutrition. Frequenting farm markets when they're set up in your area goes a long way toward making you a local and seasonal eater. A few tips for making the most of your farm market shopping expeditions:

- Know when to go—most markets are busiest in the morning. If you want the best, freshest selection, go early. But for the best deals, shop just before the market closes. Vendors are loath to pack up and take goods back to the farm and will often be open to marking prices down at the end of the day. And while it's most fun to shop at farm markets when the weather is inviting, iffy-weather days might yield more bargains.

- Farm markets are often a bit farther afield from your home than your local supermarket and often operate during some of the hottest months. If you're going to be traveling a fair distance home after shopping, bring a cooler packed with ice in which to put your produce (or at least the most perishable items, such as berries and tender greens) for the trip home.

- Farm market shopping is the time to throw your meal plans to the wind. You never know what might be offered or what might call to you. It's a chance to try new kinds of produce, so approach this kind of shopping expedition with an open spirit. That being said, don't overdo it. It's tempting to go home with tons of gorgeous produce and heartbreaking when you need to compost it a week or two down the road. Be realistic about what you'll use within a week.

- When you get home with your farm market finds, don't just stash everything in the fridge in opaque bags. A minimal amount of processing will ensure that these nutritious foods will be used and used soon. For example, you can stem, chop, wash, and dry greens to use in that night's dinner. Go one step further and massage kale (page 60) in preparation for making salads. Wash berries and put them into clear bowls to tempt those who open the fridge to snack on them. Cut up veggies that taste good raw (carrots, turnips, bell peppers) into bite-size pieces for snacking on later.

- If produce isn't certified organic, ask the vendor why that is. The produce may be virtually organic, just not certified. Getting a USDA Organic designation can be an expensive and time-consuming process for small growers.

- Farm market shopping isn't always inexpensive. The farm market in my town is on the pricey side; the one an easy thirty-minute drive from my house is bigger and far more reasonable. So my quandary is always whether to save time or to save money. I usually opt for the larger, less expensive farm market, as I also like the wider selection. So do compare the local farm markets within an hour's travel time of your home.

- Another way to save money is to browse around the entire market before you start buying. There are often price differences from one stand to another.

ADVANTAGES OF JOINING A CSA FARM

Another way to make food shopping an enjoyable ritual is to join a community-supported agriculture farm. Ask about CSAs in your area: believe it or not, CSA groups are available in urban communities, not just in the countryside.

CSA farms have burgeoned in the last decade or two as a way for communities to share the common goal of growing food locally. How it usually works is that a parcel of farmland is purchased, then a grower is hired. Those who want a share of the food grown on the land pay a membership fee. At many CSAs there's the option of a working or nonworking share. A working share means that you put in a few hours each week either harvesting or performing distribution tasks in exchange for a lower membership fee. Members are usually entitled to pick up their shares once a week, on a designated day.

Our family belonged to a CSA for some years, before my husband took up vegetable gardening. Aside from providing an abundance of locally grown organic produce for at least half the year, it was outright fun. CSAs build community, bringing together like-minded people with shared values concerning food, with potlucks and other events. Some CSAs offer more than produce. They may also offer locally made bread and bakery items, fresh flowers, and eggs and other animal products that we won't discuss here. But the focus for the most part is vegetables and fruits that go from field to table on the same day.

The advantages are manifold. Unlike produce that's shipped from one end of the country to the other, food that's grown close to your home reduces your carbon footprint. The produce is at its freshest as well as most flavorful and nutritious when this golden opportunity to use it the same day or soon after it's harvested presents itself. You'll get to experience varieties of veggies that never make it to the supermarket or that you may not think to try.

Are CSAs appropriate for singles? I asked my friend Leslie, knowing that farm markets and her CSA farm are the cornerstones of her food shopping routine. According to her, there's no reason to forgo joining a CSA just because you're single. True, weekly shares can be overly abundant for one person, but most of these organizations will allow you to split a share with another member. Being a social person, Leslie loves to participate in potlucks and other shared dining experiences, so fresh food never goes to waste.

To learn more about CSA farms and locate those in your area, explore www.local harvest.org.

Organic Produce

Given the choice, I always opt for organic; it seems a good idea to minimize exposure to toxic chemicals in our food when there are so many other environmental toxins over which we have no control. Organics are firmly entrenched in the mainstream. Proof positive: a majority of shoppers who buy organic food do so at their primary supermarket.

What is organic, anyway? Organic crops are grown in soils fertilized with organic rather than synthetic fertilizers and are not sprayed with inorganic chemicals. Natural foods stores, food co-ops, some farm markets, and a growing number of supermarkets now offer organic choices to consumers concerned about the effects of pesticides, additives, and chemical fertilizers on human health and the environment. Organically grown foods are often slightly more expensive than their conventionally grown counterparts, but not enough to make them prohibitive. Be aware that foods described as "whole" or "natural" aren't necessarily organically grown.

Many small organic farms have actually been hurt by the new organic labeling standards. To be certified as USDA Organic requires a massive amount of paperwork, which can be overwhelming for a small operation. As an alternative, some small organic farms might use the label "certified ecologically grown" or something similar. If you know and trust your local growers, you can make the decision to continue buying and supporting their products.

It can be daunting to buy 100 percent organic produce (which includes grains, legumes, nuts, seeds, and the products made with them). Do the best you can, and at least be aware of which crops are highest in pesticide residues when considering your purchases. Some studies examine pesticide residues that are classified by the Environmental Protection Agency (EPA) as probable human carcinogens, nervous system poisons, and endocrine system disrupters. Other studies focus on foods most eaten by children and thus most likely to do harm if there are residues.

The Environmental Working Group is a great source for up-to-the minute information on the kinds of produce that are most likely to be contaminated with pesticide residue, a list known as the Dirty Dozen, and the kinds of produce that are safe to consume even when they're not grown organically. This latter group is known as the Clean Fifteen. According the EWG, "The health benefits of a diet rich in fruits and vegetables outweigh the risks of pesticide exposure. Use EWG's Shopper's Guide to Pesticides to reduce your exposures as much as possible, but eating conventionally grown produce is far better than not eating fruits and vegetables at all."

THE ENVIRONMENTAL WORKING GROUP'S DIRTY DOZEN PLUS™ 2013

Each year, the EWG does an assessment of the most contaminated produce. These items should ideally be used in organic form to avoid consuming high levels of pesticide residue. Here's the current list, in alphabetical order. This list changes from year to year as farming and pest-management practices change, so it's worth checking the EWG website from time to time (www.ewg.org).

Apples
Celery
Cherry tomatoes
Cucumbers
Grapes
Hot peppers
Kale, collards, and other leafy greens
Nectarines (imported)
Peaches
Potatoes
Spinach
Strawberries
Sweet bell peppers
Zucchini and other summer squash

This list, in alphabetical order, shows the kinds of produce that are grown with the lowest amounts of pesticides and are therefore safest to consume in nonorganic form.

Asparagus

Avocado

Cabbage

Cantaloupe

Eggplant

Grapefruit

Kiwi

Mango

Mushrooms

Onions

Papayas

Pineapple

Sweet corn*

Sweet peas (frozen)

Sweet potatoes

* It should be noted, though, that nonorganic sweet corn can sometimes be GMO. Stick with organic sweet corn if you're concerned about this.

Other studies cite oranges, potatoes, and any leafy vegetable as among the top ten or twelve most likely to be treated with pesticides. Some of the produce and other plant foods rarely seen in these kinds of "top ten" lists (and therefore presumably safe to use in conventional rather than organic varieties) include broccoli, carrots, cauliflower, brussels sprouts, beans and legumes, and plums. Still, with so much variation in the lists, the strategy should be apparent: buy organic versions of produce whenever available. Simply put, it's better for you, your children, and the planet.

Five Easy Ways to Eat More Leafy Greens

Once you become a seasonal eater, a farm market shopper, a CSA member, or all three, greens will almost inevitably become part of your life. Everyone's mad for greens these days, and it's no wonder. Greens are recognized as the most nutrient-rich group of veggies, and they convey a multitude of benefits. Hardy greens, like kale, chard, and collards, are superb sources of highly absorbable calcium, a perk that's especially valuable in plant-based diets.

Greens are also one of the best sources of vitamin K, essential to bone health, and are abundant in vitamins A, B (especially folic acid), and C. Greens provide a wealth of antioxidants and chlorophyll, protect against cancer, and are anti-inflammatory. All of these are great reasons to eat more greens—aside from the fact that they're delicious, versatile, and add interest to all manner of preparations. Here are a handful of ways to enjoy them every day:

1. **Use greens in smoothies and juices.** Some greens are better for this purpose than others. Spinach tastes so mild in smoothies and juices that your taste buds barely know it's there. Kale and collards are a bit more assertive but add a very mild greens flavor. For either juices or smoothies, a big handful or two of spinach or one or two good-size kale or collard leaves per serving is about right. Greens blend well with bananas, apples, berries, and pears. A high-speed blender (such as Vitamix or Blendtec, though they're quite an investment) is needed to break kale and collards down smoothly; a regular blender is sufficient for spinach. For specific recipes, search the Internet for "green smoothies" and you'll find a wealth of ideas.

2. **Use "massaged" raw kale in salads.** Strip rinsed kale leaves from their stems (in my opinion, ordinary curly kale is best for this purpose), then chop the leaves into bite-size pieces. You can thinly slice the stems and add them to your salad later, or use them in lightly cooked vegetable dishes (or if you don't care for the stems, discard them). Make sure the kale isn't wet before starting; use a salad spinner if you like. Place the cut kale in a serving bowl. Rub a little olive oil into your palm,

then massage the kale for about forty-five seconds or a minute. It will soften up and turn bright green. To this you can add all manner of other veggies and fruits; dress the mixture as desired.

Here's a simple formula that I've been enjoying for years: toss massaged kale with dried cranberries, toasted or raw cashew pieces, vegan mayonnaise, and a little lemon juice. It's downright addictive. Massaged kale also goes well with avocados, apples, pears, napa or red cabbage, carrots, pumpkin seeds, walnuts . . . what you combine it with is limited only to what happens to be in your fridge. It can be dressed in ordinary vinaigrette, sesame-ginger dressing, tahini dressing, or the aforementioned vegan mayo and lemon juice.

3. **Add hardy greens to stir-fries.** The best greens to use for this purpose are lacinato kale (also called dinosaur kale, a flat-leaf variety), collards, or chard. Rinse and dry the leaves, then strip them from the stems (slice the stems from the kale and chard very thinly and use them as well). Stack a few leaves atop one another and roll up snugly from the narrow end. Slice very thinly. This will make long, thin ribbons; cut them once or twice across to shorten. Add these toward the end of your veggie stir-fries, as they cook pretty quickly this way. They blend well with all manner of veggies—broccoli, cauliflower, carrots, celery, bok choy (itself a leafy green), asparagus, green beans, and others. Stir-fried greens flavored with soy sauce or tamari and ginger are supertasty.

4. **Use plenty of leafy spring greens in salads.** Granted, this isn't a revolutionary idea, but look beyond lettuce to create invigorating warm-season salads. Use lots of peppery watercress (a nutritional superstar), baby bok choy, tender dandelion greens, tatsoi, and mizuna (the latter two are Japanese greens that have become increasingly available at farm markets and CSAs). Combine with baby greens and sprouts plus your favorite salad veggies and fruits for cleansing (and clean-tasting) salads.

5. **Learn to love bitter greens.** Add variety to your greens repertoire by getting to know escarole, broccoli rabe, and mustard greens. These greens mellow out considerably with gentle braising or when incorporated into soups and stews. The basics: heat a little olive oil in a large, deep skillet or stir-fry pan; sauté as much chopped garlic and/or shallots as you'd like. Add washed and chopped greens, stir quickly to coat with the oil, then add about a quarter cup water or vegetable stock. Cover and cook until tender and wilted, about five minutes. Traditional additions to this kind of braise are raisins and toasted pine nuts, salt and pepper, and a little apple cider vinegar.

Plant-Powered Families, Couples, and Singles

Here are some tips for tailoring plant-powered eating to whatever stage of life and living situation describes you and/or your family. Families might face a challenge when it comes to getting all their members on the same plate in terms of food preferences; and if that can't be done, making peace at the dinner table. Singles might need help when it comes to finding the motivation to cook for themselves. Read on for strategies and real-life stories.

GETTING KIDS ON BOARD AT THE PLANT-POWERED TABLE

Being vegetarian or vegan—even if that choice was self-directed—doesn't guarantee that children won't be finicky eaters. Plant-powered kids can be as picky their omnivore counterparts.

Raised from the start as vegetarians, my kids were pretty good eaters as children go. They could be picky about particular items—one didn't like mushrooms; the other didn't like peppers—but overall there were no huge objections. My favorite dinner strategy was to regularly introduce and reintroduce a wide variety of healthful fare. I set out simple preparations of vegetables, fruits, whole grains, beans, and soy foods to choose from instead of the classic practice of serving one big entrée that they could either eat or be punished for not liking. Arriving at adolescence and its growth spurts did wonders to expand not only their appetites but also their palates.

How do you convert finicky kids accustomed to pizza, hot dogs, and hamburgers to a plant-based diet? Give them familiar foods but in more nutritious, plant-based versions. These tips can also apply to picky eaters of the adult variety.

Give kids choices, and teach them to make good decisions. This doesn't mean handing them all the power and letting them dictate what is served at meals. But seriously, put yourself in their shoes. What if, day after day, some authority figure made all your meals and compelled you to eat them whether you liked them or not?

Giving kids choices—and I don't mean between candy and ice cream but rather between red and yellow peppers, for example—gives them a role in the process. I've seen moms with young kids at the natural foods store ask their children, "Do you think we should get some [fill in the blank: grapes, strawberries, bananas . . .]?" I don't view this as being indulgent. It's a teaching moment for children, a way to familiarize them with healthful foods.

At mealtime, serve several nutritious side dishes and let your child—or childlike eater—choose. Baby carrots with a tasty dip or dressing, grape tomatoes, very thin slices of multicolored bell peppers, diced baked tofu or baked tofu nuggets with barbecue sauce—these are just some of the possibilities. You'll find ideas for healthy bites throughout this book.

Take kids to the natural foods store or farm market with you. As I mentioned, these venues offer useful and fun opportunities for families to learn about whole foods,

and they feature far fewer undesirable items that children can whine for. Even if some wheedling takes place, it's likely to be for foods you'd want to take home.

Let picky eaters help with meal planning and preparation. Even the most intransigent eater can be swayed by having some say in meal planning. Show kids colorful photos of tasty dishes (such as the ones in this book!) and tell them that they can help plan, shop for, and prepare one meal a week. Their pride and sense of accomplishment will likely inspire better eating habits. If kids feel invested and empowered, they're more likely to enjoy the outcome.

If you don't want your kids to eat it, don't keep it in the house! When my kids were younger and we visited other families, we'd sometimes witness arguments over food—for example, a battle about how many cookies a child could have at four P.M. Guess what? If you don't stock cookies at home, there will be no argument. Save those kinds of foods for occasional treats to be eaten outside the home.

Don't bargain, and don't force: I can't think of anything that can backfire more than bargaining for bites, as in, "If you have just three bites of this, you can have dessert." That sends a strong message that the core part of the meal is a drag or a mere portal to the promised land of sweets. Kids need to get the message early on that a good meal is a reward in itself. Worse yet is punishing a child for refusing food. What a negative message that sends! Offering a wide variety of foods, simply prepared and pleasingly served, will always yield better results.

Use subterfuge: As a last resort, hide nutritious foods in tasty preparations. It's easy to sneak steamed or pureed high-nutrient veggies (broccoli, cauliflower, winter squash, carrots, and greens) into pasta or pizza sauce. Pureed silken tofu adds protein and goodness to soups, sauces, and smoothies. And it's amazing how many vegetables can disappear into a soothing pureed soup. Sweet potatoes, squash, green veggies, and even the often-spurned onions and garlic become palatable in a puree.

Smoothies are another way to concentrate vitamin-rich foods in a preparation that goes down easy. Combine fruits with nondairy milk and/or nondairy yogurt or silken tofu. If you have a high-powered blender, you can even add high-nutrient raw veggies, such as carrots, squash, or sweet potatoes, to smoothies. If you're really lucky, as my friend Kevin was, you can work your way up to adding greens to your family's smoothies. It all began when Kevin started making a fresh green smoothie each morning for himself and his wife, Cindy, as a supercharged way to start the day. He started their daughters on separate fruit smoothies. Over time, he gradually snuck greens into their batch, until finally (and, for him, quite surprisingly) they started drinking the same green smoothies as he and Cindy do. Serve smoothies as part of a vitamin-packed breakfast or snack. See "The Seasonal Smoothie," page 337, for specific ideas.

Recognize that "kid food" can be good for you when made with good ingredients. If you have young children, your shared meals might seem like "nursery food" for some time, but comfort food can be made healthful and tasty, too! Here are some ideas for kid-friendly meals that even adults can enjoy:

- When making pizza meals (pages 178–89), make simpler versions for your child using whole-grain pita or English muffins. Layer with sauce and a sprinkling of nondairy cheese, and if your child doesn't like veggies on the pizza itself, serve them on the side.

- Veggie burgers (pages 274–78) and sloppy joes (pages 279–82) often go over well with kids. Adults can opt for extra embellishments and spice things up to their own tastes.

- Pasta and noodles are great sanity savers for parents. Kids often love noodles with peanut butter sauce (page 311), macaroni and cheese (pages 175 and 176), and pasta with classic marinara sauce (page 157). As their palates develop, add more veggies to the mix.

Be persistent but not pushy. Produce is an intrinsic part of nutritious, plant-based diets. But even kids who willingly go vegetarian or vegan can be picky about vegetables in particular. Introduce less challenging veggies to picky eaters, including potatoes and sweet potatoes, carrots, and corn. Continue to put vegetables on the table, lightly cooked, raw, and incorporated into other dishes. Don't make a big deal of it. This is a case where familiarity breeds acceptance.

In addition, many studies have shown that the "clean your plate" rule, over the long term, has the tendency to backfire. The consequences include lifelong battles with weight and/or eating disorders. Round out your fresh produce repertoire with plenty of fruits, especially for those who are balky about vegetables. See "Eat More Fruit!" on page 350.

FAMILIES AND COUPLES WITH MIXED DIETARY PREFERENCES

I didn't realize what a bubble I've been living in before I started asking probing questions of those who have different kinds of eaters in their families—that is, vegetarians, vegans, and/or omnivores living under one roof. This is a tricky configuration to navigate and reminded me that I've always been lucky in this regard—first by meeting and marrying a man who immediately wanted to go vegetarian, raising stalwart vegetarian kids, going vegan as a family, and being pretty much on the same plate as far as the kinds of meals we like to eat are concerned.

But what to do if one parent is a devout vegan and the other insists on meat at every dinner? Or if a teenager or child goes vegetarian or vegan and the rest of the family isn't on board? It happens more regularly than I imagined. Before anything else can go forward, there needs to be agreement that a well-planned plant-based diet is a valid choice, whether the person taking that stance is a five-year-old or an individual parent or partner.

Respect one another's choices, even if you disagree with them. If you're a passionate vegan, you're not going to be thrilled about living and eating among meat eaters; there's just no two ways about it. I would argue that is more true than the reverse: that is, a passionate meat eater isn't likely to be turned off by living and eating among vegans. After all, becoming vegan often entails aversion to meat and all that it symbolizes. Omnivores aren't similarly offended by broccoli and kale—at least not usually. But there's just so much you can control. Find some creative ways to eat peacefully together, and if that's not possible, don't eat together (though the former is preferable).

For my friend Ricki Heller and her omnivore husband, the best way to keep the peace seems to be for both spouses to go about their own business. Occasionally Ricki's husband cooks his own meat at home and uses her meal as his side dish. "The rest of the time," she says, "he just eats what I eat at home and endeavors to eat his 'meat meal' for lunch at the office." She continues, "He's happy to eat whatever I cook and rarely turns it away. He won't consume my ultra-hard-core green smoothies or anything with too much tofu, but otherwise he seems to love whatever I make."

Set ground rules for at-home meals. If everyone agrees to a small set of guidelines, much conflict can be avoided. If a plant-based person is the primary cook, it's a lot less tricky. My friends Kathy Hester and Cheryl Purser say that since Kathy does nearly all the cooking in their household, they keep the house meat-free, making very occasional exceptions for potlucks and parties. She adds, "It's important to make sure that if the vegan is the planner to include a few things that the meat eater really likes."

Find common ground—it's not that hard to do! It's entirely possible to make a largely plant-based meal that works for everyone. Soups, salads, sandwiches, wraps, and potato dishes are just a few that don't need to be meaty. The same is true for pizza, lasagna, and chili. If plant-based eating is new to your family, then honestly, the burden of proof is on the new plant-powered eater. The best way to win your family over is to show them how delicious meatless meals can be. Die-hard meat eaters have the choice to add a hunk of meat to their plates or make their own taco fillings or spaghetti sauce. But often there's much common ground in meals that can be shared pleasurably and peacefully.

Hannah Kaminsky, this book's photographer, went vegan in her early teens, echoing some of the experiences I had. I went vegetarian in my teens, decades ago. She described some of her family's strategies: "While my mom, the primary meal provider of the household, has always been supportive of my plant-based diet, she warned that I would have to fend for myself, since she wasn't about to start cooking numerous separate meals every day. Thus becoming vegan was the catalyst that got me into the kitchen and interested in cooking."

The Kaminskys' family dinner centered on neutral dishes, such as rice or pasta, steamed vegetables, or a salad. While the family usually added one meaty protein, Hannah would prepare her own meatless protein dish. Like me, she occasionally started cooking for the entire family, and now, she says, "usually everyone will be a good sport and a bit adventurous. Cooking was the best way to ensure that I got something I wanted, gave my mom a break, and got everyone else eating vegan more often."

Another friend, Ellen Kanner, a vegan with an omnivore husband, agrees that it's important to make the main component of the meal something you can both enjoy. "Food should be a source of pleasure, bringing you together. Don't make separate meals—that only makes dinner divisive." Though meat isn't forbidden in Ellen's kitchen, at dinner "the main course is vegan—whole grains, beans and greens, a main course salad, a vegan curry, or a veggie stir-fry. On the other hand, when he's out on business, he's probably at a steak house."

Look at plant-based eating as an opportunity to improve the family diet. The family member who wishes to go plant-based can use it as a way to improve the eating habits of the other by using delicious food as the main attraction. My cousin Lee Iden follows a mostly plant-based diet but doesn't call herself vegan. "Call me a veganist, a nutritarian, someone who occasionally uses animal products as condiments, or just a person trying to follow a plant-based diet while navigating other food sensitivities," she explains. Her transition to primarily plant-based foods began after she was diagnosed with gluten sensitivity. She continued to cook "regular" foods for her family and ate around them, describing her own meals as "pathetic." When her daughter was diagnosed with gluten sensitivity as well, Lee decided to step it up and make meals for the family (which includes her husband, Bruce, their daughter, and two sons) based on a gluten-free centerpiece that she made sure was absolutely delicious. No one complained.

Once the nest was empty, Lee decided, for health reasons, to try to follow a primarily plant-based diet. She stopped serving any meat in the house once she discovered many wonderful gluten-free *and* vegan recipes. Lee and Bruce now eat mostly vegan food at home, and when eating out, Bruce orders a vegetarian entrée about 50 percent of the time. On the day I queried her, Lee described her husband's fare for the day: "He's got a veggie burger for today's lunch, and he had whole-grain cereal with almond milk for breakfast. It's a huge improvement over his old diet."

Lee improved her own diet as well as her family's by setting an example and offering tasty food rather than by imposing stringent rules.

Have the courage of your convictions. Just because I said that plant-based eaters have the burden of proof—the obligation to show how amazing plant-based food can be—that doesn't mean you need to make yourself an open target for criticism or, worse yet, ridicule. Stand up for your beliefs, quietly and firmly. Don't invite arguments, and ignore baiting. Having now spent decades as a vegetarian and then a vegan, I've rarely been hassled, as I've always stood firm, armed with food and facts. I am, however, totally on board with seducing people to the plant-powered side with irresistible food! And when people ask me the inevitable "why" questions, I always say I'm glad to tell them whatever they want to know, after the meal is over . . .

PLANT-POWERED SINGLES

Cookbooks rarely speak to single people, even though more Americans than ever now live alone. Singles might be concerned about how to adjust quantities downward in recipes and what foods they should keep on hand so they'll want to eat at home more often. Since I've never been in that situation, having gotten hitched right out of college, there are no better spokespersons for this experience than some of my single friends, who have contributed these fantastic tips and strategies, most of which might never have occurred to me.

Stock your pantry with staples you'll make most use of. There's no point in wasting space and money on foods you rarely eat. If there are certain styles of meals or cuisines you particularly enjoy, focus on those and make use of them. My friend Sharon Nazarian, for example, particularly enjoys southwestern-style meals like burritos, which can be assembled quickly after she returns from a long day at work. To that end, she keeps her pantry stocked with canned and refried beans and salsa; her freezer staples include frozen corn and her favorite whole-grain tortillas. Then, when she gets home, all she needs are a few fresh items—perhaps some avocado, tomatoes, and romaine lettuce, along with fresh fruit for dessert—and her favorite kind of meal is ready in practically no time.

Co-op your meals: Sharon has another practical and enjoyable way to stay motivated to cook and eat well as a single person—rotate meal preparation with one or more people on a regular basis. Taking turns with your family or roommates and assigning each person a specific day for dinner making—or even having a once-a-week dinner club—can go a long way toward helping make home cooking a reality for those who live solo. Sharon alternates meal preparation with her sister, who lives in the apartment next door to hers. Just as Sharon does when she creates her tortilla-based dinners, her sister, who enjoys cooking Italian-style meals, tailors her pantry staples to her preferences. For the sisters, it's double the culinary pleasure when they have one another's company at meals.

Focus on your favorite fresh produce staples, and be mindful of quantities. Recently, when our nest emptied, I had quite a time trying to adjust the amount of groceries I bought, especially when it came to fresh produce. I can now imagine how challenging the task is for a single person, especially those whose repertoires are, like mine, largely based on produce.

My friend Rachel Evans, a professional classical violinist, is always on the go. She finds that sticking with a set of basic fresh foods around which meals are built is helpful. She's also mindful of how much she buys at a time. Since she especially enjoys salads and juicing, some of the basics she generally keeps on hand are salad greens, carrots, beets, red cabbage, kale, parsley, and cilantro. Other staples include broccoli, bok choy, cucumbers, olives, and hummus. Says Rachel, "I buy organic prepared lentils and beans to throw into my salads as well as avocados when they're affordable. Ezekiel bread, nut butters, and nuts and seeds round out my pantry staples." (Ezekiel 4:9 is a brand of sprouted-grain breads made by the Food for Life Baking Company.) To someone just embarking on a plant-based lifestyle, Rachel's staples might sound spartan, but her choices are designed to yield the kinds of meals she most enjoys.

Rather than a long list of produce, if you're just plunging in, choose five types of must-have veggies and must-have fruits, varying them from one season to another and embellishing the list once you have a better feel for how much you actually use before the fresh goods are past their prime.

Make friends with helpful appliances. You need not buy dozens of machines and gadgets to live a healthful lifestyle, but certain items can make prepping single-serving meals easier and more fun. Heidi Rettig Efner's husband travels on business all week, so she needs to eat by herself on weekdays, just as she would if she were single. Since she enjoys grain-and-veggie meals, her best friend in the kitchen is a rice cooker that's set up for cooking grains in the bottom part and steaming veggies in a "hat" on the top. It cooks not only rice but also other grains, such as quinoa, to the perfect texture. Heidi has gotten creative with it: she cooks the grain in fresh carrot juice for extra nutrition and uses the steaming section for supercharged veggies such as sweet potatoes and edamame.

Heidi also swears by her high-speed blender and makes a hefty smoothie each day for breakfast. One of her favorites combines kale, pineapple, ginger, and cashews. She also enjoys using the blender to make delicious spreads that can serve as snacks or a single-serving dinner. For instance, a white-bean pâté on fresh bread, topped with sautéed mushrooms and greens and served with homemade soup (previously frozen in single servings for this very purpose), makes a splendid meal for the solo eater.

PART TWO

PLANT-POWERED RECIPES AND MENUS

Sweet-and-Sour Stir-Fried Vegetables
with Seitan or Tempeh (page 199)

The following chapters present not just the usual recipe categories (appetizers, soups, salads, entrées, and so on) but an approach that's more specific yet eminently flexible. Rather than one big catchall chapter of "main dishes," as you'll find in many cookbooks, plant-based or otherwise, the following chapters all center on themes around which to build full meals. These define the various styles of plant-based meals and make it easier and more fun to answer that eternal question, "What's for dinner?" That being said, you'll also find plenty of ideas and inspiration for the rest of the day's meals as well.

Flexible menu suggestions are given for most every centerpiece dish. Lots of mixing and matching can be done once you're familiar with the various meal options. The menu suggestions can be useful starting points for discovering what kinds of dishes go well together.

You'll find lots of variations within the recipes themselves as well. These are based on seasonality and preference. A good recipe doesn't need to be made according to stringent instructions, in one way only. To my mind, the best kind of recipe is one that has a firm foundation but allows individual cooks to play with it. I love it when readers let me know about certain recipes they were making and the swaps they made if they found they were missing an ingredient—or simply felt like a change. And, most important, I like knowing that even with such tweaks, the outcome was still a tasty dish that didn't suffer a bit.

The easy-to-accomplish recipes that follow are ones that can and, I hope, will become central to your plant-powered repertoire. Some recipes are templates—for instance, a basic quinoa pilaf can be varied in a number of ways, according to what's seasonal, available, and, most of all, what you're in the mood for. These are the essential recipes that every plant-powered cook needs in his or her repertoire—well, at least according to me.

These recipes and menus are not about me showing off my culinary skills or trying to convince you that it's worth taking two to three hours each night to make dinner. I don't have that kind of time, and, I suspect, neither do most of the readers of this book. Like you, I prefer to get dinner on the table in less than an hour. A nutritious meal in less than half an hour sounds like bliss to me, as it probably does to you, and it can be done if the right ingredients are made ahead of time (for instance, brown rice that's already cooked and ready to use). You won't find fancy concoctions like Panko-Crusted Eggplant Stacks with Sun-Dried Tomato–Macadamia Nut Tapenade and Thai Basil–Chipotle Chutney. Hmm . . . that doesn't sound half bad, even though I just made it up. If I came across it in a restaurant I'd be all over it. But I don't want to encounter such complexity in my own kitchen at six P.M., and I don't think you would, either. Instead, you'll find recipes with familiar-sounding names and easy techniques—chili and cornbread, vegetable lo mein, sloppy joes, hummus wraps.

The most common obstacle to enjoying a great homemade evening meal, after the lack of time and energy, is having no idea what to make. But few of us have that problem when faced with the delightful prospect of eating out. Do you feel like having a delicious, veggie-filled Asian meal? There's a chapter for that. How about a hearty Mexican-style meal? How about a light soup-and-salad dinner or a tasty pairing of soup and a wrap? If you approach your home meal preferences with the same spirit of anticipation as you bring to going out to eat, it makes a world of difference.

The chapters ahead will show you how easy it is to make the kinds of meals you already like in your own kitchen, in the most plant-powered way possible. If you're a rank beginner in the plant-based lifestyle, these menus will serve as a friendly introduction to how these kinds of meals are put together and, wherever you encounter Hannah Kaminsky's beautiful photos, how they look.

You'll find many ways to start with a simple ingredient and build a great meal around it. For example, that cooked quinoa you keep in the fridge can be turned into a number of enticing pilafs with a variety of legumes, veggies, herbs, seasonings, nuts, and dried fruits; or it can be the foundation of a nearly instant Middle Eastern–style platter. I encourage cooks of all levels to trust their intuition and personalize these recipes to their own and their families' tastes when making healthful, whole-foods, plant-based meals. Nothing is set in stone; there are few rules besides have fun and enjoy the food.

Explanation of Nutritional Analyses

All breakdowns are based on one serving. When a recipe gives a range in the number of servings—for example, between four and six—the analysis is based on the smaller number of servings.

When more than one ingredient is listed as an option, the first ingredient is used in the analysis. Usually, the optional ingredient or ingredients will not change the analysis significantly.

Ingredients listed as optional or called for as toppings or garnishes are not included in the analysis. When salt "to taste" is called for, its sodium content is not included in the analysis.

These analyses were done by a nutritionist with skill and expertise, but please note that they are still just estimates. When using prepared products, such as tortillas, salsa, or canned beans, nutritional content will vary depending on the brand used. For this book, analyses of recipes using prepared products were based on my preferred brands; when you use yours, the statistics may vary—not wildly, but they will vary nonetheless.

Finally, you'll see that the recipes have not been analyzed for cholesterol, which is usually included in standard analyses. This is because plant foods contain no cholesterol, and so, to avoid a great deal of redundancy, you should assume that the cholesterol content in all recipes is zero.

CHAPTER 1

Plant-Powered PROTEIN

When you transition to a plant-based diet, or even to a more plant-based diet, trust me, you're going to hear that old chestnut of a question, "Where do you get your protein?" While we longtime vegans kind of roll our eyes at this, it's not an unreasonable query. I look at it as an opportunity to enlighten, because most often it's asked in the spirit of curiosity, not confrontation. Once you peruse this chapter, you'll have ready answers. While you can think of this chapter as a primer for the others, you need not tackle this chapter's dishes before proceeding. They're here for reference as well as to provide basic, tasty ways to prepare these elemental plant foods.

Quick Quinoa Paella (page 102)

Before meat substitutes such as vegan hot dogs, sausages, burgers, crumbles, and others came along, those of us of the post-1960s vegetarian persuasion were compelled to prowl the aisles of dusty, sad-looking "health food" stores for sustenance. Our choices comprised mainly dried beans, brown lentils, and a limited number of grains. Now we have quinoa, which cooks in fifteen minutes, but back then we had wheat berries and oat groats, which took a couple of hours or so to cook. Okay, maybe it wasn't *that* long, but it seemed like it, and even when they were considered done, they seemed fairly challenging to chew and digest.

Now a gorgeous variety of grains and legumes (in addition to nuts, seeds, dried fruits, and more) is temptingly displayed in the bulk bins in natural foods stores as well as in many enlightened supermarkets. Red lentils, quinoa, rice in many hues, whole-grain couscous, millet, dried yellow peas, and other such basics never really lost the respect they deserve, but these days they're shining a bit brighter. They're not the unglamorous cousins of meat substitutes; rather, they're the very foundations of a whole-foods, plant-based diet.

Since this chapter serves as an introduction to using whole foods to create plant-based meals, attempting to be encyclopedic would be overwhelming. Instead of offering all the possibilities, I'd like to focus on a few protein-packed plant foods and simple ways to prepare them on the stove top. These are the basic preparations I hope you'll find useful to have in your repertoire: grain pilafs, bean skillets, and easy ways to prepare tofu, tempeh, and seitan.

While you'll find these ingredients used liberally in this book's other themed chapters, this chapter pulls the focus in a bit tighter, serving almost as a jumping-off point. So, for example, here you'll learn how quinoa is cooked, if it's unfamiliar to you, and discover ways to highlight it in seasonal pilafs. Later in the book, you'll be using it to make savory sloppy joes, burgers, and more. The steps for cooking dried beans from scratch are outlined here, if you choose to cook them that way, along with some supereasy ways to dress them up. Like whole foods, they'll continue to play a major role in many of this book's chapters.

Tofu Prep Basics

No worries, tofu newbies! These simple tips will help you tame those quivering, cream-colored blocks in no time. These steps apply to firm or extra-firm tofu that comes in tubs weighing between 14 and 16 ounces. Baked tofu and silken tofu are both ready to use out of their respective packages. If you're unfamiliar with the different varieties of tofu, review the brief lexicon on pages 40–41.

Cut a block of tofu crosswise into six slabs. Lay the slabs on several layers of paper towels or a clean kitchen towel, cover with more of the same, and apply a little pressure with your palms to press out some of the water. If you'd like the tofu to be even firmer, cover the top layer of paper towels or your kitchen towel with a cutting board, then place some weight on top of the cutting board.

If you use between two and four tubs of tofu per week, as I have these many years for my tofu-loving family, consider dispensing with the old-fashioned paper-towel-wasting technique and makeshift pressing methods and investing in a tofu press. I love both my TofuXpress and EZ Tofu Press. There are other brands as well, available online. Once the tofu is blotted or pressed, you can leave the six slabs intact to make cutlets, but more often recipes will call for it to be cut further in any number of ways. You can cut the tofu slabs into small or large dice, cut the slabs into strips, cut each slab in half to make two squares, or go one step further and cut each square on the diagonal to make triangles. This is a very tempting way to serve it to kids as well as to tofu skeptics.

Simple Preparations for Tofu, Tempeh, and Seitan

In the universe of plant proteins, tofu, tempeh, and seitan are three of the premier powerhouses, taking their place alongside legumes and select whole grains. Because this trio of protein foods needs only a light hand to prepare, and because they are so versatile, they're a blessing for the busy cook. If they're new to you, review the information and specifics on pages 40–41.

Here are a few easy and tasty ways to prepare tofu, tempeh, and seitan. These preparations are useful for boosting the protein content of a meal centered on vegetables, grains, pastas, and Asian noodles. You'll find plenty of additional recipes for using these proteins in the chapters ahead. For each of the following preparations, use one or two 8-ounce packages of tempeh, diced or cut into strips; about a pound of seitan, cut into bite-size chunks; or a 14- to 16-ounce tub of extra-firm tofu, cut into dice or strips.

The instructions that follow call for cooking on the stove top, but these preparations can all be made in the oven as well. If you prefer to cook them that way, arrange the pieces of protein in a small parchment-lined roasting pan. Bake for 25 to 35 minutes at 375°F to 425°F, depending on what else you've got baking, or until the protein begins to turn golden and crisp.

SWEET AND SAVORY

I've been making this simple tofu preparation since time immemorial—or at least from the time my children were small, as they absolutely loved it. To make it on the stove top, combine a tablespoon or so each of soy sauce, olive oil, and maple syrup (or agave nectar) in a wide skillet. Before the mixture gets too hot, add extra-firm tofu that has been well blotted and diced. Stir quickly to coat, then sauté over medium-high heat, stirring occasionally, until the tofu turns golden and crisp on most sides. Add a little grated ginger and/or sliced scallions if you like.

BARBECUE-FLAVORED

This is such a staple in my home that I can't imagine doing without it. Prepare the protein of your choice as described above. In a wide skillet or stir-fry pan, combine it with a generous amount of No-Cook Barbecue Sauce (page 86) or your favorite prepared natural barbecue sauce. Cook over medium-high heat until some of the protein starts to brown here and there, stirring regularly. This takes about 15 to 20 minutes. Add more sauce as needed.

CORNMEAL-CRUSTED

These crusty little nuggets are especially appealing to kids when served with ketchup or barbecue sauce. Prepare the protein of your choice as described above. If using tempeh, moisten with a little water before proceeding, as tempeh has a drier surface than tofu or seitan.

Combine ¼ cup cornmeal, ½ teaspoon salt, and 1 teaspoon salt-free all-purpose seasoning blend in a plastic food storage bag and give it a few shakes to combine. Add the protein to the bag, close off the top with one hand, and shake gently until it's evenly coated with the cornmeal mixture. Transfer to a wide nonstick skillet that has been lightly oiled. Cook, stirring occasionally, until golden and crisp. This recipe works especially well when baked (see above for directions).

CARAMELIZED ONION–SMOTHERED

Make any of the preparations above and top with a portion of Caramelized Onions with or without Bell Peppers (page 88)—I highly recommend the bell pepper option!

Barbecue-Flavored
or Gravy-Smothered Protein Skillet

Here's a superbasic preparation for tofu in combination with seitan and/or tempeh. This really is better than it might at first sound, because the proteins are truly enhanced by one of two flavorful sauces. I've made this more times than I can count; my kids just loved this preparation as they were growing up, especially as teenagers.

SERVES 4 TO 6

1 tablespoon extra-virgin olive oil or 3 tablespoons vegetable broth or water
1 tablespoon reduced-sodium soy sauce
One 14- to 16-ounce tub firm or extra-firm tofu
One 8-ounce package seitan or tempeh, cut into bite-size strips (for larger portions and even more protein, use both)
1 recipe No-Cook Barbecue Sauce (page 86) or Basic Gravy (page 87, any variation)
2 to 3 scallions, white and green parts, thinly sliced

1. Drain the tofu and cut into 6 slabs crosswise. Blot well between paper towels or clean kitchen towels (or use a tofu press), then cut each slab into strips.

2. Heat the oil, broth, or water and the soy sauce in a wide skillet. Add the tofu and seitan and/or tempeh. Sauté over medium-high heat, stirring frequently, until everything is golden and starting to turn crisp, about 8 to 10 minutes.

3. Meanwhile, prepare the sauce or gravy according to the directions. Remove the tofu mixture from the heat, pour the sauce or gravy into the skillet, and stir. Return to the heat. Cook for a minute or so, stirring constantly, then serve.

PER SERVING WITH SEITAN: Calories: 193 with oil, 163 without oil; Total fat: 9g with oil, 6g without oil; Protein: 24g; Carbohydrates: 6g; Fiber: 2g; Sodium: 375mg

PER SERVING WITH TEMPEH: Calories: 233 with oil, 203 without oil; Total fat: 14g with oil, 10g without oil; Protein: 20g; Carbohydrates: 12g; Fiber: 6g; Sodium: 170mg

Complete the Meal

For an easy meal, serve with Creamy Kale and Cabbage Slaw (page 324) and baked or microwaved sweet potatoes.

Tofu and Veggie Scrambles
(broccoli variation)

Tofu *and* Veggie Scrambles

For tofu fans, a book like this wouldn't be complete without a vegetable-filled scramble. Here you'll find not just this basic recipe but lots of variations, one or more of which could become your favorite. To get your weekdays off to a hearty start, make this the night before you want to have it. Then simply warm it the next morning. Or just prep the veggies the night before, as the scramble takes hardly any time at all to cook.

SERVES 4

One 14- to 16-ounce tub soft or firm tofu
2 teaspoons olive oil, Earth Balance, or other vegan buttery spread
½ teaspoon good-quality curry powder, or more to taste
Veggie variation of your choice (see below)
Salt and freshly ground pepper to taste
1 to 2 tablespoons nutritional yeast (optional; see Note)

1. Crumble the tofu in a small mixing bowl, then place it in a colander; gently press out some of the liquid while being careful not to squeeze out the tofu itself.

2. Heat the buttery spread in a skillet. When it begins to bubble, add the tofu and sprinkle in the curry powder.

3. Cook over medium-high heat for 8 minutes or so, stirring frequently, allowing the liquid to cook away (soft tofu tends to be watery) until the mixture develops a scrambled egg–like consistency.

4. Add the vegetables of your choice as directed below. Season with salt, pepper, and nutritional yeast (if desired) and serve.

note: Adding nutritional yeast lends flavor and a nice dose of B vitamins, including B_{12}. Find out more about nutritional yeast on page 13.

PER SERVING (BEFORE ADDING VEGGIE VARIATIONS): Calories: 89; Total fat: 6g; Protein: 8g; Carbohydrates: 2g; Fiber: 0g; Sodium: 23mg

continued

Veggie Variations

Add from one to three of the following to your scramble, in whatever combinations you wish. Vary the veggie combinations every time you make this, and it will be a quick dish that you'll never tire of. Some of my favorite combos are broccoli, tomato, and baby spinach; onions and hearty greens or onions and bell peppers; and asparagus and mushrooms. The following are just guidelines. You can add more or less than what's suggested below.

- **Broccoli:** Before starting the recipe above, combine 1 to 1½ cups finely chopped broccoli and a small amount of water (just enough to keep the pan moist) in the skillet you intend to use for the scramble. Sauté over medium heat, stirring frequently, until bright green. Proceed with the recipe as directed.

- **Tender greens:** Baby spinach, baby arugula, or watercress can be added to the skillet once the scramble is done; cover and allow to just wilt, then stir.

- **Mixed mushrooms:** Clean and slice 6 to 8 ounces cremini (also known as baby bella) or white button mushrooms. Or you can use more than one variety, adding unusual types such as shiitake or oyster mushrooms to the mix. Before starting the recipe above, wilt the mushrooms in the skillet you intend to use for the scramble, about 4 to 5 minutes, then drain off any excess liquid. Proceed with the recipe as directed.

- **Hearty greens:** Stem and thinly slice 6 to 8 ounces kale, collard greens, or chard. Steam them with a small amount of water in the skillet you intend to use for the scramble, just until bright green. Drain off any excess liquid and proceed with the recipe as directed.

- **Tomatoes and scallions:** Add 2 medium diced ripe tomatoes and 2 to 3 sliced scallions at the same time that you add the tofu, then proceed with the recipe as directed.

- **Onions:** In the skillet you intend to use for the scramble, sauté a medium or large chopped onion (as you prefer) in a little olive oil or water. Then proceed with the recipe as directed. Or simply incorporate Caramelized Onions with or without Bell Peppers (page 88) if you've made them ahead.

- **Bell pepper:** In the skillet you intend to use for the scramble, sauté a medium red or green bell pepper or two (diced or cut into short strips), or one of each, in a little olive oil or water. Then proceed with the recipe as directed.

- **Fresh herbs:** Use about ¼ to ½ cup finely chopped fresh parsley, cilantro, scallion, and/or basil or about 2 tablespoons minced fresh dill. Fresh oregano or thyme, in smaller quantities, are nice when available. Add toward the very end of cooking time to retain the fresh flavors of the herbs.

- **Zucchini and/or yellow summer squash:** Use 1 medium zucchini or yellow summer squash or 1 small squash of each variety. Cut into quarters lengthwise, then slice ¼ inch thick. Add at the same time as the tofu, then proceed with the recipe as directed. Add some strips of sun-dried tomato and/or sliced scallions to lend zip to this otherwise mild veggie.

- **Fresh chili pepper or other hot stuff:** Use a minced and seeded fresh hot chili pepper or two, such as jalapeño or serrano. Or, you can use crushed red pepper flakes or sriracha sauce for a spicy scramble.

Complete the Meal

For a delightful weekend brunch or weeknight dinner, serve with Easy Hash Brown Potatoes (page 300). To speed things up, make sure you have the potatoes ready ahead of time. Add a simple salad and/or fresh fruit. As shown in the photo, I've always enjoyed this scramble-and-hash-browns pairing with an Israeli-style salad of tomatoes, cucumbers, and bell peppers, diced fine and dressed with a little olive oil, lemon juice, and fresh dill.

Sauces *and* Toppings *to* Enhance Your Plant Proteins

No-Cook Barbecue Sauce

Though I'm all for high-quality prepared sauces and such to use as shortcuts, I've never found a bottled vegan barbecue sauce I really like. But this nearly instant sauce is so easy that I've ended the search. It's especially good with tofu, tempeh, and seitan. And though cooking on the grill isn't addressed in this book, it's a great sauce for that as well.

MAKES ABOUT 1¹/₂ CUPS

1 ¼ cups tomato sauce
2 tablespoons maple syrup
1 tablespoon molasses (optional)
1 to 2 tablespoons reduced-sodium natural soy sauce, or to taste
1 teaspoon sweet or smoked paprika
1 to 2 teaspoons good-quality chili powder, or to taste
1 teaspoon dried oregano or basil

Combine all ingredients in a mixing bowl and mix well. If time allows, cover and let stand at room temperature for an hour or so to allow the flavors to combine more fully. If you need to use it right away, go ahead—it will still be quite good.

PER ¼ CUP: Calories: 36; Total fat: 0g; Protein: 1g; Carbohydrates: 9g; Fiber: 1g; Sodium: 159mg

This sauce is used in

- Barbecue-Flavored or Gravy-Smothered Protein Skillet (page 81)
- "Simple Preparations for Tofu, Tempeh, and Seitan" (pages 79–80)
- Skillet Barbecue-Flavored Beans (page 95)
- Barbecue-Flavored Roasted Vegetables (page 295)

Basic Gravy *with* Mushroom *and* Miso Variations

Even without the extras listed in the variations, this gravy is a tasty way to enhance tofu, tempeh, and seitan as well as simple cooked grains. It's delicious on potatoes as well.

MAKES ABOUT 1½ CUPS

1¼ cups vegetable broth
2½ tablespoons reduced-sodium soy sauce
2 tablespoons arrowroot or cornstarch
Good pinch of dried thyme or dried basil
2 tablespoons nutritional yeast (optional but highly recommended)

1. Combine 1 cup of the broth and the soy sauce in a small saucepan and bring to a simmer.

2. Meanwhile, combine the arrowroot with the remaining broth in a cup or small container. Stir until smoothly dissolved.

3. When the broth reaches a steady simmer, slowly whisk in the dissolved arrowroot, whisking constantly until the mixture is thickened.

4. Remove from the heat and whisk in the dried thyme and nutritional yeast. Use at once or cover and keep warm until needed.

PER ¼ CUP: Calories: 17; Total fat: 0g; Protein: 0g; Carbohydrates: 3.5g; Fiber: 0g; Sodium: 280mg

Variations

- **Mushroom gravy:** Add 6 to 8 ounces thinly sliced mushrooms to the broth and soy sauce in the first step. Use your favorite—cremini (baby bella), shiitake, oyster mushrooms, or a combination.

- **Miso gravy:** Omit the soy sauce from the initial step; whisk in 2 to 3 tablespoons of any variety of miso (thinned in a little water) once the gravy is done. Of course, you can also make a mushroom-miso gravy by adding mushrooms as directed in the variation above. For more about miso, see the sidebar on page 214.

Caramelized Onions
with or without Bell Peppers

In "Top Ten Make-Aheads to Get You Through the Week," pages 51–52, this is one of the items on the list. Can you make it through the week without a batch of caramelized onions? Most definitely. But if you're an onion fan, you'll appreciate having these deliciously sweet onions ready and waiting to embellish all kinds of dishes.

There are no exact quantities for this, but as a guideline, I usually use two large (or three to four medium) onions and one medium red bell pepper. You can use yellow or red onions or some of each. And of course you can use bell peppers of other hues, including green, yellow, and orange. Quarter and thinly slice the onions. If using a bell pepper, cut it into short, narrow strips.

Heat a tablespoon or two of olive oil (or ¼ cup vegetable broth) in a medium or large skillet, depending on how much you're making. Add the sliced onions and sauté over low heat, covered, until soft and medium-brown in color. The slower you cook them, the more tender and sweet they'll become. This process should take no less than 20 minutes, which is why it's nice to make ahead. If you're using a bell pepper, add it (cut as described above) once the onions are golden. At this point, you can add a couple of cloves of minced garlic if you like.

Complete the meal

This preparation, with or without peppers, is fantastic for

- incorporating into Tofu and Veggie Scrambles (page 82);
- topping simply cooked grains (see "Easy Ways to Dress Up Whole Grains," page 114);
- spreading over White Pizza with Caramelized Onions and Olives (page 184);
- adding flavor to Sizzling Tempeh or Tofu Fajitas (page 230);
- topping burgers, with or without buns (pages 274 and 277);
- topping smashed potatoes (pages 303-5);
- any preparation in which you'd enjoy extra flavor.

Bean Basics

Beans, once the subject of all manner of jokes and stigmatized as a fattening "poor man's" food, have finally sloughed off their negative reputation. Available in a rainbow of earthy hues, they've emerged as lean and tasty—even gourmet—fare. They're excellent sources of protein, complex carbohydrates, and fiber.

COOKING BEANS FROM SCRATCH

For a number of years, I've relied on canned beans; I feel that eating them from a can is better than not eating them at all. But a kind of DIY revival is in the air where beans are concerned; if you want to cook your own, so much the better. It's not only more economical but also allows you to control your sodium consumption. The high salt content of canned beans is, in fact, a major drawback.

Another downside is that many cans (not just those containing beans) are made with the chemical BPA. Some brands of organic beans come in BPA-free cans and are labeled as such, so you can seek them out. Of course you'll pay a premium for beans that are not only organic but also BPA-free; even with that factored in, they're still a protein bargain.

Good-quality canned beans are great to have in the pantry at all times, but especially during warmer months, when the long soaking and cooking time required for dried beans is less than optimal. I recommend buying canned beans with no additives and rinsing the salty broth away before use.

Pressure cookers and slow cookers provide two other excellent options for cooking beans, and we'll get to that in a bit. For cooking the old-fashioned way, all you need is a large cooking pot. As a rule of thumb, dried beans generally swell to about two and a half times their volume once cooked. If you need four cups of cooked beans, for example, start with 1⅔ cups dried. As long as you're making the effort, it pays to cook more than you need for one recipe and freeze the extra beans for later use. Beans are one of the foods that freeze most successfully. Here are the basic steps:

1. Rinse the beans in a colander and look through them carefully to remove grit and small stones.

2. Combine the beans in a large pot with about three times their volume in water. This doesn't have to be exact. Cover and soak overnight. Refrigerate the cooking pot if your kitchen tends to be warm or if you're cooking the beans in the summer. For a quicker soaking method, bring the mixture to a boil, then cover and let stand off the heat for an hour or two.

3. Drain the soaking water. Though some vitamins may be lost, draining the soaking water also eliminates some of the complex sugars that many people have trouble digesting. Fill the pot with fresh water, this time in a quantity about double the volume of the beans. Again, no exact measuring is needed; just allow plenty of room for the beans to simmer. Here's a cool tip—toss a small quartered onion and a couple of bay leaves into the pot, which will add flavor as the beans cook. Discard them once the beans are done.

4. Bring the water to a boil, then lower the heat to a gentle simmer. Cover and cook the beans slowly and steadily. Set the cover slightly off the pot to prevent foaming. Most beans take about one and a half hours to cook slowly and thoroughly. To test if the beans are done, press one between your thumb and forefinger; it should yield easily. Where beans are concerned, a bit overdone is better than underdone: not cooking them enough will hinder their digestibility as well as their mouth feel.

5. Add salt to taste only when the beans are done. Salt tends to harden the skins and prolong cooking time.

PRESSURE-COOKING BEANS

A pressure cooker greatly reduces cooking time and is not the treacherous appliance many people once feared. You'll do best if you follow the manufacturer's instructions for cooking beans and other foods. I'm not being lazy here, just practical, as cooking directions will be more accurate coming from the pressure cooker's instruction manual as opposed to any general guidelines I could give you.

Certain legumes—including split peas, lima beans, fava beans, and soybeans—aren't always recommended for pressure-cooking because they foam excessively. Cookbooks by Jill Nussinow and Lorna Sass deal extensively with pressure-cooking beans and other natural foods. I defer to their expertise; please consult their books if you'd like to learn more on the subject.

SLOW-COOKER BEANS

Beans prepared in a slow cooker turn out beautifully tender and digestible, with a nice broth. Follow specific instructions provided by the manufacturer. To enhance the broth, add chopped onions and a couple of bay leaves, as suggested above for the traditional cooking method.

COOKING LENTILS

Lentils are easy to cook, and they need not be presoaked. For ordinary green and brown lentils as well as black beluga lentils, first rinse them in a fine sieve and look through them carefully for small stones, which have a habit of sneaking into batches of dried lentils. Most often, cooking one cup (about a half pound) of dried lentils is sufficient for an average recipe. Combine the rinsed lentils in a roomy saucepan with two cups of water and bring to a slow boil. Lower the heat; once the mixture reaches a gentle, steady simmer, cover (leaving the lid a bit off the pot) and cook over low heat for thirty to forty minutes, or until the lentils are tender but still hold their shape.

For red lentils, follow the same directions. These take only twenty minutes to cook and become pleasantly mushy, making them perfect for soups.

CANNED BEANS

If time is an issue, you're better off using canned beans than none at all. From a culinary perspective, the essential difference between canned beans and home-cooked beans is the sodium content, which can be pretty darn high in the former. Draining and rinsing canned beans helps mitigate the sodium content, but they still remain fairly salty, so take care when adding extra salt to recipes in which they're used. You may not need added salt at all. For a high-quality alternative, try organic cooked beans, available in natural foods stores. They're usually not nearly as salty as their nonorganic counterparts.

Another concern where canned beans—or indeed any canned products—are concerned is the chemical BPA (bisphenol A), a sealant used to coat the inside of metal products, including cans. According to the FDA, the low levels of BPA in cans is safe. So with this information you need to assess how deeply you trust the FDA. The good news is that many companies, especially those that distribute to natural foods stores, offer BPA-free cans. Search the Internet for "BPA-free cans" and the year in which you're searching to get the most up-to-date information available, including the names of companies that offer BPA-free canned goods. Anything I'd put in writing now might already be dated by the time this book is printed.

Skillet Bean Dishes

Sweet *and* Smoky Beans *and* Greens

A sweet-and-savory sauce quickly coats the beans in this dish, making them incredibly appealing. Mesquite seasoning is available in most supermarkets in the spice section, where it's shelved with grilling seasonings and rubs. It adds a deep, smoky element to food when flavor needs to develop quickly. Liquid smoke is also found in the spice section of most supermarkets, though I much prefer the mesquite.

SERVES 4 AS A MAIN DISH, 6 OR MORE AS A SIDE DISH

6 to 8 collard or lacinato kale leaves, rinsed well
1 tablespoon olive oil plus 3 tablespoons water (or ¼ cup vegetable broth or water)
2 tablespoons balsamic vinegar
1 tablespoon reduced-sodium soy sauce or tamari
2 tablespoons maple syrup or agave nectar
2 tablespoons good-quality ketchup or tomato paste
Two 15- to 16-ounce cans beans, preferably two varieties, rinsed and drained
    (try chickpeas with red or pinto beans, navy beans with black beans, or any beans
    of contrasting size and/or color)
Mesquite seasoning or liquid smoke to taste
Freshly ground pepper or crushed red pepper flakes to taste

1. Using kitchen shears, cut the collard or lacinato kale leaves fairly neatly away from the stems. Stack 4 or 5 similar-size leaf halves atop one another. Roll up snugly from one of the narrow ends, then slice into very thin ribbons. Chop the slices in a few places to shorten the ribbons.

2. Heat the oil and water (or broth or water) in a medium skillet or stir-fry pan. Add the greens and turn up the heat to medium-high. Cook, stirring frequently, until bright green and tender-crisp, about 3 to 4 minutes. If any water is left in the pan, drain it and transfer the greens to a plate.

3. In the same skillet, combine the vinegar, soy sauce, maple syrup, and ketchup. Stir together, then add the beans and stir to coat.

4. Season with mesquite (start with a few sprinkles and taste) or liquid smoke (start with ½ teaspoon). Add a bit of pepper or red pepper flakes. This is very much a season-to-taste kind of dish, so you can make it subtle or bold to your liking.

5. Continue cooking until the beans are hot and nicely glazed, about 3 to 5 minutes longer. Stir in the reserved greens. Serve at once or cover until needed.

PER SERVING WITH HOME-COOKED BEANS: Calories: 232 with oil, 203 without oil; Total fat: 3g with oil, 0g without oil; Protein: 10g; Carbohydrates: 39g; Fiber: 9g; Sodium: 435mg

Complete the Meal

- This goes well with many other dishes, not only in this chapter but also in some of the others. For example, any of the Classic Marinara Sauce variations on pages 157–58 benefit from the added protein provided when this dish is stirred in. It's also excellent paired with many of the smashed potatoes variations on pages 303–5 as well as for the Classic Potato Salad, page 312. With any of these, something fresh and crisp in the way of salad or raw veggies would be welcome.

- Pair this with any of the grits variations on page 117 or serve over polenta, either soft-cooked or prepared (page 115).

Lemon *and* Garlic Beans *or* Lentils

This basic preparation of beans or lentils is enlivened by a lemony flavor. While it may not have enough of a "wow" factor to be a stand-alone main dish, it's an easy add-on to meals for which you'd like a protein boost.

SERVES 4 AS A MAIN DISH, 6 OR MORE AS A SIDE DISH

1 tablespoon extra-virgin olive oil or 3 tablespoons vegetable broth or water
1 medium onion, quartered and thinly sliced
3 to 4 cloves garlic, minced
3½ to 4 cups cooked or two 15- to 16-ounce cans (drained and rinsed) beans or
    lentils of your choice (use two different varieties, if you like)
½ cup vegetable broth or water
Juice of ½ to 1 lemon, or 2 to 3 tablespoons bottled lemon juice, or to taste
Salt and freshly ground pepper to taste
1 to 2 teaspoons grated lemon zest (optional but highly recommended)
4 to 6 ounces baby spinach or arugula leaves or half a bunch watercress
¼ cup minced fresh parsley or cilantro, or more to taste

1. Heat the oil, broth, or water in a skillet. Add the onion and garlic and sauté over low heat until golden. Add the beans or lentils and bring to a simmer.

2. Using a potato masher, crush some of the beans—just enough to thicken the base. Add lemon juice and season with salt (omit the salt if you're using canned beans) and pepper.

3. If desired, add lemon zest to heighten the citrus flavor. Cook gently for 2 to 3 minutes longer. Add baby spinach, arugula, or watercress. Cover and cook until just wilted, then stir.

4. Stir in the chopped parsley or cilantro or pass it at the table for topping individual portions. Serve on its own or over grains or pasta.

PER SERVING WITH HOME-COOKED BEANS: Calories: 259 with oil, 229 without oil; Total fat: 5g with oil, 2g without oil; Protein: 15g; Carbohydrates: 40g; Fiber: 13g; Sodium: 10mg

Complete the Meal

See the menu suggestions for Sweet and Smoky Beans and Greens (page 92); these lemony beans and lentils can be used the same way. They also crop up in several other menu suggestions throughout this book.

Skillet Barbecue-Flavored Beans

This might well become your favorite go-to bean dish if you enjoy the flavor of barbecue sauce—its sweet and savory tang is so compatible with beans. This dish is also one of the easiest and tastiest ways to prepare beans on the stove top. I think it tastes best when made with white beans, such as navy, great northern, or cannellini, but if you prefer, try it with pink or pinto beans.

SERVES 4 AS A MAIN DISH, 6 OR MORE AS A SIDE DISH

1 tablespoon extra-virgin olive oil or 3 tablespoons vegetable broth or water
1 large onion, quartered and thinly sliced
2 cloves garlic, minced (optional)
3½ to 4 cups cooked or two 15- to 16-ounce cans (drained and rinsed) beans of your choice
½ recipe No-Cook Barbecue Sauce (page 86), or to taste

1. Heat the oil, broth, or water in a skillet. Add the onion and garlic and sauté over low heat until both are golden.
2. Add the beans and sauce and bring to a simmer. Lower the heat and cook, uncovered, for 10 to 15 minutes, or until the sauce envelops the beans nicely. Add a bit more sauce if you like; the dish should be saucy but not soupy. Serve at once.

PER SERVING WITH HOME-COOKED BEANS: Calories: 291 with oil, 261 without oil; Total fat: 4g with oil, 1g without oil; Protein: 16g; Carbohydrates: 50g; Fiber: 11g; Sodium: 250 mg

Complete the Meal

- This is a delicious companion to Quinoa Pilaf with Vegetable Variations (page 100). Add a platter of colorful raw veggies or one of the simple slaws, pages 322–25. A creamy slaw is a nice foil for the robust flavor of barbecue sauce.
- Try this with or over any simple grain dish, prepared as suggested in "Easy Ways to Dress Up Whole Grains" (page 114). For example, brown rice embellished with finely chopped spinach pairs beautifully with this. Complete the menu with one of the supereasy salads described in "Fruity, Nutty Mixed Greens Salads" (page 326) or a simple slaw.

Curried Chickpeas
or Lentils *with* Spinach

Another tasty legumes-and-greens combo, this dish is made in a snap once you've got your lentils or chickpeas cooked. You can save even more time by using canned legumes or by cooking the dried legumes the night before. Served over hot cooked grains, this is a warming, satisfying dish you'll enjoy if you're a fan of curry seasonings.

SERVES 4 AS A MAIN DISH, 6 OR MORE AS A SIDE DISH

1 tablespoon extra-virgin olive oil or 3 tablespoons vegetable broth or water
2 to 3 cloves garlic, minced
3½ to 4 cups cooked or two 15- to 16-ounce cans (drained and rinsed) chickpeas
    or lentils (see Note)
2 cups diced ripe fresh tomatoes or one 15- to 16-ounce can diced tomatoes, undrained
2 teaspoons good-quality curry powder, or more to taste
1 to 2 teaspoons minced fresh or jarred ginger
Generous pinch of ground cinnamon
6 to 8 ounces chopped fresh spinach or baby spinach leaves
2 scallions, white and green parts, thinly sliced
¼ to ½ cup chopped fresh cilantro
¼ cup raisins (optional but highly recommended)
Salt and freshly ground pepper to taste
Hot cooked brown basmati or other specialty rice, quinoa, or couscous

1. Heat the oil, broth, or water in a large skillet. Add the garlic and sauté over low heat until golden.

2. Add the chickpeas or lentils, tomatoes, curry powder, ginger, and cinnamon. Bring to a simmer, then cook for 8 to 10 minutes over low heat.

3. Add the spinach on top of the other vegetables (in batches if need be) and stir in when just wilted.

4. Stir in the scallions and cilantro (you can reserve half the cilantro for garnishing individual portions if you like).

5. Stir in the raisins, if desired. Season with salt and freshly ground pepper. Serve over hot cooked grains.

note: Use any variety of firm lentils—brown, green, or beluga—or a combination of lentils and chickpeas.

PER SERVING WITH HOME-COOKED BEANS: Calories: 307 with oil, 277 without oil; Total fat: 8g with oil, 4g without oil; Protein: 16g; Carbohydrates: 48g; Fiber: 14g; Sodium: 85mg

Variations

Substitute baby arugula, chopped tender kale, mustard greens, or escarole for the spinach.

Complete the Meal

- Omit the hot cooked grains and serve over smashed potatoes (pages 303-5), or with Brown and Wild Rice Pilaf with Mushrooms and Nuts, page 109. Add a colorful salad on the side.
- To continue the curry theme, omit the hot cooked grains and serve with Basmati Rice Pilaf with Fresh Fruit or Cauliflower, page 110. See the directions for Easy Cucumber Raita on page 147.

Quinoa Pilafs with
Vegetable Variations
(page 100)

Quinoa Basics

A grain of ancient South American origin, quinoa was once the staple nourishment of the Inca culture and is now the darling of the plant-based crowd—and beyond. Quinoa is considered a superfood for its superb nutritional profile, which includes high-quality protein. It cooks to a fluffy texture in about fifteen minutes and has a mild yet distinct flavor.

The most common quinoa variety is yellowish-tan, but red and black hues are available as well. They taste pretty much the same; their appeal is mainly visual. The colorful varieties are a bit more costly. A little less known, but making inroads into the food scene, is kañiwa, an even tinier grain than its tiny botanical cousin quinoa, with which it shares many culinary and nutritional properties.

Quinoa has a better-quality and more complete protein than any other grain aside from amaranth. It's also rich in minerals, B vitamins, and vitamin E. Busy cooks appreciate its brief cooking time; its fluffy texture and nutty flavor and aroma also make it quite versatile.

BASIC COOKED QUINOA

1. Rinse the quinoa in a very fine sieve. Many commercial types of quinoa have been pre-rinsed to remove the slightly bitter but unharmful saponins that form a natural coating on the seeds. But you never know, especially if you buy it in bulk. So take a few extra seconds and rinse it to be sure.

2. Combine the quinoa with vegetable broth or water in a 2-to-1 ratio in a small saucepan. Most often, it will be practical to use either 2 cups water to 1 cup quinoa or 3 cups water to 1½ cups quinoa, depending on how much you want to serve at a given meal. These amounts will yield 2 to 3 cups cooked quinoa respectively.

3. Bring the mixture to a rapid simmer, then lower the heat and cover. Simmer gently until the broth or water is absorbed, about 15 minutes.

This basic cooked quinoa recipe is very adaptable:

- Use it as a bed for bean or vegetable dishes in place of rice.
- Use it to make pilafs with nuts and dried fruits, which can then be served as side dishes or stuffings for vegetables.
- Make tabbouleh-style salads with it, like the one on page 315. Add diced crisp vegetables, fresh tomatoes, and minced herbs.
- Use it plain, cooked in vegetable broth instead of water for extra flavor, as a nutrition-boosting side dish.

Quinoa Pilafs

Quinoa Pilaf *with* Vegetable Variations

Here's a go-to pilaf recipe that you can vary according to season, mood, or the kinds of vegetables that happen to be in your refrigerator. Use the variations following as a guideline; take off from there with your own combinations.

SERVES 4 TO 6

1¹/₂ cups uncooked quinoa, rinsed in a fine sieve

3 cups vegetable broth or 3 cups water mixed with 1 tablespoon salt-free
    all-purpose seasoning blend

1 tablespoon extra-virgin olive oil or 3 tablespoons vegetable broth or water

1 medium yellow or red onion, chopped

3 to 4 cloves garlic, minced

Veggie Variations of your choice (see below)

¹/₂ teaspoon dried oregano, or more to taste

¹/₂ teaspoon ground cumin, or more to taste

¹/₄ to ¹/₂ cup chopped fresh parsley or cilantro to taste

Salt and freshly ground pepper to taste

1. Combine the quinoa and broth or water in a medium saucepan and bring to a simmer. Bring to a rapid simmer, then turn the heat down, cover, and simmer gently until the water is absorbed, about 15 minutes.

2. Heat the oil, broth, or water in a skillet or stir-fry pan. Add the onion and garlic and sauté over medium heat until golden.

3. Add the vegetable medley of your choice and continue to cook until the vegetables are tender-crisp.

4. Stir in the cooked quinoa followed by the oregano and cumin. Cook over low heat, stirring frequently, for 3 to 5 minutes longer. Stir in the parsley or cilantro, season with salt and pepper, then serve at once.

PER SERVING BEFORE ADDING VEGETABLES: Calories: 294 with oil, 264 without oil; Total fat: 7g with oil, 4g without oil; Protein: 9g; Carbohydrates: 50g; Fiber: 5g; Sodium: 20mg

Vegetable Variations

Add any one of these vegetable combinations after the onion and garlic sauté. Feel free to come up with your own variations as well.

- **Mushrooms, tomato, and baby spinach or baby arugula:** For an earthy pilaf, add 4 to 6 ounces sliced brown mushrooms and a diced tomato or two; cook until softened, then add 4 to 5 ounces baby spinach and cook until just barely wilted.

- **Corn, yellow squash, and scallion:** For a summery pilaf, add the kernels from 2 lightly cooked ears of corn and a medium yellow squash, cut into half-moons. Two or three sliced scallions add a nice flavor. Optional, though quite tasty: top this pilaf with chopped cilantro.

- **Kale or collard greens and butternut squash or sweet potato:** Add chopped kale or ribbons of collard greens (use several leaves, rinsed well and stemmed) plus cubes of firm-cooked butternut squash or sweet potato.

- **Cauliflower and broccoli:** Add about 2 heaping cups each finely chopped broccoli and cauliflower florets. Once the pilaf is completely done, sprinkle some toasted slivered almonds over the top if you like.

Complete the Meal

- Like the Quick Quinoa Paella (page 102), any of these quinoa pilafs are nicely balanced by salads that have a little sweetness. They all go well with those from "Fruity, Nutty Mixed Greens Salads" on page 326. For a larger meal, consider pairing this with any of the simple preparations for tofu, tempeh, and seitan (pages 79–80).

- Another delicious meal plan—serve any of these pilafs with Smoky Tempeh Strips (page 268) and Apple Slaw with Leafy Greens (page 325).

Quick Quinoa Paella

Paella is a Spanish pilaf traditionally made with white rice and seafood. We'll do away with the seafood here, of course, and since we're dispensing with tradition, let's do away with white rice as well. Using nutritious and quick-cooking quinoa instead, you can have a colorful meal in about thirty minutes.

SERVES 6

1 tablespoon extra-virgin olive oil or 3 tablespoons vegetable broth or water
3 to 4 cloves garlic, minced
1 green bell pepper, cut into 2-inch strips
1 red bell pepper, cut into 2-inch strips
1 cup sliced baby bella (cremini) mushrooms (optional)
2 cups vegetable broth
1½ teaspoons turmeric (see Note)
1 cup uncooked quinoa, rinsed in a fine sieve
2 teaspoons fresh or ½ teaspoon dried thyme
One 14- to 15-ounce can artichoke hearts, drained and quartered
2 cups frozen green peas, thawed
2 cups diced ripe fresh tomatoes
2 to 3 scallions, thinly sliced (white and green parts)
½ cup chopped fresh parsley
Salt and freshly ground pepper to taste

1. Heat the oil, broth, or water in a large, deep skillet or stir-fry pan. Add the garlic, bell peppers, and mushrooms, if desired, and sauté over medium-low heat until softened, about 2 to 3 minutes.

2. Add the broth, turmeric, and quinoa. Bring to a simmer and cook, covered, for 15 minutes.

3. Stir in the thyme, artichoke hearts, peas, tomatoes, scallions, and half the parsley. Check if the quinoa is completely done; if not, add ½ cup water. Cook, stirring frequently, just until everything is well heated through, about 5 minutes.

4. Transfer the mixture to a large shallow serving container. Sprinkle the remaining parsley over the top and serve at once.

note: As another departure from tradition, I've suggested turmeric rather than the customary saffron. Saffron is harder to obtain and very expensive, but you're welcome to try it if you have access to it. Use 1 to 1½ teaspoons saffron threads dissolved in a small amount of hot water.

PER SERVING: Calories: 222 with oil, 202 without oil; Total fat: 4g with oil, 2g without oil; Protein: 10g; Carbohydrates: 40g; Fiber: 9g; Sodium: 240mg

Complete the Meal

Serve with any of the variations from "Fruity, Nutty Mixed Greens Salads," page 326. Add a steamed green vegetable to the plate—asparagus, green beans, or broccoli work well. If you don't mind making one more simple recipe, Garlicky Hardy Greens (page 287) is excellent with this meal. To any of these green vegetable side dishes, add two cups cooked (or a 15- to 16-ounce can) chickpeas, navy beans, or other beans of your choice, as the plate needs a protein boost.

Brown Rice Basics

With its nutty taste and chewy texture, brown rice doesn't fade into the background in a meal, as white rice does. Once you switch to brown rice, there's no going back! Purchased in bulk, brown rice is quite economical. It stores well for several months, provided that storage conditions are consistently cool and dry. I like to keep mine in mason jars. Most natural-foods stores also offer organically grown brown rice at a slightly higher price.

NUTRITION NOTES

To produce white rice, the bran, polish, and germ of the rice grain are removed, leaving only the starchy white endosperm. White rice contains only about one-third of the vitamins and fiber, half the minerals, none of the vitamin E, and 80 percent of the protein in brown rice. To add some nutrition back in, white rice is often enriched with iron and three B vitamins, but it contains a fraction of the nutritional content of whole brown rice.

Brown rice is high in fiber, low in fat, and easy to digest. It provides a good range of B vitamins as well as minerals, notably, phosphorus, calcium, and potassium. Brown rice is not as high in protein as some other common grains, such as quinoa, millet, oats, and barley, but its protein content is not insignificant. This chapter is about protein-packed dishes, so to help brown rice earn its place in this chapter—and because it is a staple in many a plant-based diet—we'll help it along with legumes and nuts, with which it's highly compatible.

BROWN RICE VARIETIES

Brown rice is available in a number of varieties. The differences among them are more culinary than nutritional. When deciding which to buy, keep in mind how you plan to use the rice. The supermarket is a handy place to buy long-grain brown rice, but to explore other varieties, visit a well-stocked natural foods store or food co-op. There you'll more likely find brown basmati, jasmine, wehani, and others (though Texmati and Calmati—domestically grown brown basmatis—are often found in supermarkets). These specialty rices are exceptionally aromatic, enhancing their delicate flavors.

Long-grain brown rice cooks to a firm, fluffy texture, and its grains remain separate when cooked. The texture and mild, lightly nutty flavor make long-grain a good all-purpose rice. It's especially good in pilafs, rice salads, and as a bed for vegetables and bean dishes.

Medium-grain brown rice, like long-grain, cooks to a fluffy texture but is slightly more tender, sweet, and nutty. Like long-grain, it's a good all-purpose rice, delicious in pilafs, salads, and vegetable and bean dishes.

Short-grain brown rice, the kernels of which are almost round, cooks to a denser texture and is slightly sweeter than both long- and medium-grain brown rice. If it is cooked to more than a just-done consistency, it becomes sticky. It's a great choice for rice puddings, baked goods, and savory pancakes.

Brown basmati rice is a tender long-grain rice that originated in India. Basmati's special appeal is its extra-nutty flavor and enticing aroma. You may have tasted basmati rice in Indian eateries, but there, it's usually the refined (white) type. Brown basmati is grown in California and Texas and sold, appropriately, as Calmati and Texmati.

In bulk or packaged, brown basmati is a bit more expensive than ordinary brown rice, but not so much as to make it prohibitive. It's especially good with Indian-style fare, but it can be substituted in any recipe calling for long- or medium-grain brown rice.

BASIC COOKED BROWN RICE

The amount of water recommended for cooking long- and medium-grain brown rice varies, whether in published recipes or package directions. For any variety, I suggest starting with two parts water (or vegetable broth) to one part rice. Remember to rinse the rice well before cooking. Combine water and rice in a saucepan and bring to a gentle boil. Lower the heat, then cover and simmer for thirty to thirty-five minutes, until the water is absorbed. If the grain isn't tender enough, add a half cup additional water or broth and continue to cook until absorbed; repeat until the rice is cooked to your liking.

Spanish-Style Rice
with Red Beans *and* Olives

This classic Spanish dish is a great choice when you want something easy and hearty. Briny olives perk up the mellow flavor of brown rice and beans.

SERVES 6

1¼ cups uncooked brown rice (see Note)
1 tablespoon extra-virgin olive oil or 3 tablespoons vegetable broth or water
1 large yellow or red onion, quartered and thinly sliced
3 to 4 cloves garlic, minced
3½ cups cooked or two 15- to 16-ounce cans (drained and rinsed) small red beans
1½ cups diced ripe fresh tomato
¾ cup pimiento-stuffed green olives, chopped
3 scallions, white and green parts, thinly sliced
1 tablespoon adobo seasoning, or to taste
Crushed red pepper flakes to taste
Salt and freshly ground pepper to taste
½ cup chopped fresh cilantro or parsley

1. Combine the rice with 2½ cups water in a small saucepan and bring to a slow boil. Lower the heat and simmer gently and steadily, covered, until the water is absorbed, about 30 minutes. If you'd like a more tender grain, add another ½ cup water and cook until absorbed. This step can be done ahead, and the cooked rice can be stored in the refrigerator overnight.

2. Shortly before serving, heat the oil, broth, or water in a large, deep skillet or stir-fry pan. Add the onion and sauté over medium-low heat until translucent. Add the garlic and continue to sauté until the onion just begins to brown.

3. Add the cooked rice to the skillet along with the next six ingredients. Cook for 5 to 8 minutes, or until everything is well heated through.

4. Season with salt and pepper, then stir in half the cilantro. Pass around the remaining cilantro to top individual servings.

note: Try this with brown basmati rice for extra flavor and aroma, or use an exotic rice blend for extra color and flavor.

PER SERVING: Calories: 334 with oil, 314 without oil; Total fat: 6g with oil, 3g without oil; Protein: 13g; Carbohydrates: 59g; Fiber: 12g; Sodium: 333mg

Complete the Meal

- Serve with wilted rainbow chard or other hardy greens (see Garlicky Hardy Greens, page 287) along with a platter of stacked tomato and orange or pineapple slices, as shown in the photo below, or a platter of red and yellow peppers, artichoke hearts, cherry tomatoes, and orange slices.

- A salad of mixed greens, small orange sections, and toasted almonds is also a nice companion to this dish; add more green to the plate with steamed broccoli, broccoli rabe, or green beans.

Latin American–Style Black Beans *and* Rice

This classic preparation is characterized by a group of veggies and seasonings often referred to as sofrito—basically, the onion, garlic, bell pepper, tomato, and chili peppers, which meld together deliciously with the beans. No wonder this is a classic!

SERVES 4 TO 6

1 tablespoon extra-virgin olive oil or 3 tablespoons vegetable broth or water

1 large onion, finely chopped

3 to 4 cloves garlic, minced

1 medium green or red bell pepper, or half of each, finely diced

1 cup finely diced ripe fresh tomato

1 to 2 small fresh hot chili peppers, seeded and minced, or crushed red pepper flakes to taste (optional)

4 cups cooked or two 15- to 16-ounce cans (drained and rinsed) black beans

2 teaspoons ground cumin

1 teaspoon dried oregano

Juice of 1/2 to 1 lemon or lime, or to taste

Salt and freshly ground pepper to taste

1/4 cup chopped fresh cilantro or parsley (optional)

Hot cooked rice

1. Heat the oil in a large skillet. Add the onion and sauté over medium heat until translucent. Add the garlic and the bell pepper and continue to sauté until all have softened and are starting to turn golden.

2. Add the next six ingredients along with 1/3 cup water. Bring to a simmer.

3. Mash a small amount of the black beans with the back of a wooden spoon, just enough to thicken the base. Simmer gently, covered, over low heat for 10 minutes.

4. Season with salt and pepper, then stir in the cilantro, if desired, and serve over hot rice.

PER SERVING: Calories: 289 with oil, 259 without oil; Total fat: 4g with oil, 1g without oil; Protein: 17g; Carbohydrates: 49g; Fiber: 17g; Sodium: 10mg

Complete the Meal

This is delicious with roasted winter squash (page 290) during the cooler months, or zucchini and/or yellow squash simply sautéed in olive oil any time of year. Any of the fruity, nutty mixed greens salads (page 326) or simple slaws on pages 322–25 round out this combination nicely.

Brown *and* Wild Rice Pilaf *with* Mushrooms *and* Nuts

Filled with earthy flavors, this pilaf is as equally welcome for everyday cool weather meals as it is for holiday menus. Wild rice is nutrient-dense, with a plethora of minerals, B vitamins, and fiber.

SERVES 4 AS A GENEROUS MAIN DISH OR 6 AS A HEARTY SIDE DISH

2/3 cup uncooked wild rice
2/3 cup uncooked long-grain brown rice
3 cups vegetable broth or water
1 tablespoon extra-virgin olive oil, fragrant nut oil, or 3 tablespoons vegetable broth or water
1 medium red onion, finely chopped
2 stalks celery, diced
2 to 3 cloves garlic, minced
6 ounces brown mushrooms (try a combination of cremini and shiitake), thinly sliced
4 to 6 ounces baby spinach
Juice of 1/2 lemon, or 2 tablespoons bottled lemon juice, or to taste
1/4 cup finely chopped fresh parsley
2 to 3 teaspoons salt-free all-purpose seasoning blend (see page 121 for brands)
1 teaspoon ground cumin
1/2 cup lightly toasted chopped walnuts or slivered almonds
Salt and freshly ground pepper to taste

1. Rinse the wild and brown rice and combine them in a saucepan with the broth or water. Bring to a gentle boil, then lower the heat and cover. Simmer gently until the water is absorbed, about 35 minutes. Remove from heat.

2. Heat the oil, broth, or water in a large skillet. Add the onion and sauté over medium-low heat until translucent. Add the celery and garlic and continue to sauté until the onion is lightly browned.

3. Add the mushrooms and sauté until they have softened, about 5 minutes, then add the spinach, in two batches if needed. Cover and cook just until the spinach wilts down, which will take 30 to 45 seconds.

4. Stir in the cooked wild and brown rice mixture along with the lemon juice, parsley, salt-free seasoning blend, and cumin. Cook for 5 minutes over low heat, stirring frequently. Stir in the nuts, season with salt and pepper, and serve at once.

continued

PER SERVING: Calories: 352 with oil; 341 without oil; Total fat: 12g with oil, 11g without oil; Protein: 12g; Carbohydrates: 53g; Fiber: 7g; Sodium: 70mg

Complete the Meal

- This is wonderful with Roasted Root Vegetables (page 293) or the Cruciferous Combo (page 289) served on a bed of lentils. Though neither this pilaf nor the roasted veggies are difficult to make, I recommend preparing them when you have some time to spend—like a wintry Sunday. As with the meal suggested above, a colorful salad is welcome here.
- This goes well with Lemon and Garlic Beans or Lentils, page 94. Add a platter of raw vegetables, a simple salad, or one of the simple slaws on pages 322–25.

Basmati Rice Pilaf *with* Fresh Fruit *or* Cauliflower

A choice between fresh fruit or cauliflower might sound a bit odd, but either of these possibilities is fantastic with a fragrant basmati rice pilaf. The fruit pushes the rice toward its naturally sweet side, and the cauliflower accentuates the rice's savory flavors. Either way, what makes this pilaf particularly delectable is the addition of crunchy nuts and dried fruits. It pairs well with simple lentil dishes and curried vegetable stews.

SERVES 6 AS A HEARTY SIDE DISH

1½ cups uncooked brown basmati rice (see Note)
1 tablespoon extra-virgin olive oil or 3 tablespoons vegetable broth or water
1 medium onion, quartered and thinly sliced
2 medium sweet apples or pears, cored and diced, or 3 to 4 cups finely chopped
    cauliflower florets
½ cup raisins, dried cranberries, sliced dried apricots, or a combination
½ teaspoon turmeric
½ teaspoon ground cinnamon
Generous pinch of ground nutmeg
¼ cup orange juice, preferably freshly squeezed, or as needed to moisten
1 to 2 teaspoons grated zest from an organically grown orange (optional)
½ cup toasted cashews, chopped, or toasted slivered almonds
Salt and freshly ground pepper to taste
¼ cup chopped fresh cilantro, or more, to taste

1. Combine the rice with 3½ cups water in a saucepan. Bring to a gentle boil, then lower the heat, cover, and simmer gently for 30 minutes, or until the water is absorbed. If you'd like a more tender grain, add ½ cup more water and continue cooking until absorbed. Remove from the heat.

2. Heat the oil, broth, or water in a large skillet. Add the onion and sauté over medium heat until golden. Add the apple and sauté until it softens, about 3 to 4 minutes.

3. Stir in the cooked rice, dried fruit, and spices. Cook over low heat until piping hot and the spices are distributed throughout, stirring frequently, about 7 to 8 minutes. Stir in the juice to moisten the mixture along with the zest, if desired. Just before serving, stir in the nuts, season with salt and pepper, and stir in the cilantro.

note: You might find this rice variety marketed under the name Texmati or Calmati in the ethnic-food aisles in supermarkets. It's easy to find in natural foods stores. In a pinch, though, feel free to use long-grain brown rice; it will still be flavorful, though the aromatic quality will be sacrificed a bit.

PER SERVING WITH APPLES AND CASHEWS: Calories: 341 with oil, 321 without oil; Total fat: 9g with oil, 7g without oil; Protein: 6g; Carbohydrates: 62g; Fiber: 4g; Sodium: 6mg

Complete the Meal

- See the suggestions accompanying Curried Chickpeas or Lentils with Spinach (page 96).
- Serve with Marinated Bean Salad or any of its variations (page 313), fresh flatbread, and steamed green beans or asparagus.

Beyond Brown Rice and Quinoa: Other Grains to Explore

Carbohydrates—the food group considered "the staff of life"—often suffer from an image problem and go in and out of favor depending on the diet trend du jour. In particular, complex carbohydrates are suspect simply because they are "carbs." But in their unadulterated, unrefined form, grains are nourishing staples. Whole grains shouldn't be lumped into the same category as refined carbs and starchy foods; they're versatile, filling, and packed with nutrients.

Besides boasting a wide range of B vitamins, grains are a good source of iron, potassium, and other valuable minerals. They are also one of the best sources of dietary fiber. And grains are blessedly low in fat: a cup of cooked grains, which is more than an average serving, contains about 220 calories and, usually, less than two grams of fat.

In a book of this scope, it's impossible to talk in depth about every type of grain. Most of the time, I recommend brown rice or quinoa, the former being the most familiar and the latter the most nutritious in this group of foods. But for a change of pace, try some of the following grains:

BARLEY

The pearl variety of barley is tasty and versatile, but you may want to try pot barley for its greater nutritional impact. Pearl barley loses half its vitamin and mineral content and much of its fiber when its bran and germ are removed. Pot barley undergoes just enough "pearling" to remove the tough hull. It's a chewy, mild-tasting grain that's every bit as versatile as its more refined cousin. For a change of pace, use it instead of rice as a bed for vegetables, in pilafs and casseroles, in hot or cold soups, and in marinated grain salads.

To cook, use three to three and a half parts water to one part grain. Bring the water to a simmer in a saucepan, then stir in the grain. Simmer, covered, gently but steadily until the water has been absorbed, about forty-five to fifty minutes.

BULGUR

Bulgur is made from parboiled, dried, and cracked wheat berries. It seems to me that bulgur was popular until a decade or so ago, when quinoa came along. Quinoa has become the go-to grain for making tabbouleh, for example, though bulgur is the ingredient traditional to the original Middle Eastern recipe. Though quinoa has the advantage of being gluten-free, with higher-quality protein, bulgur is no slouch. It's chewy, hearty, and versatile, good for making pilafs, and combines well with nuts, dried fruits, beans, and fresh herbs. Think of it as a replacement for rice—and, yes, even for quinoa from time to time.

To cook, use two parts water to one part grain. The traditional way to cook bulgur is to pour the boiling water over it in a heatproof container, then cover and let stand for thirty minutes. If you need it cooked more quickly, bring water to a simmer in a saucepan. Stir in the grain, then cover and simmer gently for fifteen minutes, or until the water is absorbed.

MILLET

This small round yellow seed is nourishing and versatile, with a mild flavor and a slightly mushy texture. It's as welcome on the dinner table as it is in a hot cooked cereal for breakfast Well-cooked millet, which can be cooked ahead of serving time, makes warming, filling breakfast fare embellished with a little sweetener (such as agave or maple syrup), chopped nuts, and dried fruit. Because of its cohesive texture, millet works well in casseroles and as a stuffing for vegetables.

Millet's flavor is enhanced by toasting the grains in a dry or lightly oiled skillet for four to five minutes before cooking, though this is optional. Experiment with different water-to-grain ratios to vary the texture. Use two and a half to three and a half parts water to one part grain. The less water used, the denser the result; more water will yield a porridgelike consistency. Bring the water to a simmer in a saucepan, then stir in the grain. Simmer, covered, gently but steadily until the water has been absorbed and the grains have burst, about thirty-five to forty-five minutes.

COUSCOUS

Couscous is the name of a spicy, complex Moroccan dish; the grain used is traditionally cracked millet. But what we most often refer to as couscous is actually akin to pasta and is made from the same durum wheat. Natural foods stores often carry whole-grain couscous, which is a better choice than the refined variety. Mild and tender, couscous is versatile and easy to prepare and takes ten minutes or less to cook. Use couscous as a bed for vegetables and as a change-of-pace alternative to rice in vegetable stir-fries, curries, and bean stews. It also makes a nice base for grain salads, such as tabbouleh.

To cook, use two parts water to one part couscous—so, for example, 2 cups liquid and 1 cup couscous. Place the couscous in a heatproof bowl or casserole. Bring the amount of liquid needed to a boil, then pour it over the couscous. Cover and let stand for ten minutes, then fluff with a fork.

Easy Ways to Dress Up Whole Grains

In terms of flavor, some cooked grains are more nutty and distinctive than others, but all can be described as mild. So a few simple tweaks to boost their flavor are always welcome:

- For extra flavor, cook grains in vegetable broth instead of water.
- Stir a generous amount of barely wilted, finely chopped spinach into cooked grains. I especially like to do this with brown rice. Add a thinly sliced scallion or two, a little chopped dill, a splash each of lemon juice and olive oil, and you've created a rice dish that sings.
- Top cooked grains with Caramelized Onions with or without Bell Peppers (page 88).
- Stir in a generous amount of fresh herbs—parsley, dill, and/or cilantro—along with a small amount of minced scallions or chives to really boost the flavor of plain cooked grains.
- For a gentle Asian spin, add a dash of dark sesame oil and soy sauce; stir in some thinly sliced scallions.
- An even easier way to add Asian flavor is with some sesame-ginger dressing—homemade (page 328) or prepared.
- Stir in one tablespoon sesame or hemp seeds per cup of cooked grain. This won't affect the flavor all that much (especially in the case of hemp seeds) but will add a nice boost in nutrition.
- Replace one cup of cooking liquid with light coconut milk. Add a little flaked coconut and minced fresh ginger to give grains a Southeast Asian flavor.
- Stir in some salsa and chopped cilantro for a rice dish that suits Mexican-style and southwestern-style meals, such as those you'll find in chapter 5.
- Last but definitely not least, top any plain cooked grains with Basic Gravy with Mushroom and Miso Variations (page 87) to add a huge "yum" factor.

Polenta: Soft-Cooked or Prepared

Polenta is basically cooked cornmeal. It's a traditional preparation in Italian cuisine, providing a soft, flavorful bed of grain that can be used in place of rice or even in place of pasta. Cooked cornmeal, or polenta, is gluten-free. Look for organic cornmeal (which is by definition non-GMO) in one-pound packages or in bulk.

For convenience, you can buy prepared firm polenta, as described below, or you can also make your own firm polenta. Simply spread cooked polenta in a shallow pan and refrigerate overnight. The next day it will be firm enough to cut into squares. Warm on a lightly oiled nonstick pan or griddle, then serve topped as suggested below or on its own.

Soft-cooked or firm polenta is a delicious base for simple bean dishes, wilted greens, and of course, any of the beans-and-greens variations on pages 92–94. It can also be served as a side dish alongside Pasta with Beans and Greens (page 164) or topped with warmed leftover vegetable stews or bean dishes.

BASIC COOKED POLENTA

To make four generous or six moderate servings of cooked polenta, bring three cups of water to a simmer in a roomy saucepan. Sprinkle in a cup of cornmeal, whisking all the while. Turn the heat down to very low and cover the saucepan with the lid set slightly off the pot. Cook for fifteen to twenty minutes, whisking frequently to prevent lumping. If the mixture is too thick, whisk in an additional half to one cup of water—the quantity will vary according to how fine or coarse the cornmeal is. Stir in a tablespoon or two of Earth Balance or another brand of vegan buttery spread and season with salt.

PREPARED POLENTA

Packaged in 16- to 24-ounce cylindrical packages, this kind of polenta is basically cooked whole-grain cornmeal that is dense enough to slice. It provides an offbeat way to add variety to meals. Look for it in the refrigerated section (alongside fresh pasta) or in the gluten-free section of supermarkets or natural foods stores.

To heat, slice the polenta approximately half an inch thick. Cook the slices on a very lightly oiled nonstick griddle over medium-high heat until golden and slightly crisp on both sides, about eight minutes per side.

Serve as a bed for any of the simple bean skillets in this chapter (pages 92–97) or for vegetable medleys of all sorts. Top it, for instance, with Roasted Ratatouille, as shown in the photo on page 297. Roasted Root Vegetables (page 293) are highly compatible with this as well.

Grits 'n' Greens

Give Grits a Chance!

Grits, or hominy grits, are hulled, dried, and cracked corn kernels. To add variety to your grain repertoire, seek out stone-ground grits, which are much more flavorful than the stripped-down quick-cooking grits sold in supermarkets. Although grits are best known for their traditional role as a breakfast staple of the American South, they're terrific for dinner as well. Like coarse cornmeal, described above, grits cook to a mushy texture. They make a soft bed of naturally gluten-free grain for bean and vegetable dishes or even a pleasant side dish by themselves.

Grits can also play a starring role in simple preparations. My family has long had a thing for grits; when my kids were growing up, cheese grits were always a welcome treat. Now vegan-cheese grits are still warmly welcomed anytime.

BASIC COOKED GRITS

The directions for cooking grits are almost identical to those for polenta. Bring four cups of water to a simmer in a roomy saucepan. Sprinkle in a cup of stone-ground grits, whisking all the while. Turn the heat down to very low and cover the saucepan with the lid set slightly off the pot. Cook for fifteen to twenty minutes, whisking frequently to prevent lumping. If the mixture is too thick, whisk in an additional half cup of water. Stir in a tablespoon or two of Earth Balance or another brand of vegan buttery spread and season with salt. This makes four generous or six moderate servings. Below are a trio of simple and tasty ways to embellish grits.

VEGAN CHEEZ AND CORN GRITS

To basic cooked grits, add a half to one cup grated Cheddar-style vegan cheese and a cup or so of cooked fresh or frozen corn kernels. Though my kids are grown, they still adore this—almost as much as they still love vegan mac and cheese!

TOMATO AND CHILI PEPPER GRITS

To basic cooked grits, add one large or two medium diced ripe fresh tomatoes and one to two small fresh hot chili peppers, seeded and minced.

GRITS 'N' GREENS

Top basic cooked grits or either of the variations above with a generous amount of wilted spinach, chard, kale, or collards. If you need a formula to follow, consult Garlicky Hardy Greens, page 287. This is tasty accompanied by Smoky Tempeh Strips (page 268) or Lemon and Garlic Beans or Lentils (page 94) plus a platter of grape tomatoes, baby carrots, bell pepper strips, and olives.

CHAPTER 2

Bountiful

BOWLFULS

MAIN-DISH SOUPS AND STEWS

What's not to like about soups and stews? They're nourishing, warming, and can be comforting and invigorating all at once. This chapter focuses on the kinds of meals you serve by the ladleful, including smooth but substantial purees, thick soups of beans, legumes, and vegetables, stick-to-your-ribs chili, and chunky curries. Plant-based bowlfuls can easily serve as centerpieces for meals or as companion dishes alongside sandwiches, wraps, and salads, as will be amply demonstrated in this chapter. I adore soups and stews, not only because they marry an abundance of fresh and nutritious ingredients and put them together in one neat package but also because they can stretch over two or three meals. And as you've already discovered, I do love meals that yield leftovers!

Quick Black Bean Soup (page 126) with Greek Salad (page 318)

It was quite a challenge to choose which soups and stews merited a place as "essential" in this chapter. I mean, I could write an entire book on soups and stews. In fact, I have (that would be *Vegan Soups and Hearty Stews for All Seasons*). Having explored so many possibilities for this kind of meal made it doubly hard to limit the selections in this chapter.

In the end, I've zeroed in on soups and stews that are hearty enough to serve as the centerpieces of meals. If you make these before you need them—say, on a leisurely Sunday afternoon—the first two weekday dinners are covered. Most of these freeze well, too. With a warming pot of soup waiting for you, it's easy to complete your meal with a companionable salad, sandwich, wrap, or quesadilla.

Seasoning Tips for Plant-Powered Soups and Stews

Bouillon and seasoning bases—use with caution: Natural brands of bouillon cubes and powdered vegetable-broth bases seemed like a good choice to me until recently, when I learned that certain ingredients are secret code words for MSG and that the words "no added MSG" don't necessarily mean that a preparation contains no MSG at all. I avoid most supermarket brands of bouillon cubes for that very reason. Some of the latter also contain partially hydrogenated fats and animal ingredients. If there is "hydrolized" anything in your seasoning, for example, it could mean hidden MSG, which is a major allergen and in other ways seriously disagrees with many people. That's why I prefer the following option.

Salt-free all-purpose seasoning blends: Instead of loading your soups and stews with salt or commercial soup bases, heighten their flavor with salt-free all-purpose seasoning. A couple of teaspoons to a tablespoon of this can really perk up your meal. These blends also save you the trouble of measuring a dozen different spices or buying a lot of spices that you may not use regularly. A few good brands are Frontier (my favorite), Simply Organic (you'll find this and Frontier at natural foods stores), and Mrs. Dash (I like the "Original Blend" and "Table Blend" flavors, available in supermarkets).

Like certain organic bouillon cubes I used to use, some "natural" seasoning blends contain hydrolized soy protein, which isn't a good thing. The brands mentioned above are made only from herbs, spices, onion, garlic, and/or dried citrus zest, without added oils or questionable soy products.

Lemon or lime juice: Seasoning blends heighten flavor, and lemon or lime juice brightens them. If your soup is tasting a little flat, add just a splash of either. Be judicious and add citrus juice in small amounts, as it's easy to cross the line from bright to overly tart.

Vegetable broth: I admit that I'm too lazy to make vegetable stock. Once the decision is made to have soup, I don't have the time or patience to do a prequel, so to speak. So once in a while, I enjoy starting with a 32-ounce container of low-sodium vegetable broth, which adds a great deal of flavor to soups that don't require long simmering time. Those would include quick Asian-style soups, such as those in chapter 4. Though I don't use these broths consistently, when I do use them, I like the result. My favorite is Pacific brand organic low-sodium vegetable broth; it contains no questionable ingredients.

Fresh herbs: Parsley, dill, cilantro, basil, and other fresh herbs are the perfect way to finish soups and stews. Add them toward the very end of cooking time, or even once the soup is completely done, to retain as much of their flavor and color as possible. And passing around some chopped fresh herbs to top individual portions is always a good idea.

Red or white wine: If you have an opened bottle of dry wine (white or red), a small amount—say, about a quarter to a third of a cup—adds nice depth of flavor to soups and stews. If it's a robust stew using lots of dark-colored veggies and beans, either white or red wine will work; if your preparation has light colors and flavors, white wine works better. You don't want to end up with pink cream of cauliflower soup; on the other hand, there's nothing really wrong with that . . .

Most important, season and salt to taste: Add salt toward the end of cooking time to give the other flavors a chance to develop and to avoid oversalting. Salt a little at a time, stir thoroughly, and taste frequently. In any given recipe, here or elsewhere, use the amount of salt and other seasonings called for as a guide. Trust your own sense of taste to create just the right seasoning to suit you and yours!

Hearty Bean, Pea, *and* Lentil Soups

Curried Split Pea *or* Red Lentil Soup

This soup is the edible equivalent of a comforting blanket on a chilly day. If you prepare it on a Sunday, it will serve you well for half the week or so, depending on how large a crowd you're feeding. And once you've had enough, you can pop it in the freezer (try freezing single portions) and take it out when the craving for a thick soup strikes again. It also makes a great lunch offering when carried to work or school in a container. Though both versions are satisfying and tasty, the red lentil variation cooks far more quickly than the one using peas.

SERVES 8 OR MORE

2 tablespoons extra-virgin olive oil or 3 to 4 tablespoons vegetable broth or water
1 large onion, finely chopped
3 to 4 cloves garlic, minced
3 medium carrots, peeled and diced
2 celery stalks, peeled and diced
8 cups water (if using split peas) or 6 cups water (if using red lentils)
2 to 3 teaspoons salt-free all-purpose seasoning blend (see recommended brands, page 121)
2 cups dried green or yellow split peas or red lentils, rinsed
2 dried bay leaves
1 tablespoon good-quality curry powder, or to taste
1 teaspoon ground cumin
1 to 2 teaspoons grated fresh ginger (optional)
Pinch of ground nutmeg
Salt and freshly ground pepper to taste

OPTIONAL TOPPINGS
Minced fresh herbs, such as cilantro, parsley, scallions, and/or dill
Wilted baby spinach or arugula or chopped and wilted chard or kale

1. Heat the oil, broth, or water in a soup pot. Add the onion and sauté over medium-low heat until translucent. Add the garlic, carrots, and celery. Continue to sauté for 8 to 10 minutes, or until the vegetables are golden.

2. Add remaining ingredients except the salt, pepper, and garnishes. Bring to a rapid simmer, then lower the heat. Cover and simmer gently until the peas or lentils are mushy. The peas will take about 1 to 1½ hours; the lentils only 20 to 30 minutes. Either way, stir occasionally, and, if needed, add additional small amounts of water if the consistency gets too thick. The soup should be thick but not a solid mass.

3. When the peas or lentils are done, adjust of the consistency with more water if needed, then season with salt and pepper. Discard the bay leaves. Garnish and serve at once, or, if time allows, let the soup stand off the heat for an hour or so to develop its flavor. It thickens considerably with refrigeration; thin with additional water as needed and adjust the seasonings before serving.

PER SERVING: Calories: 217 with oil, 187 without oil; Total fat: 4g with oil, 1g without oil; Protein: 13g; Carbohydrates: 34g; Fiber: 14g; Sodium: 35mg

Variations

- Along with the split peas, add ⅓ to ½ cup uncooked brown rice or barley for an even heartier soup that will stretch further. You'll need to add at least an additional cup of water plus more as needed as the soup thickens.

- If you're making the soup with red lentils, consider adding about a half cup of uncooked quinoa, which will take about the same amount of time to cook as the lentils.

- In the red lentil variation, add a cup or two of small red or kidney beans (either cooked dried beans or drained and rinsed canned beans) for an even heartier soup with a nice visual appeal. Use cilantro to top individual portions.

Complete the Meal

- Serve with fresh whole-grain pita bread or flatbread and any of the fall and winter salads from "Fruity, Nutty Mixed Greens Salads" (page 326).
- Serve with the Middle Eastern Salad (Fattouche), page 318, in which crisp flatbread mingles deliciously with the salad ingredients.

Lentil Soup *with* Tasty Variations

A plant-powered recipe repertoire isn't complete without a robust lentil soup. It's a great make-ahead when you're planning meals for a busy week, as it lasts nicely and develops flavor as it stands. It makes a great portable lunch and pairs well with salads and wraps. High in protein and flavorful, lentils, like their fellow legumes, are enjoying a robust revival among aficionados of whole, plant-based foods.

SERVES 6

2 tablespoons extra-virgin olive oil or 3 to 4 tablespoons vegetable broth or water
1 large onion, finely chopped
3 cloves garlic, minced
3 medium carrots, peeled and thinly sliced
2 celery stalks, finely diced
1½ cups dried lentils, rinsed
One 15- to 16-ounce can diced tomatoes (try a flavorful variety such as fire-roasted
     or Italian-style)
¼ cup dry red or white wine (optional)
1 tablespoon salt-free all-purpose seasoning blend (see recommended brands, page 121)
2 teaspoons sweet paprika (or smoked paprika for a deeper, spicier flavor)
2 teaspoons ground cumin
¼ cup chopped fresh parsley, or more to taste
¼ cup chopped fresh dill
Salt and freshly ground pepper to taste

1. Heat the oil, broth, or water in a small soup pot. Add the onion and sauté over medium heat for 5 minutes, or until translucent. Add the garlic, carrots, and celery and sauté 3 to 4 minutes longer.

2. Add 6 cups of water along with the next six ingredients. Bring to a simmer, then cover and simmer until the lentils and vegetables are done, about 30 to 40 minutes.

3. Stir in the herbs and season with salt and pepper. If time allows, this soup benefits from standing for an hour or so before serving to develop its flavor. Heat through as needed before serving.

PER SERVING: Calories: 253 with oil, 213 without oil; Total fat: 5g with oil, 1g without oil; Protein: 14g; Carbohydrates: 39g; Fiber: 18g; Sodium: 50mg

Variations

- **Lentil and Grain Soup:** Add ⅓ cup brown rice or pearl barley when adding the lentils along with an additional cup of water. Or add ½ cup quinoa about halfway through the cooking time along with a cup of water. More water will be needed as the soup stands and thickens.

- **Lentil and Greens Soup:** Once the lentils are done, add short, narrow ribbons of kale, collard greens, or chard—as much as you'd like, but figure half of an average bunch. Or, once the soup is completely done, toss in a few handfuls of baby spinach, baby arugula, or a bunch of watercress leaves. Stir in until wilted. Add a tablespoon of freshly squeezed or bottled lemon or lime juice to brighten the flavor of the greens.

- **Lentil and Pasta Soup:** Cook about a cup of small pasta separately in a saucepan. Try small tubes (ditalini), tiny shells, or Israeli couscous. Once the soup is done, stir in the cooked pasta and adjust the consistency with more water. Then taste for seasoning.

Complete the Meal

- Pair this with Cucumber and Avocado Wraps with Bean Spread or Hummus (page 258) for a fantastic meal (I prefer the hummus variation). It's also great with Tossed Salad Wraps, page 259, made with your favorite dressing.

- For a larger meal, explore some of the smashed potatoes variations (which you can also make with sweet potatoes), pages 303-5. Add a simple salad or any of the simple slaws, pages 322-25.

Quick Black Bean Soup

Making a hearty bean soup in a hurry seems like a dinner-hour fantasy, but canned black beans are so flavorful that they do the job perfectly. I suggest using organic black beans. Organic canned black beans are often lower in sodium than their nonorganic counterparts. If you use the former, don't drain and rinse, as I usually suggest—the liquid from the can adds lots of flavor to the soup base. Otherwise, if using conventional black beans, drain and rinse as usual. Not only is the liquid very salty, it has a less-than-desirable consistency as well.

SERVES 4 TO 6

1½ tablespoons extra-virgin olive oil or 3 to 4 tablespoons vegetable broth or water
1 large onion, finely chopped
3 to 4 cloves garlic, finely chopped
Two 28-ounce cans black beans, preferably organic and low sodium (see Note)
2 to 3 teaspoons salt-free all-purpose seasoning blend
    (see recommended brands, page 121)
Juice of 1 lemon or lime, or more to taste
2 teaspoons ground cumin
1 teaspoon dried oregano
¼ cup finely chopped fresh parsley or cilantro
Salt and freshly ground pepper to taste

OPTIONAL TOPPINGS

Vegan sour cream (homemade, page 248, or store-bought) or Cashew Cream (page 249)
3 to 4 scallions, white and green parts, thinly sliced
Additional chopped fresh parsley or cilantro

1. Heat the oil, broth, or water in a soup pot. Sauté the onion over medium heat until translucent, about 3 to 4 minutes. Add the garlic and sauté until the onion is light golden in color, 3 to 4 minutes longer.

2. Add the remaining ingredients except the toppings along with 3 cups of water (if using organic beans and their liquid) or 4 cups of water (if using nonorganic beans, drained and rinsed). Bring to a slow boil.

3. Mash some of the beans with a potato masher—just enough to thicken the liquid base of the soup. Cover and simmer gently and steadily for 10 minutes. Adjust the consistency with more water if desired.

4. Top each serving with a dollop or swirl of vegan sour cream or cashew cream, a sprinkling of sliced scallions, and/or chopped parsley or cilantro.

PER SERVING: Calories: 340 with oil, 297 without oil; Total fat: 5g with oil, 0g without oil; Protein: 20g; Carbohydrates: 57g; Fiber: 12g; Sodium: 368mg

Variation

Instead of the garnishes suggested in the recipe, top the soup with wilted greens, diced baked butternut squash or sweet potatoes, or some sautéed onion and bell pepper.

Complete the Meal

- This is wonderful with the Greek variation in "Tossed Salads Go Global" (page 318), as shown in the photo below.
- Serve with any of the easy quesadilla variations that don't include beans (pages 240–41). Add any of the simple slaws on pages 322–25 or a basic tossed salad.

Long-Simmering Bean Soup

When time isn't an issue, simmering dried beans for many hours until they melt into a flavorful, thick soup is a pleasure. Though I'm not a slow-cooker expert, I think this would work well cooked by that method too.

1 pound dried beans (see variations)
2 tablespoons extra-virgin olive oil or ¼ cup vegetable broth or water
1 medium onion, chopped
2 large carrots, peeled and chopped
2 large celery stalks, diced
2 or 3 cloves garlic, crushed or minced
2 to 3 teaspoons salt-free all-purpose seasoning blend
    (see recommended brands, page 121)
1 teaspoon dried basil
½ teaspoon dried thyme
¼ cup dry red or white wine (optional)
Salt and freshly ground pepper to taste
Crushed red pepper flakes (optional)

OPTIONAL TOPPINGS

Vegan sour cream (homemade, page 248, or store-bought) or Cashew Cream (page 249)
3 to 4 scallions, thinly sliced
Chopped fresh parsley or cilantro

1. Rinse and sort the beans and soak them overnight in plenty of water in a large soup pot. Or, for a quicker soaking method, bring the beans and water to a boil in a large soup pot, then cover and let stand off the heat for an hour or so. In either case, drain and rinse the cooked beans and return them to the soup pot. Cover the beans with about double their volume in water.

2. Heat the oil, broth, or water in a medium skillet. Add the chopped onion, carrots, celery, and garlic. Sauté over medium heat until all are soft and golden. Add this mixture to the beans in the soup pot along with the seasoning blend, dried basil, thyme, and wine, if desired. Bring to a slow boil, then lower the heat and cover, setting the lid slightly off the pot. Simmer for 1 to 1½ hours, or until the beans are quite soft.

3. Using an immersion blender, process the soup to a texture that's as smooth or as chunky as you like. You can also do this using a potato masher and a bit of muscle power.

4. This is meant to be a thick soup, but adjust the consistency with more water if you find it overly dense. Season to taste with salt and pepper. If you'd like a bit of heat, add some crushed red pepper flakes, but use a light hand. Continue to simmer over very low heat for 10 to 15 minutes.

5. Serve at once or let stand off the heat until needed, then heat through before serving. Garnish as desired. This soup keeps well in the refrigerator for several days, and the flavor improves as it stands.

PER SERVING: Calories: 307 with oil, 287 without oil; Total fat: 3g with oil, 1g without oil; Protein: 17g; Carbohydrates: 53g; Fiber: 13g; Sodium: 44mg

Variation

Use whatever kind of beans you want or even one of those multibean mixtures. Some of my favorites are black, pinto, or small red beans, which cook to a more creamy texture than some of their fellow beans.

Complete the Meal

Follow the same suggestions given for Quick Black Bean Soup (page 126).

White Bean *and* Corn Chowder

A soothing style of thick rich soup with a milky base, chowder is easy to translate to plant-based mode. This creamy bean chowder, with potatoes and corn at center stage, gets a boost from the addition of sweet potatoes or butternut squash, making it a perfect fall or winter soup.

SERVES 6

1½ tablespoons extra-virgin olive oil or 3 tablespoons vegetable broth
1 large onion, finely chopped
2 medium potatoes, peeled and finely diced
1 medium sweet potato, peeled and finely diced, or 2 cups finely diced butternut squash
2 to 3 medium carrots, peeled and thinly sliced
2 large celery stalks, diced
One 32-ounce carton low-sodium vegetable broth or 4 cups water mixed with
    2 to 3 teaspoons salt-free all-purpose seasoning blend (see recommended brands,
    page 121)
4 cups cooked (from 1 2/3 cups dried) or two 15- to 16-ounce cans (drained and rinsed)
    navy beans or cannellini
2 cups fresh or frozen corn kernels
2 cups unsweetened rice milk or other unsweetened nondairy milk
2 medium ripe fresh tomatoes, finely diced
½ cup chopped fresh parsley
2 tablespoons minced fresh dill, or to taste (optional)
Salt and freshly ground pepper to taste

1. Heat the oil or broth in a soup pot. Add the onion and sauté over medium heat until golden. Add the potatoes, sweet potato, carrots, celery, and broth. Bring to a gentle boil, then cover and simmer gently for 15 minutes.

2. Add the beans. If you'd like a thicker soup base, puree half the beans before adding to the pot. Then add the corn.

3. Bring to a rapid simmer, then lower the heat and simmer gently for 25 to 30 minutes, or until all the vegetables are tender but not overdone.

4. Stir in the nondairy milk and tomatoes and continue to simmer gently for 5 to 10 minutes longer. Stir in the parsley and dill, then season with salt and pepper. Serve at once; or, if time allows, let the soup stand off the heat for an hour or so before serving, then heat through.

PER SERVING: Calories: 422 with oil, 392 without oil; Total fat: 6g with oil, 3g without oil; Protein: 16g; Carbohydrates: 80g; Fiber: 15g; Sodium: 189mg

Complete the Meal

- Smoky Tempeh and Avocado Reuben Sandwiches (page 265) are delicious with this soup. Add a platter of crisp raw veggies and use the rest of the Thousand Island-ish Dressing made for the sandwich as a dip (page 283).

- A nice foil to this comforting soup is an invigorating kale salad. Try Southwestern-Flavored Kale Salad (page 321) or Colorful and Luscious Kale and Avocado Salad (page 322).

Vegetable Soups

Cream *of* Broccoli Soup

A longtime favorite in our family of broccoli enthusiasts, this soup gets a thick, creamy base from pureed white beans or tofu. The addition of green peas at the end of cooking time brightens the color and heightens the flavor of the soup.

SERVES 6

1½ tablespoons extra-virgin olive oil or 3 tablespoons vegetable broth or water
1 large onion, chopped
2 to 3 cloves garlic, minced (optional)
One 32-ounce carton low-sodium vegetable broth or 4 cups water mixed with
    2 to 3 teaspoons salt-free all-purpose seasoning blend (see recommended brands,
    page 121)
5 to 6 cups coarsely chopped broccoli florets and peeled stems
2 cups frozen green peas, thawed
One 15- to 16-ounce can great northern beans or cannellini, drained and rinsed,
    or one 12.3-ounce package firm silken tofu
1 cup unsweetened rice milk or other unsweetened nondairy milk, plus more as needed

TO FINISH THE SOUP

2 cups finely chopped broccoli florets
½ cup chopped fresh dill or parsley, or a combination, plus more for garnish
Juice of ½ lemon, or 2 tablespoons bottled lemon juice, or to taste
Salt and freshly ground pepper to taste

1. Heat the oil, broth, or water in a soup pot and add the onion. Sauté over medium heat until translucent, then add the garlic if desired. Continue to sauté until the onion is golden.

2. Add the broth and broccoli. Bring to a simmer, then cover and simmer gently until the broccoli is tender but not overcooked, about 8 to 10 minutes. Add the beans or tofu and half the green peas. Continue to cook just until everything is nicely heated through.

3. The easiest way to puree this soup is to simply insert an immersion blender into the pot and puree until it's as smooth as you'd like it to be. You can also leave it a bit chunky. If

you don't have an immersion blender, transfer the mixture to a regular blender and puree (don't overprocess!), then transfer back to the soup pot. Add enough nondairy milk to give the soup a medium-thick consistency.

4. To finish the soup, add the remaining green peas, the finely chopped broccoli florets, the chopped herbs, and the lemon juice. Stir together, then season with salt and pepper. Cook over very low heat for 5 minutes longer, or until the finely chopped broccoli florets are tender-crisp, then serve.

PER SERVING: Calories: 262 with oil, 232 without oil; Total fat: 5g with oil, 2g without oil; Protein: 12g; Carbohydrates: 44g; Fiber: 13g; Sodium: 302mg

Complete the Meal

- Serve with any of the wraps on pages 257–62. I particularly like this with Hummus Wraps with Grains and Greens (page 257), as shown in the photo.
- For a fun soup-and-salad meal, serve this with the Taco Salad variation in "Tossed Salads Go Global" (page 319).

Coconut Cream *of* Orange Vegetables Soup

In addition to the mellow cruciferous veggie soup on page 132, you'll enjoy having this puree of orange veggies in your repertoire. Unlike the broccoli soup, which is dressed up with herbal notes, this one is subtly flavored with ginger and curry, which marry well with the natural sweetness from the coconut milk and the vegetables themselves.

SERVES 6

1 tablespoon extra-virgin olive oil or 3 tablespoons vegetable broth or water
1 large onion, chopped
2 large celery stalks, diced
6 heaping cups peeled and diced orange vegetables (see Variations)
4 cups water
2 to 3 teaspoons grated fresh or jarred ginger, or to taste
2 to 3 teaspoons good-quality curry powder, or to taste
Pinch of ground nutmeg (optional)
One 15-ounce can light coconut milk or 2 cups unsweetened rice milk
Salt and freshly ground pepper to taste

1. Heat the oil, broth, or water in a soup pot. Add the onion and sauté over low heat until golden.

2. Add the celery, vegetables of your choice, and water. Bring to a rapid simmer, then stir in the ginger, curry, and nutmeg, if desired. Lower the heat, then cover and simmer until the vegetables are tender, about 20 to 25 minutes.

3. Remove about half the solid ingredients with a slotted spoon and transfer to a food processor along with about ½ cup of the cooking liquid. Process until smoothly pureed, then stir the mixture back into the soup pot. Or simply insert an immersion blender into the pot and puree until partially smooth, with plenty of chunks remaining.

4. Stir in the coconut milk. The soup should have a slightly thick consistency. If it's too thick, stir in just a little more water. Season with salt and pepper, then simmer over very low heat for 10 minutes longer.

5. Serve at once or, if time allows, let stand off the heat for an hour or two. Heat through before serving.

PER SERVING: Calories: 177 with oil, 157 without oil; Total fat: 6g with oil, 4 g without oil; Protein: 2g; Carbohydrates: 30g; Fiber: 4g; Sodium: 44mg

Variations

Use any of the following orange vegetables to make 6 heaping cups. You can also combine two or all three if you like:

- Raw sweet potatoes (about 3 medium-large)
- Any kind of orange winter squash, though butternut is my favorite for soup—see page 298 for cutting and peeling instructions
- Carrots or whole baby carrots—the latter is the easiest of all the options

Complete the Meal

- For a warming fall or winter meal, serve this as a first course with one of the quinoa pilaf variations on page 101 (with the exception of the kale and butternut squash variation, as that would be a bit redundant). Any of the simple slaws on pages 322–25 would complete the meal nicely.
- Serve side by side with any of the quesadilla variations on pages 240–41. Add a simple salad or a platter of crisp raw veggies. Or try one of the salads from "Fruity, Nutty Mixed Greens Salads" on page 326—using fresh pear and walnuts in this kind of supereasy salad would complement the soup nicely.

Tomato-Based Soups

Vegetable-Barley Soup *with* Mushroom Variation

Tomato soups are sturdy and comforting, and the addition of barley is especially nice when the weather is cool. This is one of those "Sunday" soups that yields substantial dividends as you go through the week.

SERVES 8

2 tablespoons extra-virgin olive oil or 3 to 4 tablespoons vegetable broth or water
1 medium-large onion, finely chopped
1 to 2 cloves garlic, minced (optional)
¾ cup pearl barley
2 to 3 medium carrots, peeled and sliced
1 large potato, any variety, peeled and diced
2 large celery stalks, diced
2 bay leaves
1 tablespoon salt-free all-purpose seasoning blend (see recommended brands, page 121)
One 28-ounce can crushed tomatoes
¼ cup minced fresh parsley
2 tablespoons minced fresh dill, or more to taste
Salt and freshly ground pepper to taste

1. Heat the oil, broth, or water in a large soup pot. Add the onion and sauté over low heat until golden.

2. Add the garlic, barley, carrots, potato, celery, bay leaves, seasoning blend, tomatoes, and 6 cups water.

3. Bring to a simmer, then cover and simmer gently for 45 to 60 minutes, stirring occasionally, or until the grain and vegetables are done.

4. Add the parsley and dill. Adjust the consistency with more water as needed. The soup should be thick but not overly so. Season with salt and pepper. This soup will thicken as it stands. Adjust the liquid and seasonings as needed.

PER SERVING: Calories: 158 with oil, 128 without oil; Total fat: 4g with oil, 1g without oil; Protein: 4g; Carbohydrates: 29g; Fiber: 7g; Sodium: 40mg

Variation

Reduce the amount of water to 5 cups. Add 10 to 12 ounces baby bella (cremini), shiitake, or oyster mushrooms—or any combination thereof—once everything else is in and simmering. Add a cup or two of unsweetened rice milk when adding the fresh herbs at the end, which will give this soup a lovely, bisquelike quality.

Complete the Meal

Like other soups in this chapter, this one pairs well with salads, wraps, and quesadillas. Here are some of my favorite companions for this soup:

- Chunky Bean Spread (page 269), served as suggested following the recipe
- Ultimate Eggless Egg Salad (page 270), served as suggested following the recipe
- Cucumber and Avocado Wraps with Bean Spread or Hummus (page 258)
- Vegan Niçoise-Style Salad (page 306)
- Any of the easy quesadilla variations on pages 240–41

Tomato-Vegetable Soup
with Variations

Though you can make and serve this soup in its basic form, below, I highly recommend using it as a template for the variations listed after the recipe. It's delightful as is, but why stop at basic when a couple of simple tweaks can turn it into minestrone or tortilla soup?

SERVES 8 OR MORE

1 tablespoon extra-virgin olive oil or 3 tablespoons vegetable broth or water
1 large or 2 medium onions, finely chopped
2 to 3 cloves garlic, minced
2 medium carrots, peeled and diced
2 medium celery stalks, diced
Handful of celery leaves, chopped
2 medium potatoes, any variety, peeled and diced
One 15- to 16-ounce can diced tomatoes, undrained
One 15- to 16-ounce can tomato sauce
¼ cup dry red wine (optional)
2 bay leaves
2 to 3 teaspoons salt-free all-purpose seasoning blend (see recommended
　　brands, page 121)
1 teaspoon dried oregano
1 teaspoon dried thyme
½ cup chopped fresh parsley, or more to taste
Salt and freshly ground pepper to taste

1. Heat the oil, broth, or water in a soup pot. Add the onions and sauté over medium-low heat until translucent. Add the garlic and continue to sauté until both are golden.

2. Add the carrots, celery and leaves, and potatoes along with just enough water to cover. Stir in the tomatoes, tomato sauce, wine (if desired), bay leaves, seasoning blend, oregano, and thyme. Bring to a rapid simmer, then lower the heat. Cover and simmer gently until the vegetables are done but not overcooked, about 20 to 25 minutes.

3. Adjust the consistency with a small amount of additional water if the soup is too dense. Stir in half the parsley and season with salt and pepper. Simmer over low heat for at least another 20 to 30 minutes, or until the vegetables are completely tender but not overdone. Discard the bay leaves, add the remaining parsley, and serve.

PER SERVING: Calories: 104 with oil, 90 without oil; Total fat: 2g with oil, 0g without oil; Protein: 3g; Carbohydrates: 20g; Fiber: 4g; Sodium: 103mg

Variations

Transform this soup into any of these other classic tomato-based soups with a few easy tweaks:

- **Minestrone:** Add 1 to 1½ cups cooked or canned (drained and rinsed) chickpeas and 1 cup thawed frozen green peas toward the end. Serve this with the Italian variation in "Tossed Salads Go Global" (page 319) and a crusty whole-grain bread or pan-grilled rounds of prepared polenta (see page 115).

  When you have a bit more time for meal preparation, this is a fitting companion to a light pasta dish such as Vegan Pasta Alfredo (page 167) or any white pizza; my choice would be White Pizza with Caramelized Onions and Olives (page 184).

- **Tomato-Rice (or Tomato-Quinoa) Soup:** Omit the potatoes. When the soup is nearly done, stir in 1½ cups or so cooked brown rice and let it come to temperature over low heat for 10 minutes or so. If you use quinoa, simply add it when you would have added the potatoes. With this variation, add a cup or so of cooked beans (any variety you'd like—you can even consider edamame, as shown in the photo below). You'll also need to add from 1 to 2 cups of additional water, as the grains absorb the liquid quickly.

Global Stews

Classic Veggie Chili
and Ideas *for* Leftovers

From the first days of modern vegetarian publications—say, the early 1970s—to today's massive inventory of vegan cookbooks, hardly any of them (my own included) have gone to press without some sort of chili recipe. It's really *that* essential to the plant-based repertoire. The chili recipe below isn't revolutionary, but this book wouldn't be complete without it.

SERVES 6 TO 8

1 tablespoon extra-virgin olive oil or 3 tablespoons vegetable broth or water

1 large onion, chopped

3 to 4 cloves garlic, minced

1 medium or large bell pepper (any color), finely diced

4 to 5 cups cooked or two 28-ounce cans (drained and rinsed) beans of your choice (see Variations)

One 28-ounce can crushed tomatoes

1½ to 2 cups cooked fresh or thawed frozen corn kernels

1 to 2 fresh hot chili peppers (see Variations), seeded and minced, or one 4- to 8-ounce can chopped mild green chilies

1 tablespoon good-quality chili powder, or to taste

2 teaspoons ground cumin

2 teaspoons unsweetened cocoa powder (optional but highly recommended)

1 teaspoon dried oregano

Salt to taste

OPTIONAL TOPPINGS (ANY OR ALL)

Lightly cooked or raw chopped onions or scallions

Chopped fresh cilantro

Grated nondairy Cheddar-style or pepper Jack–style cheese

Diced ripe fresh tomatoes

1. Heat the oil, broth, or water in a large soup pot. Add the onion and garlic and sauté over medium heat until the onion is golden.

2. Add remaining ingredients except salt along with ½ cup water. Simmer gently, covered, for 30 minutes, stirring occasionally. Season gently with salt and adjust the other seasonings.

3. If time allows, let stand for an hour or so off the heat, then heat through as needed before serving. The chili should be very dense, but if you'd like it a bit more on the soupy side, add another ½ to 1 cup water and continue to heat through. Ladle into bowls and pass around the garnishes.

PER SERVING: Calories: 265 with oil, 245 without oil; Total fat: 4g with oil, 2g without oil; Protein: 15g; Carbohydrates: 47g; Fiber: 13g; Sodium: 25mg

Variations

- Use pink, pinto, red, or black beans, varying your choices each time you make this. Using two different beans in the same pot adds to the visual appeal.

- If using fresh chilies, for a spicier effect, use jalapeño or serrano peppers or 1 or 2 chipotle peppers in adobo sauce (the latter come in cans or jars and are supremely incendiary). For a milder effect, use poblanos.

- For added texture, stir in a cup or so of cooked grain—quinoa, whole-grain couscous, or bulgur all work well. Adjust the liquid as needed.

- Winter squash or sweet potatoes added to chili are not only delicious but also add to its visual appeal. Toward the end of cooking time, add 2 cups or so cooked diced sweet potatoes or winter squash. Butternut or sugar pumpkins are particularly good. See tips on taming winter squash, page 298.

- Add a diced medium zucchini and/or a cup or two of chopped brown mushrooms to the mix. Stir them in when adding all the other ingredients in the second step.

Complete the Meal

For a classic combo, serve with the cornbread on page 144 and a colorful salad, combining mixed greens, tomatoes, carrots, cucumbers, olives, and pumpkin or sunflower seeds. If you have a little extra time, the Cilantro-Lime variation of Vegan Ranch-Style Dressing (page 328) adds a refreshing note to this meal.

continued

Classic Veggie Chili (page 140)

Ideas for Leftovers

- **Chili-Stuffed Winter Squash:** Use as many small hard squashes as you need. Choose from acorn, golden acorn, small butternut squashes, or the smallest possible sugar pumpkins. See directions for prebaking them, which makes them easier to cut, on page 298. When the squashes are cool enough to handle, scoop out and discard the seeds and fibers. Stuff the cavity with leftover chili. Reheat in the oven or microwave if needed. Dust the tops with minced scallion or cilantro and serve. Depending on the size of the squashes, allow 1 or 2 squash halves per serving.

- **Cincinnati Chili Mac:** A classic American iteration of basic chili, Cincinnati Chili Mac is served over spaghetti. A key spice in the chili is cinnamon, for reasons unknown—but it does work well. Cook 8 to 10 ounces of whole-grain spaghetti according to package directions. Add ½ to 1 teaspoon of cinnamon to your leftover chili when reheating, depending on how much you're reheating and how much you enjoy cinnamon. Serve the chili over the spaghetti and finish with any of the usual toppings, though these are entirely optional.

- **Chili-Topped Smashed Sweet Potatoes:** Bake or microwave sweet potatoes as needed. Cut each in half and arrange cut side up on individual plates or on a serving platter. Smash gently with a potato masher and top with leftover chili. A dollop of Vegan Sour Cream (page 248) or Cashew Cream (page 249) makes this extra tasty. Two medium to large halves of chili-topped sweet potatoes make a filling main dish so good that you'll forget you're eating leftovers. For more enticing smashed potato ideas, see pages 303–5.

Corn-Kernel Cornbread
or Muffins

I know this isn't a stew, but I can't think of a better place for the cornbread recipe than after chili. Consider adding the optional chilies and nondairy cheese, which give this pan bread a moist texture as well as a major yum factor. And since cornbread is only as good as it is fresh, I'm also providing a recipe that lets you turn any leftovers into a delicious stuffing for a subsequent meal.

MAKES ONE 9-INCH PAN BREAD (12 SERVINGS) OR 1 DOZEN MUFFINS

1 cup cornmeal, preferably stone-ground
1 cup whole-wheat pastry flour or spelt flour
1 teaspoon baking soda
1 teaspoon baking powder
1 teaspoon salt
2/3 cup applesauce
2 tablespoons extra-virgin olive oil
1/3 cup unsweetened nondairy milk of your choice, or more as needed
1/2 cup frozen corn kernels, thawed
1 small hot fresh chili pepper (such as jalapeño), seeded and minced,
    or one 4-ounce can diced mild green chilies (optional)
1 cup grated nondairy cheddar-style cheese (optional)

1. Preheat the oven to 400°F.

2. Combine the first five ingredients in a mixing bowl and stir together.

3. Make a well in the center of the dry ingredients. Pour in the applesauce, oil, and nondairy milk. Stir until well combined, adding more nondairy milk if needed to make a smooth, slightly stiff batter. Stir in the corn kernels and the chilies and cheese, if desired.

4. Pour the batter into an oiled 9 × 9-inch baking pan or divide among a foil-lined 12-cup muffin tin. Bake for 20 to 25 minutes, or until the top is golden and a knife inserted in the center comes out clean. Let cool until just warm. Cut the pan bread into 12 sections; for muffins, transfer them to a serving plate, leaving them in the foil liners.

PER SERVING OR MUFFIN: Calories: 104; Total fat: 3g; Protein: 2g; Carbohydrates: 18g; Fiber: 2g; Sodium: 340mg

Leftover Cornbread Skillet Stuffing: Heat a small amount of olive oil in a medium skillet. Sauté a chopped onion and two diced celery stalks until lightly browned. Crumble leftover cornbread (I usually use ⅓ to ½ a pan) into the skillet. Drizzle with ½ to 1 cup vegetable stock or water—just enough to moisten the crumbs without making them mushy.

Season with 2 to 3 teaspoons salt-free all-purpose seasoning blend or any other kind of seasoning you enjoy, then stir in about ¼ cup chopped fresh parsley and, if you like, a couple of thinly sliced scallions. Cook over medium-high heat, stirring frequently, until the mixture is touched with golden brown here and there. Season with salt and pepper. You can even serve your leftover chili atop this mixture for a tasty variation.

Coconut Curried Vegetable Stew

Even those who aren't big on curries might very well be won over by this colorful stew. Though the vegetables are typical of Indian cuisine, this is Westernized with the lazy yet tasty technique of using curry powder rather than toasting a number of individual spices in the pan according to authentic Indian tradition. So please forgive this minor indiscretion, as otherwise this is a completely delicious meal in a bowl, offering a plethora of veggies enveloped in coconut milk.

SERVES 6 TO 8

1 tablespoon extra-virgin olive oil or 2 to 3 tablespoons vegetable broth or water

1 medium onion, finely chopped

2 to 3 cloves garlic, minced

4 medium carrots, peeled and sliced

4 medium potatoes, any variety, peeled and diced

1/2 medium head cauliflower, cut into bite-size pieces

1 to 2 teaspoons grated fresh ginger, or to taste

2 to 3 teaspoons good-quality curry powder, or to taste

1 teaspoon ground cumin

1/2 teaspoon turmeric

1 to 2 small fresh hot chili peppers, seeded and minced (optional)

One 15-ounce can light coconut milk

8 to 10 ounces green beans (fresh or organic frozen) or slender asparagus,
    cut into 1- to 2-inch lengths

3 to 4 ounces baby spinach

1/4 to 1/2 cup minced fresh cilantro, plus more for topping

Salt and freshly ground pepper to taste

1. Heat the oil, broth, or water in a large soup pot. Add the onion and garlic and sauté over medium heat until the onion is golden. Add the carrots, potatoes, and 2 cups water and bring to a rapid simmer. Lower the heat, cover, and simmer gently for 10 minutes, or until the potatoes are about half tender.

2. Add the cauliflower, ginger, curry powder, cumin, turmeric, chili peppers (if desired), and coconut milk. Return to a simmer; add the green beans or asparagus. Continue to simmer gently, covered, until the vegetables are just tender, about 10 minutes longer.

3. Mash some of the potatoes against the side of the pot with a wooden spoon to thicken the stew's base. Stir in the spinach and cilantro and cook just until the spinach is wilted. The stew should have a thick consistency, with just enough liquid to warrant serving it

in bowls rather than on a plate. Adjust the liquid with water or nondairy milk, keeping in mind that as the stew stands, it will thicken. Adjust the seasonings to taste.

PER SERVING: Calories: 296 with oil, 276 without oil; Total fat: 12g with oil, 9g without oil; Protein: 6g; Carbohydrates: 46g; Fiber: 8g; Sodium: 136mg

Variations

- Replace all or some of the potatoes with sweet potatoes.
- Use about 1½ cups frozen green peas in place of the green beans or asparagus.
- If you enjoy bitter greens, substitute an equivalent amount of mustard greens (which are traditional in some regional Indian cuisines) for the spinach, or replace half the spinach with mustard greens.

Complete the Meal

The following two simple side dishes continue the delightful theme of the meal. You can also add a fresh flatbread, though this is entirely optional.

- **Simple Dried Fruit and Nut Couscous:** In a heatproof serving bowl, pour 2 cups boiling water over 1 cup whole-grain couscous. Let stand for 10 minutes. Stir in a tablespoon or so of vegan buttery spread (such as Earth Balance) or fragrant nut oil. Add about ⅓ cup raisins or currants, about ¼ cup toasted sliced or slivered almonds, and a pinch each of cinnamon and ground nutmeg. Season to taste with salt and pepper and keep warm until ready to serve.
- **Easy Cucumber Raita:** Combine a crisp medium-size cucumber, quartered lengthwise and thinly sliced, with a 6-ounce container of coconut-milk yogurt. Stir in some chopped fresh herbs—as much or as little as you like. Consider cilantro, parsley, dill, basil, or a combination. Or, to vary the flavor, add a medium diced ripe fresh tomato or two.
- When you have more time, consider making Basmati Rice Pilaf with Fresh Fruit or Cauliflower (page 110)—choose the fresh fruit variation, since there's already plenty of cauliflower in the stew. The raita described above is a good addition to this meal as well.

Coconut Curried Vegetable Stew (page 146)

Curried Chickpea, Eggplant, *and* Green Bean Stew

This delectable dish is a Westernized mashup of two Indian favorites—chana masala, a dish that highlights chickpeas, and baingan bharta, which features eggplant. Green beans aren't traditionally used in either dish, but they work well in tandem with the chickpeas and eggplant, adding color as well as flavor. Altogether, this is a good rendition of a tomato-based curry, which contrasts nicely with the creamy coconut stew on page 146.

SERVES 4 TO 6

1 tablespoon extra-virgin olive oil or 3 tablespoons vegetable broth or water
1 large onion, chopped
2 to 3 cloves garlic, minced
4 cups cooked or two 15- to 16-ounce cans (drained and rinsed) chickpeas
1 medium eggplant, stemmed and diced
2 teaspoons good-quality curry powder, or more to taste
1/2 teaspoon turmeric
2 to 3 teaspoons grated or minced fresh or jarred ginger, or to taste
8 to 10 ounces fresh or frozen green beans, cut into 1-inch pieces
3 to 4 medium ripe fresh tomatoes, diced, or one 15- to 16-ounce can
    diced tomatoes, undrained
1 tablespoon freshly squeezed or bottled lemon or lime juice, or more to taste
1/4 cup chopped fresh cilantro, plus more for serving
Salt and freshly ground pepper to taste
Crushed red pepper flakes to taste (optional)

1. Heat the oil, broth, or water in a soup pot. Add the onion and sauté until translucent. Add the garlic and continue to sauté until the onion is golden.

2. Add the chickpeas, eggplant, curry powder, turmeric, ginger, and 1 cup water. Bring to a simmer, then cook over medium-low heat for 10 minutes, stirring occasionally.

3. Stir in the green beans, tomatoes, and citrus juice. Add a small amount of additional water, if needed, but let the consistency remain thick and stewlike rather than soupy. Cook over low heat for 10 minutes longer.

4. Stir in the cilantro and season with salt and pepper. If you'd like a bit more spice, sprinkle in some crushed red pepper flakes. Serve on its own in shallow bowls or on a plate with other components of the meal, such as plain cooked grains, as suggested on page 150.

continued

PER SERVING: Calories: 357 with oil, 327 without oil; Total fat: 8g with oil, 5g without oil; Protein: 17g; Carbohydrates: 59g; Fiber: 17g; Sodium: 25mg

Variations

- Use asparagus in place of the green beans.

- Once the dish is finished, add 3 to 4 ounces baby spinach to the pan and cover. Allow to wilt for a minute or two, then stir together.

Complete the Meal

- Follow the suggestions for accompaniments to Coconut Curried Vegetable Stew (page 146).

- Serve alongside or over hot cooked brown basmati rice. Add one of the salads from "Fruity, Nutty Mixed Greens Salads" (page 326) to complete the menu.

Southeast Asian–Style Vegetable *and* Nut Butter Stew

To round out this chapter on meals in bowls, I present one of my longtime favorites—a stew that's richly enveloped in spicy-as-you-like-it nut butter. It might be just the thing to get kids and other picky eaters to appreciate and enjoy vegetable medleys of this kind.

SERVES 6 TO 8

1½ tablespoons extra-virgin olive oil or 3 tablespoons vegetable broth or water

1 large red onion, chopped

3 to 4 cloves garlic, minced

2 medium sweet potatoes, peeled and cut into ½-inch dice

One 15- to 16-ounce can diced tomatoes, with liquid

2 teaspoon grated fresh ginger, or more to taste (see Note)

3 cups small broccoli or cauliflower florets

1 or 2 small fresh hot chili peppers, seeded and minced, or crushed red pepper flakes to taste (see Note)

½ cup natural smooth peanut butter

2 cups shredded green cabbage or thinly sliced lacinato kale or collard greens

¼ to ½ cup chopped fresh cilantro

Salt and freshly ground pepper to taste

Chopped peanuts
Thinly sliced scallions

1. Heat the oil, broth, or water in a soup pot. Add the onion and garlic and sauté over medium heat until the onion is golden.

2. Add the sweet potatoes, tomatoes, ginger, and 3 cups water. Bring to a slow boil, then lower the heat and cover. Simmer gently until the sweet potatoes are nearly tender, about 15 minutes.

3. Add the broccoli or cauliflower and chili peppers. Stir in the peanut butter, a little at a time, until it melts into the broth. Cover and simmer gently for 5 minutes.

4. Stir in the greens and continue to cook for 5 to 10 minutes longer, or until all the vegetables are tender but not overdone. Add a bit more water if needed for a moist but not soupy consistency.

5. Stir in the cilantro, then season with salt and pepper. Serve in bowls over hot cooked rice. If desired, garnish each serving with chopped scallions and/or chopped peanuts.

PER SERVING: Calories: 234 with oil, 205 without oil; Total fat: 15g with oil, 11g without oil; Protein: 8g; Carbohydrates: 22g; Fiber: 13g; Sodium: 48mg

note: To make this dish spicier, gradually increase quantities of the ginger and cayenne or red pepper flakes or use a hotter chili pepper, such as canned chipotle in adobo sauce. Taste frequently to make sure you don't overdo it! Or pass around the hot stuff and let everyone spice up their own portions. You can also pass around a bottled hot sauce, such as sriracha, instead of using dried spices.

Variations

- Replace peanut butter with cashew or almond butter.
- To bolster protein content, add 8 ounces diced, lightly sautéed tempeh or baked tofu.
- To make this stew richer, substitute a 15-ounce can of light coconut milk for 2 cups of the water.

Complete the Meal

Add some cooked grain to the meal. Brown basmati rice, millet, or quinoa can be used as a bed for the stew. Or to use any of these grains as a simple side dish, cook them in vegetable broth for extra flavor, and then, once done, stir in a tablespoon or so of vegan buttery spread or a fragrant nut oil. And since the stew is so abundant in veggies, the simple grated carrot and raisin salad described on page 175 completes the plate nicely.

CHAPTER 3

Plant-Powered
PASTA AND PIZZA

In this chapter, we go out for Italian. Actually, we stay in for Italian. Many of these recipes offer twists on their Italian-restaurant counterparts and may not employ the exact techniques and ingredients a traditional Italian home cook might use to make them. Still, the dishes in this chapter are built upon traditional formulas for pasta and pizza, two beloved types of meals no matter where you live. They're comforting, familiar, and easy to prepare at home. If you already love this kind of fare, you'll find much to enjoy in this chapter.

Pasta with Hearty Lentil and Spinach Sauce (page 159)

Pasta is a staple in almost every kitchen; it's a good value for its modest cost and a special friend to harried parents—few kids will refuse it. The amazing array of shapes and, now, the growing variety of whole-grain and gluten-free pastas make them fantastic vehicles for fresh vegetables and delicious sauces. Stock your pantry with a variety of pastas and noodles; with companionable fresh ingredients, many go-to meals are forty-five minutes away—or less!

Pizza has long been a favorite in our home. When my kids were young, we'd often have a pizza-and-movie night on Fridays as a way to unwind from the week. I must admit that these started out as deliveries from the local pizza parlor before we all went vegan. At least, though, we ordered the veggie pizza, which was topped with a fair amount of broccoli, mushrooms, eggplant, peppers, and olives. Making our transition to plant-based fare dovetailed with the burgeoning availability of options in the way of prepared crust, organic tomato-based sauces, and the improvement in vegan cheeses. I calculated that a homemade pizza, made differently each time depending on which vegetables "called" to us, could be on the table in less time than it took to wait for a pizza to be ordered and delivered—or even picked up. And a really good salad could be made while the pizza was in the oven.

While I do recommend seeking out prepared, whole-grain crusts for homemade pizzas, if you're a completely DIY kind of person, I provide basic crust recipes (one whole wheat, one gluten-free). Personally, I'd rather take the time to prep lots of veggies than to make crust from scratch, but I want to make everyone happy. And this chapter, I promise, contains many paths to happiness.

Easy Salads to Go with Pasta and Pizza

To my mind, there's no better pairing for pizza or a pasta dish than a colorful, bountiful salad. Start with mixed baby greens, a mix of romaine lettuce and baby spinach or baby arugula, or tender lettuce like Boston or Bibb, then add any of the following:

- Diced fresh tomatoes, thinly sliced bell pepper (any color), sliced cucumber, diced cooked beets, toasted sunflower seeds, strips of sun-dried tomatoes, and/or black olives

- Artichoke hearts (marinated or not, as you prefer), chickpeas, corn kernels, cherry or grape tomatoes, and toasted pumpkin seeds

- Thinly sliced radicchio or red cabbage, golden cherry tomatoes, green olives, and sliced celery or fennel

- Chickpeas, scallions, diced fresh tomatoes, diced avocado, and lots of basil

- Consider the Italian variation in "Tossed Salads Go Global," page 319

Dress any of these salad combinations with extra-virgin olive oil and lemon juice or any favorite homemade (pages 327–31) or prepared salad dressings you enjoy.

Pasta Nutrition Notes

Pastas and noodles have at last shed their old "fattening" image—it's not what's in them, after all, it's what you put on them. An average serving of two ounces of plain cooked pasta contains only one to two grams of fat. It's well known that a big plate of pasta has become the traditional food for competitive runners before a race. This is because pasta is high in complex carbohydrates, which provide a quick supply of fuel for the body.

Nutritional qualities of the various varieties of pastas and noodles depend on the particular flours used in making them. In general, however, most pastas and noodles, in addition to being good sources of complex carbohydrates, are good sources of protein (ranging from about six grams in a two-ounce serving of refined pasta to ten grams per two-ounce serving of whole-grain pastas) and are rich in iron and the B vitamins.

Though even ordinary durum wheat pastas can claim the aforementioned benefits, which are conferred during the enrichment process, pastas and noodles made from whole-grain flours provide greater amounts of protein and fiber and contain a wider range of vitamins and minerals, including calcium, magnesium, phosphorus, zinc, vitamin B_6, and Vitamin E.

Some varieties to explore include those including the flours of artichoke (that is, Jerusalem artichoke, a starchy tuber), corn (organic corn flour ensures that it's non-GMO), quinoa, spelt, and, of course, whole wheat. Other pastas have dried vegetables added to them, notably, spinach and tomato, which add subtle color and flavor. Pasta comes in shapes and varieties too numerous to mention; if you're a pasta fan, look beyond the standard durum wheat varieties to add interest and nutrition to these kinds of meals.

Aside from what we put in the category of pasta, there's also a world of Asian noodles, which we touch on in chapter 4.

Gluten-Free Pasta

Like all gluten-free items, gluten-free pastas have improved in flavor over the past few years, and the number of varieties has expanded as well. Time was, the only option was rice pasta, which used to have (and still sometimes does have) a tendency to be gummy and fall apart. But not necessarily—my cousin Lee's favorite is the penne from Bionaturae, which is made (in Italy) from rice flour, rice starch, and organic soy flour. She enjoys the consistency, and since she has celiac disease, she appreciates knowing that this brand is made in accordance with the strictest gluten-free standards.

My friend Rachael's favorite is the quinoa pasta offered by Ancient Harvest. She also advises home cooks not to adhere strictly to the cooking time printed on boxes of gluten-free (GF) pasta. She finds that if the pasta takes six minutes to cook the first time she makes it, the next time it might take ten to twelve minutes—even if it's the same brand and shape. It's best to watch the pasta carefully as it cooks, stir gently, and be sure not to overcook it. GF pasta tends to fall apart more easily than standard pastas.

Another option is Asian rice noodles, which hold up better than domestically produced rice pasta. To avoid cross-contamination, make sure that the noodles you intend to use aren't made in facilities that may also produce products containing gluten. Other GF pasta brands include RP's Pasta Company, Jovial, Schär, and Tinkyáda, which you can look for in specialty foods stores, natural foods stores, well-stocked supermarkets, and online. Very often, it's a matter of personal preference.

Classic Pasta Dishes, Updated

Classic Marinara Sauce *with* Variations

There are many excellent pasta sauces on the market, and they can't be beat for convenience. But they can't compare to a homemade marinara and the wonderful aroma that will permeate your kitchen as it cooks!

SERVES 6 TO 8; ENOUGH FOR 1 POUND OF COOKED PASTA

1 tablespoon extra-virgin olive oil or 3 tablespoons vegetable broth or water
3 to 4 cloves garlic, minced
1 medium onion, finely chopped
1 cup thinly sliced small mushrooms (optional)
One 28-ounce can pureed tomatoes
One 14- to 16-ounce can tomato sauce
¼ cup dry red wine (optional)
½ teaspoon each dried oregano, basil, thyme, and marjoram (or substitute
    2 teaspoons Italian seasoning)
Salt and freshly ground pepper to taste

1. Heat the oil, broth, or water in a large saucepan. Add the garlic and onion and sauté over low heat until golden.

2. Add all remaining ingredients except the salt and pepper and bring to a gentle simmer. Cover and simmer very gently for 30 minutes. Season with salt and pepper. Serve over hot cooked pasta or use as a sauce for pasta, pizza, or lasagna.

PER SERVING: Calories: 102 with oil, 82 without oil; Total fat: 3g with oil, 0g without oil; Protein: 3g; Carbohydrates: 19g; Fiber: 4g; Sodium: 120mg

Variations

- **Puttanesca:** Substitute 1 medium red or green bell pepper for the mushrooms; add ¾ to 1 cup chopped pitted black and green olives and ¼ to ½ cup minced fresh parsley before simmering.

- **Arrabbiata:** Add 4 to 6 chopped pickled pepperoncini (from a jar) or cherry peppers, and crushed red pepper flakes to taste before simmering.

continued

- **Eggplant and Peppers:** Stem and dice a medium eggplant (leave the peel on if you like). Dice a medium bell pepper or Italian pepper or two of any color. Add them, along with crushed red pepper flakes to taste, to the rest of the ingredients before simmering. Pass around fresh sliced basil for topping each portion.
- **Garden Vegetable:** Add 2 to 3 heaping cups of steamed chopped vegetables, such as broccoli, broccoli rabe, carrots, cauliflower, or chard—or preferably a mixture of two or three of these—before simmering. Passing around fresh sliced basil at the table is welcome here as well.

Complete the Meal

- Lemon and Garlic Beans or Lentils (page 94) or Sweet and Smoky Beans and Greens (page 92) are both good options for boosting the protein content of this dish. Round the meal out with any of the easy salads to go with pasta and pizza described on page 155.
- Keep the meal simple by serving with a colorful green salad with beans or chickpeas tossed in. For a larger meal, add a steamed green vegetable such as broccoli or green beans (top with toasted almonds or pine nuts if you like) and a crusty whole-grain bread.

Pasta *with* Hearty Lentil *and* Spinach Sauce

This recipe is a longtime family favorite. Easy and substantial, this can easily become your go-to plant-powered pasta dish.

SERVES 6

8 to 10 ounces rotini, miniature penne, or other short, chunky pasta
1 tablespoon extra-virgin olive oil or 3 tablespoons vegetable broth or water
1 medium onion, finely chopped
3 to 4 cloves garlic, minced
1 medium red bell pepper, diced
1 to 1½ cups sliced white or cremini mushrooms (optional)
One 28-ounce jar good-quality marinara sauce (see Note)
One 14- to 16-ounce can diced tomatoes undrained, or 2 cups diced ripe fresh tomatoes
3 to 3½ cups cooked or two 15- to 16-ounce cans (drained and rinsed)
     brown lentils (see Note)
1 teaspoon dried oregano
1 teaspoon sweet or smoked paprika
6 to 8 ounces baby spinach, rinsed well
¼ cup minced fresh parsley or sliced fresh basil, or more to taste
Salt and freshly ground pepper to taste
Crushed red pepper flakes to taste (optional)

1. Cook the pasta in plenty of steadily boiling water in a large pot until al dente, then drain.

2. Meanwhile, heat the oil, broth, or water in a medium skillet. Add the onion and sauté over medium-low heat until the translucent. Add the garlic, bell pepper, and mushrooms, if desired, and continue to sauté until the onion is golden and the bell pepper is tender.

3. Return the cooked pasta to the large pot and stir in the marinara sauce, diced tomatoes, lentils, oregano, and paprika along with the vegetable mixture in the skillet. Simmer gently over medium-low heat for 5 to 8 minutes, or until everything is well heated through.

4. Add the spinach, about half at a time, cover, then stir in once it's wilted.

5. Stir in the parsley or basil and season with salt and pepper. If you'd like a little heat, add a pinch of crushed red pepper flakes. Serve at once.

continued

note: Using canned lentils makes this a breeze, but when you aren't in a hurry, by all means use home-cooked lentils. For this recipe, use 1 cup dried lentils. Rinse and sort them and combine them in a saucepan with 2 cups water. Bring to a rapid simmer, then lower the heat and simmer gently, covered, for 30 minutes, or until the lentils are tender and still hold their shape. Drain any excess water. This step can be done ahead of time. The same goes for the marinara sauce—if you'd like to use a homemade version, use the recipe on page 157.

PER SERVING: Calories: 357 with oil, 338 without oil; Total fat: 4g with oil, 1g without oil; Protein: 17g; Carbohydrates: 67g; Fiber: 17g; Sodium: 621mg

Variation

Use any leafy green you like in place of the spinach—tender kale and chard are especially good substitutions.

Complete the Meal

This hearty dish needs nothing more than a colorful tossed salad on the side. See some ideas for recipe-free salads that go well with pasta, page 155. Fresh olive bread is a lovely addition, too, though entirely optional. If you'd like more veggies with the meal, combine broccoli florets or chopped broccoli rabe—as much as you'd like—with a thinly sliced red or yellow bell pepper in a skillet with just enough water to keep the bottom moist. Cover and steam until the broccoli or broccoli rabe is bright green and tender-crisp.

‹ Pasta with Hearty Lentil and Spinach Sauce
(page 159)

Mixed Vegetable Lasagna

Lasagna has a timeless appeal and is always such a hit, whether you make it for your family or take it to social or holiday gatherings. It almost goes without saying that you can vary the vegetables called for here; suggestions follow the recipe. Any vegetables you use should be lightly steamed or sautéed first. I use no-boil lasagna noodles, which makes the whole enterprise a snap. Though you might have to search a bit farther afield, you will probably be able to find whole-grain no-boil lasagna noodles as well.

SERVES 12

1 medium red bell pepper, diced
1 medium zucchini, sliced
8 to 10 ounces white or baby bella (cremini) mushrooms, sliced
5 to 6 ounces baby spinach
One 12.3-ounce package firm or extra-firm silken tofu
1 recipe Classic Marinara Sauce (page 157) or one 28-ounce jar good-quality
    marinara sauce plus one 15- to 16-ounce can crushed tomatoes
12 to 15 no-boil lasagna noodles (see Note)
8 ounces grated nondairy mozzarella-style cheese (Daiya brand works very well)

1. Preheat the oven to 375°F.

2. Combine the bell pepper, zucchini, and mushrooms in a skillet or stir-fry pan. Add a little water to the pan, cover, and steam over medium heat until the vegetables are tender-crisp. Add the spinach, a little at a time, and cook until each batch is just wilted. Drain the vegetables well and set aside, uncovered.

3. In a mixing bowl, mash the silken tofu finely.

4. Have the sauce ready, either by making the marinara ahead of time or whisking the jarred marinara sauce with the crushed tomatoes in a bowl.

5. Thinly coat the bottom of a shallow 9 × 13-inch pan with a small amount of sauce. Arrange 4 to 5 lasagna noodles on top of the sauce so that they cover the bottom of the pan (you might need to break up one of the noodles to fill in odd spaces).

6. Spread about 1/3 of the remaining sauce over the noodles, followed by the tofu (distribute as evenly as you can). Sprinkle half the cheese evenly over the tofu. Follow with another layer of noodles, another 1/3 of the remaining sauce, then an even layer of the entire vegetable mixture.

7. Top the veggies with the remaining noodles, the remaining sauce, and the remaining cheese. Don't worry if you get these layers out of order, as long as you end with noodles, sauce, and cheese on top. It will taste great no matter what order you put things in.

8. Cover with foil and bake for 45 to 55 minutes, or until the noodles are tender (test them by piercing all the layers with a fork). Remove from the oven, let the lasagna stand for 5 minutes, then cut into 12 squares and serve.

PER SERVING: Calories: 196; Total fat: 6g; Protein: 8g; Carbohydrates: 30g; Fiber: 5g; Sodium: 280mg

note: Some brands of no-boil lasagna noodles contain egg, so read labels. DeCecco lasagna noodles aren't specifically no-boil, but they work well as such, and other brands might as well.

Variations

• Substitute other veggies for those recommended here. Small broccoli or cauliflower florets, chopped chard or kale, and diced eggplant are all great choices. You'll want to use 4 to 5 cups lightly steamed veggies total.

• For gluten-free lasagna, use corn tortillas. Simply layer whole tortillas, overlapped somewhat, in place of the noodles. This will have a different flavor, but it will still be delicious. Reduce baking time to 30 to 35 minutes.

Complete the Meal

Consider increasing the veggie power of this meal by roasting asparagus or green beans in the oven alongside the lasagna while it cooks. See notes on this process on pages 288–90. This is entirely optional, since there are plenty of vegetables in the lasagna. As with all hearty pasta dishes, a good salad is all that's really necessary to complete the meal. See "Easy Salads to Go with Pasta and Pizza," page 155.

Pasta with Beans *and* Greens *with* Variations

The trio of pasta, beans, and greens is a classic combination in Italian cuisine. And it rarely gets better than this, especially if you use a whole-grain pasta. Nourishing and versatile, this kind of pasta dish will satisfy the heartiest of appetites. Not only can you vary the types of pasta, greens, and beans each time you make it, you can also give the dish a traditional Tuscan touch with a few raisins or a briny lilt with olives, as noted in the variations below.

SERVES 4 TO 6

One 10- to 12-ounce bunch greens, any variety (see Variations)
10 to 12 ounces pasta (any short, chunky shape, preferably whole-grain)
1½ tablespoons extra-virgin olive oil or 3 tablespoons vegetable broth or water
1 large onion, quartered and thinly sliced
3 to 4 cloves garlic, minced
¼ cup dry white wine or water
1½ pounds diced ripe fresh tomatoes or one 28-ounce can diced tomatoes, undrained
2 cups cooked or one 15- to 16-ounce can (drained and rinsed) beans of your choice
    (see Variations)
1 tablespoon fresh oregano leaves or 1 teaspoon dried oregano
½ cup chopped fresh herbs (parsley, basil, or a combination)
⅓ cup raisins or sliced sun-dried tomatoes (optional)
Crushed red pepper flakes
Salt and freshly ground pepper to taste

1. If using chard, kale, or collards, cut the leaves away from the stems of the greens, but don't discard the stems. Chop the leaves coarsely and slice the stems thinly. Rinse both well.

2. Bring water to a boil in a large pot. Cook the pasta in rapidly simmering water until al dente, then drain and set aside.

3. Meanwhile, heat the oil, broth, or water in an extra-large saucepan or stir-fry pan. Add the onions and garlic and sauté over medium heat until the onion is golden.

4. Add the wine or water and the greens with their stems. Cover and cook just until the greens wilt down, stirring once or twice, about 3 minutes.

5. Stir in the tomatoes, beans, oregano, and herbs and cook just until everything is well heated through, 4 to 5 minutes longer. Stir in the raisins or sun-dried tomatoes, if desired.

6. Combine the cooked pasta with the sauce in a large serving bowl. Stir, then season to taste with red pepper flakes, salt, and pepper. Serve at once.

PER SERVING: Calories: 523 with oil, 478 without oil; Total fat: 7g with oil, 2g without oil; Protein: 23g; Carbohydrates: 100g; Fiber: 16g; Sodium: 273mg

Variations

Standard choices for this dish are chard (green, Swiss, or rainbow) or kale (curly or lacinato). Spinach is always welcome, of course. If you enjoy mildly bitter greens, try escarole or broccoli rabe. Here are some greens-and-beans pairings I enjoy:

- Chard with chickpeas, cannellini, red, or pink beans

- Spinach, chard, or kale with chickpeas

- Navy beans, cannellini, or great northern beans with escarole or broccoli rabe

- Use 1/3 cup briny black olives instead of raisins for a different kind of flavor accent

Complete the Meal

As shown in the photo on page 166, serve this with a simple, colorful salad. A tasty optional addition, also seen in the photo, is pan-grilled rounds of polenta. Use an 18-ounce package of polenta; cut into 1/2-inch-thick rounds and cook on a nonstick skillet or griddle sprayed with cooking spray until touched with light brown spots on both sides. Top with marinara sauce, if you like, and a sprinkling of mozzarella-style nondairy cheese. For more information on prepared polenta, see page 115.

Pasta with Beans and
Greens with Variations
(page 164)

Vegan Pasta Alfredo
with Two Stroganoff Variations

Here's a healthful nondairy version of creamy Alfredo sauce; it's just a bit more sophisticated than vegan mac and cheese and every bit as comforting. Young eaters might like this just as is, but do try to nudge them toward the veggie toppings or the stroganoff variations.

SERVES 4 TO 6

10 to 12 ounces pasta of your choice (see Note)
1 tablespoon extra-virgin olive oil or 3 tablespoons vegetable broth or water
2 to 3 cloves garlic, minced
One 12.3-ounce package firm silken tofu
½ cup unsweetened rice milk or other unsweetened nondairy milk
Freshly ground pepper to taste
1 teaspoon salt, or to taste

OPTIONAL TOPPINGS

Minced fresh parsley
Steamed broccoli florets
Wilted spinach
Sliced sun-dried tomatoes

1. Cook the pasta according to package directions until al dente, then drain.

2. Meanwhile, heat the oil, broth, or water in a small skillet. Add the garlic and sauté over low heat for 2 to 3 minutes, until golden. Remove from heat.

3. Combine the sautéed garlic and any oil or broth that remains in the skillet with the tofu and rice milk in a food processor. Process until completely smooth and creamy.

4. Combine the pasta and tofu mixture in a large serving bowl and toss together. Season with pepper and taste to see if you'd like to add salt. If the mixture needs to be moister, add a small amount of additional rice milk and toss again.

5. If desired, spoon the parsley, steamed broccoli, spinach, and sun-dried tomatoes over the pasta or on the side; serve at once.

note: This works well with the traditional pasta choice—fettuccine—and is also nice with other ribbon pastas such as pappardelle and linguine. Try it with whole-wheat pasta and spelt pasta for even more nutrition.

continued

PER SERVING: Calories: 344 with oil, 314 without oil; Total fat: 7g with oil, 3g without oil; Protein: 17g; Carbohydrates: 59g; Fiber: 6g; Sodium: 630mg

Variations

- **Mushroom Stroganoff:** Clean, stem, and slice 1 to 1½ pounds mushrooms. I like to combine a couple of medium-size portobello caps, thinly sliced, with some baby bellas (also known as cremini). A small amount of shiitake mushrooms added to the mix is nice, too. Start by sautéing a finely chopped medium onion in a tablespoon of olive oil or vegetable broth in a medium skillet (or in enough water or broth to keep the skillet moist) until golden. Add the mushrooms and cover. Cook until they've wilted down to your liking, about 5 to 8 minutes.

  If there's plenty of liquid in the pan from the mushrooms, rather than drain it, thicken it with a couple of teaspoons of cornstarch dissolved in water or vegetable broth. To serve, ladle some of the mushroom mixture on top of individual servings of the pasta. Top with plenty of minced parsley and, for added plant power, some steamed fresh or frozen green peas.

- **Mushroom-Seitan Stroganoff:** Give this dish some plant-based "beefiness" courtesy of seitan. Follow the recipe above, adding 8 to 16 ounces chopped seitan once the onion is translucent. Drizzle in a tablespoon or two of soy sauce. Cook over medium-high heat until the seitan is lightly browned, stirring often. Then proceed with the mushrooms, following the instructions for regular mushroom stroganoff above.

Complete the Meal

As shown in the opposite photo, no matter which variation you choose, this flavor- and texture-packed dish is completed very simply. The steamed broccoli (or spinach) suggested in the basic recipe can be served on the side of the pasta dish. Add a basic tossed salad. For salad inspirations, see ideas on page 155. Or instead of salad, you can serve this with one of the simple slaws on pages 322–25.

< Vegan Pasta Alfredo (Mushroom-Seitan Stroganoff variation)

Pasta Primavera

This dish is so packed with veggies that even when it's made with just a half pound of pasta it provides generous helpings for four people. In this case the pasta acts in service of the vegetables rather than the other way around. Admittedly there's a bit of chopping involved with this recipe, but it's not something that can't be accomplished during the pasta's cooking time. Perhaps I won't designate this as a go-to dinner after a tiring day, but this ever-so-slightly more leisurely preparation results in a great meal for a weekend or special occasion.

SERVES 4 TO 6

8 ounces pasta (any short, chunky shape, preferably whole-grain)
1 tablespoon extra-virgin olive oil or 3 tablespoons vegetable broth or water
1 medium to large red onion, quartered and thinly sliced
3 cloves garlic, minced
¼ cup dry white wine or water
4 cups broccoli or cauliflower florets (or 2 cups of each)
8 ounces slender asparagus, cut into 1-inch lengths
6 to 8 ounces baby bella (cremini) mushrooms, sliced
1 small zucchini or yellow summer squash, diced
3 medium ripe fresh tomatoes, diced, or one 15- to 16-ounce can diced tomatoes
¼ cup thinly sliced sun-dried tomatoes
1 teaspoon dried oregano
½ teaspoon dried thyme
¼ to ½ cup chopped fresh parsley
Thinly sliced fresh basil to taste, plus more for topping
Salt and freshly ground pepper to taste
Vegan Parmesan-Style Cheez (page 173) for topping (optional)

1. Cook the pasta in plenty of rapidly simmering water until al dente, then drain and set aside.

2. Meanwhile, heat the oil, broth, or water in an extra-large skillet or stir-fry pan. Add the onion and sauté over medium heat until translucent. Add the garlic and continue to sauté until the onion is golden.

3. Add the wine, broccoli, asparagus, and mushrooms. Cover and cook for 2 minutes, until the broccoli is bright green.

4. Stir in the zucchini, fresh and dried tomatoes, and dried herbs. Cover and cook over medium heat for 3 to 5 minutes longer, or until all the vegetables are tender-crisp.

5. Remove from the heat, then stir in the fresh herbs. Season with salt and pepper.

6. Transfer vegetable mixture to a large serving bowl and toss with the cooked pasta. Serve at once. Pass around Vegan Parmesan-Style Cheez and additional basil for topping individual portions, if desired.

PER SERVING: Calories: 326 with oil, 296 without oil; Total fat: 5g with oil, 2g without oil; Protein: 15g; Carbohydrates: 62g; Fiber: 10g; Sodium: 117mg

Complete the Meal

While this pasta dish is quite satisfying and needs little more than a salad to complete it, make sure that the salad component of the meal offers added protein. A mixed greens and tomato salad with chickpeas, lentils, or any of your favorite beans will do nicely, or consider the Italian variation in "Tossed Salads Go Global" (page 319). If you'd like a heartier meal, fresh olive bread is always welcome, or try pan-grilled polenta rounds, as suggested on page 115.

Pasta *with* Leafy Greens *and* Basil Pesto

I've long enjoyed pesto sauce that combines basil with spinach or other leafy greens more than basil-only pesto, which can be overpowering in flavor and which turns brown all too quickly. This makes a lovely no-cook sauce for summer pasta, but don't stop there. Try it as a tasty topping for sautéed potatoes, an offbeat dressing for potato salad, on grains, or as a garnish for cold soups.

SERVES 4 TO 6

10 to 12 ounces pasta (any long shape, such as spaghetti or linguine, or any short, chunky shape, such as miniature penne, farfalle, or rotelle)

LEAFY GREENS AND BASIL PESTO

1 tablespoon extra-virgin olive oil or 3 tablespoons water or vegetable broth
1 to 2 cloves garlic, crushed (optional)
½ to 1 cup firmly packed fresh basil leaves, or to taste
Juice of ½ lemon or 2 tablespoons bottled lemon juice, or more to taste
½ cup walnut halves or shelled unsalted pistachios or ¼ cup pine nuts (omit nuts if you'd like a less caloric pesto)
6 ounces baby spinach, arugula, watercress, or a combination
Salt and freshly ground pepper to taste
Vegan Parmesan-Style Cheez (opposite) for topping (optional)

1. Cook the pasta in plenty of rapidly simmering water until al dente, then drain and transfer to a serving container. Keep warm.

2. Combine the next six ingredients in a food processor and pulse until the mixture is evenly combined yet still coarse in texture. You may need to add the spinach in batches if your processor has a small or medium-size container.

3. Stop the machine and season the mixture gently with salt and pepper; taste to see if you'd like to add more lemon juice, then pulse a few times to mix. Transfer to the serving container, toss with the warm pasta, and serve.

PER SERVING WITH WALNUTS: Calories: 390 with oil, 360 without oil; Total fat: 14g with oil, 11g without oil; Protein: 15g; Carbohydrates: 59g; Fiber: 9g; Sodium: 68mg

Variations

- Turn this into a pasta salad by adding 2 to 3 cups of diced fresh vegetables. Tomatoes, summer squash, bell peppers, carrots, or anything you have in the crisper that tastes good raw will add color and flavor.

- Try substituting fresh parsley for the basil or using half of each.

Complete the Meal

- For an easy warm-weather dinner, serve with Marinated Bean Salad (page 313) or an even simpler salad of diced ripe tomatoes, chickpeas, and cucumbers dressed in lemon juice and just a little olive oil. Add corn on the cob or grilled vegetables if you're so inclined.

- For a glorious warm-weather meal, pair this with Vegan Niçoise-Style Salad, page 306.

Vegan Parmesan-Style Cheez

This dairy-free cheeselike topping is especially delicious on pasta dishes and can be used to top casseroles and salads. It's addictively delicious and features calcium-rich sesame seeds and/or omega-rich hemp seeds: alternate them each time you make this recipe or use them in tandem.

1. Combine 1 cup raw cashews, ¼ cup nutritional yeast, ¼ cup sesame or hemp seeds (or ⅛ cup of each), and a teaspoon of salt in a food processor.

2. Pulse until the mixture is finely and evenly ground.

3. Serve immediately or transfer to a tightly sealed container and store in the refrigerator, where it will keep for several weeks.

Vegan Macaroni and Cheez

Vegan Macaroni *and* Cheez *with* Variations

This basic vegan macaroni and cheese is rich and comforting. Using pureed silken tofu as a base makes it supereasy. Make it for the kids for dinner, then reheat leftovers and pack them in a Thermos for the next day's brown-bag lunch.

SERVES 4 TO 6 ADULTS OR 6 OR MORE CHILDREN

10 to 12 ounces pasta (any short shape; kids like elbows, or try cavatappi or rotini)
One 12.3-ounce package firm or extra-firm silken tofu
2 tablespoons Earth Balance or other vegan buttery spread
1½ cups Cheddar-style nondairy cheese
Salt to taste

1. Cook the pasta in plenty of rapidly simmering water until al dente, then drain.

2. While the pasta cooks, puree the tofu until perfectly smooth in a food processor or blender. Transfer to a medium saucepan and add the Earth Balance and nondairy cheese. Slowly bring to a gentle simmer, stirring often, then cook over low heat until the cheese is thoroughly melted.

3. Combine the cooked pasta and sauce, either in a serving bowl or in the pot used for cooking the pasta, and stir. Season with salt to taste and serve at once.

PER ADULT-SIZE SERVING: Calories: 483; Total fat: 18g; Protein: 18g; Carbohydrates: 66g; Fiber: 7g; Sodium: 462mg

Variation

Baked Macaroni and Cheez with Crisp Bread Crumbs: Transfer macaroni and cheese (plain or embellished with sweet potato or squash) to a 2-quart casserole dish. Top with ½ to ¾ cup fresh bread crumbs. Bake at 400ºF until the top is golden and crusty, about 20 to 25 minutes.

Complete the Meal

For a simple, kid-friendly meal (we're talking kids of all ages, of course!) serve as shown in the photo on the facing page—with steamed green beans or broccoli and a classic carrot-raisin salad. Combine about 8 ounces peeled and grated carrots with ½ cup or so raisins. Add lemon juice and agave nectar or maple syrup to taste (start with about a tablespoon of each, then add more until the sweet-tart balance is to your liking) and a generous pinch of ground cinnamon.

Macaroni *and* Almost-Raw Cheez Sauce

An alternative to the tofu-based sauce on page 175, this recipe takes classic mac and cheese from comfort food to superfood—with raw cashews for protein, hemp seeds for valuable omegas, and nutritional yeast for vitamin B_{12}. This sauce is also tasty on smashed potatoes or lightly steamed vegetables—especially broccoli and cauliflower. Another fun use for this is as a queso sauce to pour over nachos (see Fully Loaded Emergency Nachos, page 239). The optional vegan cheese adds extra cheesy flavor, but you can definitely leave it out.

SERVES 6

12 to 16 ounces pasta (any short, chunky shape)

ALMOST-RAW CHEEZ SAUCE

1 cup raw cashews
1/2 to 2/3 cup whole baby carrots or peeled and coarsely chopped medium carrots
1/4 cup hemp seeds
1/4 cup nutritional yeast
1 cup unsweetened rice milk, hemp milk, or almond milk
1/2 teaspoon powdered mustard
1/2 teaspoon sweet paprika
1 teaspoon salt, plus more to taste
1/2 to 1 cup grated nondairy cheese (optional)

1. Cook the pasta in plenty of rapidly simmering water until al dente, then drain.

2. While the pasta cooks, combine all the ingredients in a high-speed blender and let it run until the mixture is smooth and creamy and you feel the container getting nice and warm.

3. Combine the cooked pasta and sauce, either in a serving bowl or in the pot used for cooking the pasta, and stir. Taste to see if you'd like additional salt and serve at once.

PER SERVING: Calories: 423; Total fat: 16g; Protein: 21g; Carbohydrates: 57g; Fiber: 8g; Sodium: 419mg

Complete the Meal

- As suggested in Vegan Macaroni and Cheez, page 175, combine with steamed green beans or broccoli and a classic carrot-raisin salad (page 175).
- Serve with any of the salad ideas suggested in "Easy Salads to Go with Pasta and Pizza" (page 155) along with Steamed Broccoli and Yellow Squash (page 251).

Veggie Toppings for Macaroni and Cheez

Give any of the "mac and cheez" variations on the previous pages a plant-powered twist with the following toppings:

Steamed greens and sun-dried tomatoes: Rinse a good-size bunch of chard or kale and chop finely (use stems or not, as you prefer). Or use whole baby spinach. Simply combine with just enough water to keep the bottom of a medium skillet or saucepan moist, and steam until bright green. Spinach needs only a minute or two; chard and kale require five minutes or so. Serve over macaroni and cheese with a few slices of sun-dried tomatoes—preferably moist, but not oil-packed.

Broccoli and red bell pepper: Broccoli is good served atop mac and cheese as well as on the side. Finely chop a broccoli crown or two. Transfer to a medium skillet and combine with a diced red bell pepper and just enough water to keep everything moist. Steam over medium heat, covered, until the veggies are tender-crisp.

Sautéed onions (with optional garlic): Chop a large onion (along with a few cloves of garlic, if you like) and sauté in a small amount of olive oil over medium heat until golden brown. You can also add some bell pepper in addition to or instead of the garlic. See Caramelized Onions with or without Bell Peppers on page 88 if you need further directions.

Mushrooms and fresh herbs: Clean, stem, and slice 8 to 12 ounces of cremini (baby bella) mushrooms. Or use a combination of these brown mushrooms and a small amount of another variety, such as shiitake or porcini. Add a small amount of water and cook, covered, over medium heat until tender. Drain well. Serve over macaroni and cheese with fresh herbs—about a quarter or a half cup of chopped fresh parsley, basil, dill, or a combination.

Veg-Centric Pizzas

Pizza can fall anywhere on the culinary continuum from serious junk food (if made with massive amounts of dairy cheese and other animal products piled on white-flour crust) to delicious, nutritious vegetable delivery systems. I'm sure you can guess which direction we'll be taking.

As with stir-fries, I'm going to present a few formal pizza recipes as jumping-off points and as benchmarks for basic nutritional data. However, I encourage you to segue into improvising; to that end, you'll find a number of tempting "semirecipes" following the formal recipes. Without having to read and follow step-by-step instructions and measure exact amounts of this or that, most home cooks find that pizza is one of the easiest and most fun go-to types of meals.

For those of you who like to make everything from scratch, there are recipes in this book for whole-grain crust (page 180) and marinara sauce (page 157). But mostly, I'm going to give you the same "pass" I bestow on myself. I use a whole-grain prepared crust and whatever organic marinara sauce catches my eye (unless I'm making one of the other pizza sauces suggested below—white, pesto, or fresh tomato). But what I won't give myself—or you—a pass on is the toppings. Mere crust, sauce, and cheese—even vegan cheese—don't quite cut it. Remember, pizza is now a veggie delivery system, so partake of the toppings suggested here or improvise your own, and pile them on lavishly!

Briefly described in the next few paragraphs are four basic pizza styles, each named after the type of sauce that's spread on the crust. Since pizza with a red sauce is most familiar, you may gravitate toward that more than, say, a pesto pizza, but I hope you'll try all these variations.

Red pizza: Good store-bought varieties of red sauce are so widely available and make the process of pizza making so easy that it's almost impossible to resist them. Of course, you're free to cook your own marinara sauce using the recipe that your great-grandmother passed down or, barring that, to use the one on page 157. Otherwise, choose the most natural, lowest-sodium, sugar-free prepared sauce you can find. Though any tomato-basil sauce is fine, those with mushrooms, fire-roasted tomatoes, garden vegetables, and the like add extra kick to the overall flavor.

White pizza: I'm a big fan of white pizza because the toppings have a chance to shine rather than compete with the strong flavor of marinara sauce. Basically, white pizza sauce consists of pureed silken tofu and a little salt. It doesn't sound exciting, but it works very well.

Pesto pizza: Arranging tasty toppings on a pesto base is an offbeat treatment, one that adds a great deal of plant power to your pizza. For this basil-rich sauce, use the recipe on page 172 or use your favorite prepared brand: but be aware that store-bought pesto often contains dairy products.

Fresh tomato pizza: Instead of marinara sauce, make late-summer pizzas using flavorful ripe tomatoes, sliced about a quarter-inch thick and arranged in circles on the pizza crust.

This kind of treatment is the basis of the classic pizza Margherita, a variation on which is found on page 187.

You'll find one example of each of these pizza styles, with complete recipes, just ahead, but then please do explore the nearly recipe-free pizzas on page 189. Truly, the beauty of pizza meals is that you can improvise, tailoring them to the number of people you're feeding and the size of crust you have on hand.

A WORD ABOUT PIZZA CRUST

There are a number of natural prepared whole-grain pizza crusts available, especially at natural foods stores. Most are twelve to fourteen inches in diameter, and the four formal recipes on pages 182–87 are geared to this crust size. But don't limit yourself to these; you can use sturdy flatbreads, such as whole-grain ciabatta or pita, or even whole-grain Italian bread (the wide, flat loaves—long, narrow ones don't have enough surface area). If using such breads as alternatives to pizza crust, bake at 400°F rather than 425°F to ensure that they don't bake too quickly. There are also plenty of gluten-free pizza crust options; you can make your own at home with a mix, such as those offered by Bob's Red Mill and other brands, or choose a ready-made crust, such as the one offered by Rudi's.

AND ANOTHER WORD ABOUT VEGAN CHEESE

Note that vegan cheese is optional in all recipes and recipe ideas. Yes, vegan cheese, especially one that melts well (such as the Daiya brand), adds a huge yum factor; but it isn't entirely necessary. I like to think of vegan cheese as a condiment, because that's exactly what it is. Use it or not; use as much as is recommended in the recipes (one cup per twelve-inch pizza) or a bit more, but be aware that most vegan cheeses are scant on protein and other nutrients; they may not be unhealthful, but they're not exactly a health food, either. And if you're looking to impress guests with how delicious plant-powered pizza can be, a judicious sprinkling of vegan cheese goes a long way!

COMPLETE YOUR PIZZA MEALS

To my mind, the best companion for most any kind of pizza is a big salad. It need not be anything out of the ordinary—just an abundant bowlful of mixed greens or lettuces, tomatoes, peppers, carrots, cucumbers, and the like, with your favorite salad dressing. If you want to boost the protein content, just add plenty of beans or chickpeas as well as some sunflower or pumpkin seeds. If you'd like some specific salad ideas to accompany pizza, see "Easy Salads to Go with Pasta and Pizza," page 155.

If you'd like to add something more to the meal, serve soup as a first course. Good choices are Cream of Broccoli Soup (page 132) with red pizzas and Tomato-Vegetable Soup (page 138)—preferably the Minestrone variation—with white or pesto pizzas.

Whole-Wheat Pizza Crust

I've already admitted that I'm usually too lazy to make pizza dough from scratch, what with good, natural brands of prepared crust so widely available. Once in a blue moon, though, I like to indulge; it's really not that difficult. This is a recipe I've relied on for years when those blue moons come along.

MAKES TWO 12- TO 14-INCH PIZZA CRUSTS OF 6 SLICES EACH

2 envelopes active dry yeast
¼ cup safflower or extra-virgin olive oil
2 tablespoons natural granulated sugar
2 cups whole-wheat flour
3 cups unbleached all-purpose flour
1 teaspoon salt

1. Combine the yeast with 2 cups warm water in a medium bowl. Let stand for 10 minutes to dissolve. Stir in the oil and sugar.

2. In a large mixing bowl, combine the flours and salt. Make a well in the center and stir in the yeast mixture. Work everything together, first with a wooden spoon and then with your hands, to form a dough.

3. Turn out the dough onto a well-floured board and knead it for 8 minutes, adding flour until the dough loses its stickiness. Place the dough in a floured bowl, cover it with a tea towel, and put it in a warm place. Let it rise until doubled in bulk, about 1 to 1½ hours.

4. Punch the dough down and divide it into two rounds. Roll out one round on a well-floured board into a circle about 12 to 14 inches in diameter. Repeat with the other round.

5. Sprinkle two 12- to 14-inch pizza pans with cornmeal. Lay the rounds on the pans and stretch to fit. Arrange the toppings of your choice on the dough and bake as directed.

PER SLICE: Calories: 232; Total fat: 5.5g; Protein: 6.5g; Carbohydrates: 40g; Fiber: 3.5g; Sodium: 196mg

Gluten-Free Poured Pizza Crust

This recipe is a lovely gift to this book from Colette Martin, author of *Learning to Bake Allergen-Free.* You can buy gluten-free crust, but if you're a DIY kind of person, this crust is even easier to make than the standard variety, with no need for rising and rolling or stretching. Because this kind of crust needs to bake at a lower temperature than regular crust, it needs to be in the oven for nearly twice as long as standard pizza preparations.

MAKES ONE 8-SLICE PIZZA CRUST

1¾ cups gluten-free flour blend (use your favorite brand)
¼ teaspoon xanthan gum (omit if your flour blend contains xanthan gum)
1 teaspoon salt
1 teaspoon baking soda
4 tablespoons Earth Balance Natural Shortening, melted
1 cup unsweetened hemp milk or rice milk
1 tablespoon rice vinegar

1. Preheat the oven to 350°F.
2. Combine the flour, xanthan gum (if needed), salt, and baking soda in a medium bowl and set aside.
3. Using an electric mixer set on low speed, combine the shortening, hemp milk, and vinegar in a large bowl. Mix for 1 minute.
4. Add the flour mixture to the wet ingredients and blend for 2 to 3 minutes on medium speed.
5. Pour the batter into a 12- to 14-inch pizza pan (make sure to use a pan with a lip, and of course, without perforations on the bottom). Use a spatula (or the back of a soup spoon) to spread the batter evenly to the edges.
6. Bake in the preheated oven for 15 minutes. Remove the partially baked crust from the oven, then use a spatula to gently flip the crust over so that the browned side is on top. Add the desired toppings.
7. Bake for 12 to 18 minutes more, or until the bottom of the crust is golden brown.

PER SLICE: Calories: 182; Total fat: 6.5g; Protein: 2.8g; Carbohydrates: 36g; Fiber: 2.5g; Sodium: 492mg

Red Pizza *with* Bell Peppers *and* Artichokes

Let's start with a classic—red pizza. The combination of red bell peppers, artichokes, and basil in this pizza is absolutely splendid. Though it's filling, it goes down easy, so double the recipe if you're feeding a hungry group. Though completely optional, thin slices of fresh tomato layered between the sauce and the vegan cheese enhance the summery flavor of the fresh basil.

MAKES ONE 6-SLICE PIZZA

1 tablespoon extra-virgin olive oil or 3 tablespoons vegetable broth or water
1 medium onion, quartered and thinly sliced
2 cloves garlic, minced (optional)
1 medium red bell pepper, cut into short, narrow strips
1 cup quartered artichoke hearts (canned or frozen; not marinated)
1 good-quality 12- to 14-inch pizza crust
1 cup marinara or pizza sauce (homemade, page 157, or your favorite prepared brand),
    or more as needed
3 to 4 medium ripe fresh tomatoes, sliced about ¼ inch thick (optional)
1 cup grated mozzarella-style nondairy cheese (optional)
Sliced fresh basil leaves for topping (optional)

1. Preheat the oven to 425ºF.

2. Heat the oil, broth, or water in a medium skillet. Add the onion and garlic and sauté over medium-low heat until just golden.

3. Add the bell pepper and continue to sauté until the onion is soft and lightly browned. Stir in the artichoke hearts. Remove from heat and cover.

4. Place the crust on a 12- to 14-inch pizza pan. Spread the marinara sauce on the crust, then arrange the tomatoes over it, if desired. Top with the cheese and basil leaves, if desired.

5. Bake for 10 minutes, or until the crust is golden on the bottom and the cheese, if using, is completely melted. Remove from the oven and spread the mixture from the skillet over the surface of the pizza. Return to the oven for 2 to 3 minutes longer.

6. Remove from the oven, let stand for a minute or two, then cut into slices and serve.

PER SLICE: Calories: 325 with oil, 305 without oil; Total fat: 10g with oil, 7g without oil; Protein: 9g; Carbohydrates: 54g; Fiber: 7g; Sodium: 303mg

< Red Pizza with Bell Peppers and Artichokes

White Pizza *with* Caramelized Onions *and* Olives

While working on this book, I hosted a dinner gathering for a few friends, using them as guinea pigs for a few new pizza ideas I was trying out. I served four different varieties that evening, and they all passed with flying colors. This one, perhaps the most offbeat, was far and away the favorite. Based on a traditional Mediterranean recipe that calls for lots of onion and olives and no tomatoes, it uses a simple base of pureed silken tofu to give it substance.

MAKES ONE 6-SLICE PIZZA

1 tablespoon extra-virgin olive oil or 3 tablespoons vegetable broth or water
2 large or 3 medium onions, quartered and thinly sliced (see Note)
One 12.3-ounce package firm silken tofu
1 teaspoon salt
1 good-quality 12- to 14-inch pizza crust
½ cup chopped pitted briny black olives (such as kalamata)
Finely chopped fresh parsley or thinly sliced basil leaves

1. Preheat the oven to 425ºF.

2. Heat the oil, broth, or water in a medium skillet. Add the onions and sauté over medium-low heat until lightly and evenly browned, stirring frequently, about 15 to 20 minutes.

3. Meanwhile, puree the tofu with the salt in a food processor or, using an immersion blender, in its container.

4. Place the crust on a 12- to 14-inch pizza pan or a pizza stone. Spread the pureed tofu evenly over the surface of the crust with a silicone spatula or wooden spoon. When the onion mixture is done, spread it evenly over the pureed tofu.

5. Bake for 10 to 12 minutes, or until the crust is golden. Remove from the oven, then sprinkle the olives and fresh herb of your choice over the surface. Let stand for a minute or two, then cut into slices and serve.

note: The most time-consuming part of this pizza is making the caramelized onions, so if you fall in love with this recipe you might consider making a batch ahead of time, as suggested on page 88.

PER SLICE: Calories: 320 with oil, 300 without oil; Total fat: 11g with oil, 8g without oil; Protein: 11g; Carbohydrates: 48g; Fiber: 8g; Sodium: 705mg

Variations

- Bake or microwave a medium sweet potato until done but still firm. Let cool, then peel and thinly slice it; after spreading the onion on the surface, arrange the sweet potato slices on top of the pizza in concentric circles (or just scatter them about), then top with the olives.

- Add 3 to 4 cloves minced fresh garlic to the onion sauté once the onions are translucent.

- If you make this in the late fall or winter, consider sprinkling a few fresh rosemary leaves over the top in place of parsley or basil.

Pesto Pizza *with* Roasted Mixed Vegetables

Make your veggie pizza even greener with a pesto base. What's nice about this recipe is that the vegetables are roasted while the pizza bakes, bringing out their natural sweetness.

MAKES ONE 6-SLICE PIZZA

1½ cups small broccoli florets
1 medium red or green bell pepper, cut into narrow strips
1 heaping cup diced unpeeled eggplant or 1 small unpeeled Japanese eggplant, sliced
1 tablespoon extra-virgin olive oil
1 good-quality 12- to 14-ounce pizza crust
3⁄4 to 1 cup pesto (page 172), or more as needed
1 cup grated mozzarella-style nondairy cheese (optional)
1⁄3 cup sun-dried tomatoes (not oil-cured), cut into strips
A few leaves fresh basil, thinly sliced, or ½ teaspoon dried basil

1. Preheat the oven to 425°F.
2. Combine the broccoli, bell pepper, eggplant, and oil in a mixing bowl. Stir together and transfer to a lightly oiled roasting pan. Place in the preheated oven and roast for 10 minutes.
3. Meanwhile, place the crust on a 12- to 14-inch pizza stone or pizza pan. Distribute the pesto over the surface of the crust. Sprinkle with the cheese, if desired, then place the crust in the oven alongside the vegetables.
4. Give the vegetables a stir after the pizza goes in the oven. Bake for an additional 12 to 15 minutes, or until the vegetables are nicely roasted and the pizza crust begins to turn golden.
5. Remove from the oven and distribute the vegetable mixture evenly over the surface of the pizza. Scatter the sun-dried tomatoes over the vegetables and sprinkle with basil. Allow to stand for a minute or two, then cut into 6 slices and serve.

PER SLICE: Calories: 322; Total fat: 12g; Protein: 10g; Carbohydrates: 49g; Fiber: 7g; Sodium: 306mg

Variation

Substitute zucchini, yellow squash, asparagus, or mushrooms for any or all the vegetables suggested above.

Fresh Tomato Pizza *with* Mixed Mushrooms *and* Fresh Herbs

The most basic variety of fresh tomato pizza is the delicious pizza Margherita, which consists simply of sliced fresh tomatoes, mozzarella, and basil on a plain crust. Here we'll gild the lily with a plethora of tasty mushrooms, which add so much flavor that the vegan cheese is optional.

MAKES ONE 6-SLICE PIZZA

10 to 12 ounces mixed mushrooms (such as cremini, portobello, and shiitake), sliced

1 good-quality 12- to 14-ounce pizza crust

3 to 4 medium ripe fresh tomatoes (both red and yellow varieties, if available) sliced about ¼ inch thick

1 cup grated mozzarella-style nondairy cheese (optional)

½ cup chopped pitted briny black olives (such as kalamata)

2 to 3 scallions, thinly sliced (white and green parts)

¼ cup minced fresh parsley

½ cup sliced fresh basil leaves

1. Preheat the oven to 425ºF.

2. Combine the mushrooms in a skillet with a little water. Cover and cook until wilted, then drain well.

3. Meanwhile, place the crust on a 12- to 14-inch pizza pan or pizza stone. Arrange the tomatoes in concentric circles over the surface, followed by the nondairy cheese (if desired), cooked mushrooms, olives, and scallions.

4. Bake for 10 minutes, or until the bottom of the crust is golden. Remove from the oven, then scatter the parsley and basil over the surface.

5. Let stand for a minute or two, then cut into 6 slices and serve.

PER SLICE: Calories: 270; Total fat: 7g; Protein: 9g; Carbohydrates: 47g; Fiber: 5g; Sodium: 305mg

Variation

Use marinara sauce (your favorite brand or homemade, page 157) in addition to or in place of the fresh tomatoes.

Pesto and Heirloom
Tomato Pizza (page 189)

Nearly Recipe-Free Pizza Ideas

Choose a crust and one of the sauces described on pages 178–79, then top as lavishly as you desire. Vegan mozzarella-style cheese is optional in any of these variations. I don't give exact amounts for the topping ideas, because if you make too much, there are no worries: you can use the extra as a side dish, stir it into a grain, or roll it into a wrap with fresh greens the next day. As with all the other pizza recipes, preheat the oven to 425°F for a standard pizza crust or 400°F for flatbreads or Italian bread.

Potato or Sweet Potato and Arugula Pizza: Potato and arugula pizza is actually a classic combo, and while it does sound odd, it's very good. Spread the crust with white pizza sauce, then arrange slices of firm-cooked peeled potatoes or sweet potatoes over the top (you'll need about two medium-large potatoes to cover a twelve- to fourteen-inch crust; choose large, fat, round potatoes as opposed to thin, oblong potatoes). Sprinkle with a cup or so of shredded mozzarella-style nondairy cheese. After removing the pizza from the oven, sprinkle the top with lots of baby arugula leaves. Return to the oven for just a minute or two longer, until the arugula wilts.

Asparagus and Spinach Pizza: This is a lovely idea for spring and makes a good red or white pizza. Cut plenty of slender asparagus into one-inch lengths and steam until just tender-crisp in a large pan. Wilt down lots of spinach in the same pan. Drain the vegetables well. Cover the crust with sauce and bake. Spread the steamed vegetables evenly on the baked pizza, then finish with a scattering of chopped pitted briny olives or strips of sun-dried tomatoes.

Kale, Mushroom, and Red Onion Pizza: My assistant, Rachael, came up with this delightfully hearty variation. Sauté a quartered and thinly sliced red onion (and a couple cloves of minced garlic, if desired). Add a cup or more of sliced brown mushrooms, cover, and cook until wilted. Add as much stemmed and thinly sliced kale (curly green or lacinato) as you'd like and continue to cook until tender-crisp. Drain well. Cover the crust with red or white sauce and bake. Spread the vegetables evenly on the baked pizza, then return to the oven for a minute or two to allow the flavors to meld.

Eggplant Pizza with Green Olives and Basil: Here's a nice end-of-summer idea. Cut a smallish eggplant into dice, or, better yet, slice a long Japanese eggplant one-quarter inch thick. Toss the eggplant with a modest amount of olive oil and roast at the same time as the pizza is baking. This is good with red sauce; add slices of fresh tomatoes if desired.

Ratatouille Pizza: Use the versatile recipe for Roasted Ratatouille on page 296 to make a delicious pizza topping. This is especially good on a fresh tomato pizza, but it works well with all the other variations as well—red, white, or pesto.

Pesto and Heirloom Tomato Pizza: Bake or grill a crust or small flatbreads. Spread with pesto (page 172), then load up with sliced heirloom tomatoes, mixing yellow and red varieties. Sprinkle with salt and pepper and top with plenty of thinly sliced basil leaves. Some fresh oregano leaves would add a nice touch, too. This can be served at room temperature.

CHAPTER 4

ASIAN *Express*

My favorite kind of food to go out for is Asian. Chinese, Japanese, Thai—they're all fantastic, even if American restaurant versions of this fare aren't quite authentic. There's always a decent selection on the menu for those of us of the plant-based persuasion. Dishes featuring lightly cooked vegetables, hearty noodles, light soups, and the plant protein trio of tofu, tempeh, and seitan offer a myriad of sensory pleasures when dining out and are easy and economical to re-create at home. An added bonus is that homemade Asian-style fare can be made with a lot less oil and salt.

Asian Noodle Bowl (page 218)

I love this kind of cuisine so much that I've long attempted my own homemade versions of it. If restaurant renditions are less than faithful to the originals, then mine are possibly even more fanciful renditions. Still, my family has always enjoyed my homemade Asian-style meals, and I hope you'll savor them as well. What I like best about them is their inherent veg-friendliness. I mean, what's a stir-fry if not an amalgam of colorful vegetables?

Asian-style meals can be served as spontaneous weeknight fare for those of us who stock our pantry and fridge in a certain way. If brown rice, a variety or two of noodles, soy sauce, garlic, ginger, and tofu are available in your kitchen, for example, all you need are a few fresh vegetables to make an excellent meal without a whole lot of planning.

Stir-fries, in fact, are just about the easiest ways to use up the leftover vegetables lingering in your crisper or the just-bought vegetables you've brought home from the farm market or CSA farm. And the savory sauce that you choose to flavor them with might bring around even the most vegetable-shy eater. Colorful, minimally cooked vegetables, delectable rice and noodle dishes, nearly instant gingery soups, garnishes of nuts, sesame seeds, and scallions—even writing about it makes me hungry. So heat up your stir-fry pan or wok, and let's go!

Basic Tofu Preparations

Double Fruit-Glazed Tofu

Fruit preserves, orange juice, and soy sauce make a luscious glaze for tofu without adding fat. If you're serving a hungry group of tofu fans, consider doubling this recipe—it's addictive! This also might be just the thing to convert tofu skeptics.

SERVES 3 TO 4

One 14- to 16-ounce tub extra-firm tofu
¼ cup apricot or peach preserves or orange marmalade
¼ cup orange juice (preferably freshly squeezed)
2 tablespoons reduced-sodium natural soy sauce, tamari, or hoisin sauce
2 teaspoons grated fresh or jarred ginger

OPTIONAL TOPPINGS
Thinly sliced scallions
Black or white sesame seeds

1. Drain the tofu and blot well between paper towels or clean tea towels (or use a tofu press), then cut so you have 12 little squares of tofu.

2. Combine the preserves, juice, soy sauce, and ginger in a small bowl and whisk together.

3. Heat a medium skillet and pour in the preserves mixture. When it starts bubbling, arrange the tofu in the pan in a single layer. Turn the heat up to medium-high and cook each side for 5 minutes, or until the tofu is nicely glazed and most of the liquid has been absorbed.

4. Serve at once, scooping up any remaining glaze to top the tofu pieces. Garnish individual servings with scallions and/or sesame seeds.

PER SERVING: Calories: 300; Total fat: 12g; Protein: 21g; Carbohydrates: 35g; Fiber: 1g; Sodium: 632mg

Complete the Meal

- Serve with Asian Noodle Bowls (page 218) and a platter of baby carrots and cherry or grape tomatoes, as shown in the photo on page 191.
- Cold Peanut Butter–Sesame Noodles with Crisp Veggies (page 311) is a delicious companion dish.

Skillet Tofu Teriyaki

This simple recipe is all about the sauce, which is absorbed by the tofu to make it remarkably flavorful. As I suggested on page 193, double this if you're feeding a hungry group of tofu fans. You'll need half a recipe of Teriyaki Sauce for each tub of tofu, so you may as well make the entire sauce recipe—if you don't double this tofu recipe, you can always use the remaining sauce for another purpose.

SERVES 2 TO 4

One 14- to 16-ounce tub extra-firm tofu
½ recipe Teriyaki Sauce (page 220)

1. Drain the tofu and cut into 6 slabs crosswise. Blot well between paper towels or clean tea towels (or use a tofu press), then cut each slab into strips. If you can press the tofu ahead of time (see page 79), so much the better.

2. Heat ¼ cup of the teriyaki sauce in a wide skillet (make sure to whisk well before measuring). Arrange the tofu slices in a single layer in the pan. Cook over medium-high heat until the bottoms are nicely browned, about 5 to 7 minutes.

3. Drizzle in the remaining sauce; flip the tofu slices and brown them on the second side, which will likely take less time than the first. Serve at once.

PER SERVING: Calories: 243; Total fat: 12g; Protein: 21g; Carbohydrates: 15g; Fiber: 1g; Sodium: 616mg

Complete the Meal

- A stunning meal centered on this simple tofu dish is shown in the facing photo. Serve the Tofu Teriyaki over steamed broccoli. Add a simple salad of crisp greens and veggies. For an authentic flavor, pass around Japanese-Style Carrot-Ginger Dressing (page 331). Store-bought vegetable sushi rolls add a "wow" factor to the meal. (You didn't think I was going to have you make them from scratch for a weeknight meal, did you?)

- For a meal with a Chinese flair, serve this with either of two simple stir-fries described on page 222—Baby Carrots, Broccoli, and Baby Corn or Spicy or Gingered Broccoli, Asparagus, or Green Beans. Try serving this tofu and one of these vegetable dishes in a bowl over cooked long-grain brown rice. Top with toasted cashews or peanuts. Add a platter of colorful sliced bell peppers and sliced tomatoes.

< Skillet Tofu Teriyaki

Building Sensational Stir-Fries

Though several recipes follow for delectable, vegetable-laden stir-fries, this is the kind of meal centerpiece I encourage everyone to master and be able to make without following a specific recipe. Okay, maybe you can refer to one of the handful of sauce options on pages 219–21, but when it comes to choosing and combining veggies for the stir-fry, learn to use what's in season as well as what happens to be in your crisper. Cooked quickly and over high heat, vegetables retain their color and nutrients. Here are the steps:

Choose your carbs. While this is entirely optional, a stir-fry perched on grains or noodles makes a more filling meal than just the veggies by themselves. The obvious choices are brown rice or Asian noodles. If need be, consult the basic cooking tips for brown rice on page 105 and look over the mini lexicon of varieties of Asian noodles on page 207. There are other options—for example, there's no reason you can't mix it up and choose quinoa or whole-grain couscous instead of rice or noodles. Whatever your choice, start making your carbs before the stir-fry. While these are cooking, go on to the next steps, and once they're done, transfer to a covered container to keep warm.

Make the sauce. My preference for stir-fries is Basic Chinese Sauce (page 220)—consider the miso variation from time to time. And for a change of pace, try Sweet-and-Sour Sauce (page 221). Make the sauce before you stir-fry the vegetables and set the sauce aside until needed.

Prepare the vegetables. Remember, there are no set amounts. Learn what fits comfortably in your stir-fry pan, and choose four to six different varieties. If you need a point of departure, choose from within the following groupings and prepare as suggested:

- *Hard vegetables:* Turn the heat under your pan to high and start the stir fry with the vegetables that take longest to cook (that's relative, of course, as all vegetables cook pretty quickly this way), such as diagonally sliced broccoli, cauliflower, celery, and carrots.

- *Soft vegetables:* Choose from among bell pepper strips, mushroom slices or small whole mushrooms, diced unpeeled eggplant, thickly sliced green cabbage or napa cabbage, diced or matchstick-cut turnips or daikon radish, hardy greens such as kale or collards (cut into ribbons), and zucchini or yellow squash (sliced into quarter-inch-thick half-moons).

- *Quick-cooking vegetables:* If using any of these, just toss them in at the end so that they don't get overcooked. These include bok choy or baby bok choy (both thickly sliced on the diagonal), snow peas (with their stems trimmed), canned baby corn, mung bean sprouts, chopped Asian greens, whole baby spinach, watercress leaves, and sliced scallions.

Choose a protein. If you don't plan to serve a separate tofu, tempeh, or seitan dish, you may want to fold some of these plant proteins into the stir-fry at the end. Use a 14- to 16-ounce tub of tofu (very well drained and blotted, or pressed in a tofu press), an 8-ounce package of baked tofu, an 8-ounce package of tempeh, or 8 to 16 ounces of seitan. Heat a small amount of safflower or other neutral-flavored vegetable oil and reduced-sodium natural soy sauce or tamari in the pan you intend to use for the stir fry, or you can cook the protein in a separate pan. Sauté the protein of your choice over medium-high heat until golden and crisp on most sides. If using one pan for both the protein and the vegetables, transfer the cooked protein to a plate until needed.

Start your stir-fry. Heat a little oil in the pan—use an oil tolerant of high heat, such as safflower oil or sunflower oil—and add a little bit of dark sesame oil for flavor. If you're a no-oil person, heat about a quarter cup of vegetable broth or water. Do a quick sauté with a finely chopped medium onion or a few shallots, if you like. But do start with garlic; that's mandatory! If you skip the onion or shallots, add some sliced scallions as you're finishing the stir-fry.

Add vegetables from the first grouping and stir-fry until about halfway to tender-crisp. Depending on how many vegetables are filling the pan, this means roughly 3 to 4 minutes. I should mention that stir-frying means just that—cooking while stirring nearly continuously. Add vegetables from the second grouping and stir-fry until everything is just tender-crisp. Finally, add vegetables from the last grouping, and stir-fry just until they're heated through.

Finish with the sauce and protein. Whisk the sauce, then pour it into the pan. Stir in the protein, if desired, and cook just until the sauce has thickened. Remove from the heat.

Serve at once. Fresh vegetable stir-fries are best served right away, straight from the pan. Spoon the vegetables over the grain or noodles of choice, and pass around extra soy sauce along with hot sauce and crushed nuts (peanuts, cashews, almonds, or walnuts) for topping individual servings.

Complete the meal. A stir-fry is a meal in itself, but as you've seen by now, I always like to add something raw to the mix. Try my simple Bok Choy, Spinach, and Romaine Salad (page 223) or Creamy Kale and Cabbage Slaw (page 324). Turn this meal into a feast by adding natural vegetable spring rolls from the freezer case at your natural foods store.

Sweet-and-Sour Stir-Fried Vegetables
with Seitan or Tempeh

Sweet-*and*-Sour Stir-Fried Vegetables *with* Seitan *or* Tempeh

This sweet-and-sour stir-fry has several steps but can be made easily and at a leisurely pace. Best of all, it results in a delicious and nourishing meal.

SERVES 6

1 tablespoon safflower or other high-heat oil or ¼ cup vegetable broth or water
1 pound seitan, cut into bite-size chunks, or one 8-ounce package tempeh, diced
  (see Note)
1 medium onion, quartered and thinly sliced
2 to 3 cloves garlic, minced
2 large broccoli crowns, cut into bite-size pieces
2 medium red bell peppers, cut into 1-inch pieces
1 medium zucchini or yellow squash, halved lengthwise and cut into ½-inch chunks
2 medium ripe fresh tomatoes, diced
2 cups fresh pineapple chunks (about ¾ inch thick) or one 20-ounce can
  unsweetened pineapple chunks in juice, drained and liquid reserved
1 recipe Sweet-and-Sour Sauce (page 221)
Hot cooked rice, quinoa, or noodles (see Note)

OPTIONAL TOPPINGS

Chopped cashews or walnuts
Reduced-sodium natural soy sauce or tamari
Sriracha or other Asian hot sauce

1. Heat half the oil, broth, or water in a stir-fry pan or wok. Add the seitan or tempeh and stir-fry over medium-high heat until lightly browned, stirring frequently, about 5 minutes. Transfer to a plate and set aside.

2. Heat the remaining oil, broth, or water in the pan. Add the onion and sauté over medium heat until golden. Turn up the heat; add the garlic, broccoli, and bell peppers and stir-fry for 5 minutes.

3. Stir in the zucchini and stir-fry just until everything is tender-crisp, about 2 minutes longer, then stir in the tomatoes and pineapple chunks.

4. Stir in the sauce and cook until it thickens. Taste and adjust the sweet-sour balance with more agave and/or vinegar (as called for in the sauce recipe) to your liking.

5. Serve at once over hot cooked grains or noodles. Pass around any of the optional items for topping individual portions.

continued

note: Why a pound of seitan but just 8 ounces of tempeh? Seitan is more moist and less dense; a pound of tempeh would be quite intense in this dish. But if you're a big fan of tempeh and want a higher-protein dish, go for it—use two 8-ounce packages.

This is especially good served over bean-thread noodles or Asian brown rice vermicelli, but soba or udon work well, too. Long-grain brown rice and brown basmati rice are good choices as well.

PER SERVING WITH SEITAN: Calories: 264; Total fat: 7g; Protein: 22g; Carbohydrates: 32g; Fiber: 4g; Sodium: 516mg

PER SERVING WITH TEMPEH: Calories: 237; Total fat: 9g; Protein: 10g; Carbohydrates: 34g; Fiber: 6g; Sodium: 237mg

Variations

- Vary the vegetables as you'd like; green beans can take the place of squash; cauliflower can replace all or half of the broccoli.

- Once the dish is finished, you can add a couple of big handfuls of baby spinach or arugula (unless, of course, you're serving the stir-fry with Wilted Sesame Greens, page 222). Stir them in, and they'll wilt quickly.

Complete the Meal

Asian-Flavored Kale Salad (page 322) is a perfect companion to this. Otherwise, Wilted Sesame Greens (page 222) complement the dish nicely if you make sure that the greens are barely wilted. For a fun (though entirely optional) addition to the meal, consider vegetable spring rolls from your natural foods store's freezer case.

Spicy Eggplant *in* Garlic Sauce

Most longtime vegetarians or vegans have at one time or another ordered spicy eggplant, a dish that's a standard on Chinese take-out menus. I have, though I've sometimes regretted it, as more often than not it comes drenched in oil—and it doesn't sit too well in the digestive system afterward. But this low-fat version is equally craveworthy and comes with none of the regrets.

SERVES 4

2 small-to-medium eggplants or 4 Japanese eggplants, about 1 pound total
1 tablespoon safflower or other high-heat oil or 3 tablespoons vegetable broth or water
1 small onion, minced
5 to 6 cloves garlic, minced
¼ cup dry red or white wine
¼ cup vegetable broth or water
1 teaspoon grated fresh ginger
¼ cup hoisin sauce
1 tablespoon natural low-sodium soy sauce or tamari, or more to taste
1 teaspoon dark sesame oil (optional)
Sriracha or other Asian hot sauce to taste
4 large stalks bok choy or celery, thinly sliced on the diagonal
Hot cooked brown rice, quinoa, or Asian noodles (see page 207)
Thinly sliced scallion and/or minced fresh cilantro for garnish

1. If using small-to-medium eggplants, stem them and cut into ½-inch-thick slices. Slice the rounds into half circles, then into ¼-inch-thick strips. If using Japanese eggplants, stem them and cut into ¼-inch-thick slices.

2. Heat the safflower oil, broth, or water in a wok or stir-fry pan. Add the onion and garlic and sauté over low heat until golden.

3. Add the wine, broth or water, ginger, and eggplant. Cover and cook over medium heat for 5 minutes. Stir once or twice during that time.

4. Stir in the hoisin sauce, soy sauce, sesame oil (if desired), and hot sauce. Cook, uncovered, until the eggplant is tender but not overdone, 5 to 8 minutes longer.

5. Stir in the bok choy and continue to cook just until heated through, not more than a minute longer.

6. Serve at once over hot cooked grain or noodles. Pass around thinly sliced scallions and/ or chopped cilantro, as well as extra hot sauce, for individual servings.

continued

PER SERVING: Calories: 106 with oil, 76 without oil; Total fat: 4g with oil, 1g without oil; Protein: 2g; Carbohydrates: 15g; Fiber: 3g; Sodium: 452mg

Variation

Easily add some protein to the dish with an 8-ounce package of baked tofu. Cut it into thin strips and stir it in along with the bok choy.

Complete the Meal

- Delicious as this dish is, it needs a protein boost, so if you don't add baked tofu, as suggested above, see "Simple Preparations for Tofu, Tempeh, and Seitan" on pages 79–80; there you'll find directions for the Sweet and Savory variation, which you can serve as a side dish. This plate also needs some color, so Red Cabbage and Carrot Salad on page 223 does the job with ease.

- For a bit of a feast, but not a difficult one to prepare, serve this with Asian Succotash (page 222), Asian-Flavored Kale Salad (page 322), and vegetable spring rolls from your natural foods store's freezer.

Stir-Fried Tofu *with* Leafy Greens

If you're learning to love both tofu and leafy greens, this light, leafy stir-fry is a perfect way to nudge your palate in that direction.

SERVES 4 TO 6

One 14- to 16-ounce tub extra-firm tofu
1 tablespoon safflower or other high-heat oil or 3 tablespoons vegetable broth or water
2 tablespoons reduced-sodium natural soy sauce or tamari, plus more to taste
8 to 10 ounces chard, kale, collard greens, or any combination of dark, leafy greens, rinsed well
4 to 6 medium stalks bok choy, with leaves, or 4 to 6 baby bok choy, quartered lengthwise
1 whole shallot, 1 medium leek, or 1 medium onion, finely chopped
2 to 4 cloves garlic, minced
1 to 2 teaspoons dark sesame oil, or to taste
2 to 3 teaspoons minced fresh ginger, or to taste
Freshly ground pepper to taste
Crushed red pepper flakes to taste
Cashews or sesame seeds for topping (optional)

1. Drain the tofu and cut into 6 slabs crosswise. Blot well between paper towels or clean kitchen towels (or use a tofu press), then cut each slab into ½-inch-thick strips.

2. Slowly heat half the oil, broth, or water along with the soy sauce in a stir-fry pan or wide skillet, stirring constantly. Add the tofu and stir quickly to coat with the liquid. Sauté over medium-high heat until golden brown and crisp on most sides, about 10 minutes. Transfer to a plate.

3. Using kitchen shears, cut the greens fairly neatly away from the stems. Stack 4 or 5 similar-size leaf halves atop one another. Roll up snugly from one of the narrow ends, then slice into very thin ribbons. Chop the slices in a few places to shorten the ribbons.

4. Heat the remaining oil, broth, or water in the same pan in which you cooked the tofu. Add the shallots and garlic and sauté over medium-low heat until all are golden.

5. Stir the greens in quickly to coat with the oil, then turn the heat up to high. Stir-fry a minute or so, then add the bok choy. Continue to stir-fry until both are tender-crisp, about 2 to 3 minutes. Don't cook this a minute longer that you have to!

6. Season with sesame oil, ginger, pepper, crushed red pepper flakes, and additional soy sauce to taste. Sprinkle with cashews or sesame seeds, if desired, and serve at once.

continued

Stir-Fried Tofu with Leafy Greens

PER SERVING: Calories: 173 with oil, 143 without oil; Total fat: 11g with oil, 8g without oil; Protein: 13g; Carbohydrates: 10g; Fiber: 2g; Sodium: 446mg

Variations

- Substitute broccoli florets (from about two good-size crowns) for either the dark, leafy greens or the bok choy.

- If you have the really small variety of baby bok choy (3 to 4 inches in length), simply cut through the stem lengthwise. These look so pretty in the dish!

- Toss in a bunch of watercress at the end to boost nutrition and add a unique flavor.

- Use Asian greens, such as tatsoi or mizuna, if available, in place of the dark, leafy greens.

Complete the Meal

As shown in the photo on page 204, serve with brown rice or Asian noodles (any of the varieties on page 207), a platter of orange wedges, and Red Cabbage and Carrot Salad, page 223.

Plant-Powered Pepper Steak

This Chinese restaurant classic is usually beefy and thus out of the realm of possibility for those of us who don't eat that way. But this version is just as hearty as the real thing, and with plant protein accompanying the plethora of peppers, it is much better for you. Seitan is particularly "meaty," though you can make this with tempeh or tofu as well.

SERVES 4 TO 6

14 to 16 ounces seitan
2 tablespoons safflower or other high-heat oil or 3 to 4 tablespoons vegetable
    broth or water
1 tablespoon reduced-sodium natural soy sauce or tamari
1 large onion, quartered and thinly sliced
2 cloves garlic, minced
1 medium green bell pepper, cut into 2-inch-thick strips
2 medium red bell peppers, cut into 2-inch-thick strips (or use 1 red pepper and
    1 yellow or orange pepper)
2 teaspoons grated fresh ginger, or more to taste
1 recipe Basic Chinese Sauce (page 220)
Hot cooked brown rice

1. Cut the seitan into bite-size strips or chunks.

2. Slowly heat half the oil, broth, or water along with the soy sauce in a stir-fry pan. Add the seitan, stir quickly to coat, and turn the heat up to medium-high. Stir-fry until most of the sides are lightly browned. Transfer to a plate until needed.

3. Heat the remaining oil, broth, or water in the pan. Add the onion and sauté over medium heat until golden. Add the garlic and bell peppers, turn the heat up, and stir-fry until the peppers are tender-crisp, about 2 to 3 minutes.

4. Stir in the ginger and cook until everything is well heated through, just a minute or so longer. Stir the seitan back into the pan.

5. Stir in the sauce and cook until it has thickened. Serve at once over hot cooked brown rice, passing around extra soy sauce if desired.

PER SERVING: Calories: 274 with oil, 214 without oil; Total fat: 10g with oil, 3g without oil; Protein: 28g; Carbohydrates: 20g; Fiber: 5g; Sodium: 900mg

Variations

- Vary this by using a 14- to 16-ounce tub of extra-firm tofu or an 8-ounce package of tempeh. If using tofu, drain and cut into 6 slabs crosswise, blot very well (or use a tofu press), then cut into dice. If using tempeh, cut the block in half lengthwise then into ¼-inch-thick slices. You can even combine two of the proteins for a higher-protein dish—seitan and tofu or tofu and tempeh, for example.

- A handful of snow peas or snap peas makes a nice addition to this, as do about 6 to 8 ounces of sliced baby bella (cremini) mushrooms. Either or both can be added just after the peppers start to soften.

Complete the Meal

- This is delicious with the easy Bok Choy, Spinach, and Romaine salad on page 223.
- Serve with Wilted Sesame Greens or Spicy or Gingered Broccoli, Asparagus, or Green Beans (both on page 222) and a platter of raw baby carrots and crisp raw turnip sticks.

ASIAN NOODLES: A MINI LEXICON

There's no need to scour specialty groceries for Asian noodles, which add authenticity (not to mention fun) to Asian-style meals. Look no farther than the natural foods store or the Asian foods section of supermarkets. It's always best to follow package directions for cooking Asian noodles.

Buckwheat noodles (soba): This spaghetti-shaped noodle combines hearty buckwheat flour with wheat or whole-wheat flour.

Bean threads (also called cellophane noodles, harusame, saifun, and mung bean noodles): These fine, delicately flavored, transparent noodles are made of mung bean starch and are completely wheat-free. They add a pleasant and somewhat slippery texture to Asian preparations.

Rice vermicelli (also called mei fun and rice sticks): These superlong fine noodles are commonly made of white rice flour, but if you search a bit farther afield, brown rice vermicelli are also available. With the same mild flavor and tender texture as rice, these noodles offer a nice gluten-free option without the usual gumminess of rice pastas. Related to these in flavor are the wide, flat rice noodles popular in Thai cuisine—if you've had pad thai, you've had these.

Udon: Used in Chinese cuisine, these long, somewhat thick noodles are comparable to linguine in appearance. Whole-wheat versions of these noodles are often available in natural foods stores; they have a smoother texture and milder flavor than domestic whole-wheat pastas.

Asian-Style Rice *and* Noodle Dishes

Chinese-Style Vegetable Fried Rice

This tasty version of the Chinese take-out favorite can be made quickly—especially if you've cooked the rice ahead of time. This basic recipe is one that I've been making for years; it can be one of your go-to favorites if you enjoy brown rice.

SERVES 6

1¼ cups uncooked brown rice
1 tablespoon safflower or other high-heat oil or 3 tablespoons vegetable broth or water
2 cups frozen green peas, thawed
1 cup cooked fresh or thawed frozen corn kernels
4 to 5 scallions, white and green parts, minced
1 teaspoon dark sesame oil
1 to 2 teaspoons grated fresh or jarred ginger
2 tablespoons reduced-sodium natural soy sauce or tamari, or to taste
Freshly ground pepper to taste
Crushed red pepper flakes (optional)
Sriracha or other Asian hot sauce (optional)

1. Bring 3 cups water to a simmer in a saucepan. Stir in the rice; cover and cook at a gentle, steady simmer until the water is absorbed, about 35 minutes.

2. Heat the oil, broth, or water in a stir-fry pan or large skillet. Add the peas, corn, and scallions. Stir-fry over medium-high heat for 5 minutes.

3. Stir in the cooked rice, sesame oil, and ginger. Season with soy sauce, pepper, and the crushed red pepper flakes and/or sriracha (if desired). Stir-fry for 2 to 3 minutes more, then serve.

PER SERVING: Calories: 240 with oil, 220 without oil; Total fat: 5g with oil, 2g without oil; Protein: 7g; Carbohydrates: 44g; Fiber: 5g; Sodium: 245mg

Complete the Meal

- See "Simple Preparations for Tofu, Tempeh, and Seitan" on pages 79–80; there you'll find directions for the Sweet and Savory variation, which goes perfectly with this fried rice. To give the tofu dish more greenery, add some broccoli florets to the skillet once the tofu is nearly done. Drizzle in a little water, cover the skillet, and cook until the broccoli is bright green. Uncover and stir-fry until both the tofu and broccoli are done to your liking.

- Serve with the easy Red Cabbage and Carrot Salad, page 223, or a platter of sliced bell peppers, tomatoes, and cucumbers.

- Serve with Baby Carrots, Broccoli, and Baby Corn (page 222).

Thai-Style Pineapple-Coconut Rice

This Thai restaurant favorite is easily re-created at home and makes a lovely centerpiece for a meal. Pineapple adds a refreshing note. The result is a hearty, veggie-filled rice dish that turns an everyday meal into a special occasion.

SERVES 6

1½ cups uncooked long-grain brown rice, such as brown basmati
1 cup light coconut milk (about half a 15-ounce can), or more as needed
1 tablespoon safflower or other high-heat oil or 3 tablespoons vegetable broth or water
1 large onion, preferably red, chopped
2 cups small broccoli florets
1 medium red or green bell pepper, diced
2 medium carrots, peeled and sliced
2 medium ripe fresh tomatoes, diced
2 cups fresh pineapple chunks (about ¾ inch thick) or one 20-ounce can unsweetened pineapple chunks in juice, drained (reserve liquid for another use)
1 to 2 teaspoons good-quality curry powder
2 teaspoons minced fresh or jarred ginger, or more to taste
Salt to taste
Crushed red pepper flakes to taste
Crushed peanuts or cashews for topping (optional)

1. Combine the rice with 2 cups water and the coconut milk in a saucepan. Bring to a rapid simmer, then cover and simmer gently until the water is absorbed, about 30 to 35 minutes.

2. Meanwhile, heat the oil in a stir-fry pan or a wide skillet. Add the onion and sauté over medium heat until golden.

3. Add the broccoli, bell pepper, and carrots. Turn the heat up to medium-high and stir-fry for 3 to 4 minutes, or until the vegetables are just tender-crisp.

4. Add the tomatoes and pineapple chunks and continue to stir-fry for a minute or two, just until the tomatoes soften slightly.

5. Stir in the cooked rice, curry powder, and ginger. Stir gently until all the ingredients are completely combined. Since about half the can of coconut milk is remaining, if you'd like the mixture to be a bit more moist, add ¼ cup or so more, but take care not to make the mixture soupy.

6. Season with salt and red pepper flakes. Serve at once, passing around crushed nuts to top individual servings, if desired.

PER SERVING: Calories: 278 with oil, 258 without oil; Total fat: 6g with oil, 4g without oil; Protein: 6g; Carbohydrates: 53g; Fiber: 4g; Sodium: 45mg

Complete the Meal

- Team this with the Sweet and Savory variation in "Simple Preparations for Tofu, Tempeh, and Seitan" (pages 79–80) and the Thai variation of "Tossed Salads Go Global" (page 318) for an especially flavorful Asian-style meal (see photo below).
- Keep the accompaniments simple by serving with a platter of sliced baked tofu, cucumbers, tomatoes, and baby carrots.

Veggie Lo-Mein

Veggie Lo Mein

It's so easy to make this Chinese take-out favorite at home—and it's lighter and less heavy on the oil than its restaurant counterpart.

SERVES 4 TO 6

8 ounces udon or soba, preferably whole-grain
1 tablespoon safflower or other high-heat oil or 3 tablespoons vegetable broth or water
2 teaspoons dark sesame oil (optional but highly recommended)
½ small head green or napa cabbage, cut into long, narrow ribbons (see Note)
2 cups small broccoli florets
2 cups fresh green beans, trimmed and cut in half (see Note)
1 cup sliced mushrooms (optional)
3 to 4 scallions, white and green parts cut into 1-inch-long segments
Vegetable broth or water for moistening
Reduced-sodium natural soy sauce or tamari to taste
Freshly ground pepper to taste

1. Cook the noodles according to package directions in plenty of rapidly simmering water until al dente, then drain.

2. Meanwhile, heat the safflower oil, broth, or water and 1 teaspoon of the sesame oil (if desired) in a stir-fry pan. Add the cabbage, broccoli, and green beans. Cover and cook for 2 to 3 minutes.

3. Add the mushrooms, if desired, and scallions and stir-fry over medium-high heat for 5 minutes or until the vegetables are just tender-crisp. Add a small amount of vegetable broth or water, just enough to keep the pan moist.

4. Add the cooked noodles to the stir-fry pan and toss together. Add the remaining teaspoon of sesame oil, if using, then season with soy sauce and pepper to taste. Serve at once.

note: When you're in a hurry, you can substitute 8 ounces of preshredded coleslaw (preferably with carrots included) for the green or napa cabbage. And fresh, slender green beans are hard to come by for much of the year, so I give you my full blessing to use frozen organic whole baby green beans, which are consistently excellent—and also save you the time and trouble of trimming the ends.

continued

PER SERVING: Calories: 264 with oil, 234 without oil; Total fat: 4g with oil, 1g without oil; Protein: 11g; Carbohydrates: 52g; Fiber: 3g; Sodium: 473mg

Variations

- Use whatever you've got in the fridge in place of or in addition to some of the veggies called for in the recipe—romaine lettuce, mung bean sprouts, and/or bok choy in place of cabbage; broccoli rabe or Chinese broccoli instead of regular broccoli—it's all good!

- Turn this into a heartier dish by adding 8 ounces seitan, cut into narrow strips, along with the cabbage, broccoli, and green beans.

Complete the Meal

As shown in the photo on page 213, serve with Asian Succotash (page 222) and a simple crisp salad dressed in sesame-ginger dressing (homemade, page 328, or prepared).

Asian-Style Soups

MISO

Miso soup has long been a breakfast staple in Japan, but in the West, you're most likely to partake of it in Japanese restaurants, where a very simple brothy miso soup is a ubiquitous appetizer. Salty and pungent, miso is a paste made of fermented soybeans. It adds a robust flavor to soups and sauces. Natural foods stores are more likely to carry it than supermarkets. Note that once miso is added to soup or any other preparation, it shouldn't be boiled, lest its beneficial enzymes be destroyed.

Miso comes in several varieties. The basics are pure soybean, soybean with barley, and soybean with rice. Pure soybean (hatcho) miso is the most intense; soybean-and-rice varieties, of which there are several, are the mildest, and soybean-with-barley (mugi) miso falls somewhere in the middle. Shiro miso is a variety of mild, yellowish miso sometimes labeled "mellow white miso." Which to choose is entirely up to you and your palate. Because they're aged and fermented, miso and tempeh are considered the two most healthful and most digestible forms in which to enjoy soy foods.

Gingery Miso Soup

You don't absolutely have to have a miso soup in your back pocket (or, more appropriately, on your back burner) to enjoy vegan Asian-style meals, but if you don't you'll be missing out on one of the simplest and most delicious sources of good nutrition. Like other Asian-style soups, this one is best eaten as soon as it's made. And unlike many European-style soups, it doesn't benefit from long simmering or overnight refrigeration. That's why this recipe and the recipe for Asian-Style Tofu and Vegetable Soup (page 217) yield small quantities.

This basic recipe results in something very much akin to the appetizing hot soup served in Japanese restaurants. But by embellishing the soup with the optional add-ins listed below, you can turn it into a centerpiece that's a great introduction to or companion for Asian-style rice or noodle dishes.

SERVES 4 TO 6

4 cups water or one 32-ounce container low-sodium vegetable broth
2 teaspoons minced fresh ginger, or more to taste
3 scallions, thinly sliced (white and green parts)
7 to 8 ounces soft or firm tofu (about half a 14- to 16-ounce tub) or 6 to 7 ounces
    firm silken tofu (about half a 12.3-ounce package), cut into ¼-inch dice
2 to 4 tablespoons miso (any variety), or to taste
Freshly ground pepper to taste

1. Combine the water and stock base or broth with the ginger in a small soup pot and bring to a rapid simmer.

2. Stir in the scallions and tofu and heat gently until piping hot.

3. Dissolve the miso in enough water to make it smooth and pourable. Start with 2 table-spoons miso if you're unfamiliar with its strong, salty flavor—you can always add more. Stir the dissolved miso into the soup. If the soup is too dense, add water as needed and heat through very gently. Don't boil once the miso is in the soup, as that will destroy its beneficial enzymes. Season with pepper and serve at once.

PER SERVING: Calories: 54; Total fat: 1g; Protein: 3g; Carbohydrates: 7g; Fiber: 0g; Sodium: 470mg

continued

Variations

I recommend adding no more than two or three items from this list to the soup at any one time; each time you make it, you can choose different ingredients. Note, though, that as you add more ingredients to the soup you'll also need to add additional water. Figure on 1 to 2 cups more water for every two or three ingredients you add. Correct the flavor with more dissolved miso plus extra pepper and/or ginger, if need be.

> 2 medium carrots, peeled and thinly sliced or grated
>
> 2 cups or so finely shredded romaine lettuce
>
> 1 or 2 baby bok choy, thinly sliced
>
> 1 cup or so finely diced turnip or daikon
>
> 2 to 3 ounces baby spinach or arugula or leafy Asian greens such as tatsoi or mizuna
>
> 2 to 4 ounces soba, bean threads, or fine Asian rice noodles, cooked separately and cut into 2- to 3-inch lengths
>
> ¼ to ½ cup chopped fresh cilantro (stir it in or use it as a topping)
>
> 4 to 6 ounces mushrooms (such as baby bella, shiitake, oyster mushrooms, or a combination), chopped
>
> Caramelized onions to taste

Complete the Meal

- Omit the tofu and serve as a first course or alongside Stir-Fried Tofu with Leafy Greens (page 203) or Skillet Tofu Teriyaki (page 195). Add some cooked brown rice to bolster the meal. Or, for a fun option, serve with prepared brown-rice vegetable sushi from the supermarket.
- This makes a delicious light meal when served with the Composed Asian-Flavored Salad Platter (page 308). Prepare the soup with added noodles for a bit more heft.

Asian-Style Tofu *and* Vegetable Soup

On chilly days, I love having a long-simmering soup or stew on the burner. But when soup yearnings won't wait, Asian-style soups are the next best thing. If you have the ingredients on hand, you can go from craving to table in less than thirty minutes—sometimes much less.

SERVES 4 TO 6

One 32-ounce carton low-sodium vegetable broth
One 14- to 16-ounce tub firm tofu
2 medium carrots, peeled and thinly sliced on the diagonal
2 large celery stalks (strings peeled if you prefer), thinly sliced on the diagonal
1 medium broccoli crown, cut into small florets
2 teaspoons minced fresh or jarred ginger
2 to 3 scallions, thinly sliced (white and green parts)
1 teaspoon dark sesame oil (optional)
2 tablespoons reduced-sodium natural soy sauce or tamari, or to taste
Freshly ground pepper to taste

1. Bring the broth and 1 cup water to a rapid simmer in a small soup pot.

2. Meanwhile, drain the tofu and cut into 6 slabs crosswise. Blot well between paper towels or clean kitchen towels (or use a tofu press), then cut each slab into ½-inch dice.

3. Add the tofu and remaining ingredients to the pot, return to a simmer, then lower the heat and cook for not longer than 5 minutes, or just until the veggies are brightly colored and tender-crisp.

4. If the broth feels too crowded, add another cup or so of water and a bit more soy sauce and pepper if need be. Serve at once.

PER SERVING: Calories: 115; Total fat: 5g; Protein: 10g; Carbohydrates: 11g; Fiber: 2g; Sodium: 495mg

Variation

You can vary this soup each time you make it by adding or substituting two or three of the ingredients recommended for the miso soup, on pages 215–16.

Complete the Meal

For a tasty light meal, serve with Cold Peanut Butter–Sesame Noodles with Crisp Veggies (page 311).

Asian Noodle Bowls

Once you get the hang of this recipe, which is about equal parts soup and noodle dish, you'll want to make it whenever you crave a warming Asian-style meal that's ready in minutes. Make sure to gather up and prepare your veggies before starting, as the entire procedure goes very quickly after the noodles are soaked. Also, make sure the veggies are barely cooked so that they retain the maximum amount of flavor, color, and crunch. Bean threads are readily available in the Asian foods section of many supermarkets as well as in natural foods stores. You can also use other kinds of noodles, cooked according to package directions, and other vegetables, according to what you have on hand.

SERVES 4

Three 2-ounce bundles bean threads
One 32-ounce container low-sodium vegetable broth
2 to 3 teaspoons minced or grated fresh ginger
1 to 1½ cups sliced brown mushrooms, such as shiitake or baby bella
2 large celery or bok choy stalks, sliced diagonally, or 1 to 2 baby bok choy, sliced on a
    slight diagonal
1 medium red bell pepper, cut into short, narrow strips
1 cup frozen green peas, thawed
2 tablespoons reduced-sodium natural soy sauce or tamari
2 to 3 big handfuls baby spinach
3 scallions, thinly sliced (white and green parts), plus more for garnish if desired
Freshly ground pepper to taste

1. Place the noodles in a shallow heatproof container. Add boiling water to cover, then cover the container and let the noodles soak for 15 minutes, or until al dente.

2. Heat the broth in a small soup pot with the ginger and the mushrooms. When it comes to a gentle boil, add the celery or bok choy, bell pepper, and peas.

3. Return to a simmer and stir in the soy sauce, spinach, and scallions. Remove from the heat and grind in some pepper.

4. Once the noodles are done, drain them and cut here and there with kitchen shears or a knife to shorten, as they are very long. Divide them among four large soup bowls. Ladle the soup over them, garnish with scallions, if desired, and serve at once.

PER SERVING: Calories: 219; Total fat: 0g; Protein: 4g; Carbohydrates: 50g; Fiber: 4g; Sodium: 500mg

Complete the Meal

- Serve with Double Fruit-Glazed Tofu (page 193) and a platter of baby carrots and cherry or grape tomatoes.
- This serves as a nice introduction to Chinese-Style Vegetable Fried Rice (page 208) and any of the simple salad ideas on page 223.

Sauces

Peanut or Cashew Butter Sauce

Serve this delectable nut butter sauce over noodles or grains; it's also good over sautéed tofu or tempeh. Tailor the spiciness to your taste!

MAKES ABOUT 1½ CUPS

½ cup natural peanut or cashew butter, at room temperature
2 tablespoons reduced-sodium natural soy sauce or tamari, or to taste
1 scallion, green parts only, coarsely chopped
1 to 2 teaspoons grated fresh or jarred ginger
2 tablespoons agave nectar or maple syrup
2 tablespoons rice vinegar or freshly squeezed or bottled lime juice
Crushed red pepper flakes, cayenne pepper, or Asian hot sauce (such as sriracha) to taste

1. Combine all the ingredients in a medium bowl along with ½ cup water. Whisk until completely smooth. If your peanut butter is very dense, you can also do this in a food processor.
2. Serve the sauce at room temperature, gently warmed in a saucepan, or as directed in recipes.

PER ¼ CUP: Calories: 150; Total fat: 10.5g; Protein: 5g; Carbohydrates: 11g; Fiber: 1g; Sodium: 200mg

Suggested Uses

- Toss with hot or cold Asian noodles, such as those in the mini lexicon on page 207.
- Serve over pan-sautéed tofu or tempeh.
- Serve over plain cooked grains or lightly steamed vegetables.

Basic Chinese Sauce

Here's a go-to sauce for veggie stir-fries. I recommend putting it together before you start the stir-fry, then adding it once the vegetables are just done. I also suggest preparing the sauce with vegetable broth instead of water for maximum flavor. And if you really want your taste buds to sing, start your stir-fry with some minced garlic for added depth; it will meld nicely with this sauce in the finished dish.

MAKES ABOUT 1½ CUPS

2 tablespoons arrowroot or cornstarch
1¼ cups low-sodium vegetable broth or water
2 teaspoons dark sesame oil (optional)
2 tablespoons reduced-sodium natural soy sauce or tamari, or to taste
2 tablespoons dry red or white wine (optional)
2 teaspoons grated fresh or jarred ginger, or to taste

1. Dissolve the cornstarch with about ¼ cup of the broth or water to make it smooth and pourable.

2. Combine the dissolved cornstarch with the remaining broth and the rest of the ingredients in a mixing bowl. Whisk together until smooth.

3. Add the sauce to your stir-fry in the pan when the vegetables are just about done. Assuming your stir-fry pan or wok is placed over fairly high heat, the sauce will thicken up quickly.

PER ¼ CUP: Calories: 16; Total fat: 0g; Protein: 0g; Carbohydrates: 3.5g; Fiber: 0g; Sodium: 230mg

Teriyaki Sauce

This nicely flavored sauce has a hint of sweetness but also emphasizes the salty notes of soy sauce. It's good with any veg-centric stir fry and can also be used as a marinade for plant proteins that you cook on the stove top, grill, or in the oven.

MAKES ABOUT 1 CUP

¼ cup reduced-sodium natural soy sauce or tamari
¼ cup sake, white wine, vegetable broth, or water
2 teaspoons dark sesame oil (optional)
2 tablespoons agave nectar or other liquid sweetener
2 tablespoons rice vinegar or white wine vinegar
1 to 2 cloves crushed or minced garlic
1 teaspoon freshly grated ginger

Combine all ingredients in a small container and whisk together. Use as directed in recipes.

PER ¼ CUP: Calories: 63; Total fat: 0g; Protein: 1g; Carbohydrates: 11g; Fiber: 0g; Sodium: 600mg

Sweet-*and*-Sour Sauce

When we think of Asian flavors, a salty, savory sauce like teriyaki may be the one that comes immediately to mind, but this sauce, with a sweet edge provided mainly by fruit juice, makes a nice change of pace.

MAKES 1½ CUPS

½ cup fruit juice (pineapple juice works best; mango is good, too)
2½ tablespoons arrowroot or cornstarch
½ cup vegetable broth or water
¼ cup rice vinegar
2 tablespoons reduced-sodium natural soy sauce or tamari, or to taste
2 tablespoons agave nectar
1 to 2 teaspoons grated fresh or jarred ginger

1. Combine the fruit juice with the arrowroot in a mixing bowl and stir until dissolved.

2. Add the remaining ingredients and whisk together. Add to sweet-and-sour stir-fries and noodle dishes toward the end of their cooking time and cook until thickened.

PER ¼ CUP: Calories: 50; Total fat: 0g; Protein: 0g; Carbohydrates: 13g; Fiber: 0g; Sodium: 213mg

Asian Express Sides and Salads

Asian Succotash: This easy side dish adds extra protein to Asian-style meals. Combine one to one and a half cups fresh or frozen shelled edamame in enough water to cover in a medium saucepan. Bring to a slow boil, then simmer until done, about eight minutes. If you're using fresh corn, scrape the kernels off the cob and into the saucepan with the edamame after they've been cooking for five minutes. Thawed frozen corn kernels can be added once the edamame are nearly done; cook just until heated through. Either way, you'll want to use about two cups of corn kernels.

Once everything is done, drain. Return to the saucepan, add some very thinly sliced scallions, then season with salt and pepper. If you like, you can also stir in a teaspoon or two of dark sesame oil for a richer flavor and a small amount of black sesame seeds for visual appeal. Cover and keep warm until needed. See the photo of this on page 212, served with Veggie Lo Mein.

Spicy or Gingered Broccoli, Asparagus, or Green Beans: Heat a little reduced-sodium natural soy sauce or tamari, some sesame or safflower oil, a teaspoon or so of natural granulated sugar, and a couple of tablespoons of water in a stir-fry pan. Add a good amount of bite-size pieces of broccoli, asparagus, or green beans (or a combination of any two of these). Turn up the heat to high and stir-fry just until the veggies are bright green and tender-crisp. Remove from the heat and season with crushed red pepper flakes or sriracha sauce to taste. Stir in some grated fresh ginger as well—or instead—if you like.

Wilted Sesame Greens: This gives a nice Asian spin to kale, collards, chard, and spinach—but you can use whatever greens you've got. If you're adventurous, use Asian greens—Chinese broccoli, tatsoi, mizuna, or bok choy (regular or baby).

Heat a small amount of dark sesame oil in a wok or stir-fry pan. Add a small amount of chopped onion, shallots, and/or garlic and sauté over medium-low heat until golden. Stir the greens in quickly to coat with the oil, then turn the heat up to high. If you're using tender greens, you don't need to add any water: just the water clinging to the leaves is sufficient. If you're using hardy greens, add a little water to the pan—just enough to keep them moist.

Add a sprinkling of salt. Stir-fry until the greens are just barely wilted—a minute or two for tender greens, a bit longer for hardy greens. Sprinkle in some white or black sesame seeds.

Baby Carrots, Broccoli, and Baby Corn: This simple, colorful stir-fry is a nice addition to the table whenever you're serving a meal that could benefit from a few more vegetables. Heat a small amount of high-heat oil and/or a little dark sesame oil in a skillet or stir-fry pan. Add a more or less equal amount of small broccoli florets, thin baby carrots, and a drained 15-ounce can of baby corn. Stir-fry over high heat for three to four minutes, or until the broccoli is bright green and all the vegetables are tender-crisp. Season to taste with pepper and reduced-sodium natural soy sauce or tamari. More options:

- Add some grated fresh ginger and/or sesame seeds just before serving.

- Add a little minced garlic to the oil as it heats in the pan.

- Skip the oil altogether and use some of the liquid from the can of baby corn to steam the vegetables (covered) rather than stir-fry them.

Bok Choy, Spinach, and Romaine Salad: Combine a baby bok choy or two, or a few stalks of regular bok choy, with a few leaves of thinly sliced romaine and as much baby spinach (or baby arugula or watercress) as you like. Add some halved cherry or golden cherry tomatoes and a sprinkling of toasted sliced almonds or roasted sunflower seeds (unless you're serving this salad with a dish that already contains nuts). Dress with a splash of dark sesame oil and rice vinegar or with Japanese-Style Carrot-Ginger Dressing (page 331).

Red Cabbage and Carrot Salad: Make a simple salad combining red cabbage with baby carrots cut into quarters lengthwise. Add some thinly sliced scallions and dress in a sesame-ginger dressing (homemade, page 328, or prepared)—or double the carrot power with Japanese-Style Carrot-Ginger Dressing (page 331). If you like, sprinkle with toasted sliced almonds or chopped peanuts. See the photo on page 204, in which this is served with Stir-Fried Tofu with Leafy Greens.

CHAPTER 5

TORTILLA *Specialties*

Call this style of cooking what you will—Tex-Mex, southwestern, Mexican. I call it easy, flexible, and crowd-pleasing. Many of these are nearly instant meals that require you to make only one central, uncomplicated preparation. For example, with quesadillas and tacos, you need only focus on a filling (which can often be made ahead of time), and most of the embellishments can go on the table, allowing people to assemble their own meals to their individual tastes.

Fully Loaded Emergency Nachos (page 239)

Black Bean Tostadas (page 228)

In many of these dishes, the protein, veggies, and even salad-type elements mingle companionably and constitute almost the entire meal in themselves, so completing the menu is simple. Accompaniments that go well with tortilla dishes include leafy greens, corn, potatoes, sweet potatoes, brown rice, quinoa, bell peppers, chili peppers, and tomatoes. What I especially like about the kinds of meals in this category is that they're fantastic vehicles for beans, either as indispensable stars of the main dish or as protein-packed companions.

As I do in many of these chapters, I give you the option of either making some items (particularly condiments) from scratch or using prepared products. Here, refried beans, salsa, and vegan sour cream are among those that can be either prepared at home or purchased. None of them is difficult or complicated to make, but as someone who at one point juggled two toddlers and three deadlines at the same time, I know how important it is to be able to create nearly instant dinners that don't resemble emergency fare.

That being said, this chapter isn't all about emergency meals. These recipes are also suitable for preparing and serving in a leisurely fashion (possibly with a margarita or mojito in hand) when company is coming. It will look like you're hosting a party . . . but only you need to know that you haven't been slaving all day over a hot stove—not nearly!

Classic Tortilla Dishes

Black Bean Tostadas

A tostada is a crisp tortilla piled generously with a variety of toppings, often including beans, lettuce, and salsa. Add a salad and more veggies and you've got a quick weeknight meal or fun fare to share with company.

SERVES 4 TO 6 (1 TO 2 TOSTADAS PER SERVING)

8 good-quality corn tortillas
1 tablespoon extra-virgin olive oil or 3 tablespoons vegetable broth or water
1 medium onion or two shallots, finely chopped
2 to 4 cloves garlic, minced
3 to 3½ cups cooked or two 15- to 16-ounce cans (drained and rinsed) black beans
Juice of ½ lime or lemon, or to taste
1 to 2 small fresh hot green chili peppers, seeded and sliced (optional)
Salt and freshly ground pepper to taste
2 teaspoons ground cumin

GARNISHES

Shredded lettuce, baby greens, or baby spinach
Plenty of mild, medium, or hot chunky salsa, such as chipotle, peach, or mango
1 medium avocado, peeled and cut into small dice and tossed with a little
    lemon or lime juice
Vegan Sour Cream (page 248) or Cashew Cream (page 249), optional

1. To toast the tortillas in the oven, preheat the oven to 375ºF. Spread the tortillas on a baking sheet. Bake for 10 minutes, or until crisp and dry and touched with golden brown spots. Remove from the oven and place on a serving platter.

2. To toast the tortillas on a stovetop, heat a large dry skillet. Toast the tortillas over medium heat (two or three at a time, depending on the size of the skillet) for about 5 minutes or so on each side, until crisp and touched with golden brown spots. Don't be afraid to let them get nice and crisp—that's better than ending up with a soggy tostada.

3. Heat the oil, broth, or water in medium skillet. Add the onion and garlic and sauté until golden, about 5 minutes.

4. Add the remaining ingredients (aside from the garnishes, of course), along with ¼ cup water and bring to a simmer. Using a potato masher, mash some of the beans so that the liquid becomes thick and saucy.

5. Place the shredded lettuce, salsa, and avocado in separate serving bowls and let everyone assemble their tostadas as follows: a layer of shredded lettuce, the black bean mixture, salsa, avocado, and optional sour cream. Pick up the tostadas and eat out of hand (with plenty of napkins!).

PER TOSTADA: Calories: 140 with oil, 126 without oil; Total fat: 2g with oil, 1g without oil; Protein: 7g; Carbohydrates: 25g; Fiber: 4g; Sodium: 100mg

Complete the Meal

- As shown in the photo on page 226, serve with a side dish of Steamed Broccoli and Yellow Squash, or try it with Sautéed Zucchini, Corn, and Bell Pepper, both on page 251. Like many of the meals in this chapter, this one is nicely rounded out with Fresh Tomato Salsa (page 246) or your favorite store-bought brand. Fresh Tomato Guacamole (page 248) and Vegan Sour Cream (page 248) or Cashew Cream (page 249) are optional but always welcome.

- Other recipe-free accompaniments include baked potatoes or sweet potatoes and fresh corn on the cob. Add a simple tossed salad or Southwestern Slaw (page 251).

Sizzling Tempeh *or* Tofu Fajitas

Fajita dinners are so much fun, those you've made dinner for will hardly notice that, for the most part, they're actually making their own meals right at the table. The cook hardly has to do any work, and the fajitas can be tailored to each person's own taste. I recommend setting out the toppings before you start to cook, as the actual cooking goes quickly.

SERVES 4 TO 6 (1 TO 2 FAJITAS PER SERVING)

FOR SERVING

Shredded lettuce, preferably romaine
Fresh Tomato Salsa (page 246), or your favorite store-bought variety
Fresh cilantro sprigs
Vegan Sour Cream (page 248) or Cashew Cream (page 249), or your favorite store-bought brand (optional)
Picante sauce or other hot sauce (optional)

FOR THE FAJITAS

8 good-quality whole-grain flour tortillas, 6 to 8 inches each
3 tablespoons freshly squeezed or bottled lime or lemon juice
1½ tablespoons extra-virgin olive oil or 3 tablespoons vegetable broth or water
2 teaspoons good-quality chili powder
1 teaspoon ground cumin
½ teaspoon dried oregano
One 8-ounce package baked tofu or one 8-ounce package tempeh
1 medium green bell pepper, cut into long, narrow strips
1 medium red bell pepper, cut into long, narrow strips

1. Place the lettuce, salsa, cilantro sprigs, and sour cream or cashew cream in separate serving bowls on the table. Place a bottle of picante sauce on the table for those who like hot stuff.

2. If you'd like to warm the tortillas, wrap them in foil and heat for 5 minutes or so in a 300°F oven or toaster oven. If they're fresh and pliable, you can skip this step, but do bring them to room temperature.

3. Combine the lime juice, oil, chili powder, cumin, and oregano in a medium mixing bowl and whisk together.

4. Cut the tofu or tempeh into narrow strips about 2 inches in length. Add them to the mixing bowl and toss gently (if you're using tempeh, you might want to add a pinch of salt; you won't need it if using baked tofu). Add the bell pepper strips and toss again.

5. Heat a large skillet, then add the tempeh or tofu mixture, liquid and all. Turn the heat up to high and cook, stirring frequently, for 5 to 7 minutes, or until sizzling hot and the tofu or tempeh is touched with brown spots. Remove from the heat and cover.

6. Distribute one or two tortillas (depending on appetite and what else is being served) to everyone. Have everyone place a few strips of the tempeh or tofu and peppers in the center of their tortillas and garnish them as they wish. Roll up the tortillas and pick them up to eat out of hand.

PER 2-FAJITA SERVING WITH TOFU: Calories: 344 with oil, 298 without oil; Total fat: 13g with oil, 8g without oil; Protein: 17g; Carbohydrates: 46g; Fiber: 7g; Sodium: 600mg

PER 2-FAJITA SERVING WITH TEMPEH: Calories: 364 with oil, 350 without oil; Total fat: 13g with oil, 8g without oil; Protein: 17g; Carbohydrates: 52g; Fiber: 11g; Sodium: 350mg

Variations

- For a "meaty" texture, try 8 or 10 ounces of seitan in place of tempeh or tofu.

- If you'd like to add onion to the mix, quarter and slice a medium or large onion and combine with everything else in the marinade.

- Add one thinly sliced portobello mushroom cap to the protein-and-peppers mixture, as shown in the photo on page 232. Use a little extra lime juice and/or oil if needed.

Complete the Meal

- Serve with a simple side of brown rice or quinoa, either plain or lightly embellished (see pages 99–111 for suggestions). For something fresh and raw, choose from a platter of fresh fruit or Southwestern Slaw (page 251).
- Tomato, Corn, and Avocado Salad (page 250) is delicious with these fajitas. For a heftier meal, add an easy potato dish (consider Sautéed Paprika Potatoes, page 302) or baked sweet potatoes.

Sizzling Tempeh
or Tofu Fajitas
(page 230)

CHOOSING GOOD TORTILLAS

Not surprisingly, the key to making successful tortilla dishes is to use good-quality tortillas, whether corn or wheat. But as good as some of the products are in the Mexican foods section of supermarkets, I'm sorry to say that the flimsy corn tortillas and white wheat tortillas found there don't do it for me. The corn tortillas are tasteless and dry and often splinter and fall apart under the least amount of heat or manipulation. And since they're not organic, I worry that they're made from genetically modified (GMO) corn (though I don't want to start any rumors to that effect). As to the white wheat tortillas, there's no good reason to eat anything made of white wheat, from the perspective of either flavor or nutrition.

Eons ago, after falling in love with southwestern cuisine on a trip to New Mexico, I was disappointed to return to the Northeast and realize that I couldn't find a place to buy good tortillas. Fortunately that's changed, as whole-grain and even organic tortillas are readily available in natural foods stores. Wheat tortillas are now available in multigrain, sprouted, and even tomato- and spinach-flavored varieties. Finding gluten-free corn tortillas isn't too difficult, either, but be aware that not all corn tortillas are necessarily gluten-free; some varieties are mixed with a little whole wheat.

My favorite brands of tortillas include Sonoma and Maria and Ricardo's, both of which seem to be favorite natural foods store brands. But do explore and read labels—there may be regional brands and local options as well.

Tofu *and* Black Bean Rancheros

On a trip to the American Southwest many years ago, when we were vegetarians and not yet vegans, my husband and I discovered huevos rancheros, which are scrambled eggs perched atop corn tortillas and topped with an incendiary sauce. It's not a big stretch to make a plant-based version of this recipe, in which a tasty mélange of tofu, tomatoes, and beans is spooned atop corn tortillas. Serve as a quick dinner or a hearty brunch.

SERVES 4 TO 6 (1 TO 2 TORTILLAS PER SERVING)

One 14- to 16-ounce tub firm tofu
3 tablespoons cornmeal
Pinch of salt
1½ tablespoons extra-virgin olive oil or 3 tablespoons vegetable broth or water
1 medium onion, quartered and thinly sliced
1 medium red bell pepper, cut into short, narrow strips
1 small fresh chili pepper, seeded and minced, or one 4-ounce can diced mild green chilies
3 to 4 medium ripe fresh tomatoes, diced, or one 15- to 16-ounce can diced tomatoes
    (try fire-roasted), undrained
1 cup cooked or canned (drained and rinsed) black beans
1 teaspoon ground cumin
1 teaspoon good-quality chili powder or mesquite seasoning
¼ cup chopped fresh cilantro, or more to taste
6 to 8 good-quality corn or whole-grain flour tortillas, 6 to 8 inches each

OPTIONAL TOPPINGS

Fresh Tomato Salsa (page 246), or your favorite store-bought salsa
Picante sauce or other hot sauce
¾ cup grated nondairy Cheddar-style or nacho-style cheese

1. Drain the tofu and cut into 6 slabs crosswise. Blot well between paper towels or clean kitchen towels (or use a tofu press), then cut each slab into small dice. Combine it with the cornmeal in a large plastic food storage bag and add a pinch of salt. Shake gently until the tofu is evenly coated.

2. Heat about half the oil, broth, or water in a wide skillet. Add the tofu and sauté over medium-high heat, stirring frequently, until golden on most sides, about 8 to 10 minutes. Transfer to a plate and set aside.

3. Heat the remaining oil, broth, or water in the skillet. Add the onion and sauté over medium heat until translucent. Add the bell pepper and chili pepper and continue to sauté until both are golden.

4. Add the tomatoes, beans, cumin, and chili powder. Bring to a simmer, then cook over medium heat for 5 to 8 minutes. Stir in the cilantro and gently fold in the sautéed tofu.

5. To assemble, place 1 or 2 tortillas on each serving plate. Divide the skillet mixture among them and serve the tortillas unrolled and open, to be eaten with a knife and fork. Pass around salsa and/or picante sauce and grated cheese, if desired, for topping individual servings.

PER 2-TORTILLA SERVING: Calories: 295 with oil, 251 without oil; Total fat: 11g with oil, 6g without oil; Protein: 16g; Carbohydrates: 38g; Fiber: 9g; Sodium: 100mg

Complete the Meal

- The Taco Salad variation in "Tossed Salads Go Global," page 319, is a fitting companion. Since the Tofu Rancheros has only a cup of beans, you can go ahead and use beans in both the tofu dish and the salad if desired.
- For a tasty meal trio, team this with baked sweet potatoes and the Tomato, Corn, and Avocado Salad on page 250.

Veggie Burritos

I first discovered vegetable burritos in southwestern-style restaurants, where they often seem like the most appealing option on the menu. Sometimes refried beans are served on the side; otherwise, they're inside the burrito, as presented here. I enjoy it that way, as the refried beans not only make the burritos more substantial but also help hold everything together.

MAKES 8 BURRITOS (4 TO 8 SERVINGS)

8 good-quality flour tortillas, 10 inches each
½ recipe Refried Pinto Beans (page 250; see Note)
1 tablespoon extra-virgin olive oil or 3 tablespoons vegetable broth or water
1 large onion, quartered and thinly sliced
1 medium red bell pepper, cut into 2-inch strips
1 small zucchini or yellow squash, sliced
1 cup sliced mushrooms
1 large ripe fresh tomato, diced
3 to 4 ounces baby spinach or finely chopped kale, rinsed well
1 to 2 fresh hot chili peppers or one 4-ounce can diced mild green chilies
½ teaspoon each good-quality chili powder and ground cumin
1 cup grated nondairy Cheddar-style cheese (optional)
Fresh Tomato Salsa (page 246) or your favorite store-bought salsa

1. Preheat the oven to 250°F.

2. Wrap the tortillas in foil and place in the oven until needed. Heat the refried beans in a small saucepan until just heated through.

3. Heat the oil, broth, or water in a large skillet. Add the onion and sauté over medium heat until translucent.

4. Add the bell pepper, zucchini, mushrooms, tomato, spinach, chilies, chili powder, and cumin, and stir well. Cover and cook for 5 minutes more, or until all the vegetables are just tender. Remove from the heat and drain off any liquid.

5. To assemble, spoon a small amount of the refried beans down the center of each warmed tortilla followed by some of the vegetable mixture and a sprinkling of cheese, if desired. Fold one side over the other to enclose, then distribute among individual plates.

6. Serve at once, passing around the salsa at the table. These moist burritos are best eaten with a knife and fork.

note: If you're short on time, substitute one 15- to 16-ounce can vegan refried beans for the homemade refried beans. Warm them up in a small saucepan, adding about ¼ cup water to loosen the consistency.

PER BURRITO: Calories: 313 with oil, 299 without oil; Total fat: 8g with oil, 6g without oil; Protein: 11g; Carbohydrates: 52g; Fiber: 7g; Sodium: 465mg

Variation

Use other vegetables in place of those suggested here: broccoli, cauliflower, winter squash, sweet potatoes, fresh corn, and eggplant all work well in various combinations.

Complete the Meal

Creamy Kale and Cabbage Slaw (page 324) or Apple Slaw with Leafy Greens (page 325) go well with this, as do Southwestern Slaw (page 251) and Tomato, Corn, and Avocado Salad (page 250). If you'd like more heft to the meal, add some simply cooked brown rice or quinoa with salsa and cilantro stirred in for extra flavor.

Fully Loaded Emergency Nachos

Fully Loaded Emergency Nachos

Every chapter in this book presents at least one full-fledged "emergency" meal—that last bastion of hope before you reach for the take-out menus. Here's my choice for this chapter—nachos that can be made with pantry and refrigerator staples in a matter of minutes. I provide a few from-scratch variations in case you're not completely pressed for time—nachos are fun fare no matter what.

SERVES 4 TO 6

4 to 5 ounces natural, stone-ground, organic tortilla chips
1 cup grated cheddar- or nacho-style nondairy cheese
1 to 2 fresh jalapeño peppers, seeded and thinly sliced, or one 4-ounce can diced mild green chilies
½ cup lightly cooked fresh or thawed frozen corn kernels
½ cup cooked or canned (drained and rinsed) black, red, or pinto beans
1 medium ripe fresh tomato, finely chopped
2 or 3 big handfuls baby spinach, rinsed well
Fresh Tomato Salsa (page 246) or your favorite store-bought salsa

OPTIONAL TOPPINGS

Fresh Tomato Guacamole (page 248)
Vegan Sour Cream (homemade, page 248, or store-bought) or Cashew Cream (page 249)
Thinly sliced romaine lettuce

1. Preheat the oven to 350°F unless you plan to use the microwave.

2. Arrange the tortilla chips on a large platter or a shallow round casserole dish about 14 inches in diameter. Sprinkle evenly with the cheese, followed by the chili peppers, corn, beans, and tomato.

3. Bake for 8 minutes, more or less, until the cheese is well melted. Or microwave for 3 minutes on high.

4. Scatter the spinach over the top and return to the oven for 2 minutes or so (or to the microwave for another minute), just until it wilts.

5. Serve at once. Pass around the salsa as well as the optional toppings at the table.

PER SERVING: Calories: 282; Total fat: 13g; Protein: 6g; Carbohydrates: 36g; Fiber: 6g; Sodium: 415mg

continued

Variations

- If you have time, these can be made with a homemade queso sauce—use the recipe for Almost-Raw Cheez Sauce on page 176 and/or make your own salsa; see the recipe and variations on page 246.

- This is delicious with sliced mushrooms. Cook them lightly and add at the same time as all the other toppings.

Complete the Meal

- Omit the beans and serve with Beer-Stewed Pinto or Pink Beans, page 250. Fruit adds a refreshing note; serve it with or after the meal. Cool-weather choices include sliced pears and/or orange wedges; for warm-weather meals, a variety of melons (cantaloupe, watermelon, and/or honeydew) adds a nice touch.

- Omit the corn and serve with Southwestern Slaw, page 251, or any of the other simple slaws, pages 322–25.

Easy, Flexible Quesadillas

Think of quesadillas as a Mexican or southwestern grilled cheese sandwich. In our case, of course, that would mean a sandwich made with vegan cheese. Because they're built atop flour tortillas, quesadillas are less bready than sandwiches. And you can slip all manner of veggies into them. Quesadillas can be the centerpiece of a meal if they're loaded; when they're more lightly filled, they go well with soups and salads.

Quesadillas can be cooked on a griddle if you're only making one or two. But when you're feeding a large family or a small crowd, baking a few at once quickly in a hot oven is more efficient. Here are the basic steps:

1. Choose the tortillas you'd like to use. Flour tortillas are customary for quesadillas; please choose a whole-grain variety without questionable additives. Eight-inch tortillas work well. If you need a gluten-free option, corn tortillas are fine, though they make smaller quesadillas; but then you can make more of them if need be.

2. Choose two or three additional ingredients in addition to cheese for the filling. Here are some suggestions:
   - Cooked or canned (drained and rinsed) pinto, pink, red, or black beans
   - Lightly cooked fresh or thawed frozen corn kernels
   - Finely diced or thinly sliced ripe fresh tomatoes
   - Peeled and thinly sliced avocado
   - Sliced black olives
   - Thinly sliced green or red bell peppers

- Green chilies (use mild or hot canned diced chilies or fresh chili peppers of your choice, seeded and minced)
- Sliced and lightly sautéed brown mushrooms
- Wilted spinach or chard
- Thinly sliced baked sweet potato
- Fresh Tomato Salsa (page 246) or your favorite store-bought salsa (or you can pass salsa around when serving)
- Salsa verde (tomatillo salsa)

Here are some of my favorite combinations for quesadillas:

- Avocado and sweet potato
- Zucchini or yellow squash, sweet potato, and corn
- Black or pinto beans, corn, and red bell pepper
- Wilted spinach and mushrooms
- Arugula, tomato, and avocado

3. If baking in the oven, preheat to 400ºF. Arrange four or six 8-inch flour tortillas on two baking sheets. If cooking on a griddle, skip this step.

4. Sprinkle a modest amount of grated cheese over each tortilla—a quarter or a half cup for the entire quesadilla is about right, depending on the size of the tortillas, so start by using half of that amount for the bottom. Arrange any other ingredients (see suggestions above, plus my favorite combinations, following) over the cheese. Sprinkle with a little more cheese, and cover with another tortilla. By the way, any flavor of vegan cheese works—Cheddar- or mozzarella-style are good, but a spicy variety like pepper Jack is even better.

5. If using the oven, bake until the tortillas turn golden and crisp on both sides, about 12 to 15 minutes. If cooking on a griddle on the stove top, set it over medium-high heat, then cook quesadillas on both sides until crisp and golden. This will take about 5 to 8 minutes per side depending on the heat level of your griddle. If everything is prepped, you can even assemble the quesadilla right on the griddle, as shown in the photos on page 242.

6. To serve, cut each quesadilla into four equal wedges. Allow two to four wedges per serving, depending on what else is being served. Pass around salsa at the table, whether or not you use some inside the quesadilla.

What if you don't like vegan cheese, or if you're in the camp that doesn't want to use it, even in modest amounts? No worries: you can still make quesadillas. Simply spread refried

beans, homemade (page 250) or canned, on each side of the tortilla. I'm not sure you can officially call them quesadillas, without there being *queso* (cheese) of any kind in them, but you can still make them taste good.

Soft Tacos

Soft tacos can be made with flour or corn tortillas. Unlike quesadillas (whose name, after all, is derived from *queso,* which means "cheese" in Spanish), soft tacos don't have to include cheese. And, like fajitas, tacos are very much of an assemble-at-the-table kind of meal—the only real work (and it's not much work, really) is to make the hot filling. Everything else goes on the table, and everyone makes his or her own, embellishing to personal taste.

To make soft tacos, start with corn tortillas or small flour tortillas (soft taco size). It's particularly important to use good-quality tortillas for soft tacos, so consider looking for them in natural foods stores; see the sidebar "Choosing Good Tortillas" on page 233. Fresh, pliable, whole-grain options make a big difference. Bring refrigerated tortillas to room temperature, or warm them by wrapping in foil and placing in an oven set at 250°F. Then follow these easy steps:

1. Arrange the desired filling down the center of each tortilla, being careful not to overfill. See Tempeh and Walnut Soft Taco Filling, page 245, or "More Ideas for Soft Tacos," page 246.

2. Embellish with any or all of the items listed below and fold the tortilla gently over the fillings.

3. Serve separate small bowls of the following, with which everyone can embellish their own individual servings. No need to include all of them, but must haves, in my opinion, are the first four. Eat out of hand for a sensually messy experience, or use a fork (and knife, if need be).

   - Shredded lettuce
   - Finely diced or thinly sliced fresh ripe tomatoes
   - Fresh Tomato Salsa (page 246) or your favorite store-bought salsa
   - Peeled and diced avocado
   - Vegan Sour Cream (page 248), Cashew Cream (page 249), or store-bought vegan sour cream
   - Grated vegan Cheddar- or Jack-style cheese (the least essential ingredient)
   - Picante, sriracha, or other hot sauce

Soft Tacos with Tempeh and Walnut Filling

Tempeh *and* Walnut Soft Taco Filling

Tacos, like quesadillas, don't necessarily need a formal recipe. Two high-protein foods (with lots more going for them nutritionally) team up in a tasty taco filling that goes a long way. Use leftovers to boost protein and add texture to bean dishes and stews. Or you can freeze half of it for a future taco dinner.

FILLS 8 LARGE OR 12 SMALL SOFT TACOS (4 TO 6 GENEROUS SERVINGS)

1 tablespoon extra-virgin olive oil or 3 tablespoons vegetable broth or water
1 medium-large onion, chopped
1 medium red or green bell pepper, finely diced
One 8-ounce package tempeh
1 cup walnut pieces
One 15- to 16-ounce can tomato sauce
1 tablespoon good-quality chili powder
1 tablespoon sweet paprika
1 teaspoon ground cumin
Salt to taste
Picante or sriracha sauce to taste (optional; see Note)

1. Heat the oil, broth, or water in a large skillet. Add the onion and sauté until translucent. Add the bell pepper and continue to sauté until the onion is lightly browned.

2. Cut the block of tempeh into 10 or 12 chunks. Place in a food processor and pulse a few times. Add the walnut pieces and the onion and pepper mixture and pulse until everything is finely and evenly chopped. Be careful not to overprocess—you don't want this to turn into a puree.

3. Transfer the mixture to the skillet. Add the tomato sauce and seasonings. Stir together, bring to a simmer, then allow to cook over low heat for 15 to 20 minutes so the flavors can heighten and blend.

4. Serve straight from the skillet or transfer to a serving container, allowing everyone to construct individual soft tacos using the embellishments suggested on page 243.

note: If you'd like a milder flavor, omit the hot sauce here and pass it at the table.

PER SERVING (PER 2 LARGE TACOS): Calories: 400 with oil, 371 without oil; Total fat: 28g with oil, 25g without oil; Protein: 17g; Carbohydrates: 26g; Fiber: 10g; Sodium: 148mg

continued

Complete the Meal

Like other dishes in this chapter, soft tacos go well with baked russet potatoes or sweet potatoes. Or, if you'd like something just a tad fancier, consider some of the smashed potatoes ideas on pages 303–05. For a nice boost to the veggie content of the meal, add Southwestern-Flavored Kale Salad (page 321).

More Ideas for Soft Tacos

Frijoles Borrachos Soft Tacos: See page 250 for this delicious bean recipe. Just swap it for the tempeh and walnut filling, then finish and embellish the tacos as directed in the recipe.

Pinto Bean and Quinoa Soft Tacos: The ingredients in Pinto Bean and Quinoa Sloppy Joes (page 279) make a great taco filling. Just swap the burger bun for tortillas and the recommended embellishments.

Veggie Soft Tacos: Any kind of simple steamed or sautéed vegetable dish can be turned into delicious soft tacos. Spread some refried beans (homemade, page 250, or warmed canned refried beans) on your tortilla. Top with some warm vegetables, then finish with the recommended embellishments. Steamed Broccoli and Yellow Squash (page 251), for example, is excellent on tacos.

Salsa, Guacamole, *and* Sour Cream *to* Accompany Tortilla Specialties

Fresh Tomato Salsa

Fresh tomato salsa, sometimes known as salsa fresca, is the most basic condiment in Mexican and southwestern-style cuisine. Store-bought salsas are generally quite good, not to mention convenient, but there's nothing like the fresh, homemade kind.

MAKES ABOUT 2 CUPS

2 cups chopped ripe fresh tomatoes

1 small onion, quartered, or 2 scallions, sliced

1 to 2 fresh jalapeño peppers, seeded and coarsely chopped or
one 4- to 8-ounce can diced mild green chilies (see Note)

¼ to ½ cup minced fresh cilantro
1 tablespoon freshly squeezed or bottled lemon or lime juice, or more to taste
½ teaspoon ground cumin
¼ teaspoon salt, or to taste

1. To prepare in a food processor, simply combine all the ingredients in the container and pulse on and off until the ingredients are coarsely pureed.

2. To prepare by hand, finely chop the tomatoes, onion or scallions, and jalapeños, if using (canned chilies are sufficiently chopped; simply add them). Stir in the remaining ingredients.

3. Serve at once. Leftovers can be stored in an airtight container in the refrigerator for several days, but it's best fresh.

note: The use of one jalapeño will result in a reasonably hot salsa, while two will make this pretty fiery. Those with more experienced palates are free to use as many jalapeños as they'd like. You can use other fresh chilies of your choice, such as serrano and habanero, if you enjoy distinctive heat.

PER ¼-CUP SERVING: Calories: 12; Total fat: 0g; Protein: 0g; Carbohydrates: 2.5g; Fiber: 1g; Sodium: 90mg

Variations

• To make a fruity salsa, add a cup or so of finely chopped pineapple, peach, or mango—preferably fresh in all cases.

• Add ½ cup each of corn kernels (preferably fresh; either lightly cooked or raw) and finely diced red or orange bell pepper.

Fresh Tomato Guacamole

Here's a delicious rendition of guacamole with a bit more emphasis on the tomatoes than the avocados, which is great when a large quantity is needed. This also has more staying power than when avocado stands alone. Serve it as an accompaniment to quesadillas, soft tacos, and the other tortilla dishes in this chapter or on its own as a dip with stone-ground tortilla chips.

MAKES ABOUT 2 CUPS (8 OR MORE SERVINGS AS AN APPETIZER OR GARNISH)

3 medium ripe fresh tomatoes (try an heirloom variety or two)
1 medium ripe avocado
Freshly squeezed juice of 1 lemon or lime, or to taste
1 clove garlic, crushed (optional)
1 to 2 small fresh hot chilies seeded and coarsely chopped,
    or one 4- to 8-ounce can whole mild green chilies
2 scallions, sliced
¼ cup chopped fresh cilantro, or more to taste
½ teaspoon ground cumin
Salt and freshly ground pepper to taste

1. Cut the tomatoes into quarters. Peel and pit the avocado and cut into large chunks. Put the tomatoes and avocado in the container of a food processor along with the remaining ingredients.

2. Pulse until the ingredients are evenly and coarsely chopped. Leave the salsa a bit chunky; be careful not to overprocess. Serve at once. This is best used right away, but if you do have any left over, cover tightly and use within a day.

PER ¼-CUP SERVING: Calories: 42; Total fat: 3g; Protein: 1g; Carbohydrates: 5g; Fiber: 2g; Sodium: 6mg

Vegan Sour Cream

Here's an easy preparation that's quite useful for the dishes in this chapter. It's recommended as a garnish for hot or cold soups and as a homemade replacement for the commercial vegan sour cream or vegan mayonnaise called for in some recipes in this book.

MAKES A HEAPING CUP

1 cup crumbled firm or extra-firm silken tofu
3 tablespoons unsweetened rice milk or other nondairy milk
2 teaspoons freshly squeezed or bottled lemon juice, or more to taste
¼ teaspoon salt, or to taste

1. Combine all ingredients in a food processor and process until very smoothly pureed. Alternatively, combine all ingredients in a deep container and puree with an immersion blender.

2. Transfer to a small bowl and serve at once, or transfer to a container with an airtight lid and refrigerate until needed.

PER 2-TABLESPOON SERVING: Calories: 18; Total fat: .5g; Protein: 2g; Carbohydrates: 1g; Fiber: 0g; Sodium: 83mg

Cashew Cream

This contemporary recipe is a great substitute for dairy- or soy-based sour cream or even as a homemade replacement for commercial vegan mayonnaise. Use it for topping soups or as a simple sauce for vegetables or grains.

MAKES ABOUT 1 CUP

1 cup raw cashews
2 tablespoons unsweetened rice milk or other nondairy milk, or as needed
1 tablespoon freshly squeezed or bottled lemon juice, or to taste
½ teaspoon salt

1. Place the cashews in a small, heatproof bowl and cover them with boiling water. Let stand for at least 30 minutes or up to an hour.

2. Drain and transfer to a food processor along with the remaining ingredients. Process until smoothly pureed, stopping to scrape the sides down as needed. Add a little more rice milk if you need to thin the consistency a bit.

3. Transfer to a small bowl and serve at once, or transfer to a container with an airtight lid and refrigerate until needed.

PER 2-TABLESPOON SERVING: Calories: 99; Total fat: 7.5g; Protein: 3g; Carbohydrates: 5.5g; Fiber: .5g; Sodium: 148mg

Perfect Accompaniments for Tortilla Specialties

Here are a few easy, tasty preparations that go well with the entrées in this chapter. Yes, they're great sidekicks, but you can even combine some of them to create a flavorful meal in and of themselves; for example, Beer-Stewed Pinto or Pink Beans; Tomato, Corn, and Avocado Salad; and Steamed Broccoli and Yellow Squash are a fantastic combination—just add fresh tortillas.

Refried Pinto Beans (Frijoles Refritos): Basic to southwestern and Mexican cuisine, refried beans give a good protein boost to meals in this chapter that don't themselves contain beans. They're also a nice filling for burritos and quesadillas.

Make this with home-cooked or canned beans. Use 3½ to 4 cups well-cooked beans or two 15- to 16-ounce cans, drained and rinsed. Heat just enough olive oil to coat the bottom of a large skillet. Or skip the oil and use vegetable broth or water. Either way, sauté a finely chopped medium onion until golden; add the beans and sauté over medium heat for 5 to 8 minutes. Add ½ cup water and mash with a potato masher. Continue mashing, cooking, and adding small amounts of water until the beans reach the consistency of a thick sauce. If you're using home-cooked beans, season to taste with salt (canned beans won't need extra salt).

That's it for the basic recipe, but if you'd like to add a little savor and flavor, stir in 1 to 2 small fresh hot chili peppers, such as jalapeño, seeded and minced, or a 4-ounce can of diced mild green chilies. You can also add ¼ cup or so of minced fresh cilantro. This makes 6 or so servings.

Beer-Stewed Pinto or Pink Beans: In Spanish, the name for this classic bean dish is frijoles borrachos, which means "drunken beans." Simmering pinto beans in beer and adding plenty of fresh cilantro give them a unique flavor. To be honest, I can't stand to drink beer, but I just love what a small amount of it does for beans. This makes an awesome filling for soft tacos and a delicious accompaniment to tortilla dishes that don't themselves contain beans.

Combine 4 cups cooked (or two 15-to 16-ounce cans, drained and rinsed) pinto beans in a saucepan with ½ cup beer and 1 seeded and minced fresh chili pepper (or for a milder flavor, use a 4-ounce can of diced mild green chilies). Bring to a rapid simmer, then mash some of the beans with a potato masher until the base is nice and thick. Leave most of the beans intact. If you're using home-cooked beans, season to taste with salt (canned beans won't need extra salt). Stir in ¼ cup cilantro or more to taste. This makes 6 or so servings.

Tomato, Corn, and Avocado Salad: Combine an equal amount of diced ripe fresh tomatoes, lightly cooked fresh or thawed frozen corn kernels, and diced avocado. Embellish with scallions, cilantro, a little olive oil (if you like), and freshly squeezed or bottled lime juice. This is so good with bean dishes!

Southwestern Slaw: Combine as much finely shredded green cabbage (or, for a shortcut, packaged shredded cabbage) as you like with some lightly cooked fresh or thawed frozen corn kernels. Dress with a lime vinaigrette (page 327) or any prepared dressing of your choice. You can stop there or add thinly sliced kale, finely diced red bell pepper, thinly sliced scallion, chopped cilantro, and/or pumpkin seeds.

Sautéed Zucchini, Corn, and Bell Pepper: Sauté thinly sliced zucchini, the kernels from an ear or two of corn (or a cup or so of thawed frozen kernels), and a thinly sliced red bell pepper in olive oil just until golden. Or make the dish oil-free by steaming the vegetables in a little water. Finish with a sprinkling of ground cumin, salt and freshly ground pepper, and thinly sliced basil leaves or chopped cilantro. If you like, sprinkle some pumpkin seeds on the finished dish.

Steamed Broccoli and Yellow Squash: This is nothing fancy, but it's an appealing combination that goes well with the meals in this chapter—and others. In a wide skillet, lightly steam broccoli florets (from a medium crown) in a little water, vegetable broth, or wine until just bright green. Add a sliced yellow summer squash and continue to steam until both are tender-crisp. Serve as is or top with strips of sun-dried tomato and/or pumpkin seeds. You can even use this as a filling for soft tacos (see page 243). This colorful side dish is shown with Black Bean Tostadas in the photo on page 226.

CHAPTER 6

WRAPS, SANDWICHES, *and* BURGERS

In this chapter, which is geared toward bready kinds of meals, I've nevertheless tried to make the recipes as little about the bread as possible. In delectably leafy wraps, protein-packed sandwiches, and flavorful burgers and sloppy joes, the bread is merely the vehicle. It's what's inside that needs to grab your attention.

Barbecue-Flavored Chickpea Sandwiches (page 263)

I'm a big fan of wraps because they serve at least three useful functions. First and foremost, many wraps can often actually be salads disguised as sandwiches. Though my kids were good eaters when they were growing up, salad wouldn't have topped their list of favorite foods. But if I took what was in a salad bowl and wrapped it up, that was a different story. Second, wraps make leftovers a whole lot more exciting. Roasted vegetables, sloppy joe filling, and most any tofu or tempeh preparation are more enticing when combined with a tasty spread and tender leafy greens in a wrap. Finally, wraps make portable lunches a little more interesting. Come to think of it, they make breakfast more interesting, too. If I find half a leftover hummus and avocado wrap in the fridge in the morning, I'm all over it.

The supremely savory sandwich fillings, veggie burgers, and sloppy joes in this chapter are mostly about beans (notably, chickpeas), tofu, tempeh, and quinoa. Some of the results can be downright meaty in their heartiness, though imitating meat isn't the goal. Many of these recipes, especially the cold fare, will offer fresh inspiration for portable lunches that can be taken to school and work. They're equally welcome at dinner. When you serve wraps, sandwiches, or burgers for the evening meal, the message is easy, casual, and fun. And who can't use more of that?

Plant-Powered Wrapsody

Following are a few recipes for making wraps, but honestly, once you add wraps to your regular lunch or dinner rotation, there's hardly a need for formal recipes. These are here to get you started. Wraps are a truly easy way to be creative and enjoy varied ingredients in a carefree dinner or a luscious lunch.

These types of quick sandwiches can be made one at a time, as a single portable lunch or solo dinner, or en masse—for a family or large group, simply place the ingredients on the table and have people create their own. In these recipes, the amount of filling called for is often just an estimate, as the size of the wrappers varies—usually they're between eight and twelve inches in diameter. Lots of colors and flavors are available: spinach, sun-dried tomato, garlic and herb, and others. You'll find wrappers made with various grains as well; whole-grain wraps are preferable, of course. Look for wraps with natural ingredients—nothing you can't pronounce; no questionable oils or additives.

Apart from traditional round wraps, lavash—a thin, flexible Middle Eastern flatbread that comes in various shapes, including rectangles—can be used as a change of pace. These enclose fillings fairly snugly, though you can't tuck in the ends. So remember to eat them over your plate! If you're packing your wrap to take with you, use a sturdy container that will protect it from getting crushed.

Gluten-free wrap options exist, though my cousin Lee and others say they're not perfect and don't usually come in large sizes; they're more like tortillas. Having tried many of the options on the market, she had this to say: "The Engine 2 brown rice tortillas are similar to wheat-flour wraps but smaller. Rudi's makes a decent tortilla-size wrap in three different flavors. If you want something close to a regular flour wrap, Toufayan Bakeries has a large one that is easily found on traditional store shelves."

Hummus Wraps with Grains and Greens

Hummus Wraps
with Grains *and* Greens

This hummus wrap is chock-full of flavor and a good use of leftover grains of all kinds. Once you have your grain cooked, the wrap comes together in minutes. The recipe also doubles easily.

MAKES 2 WRAPS

Two 10-inch wraps, at room temperature
1/2 to 3/4 cup hummus, homemade (page 272) or store-bought, or as needed
2 tablespoons hemp seeds or 1 tablespoon sesame seeds (optional)
1/2 cup or so cooked quinoa, brown rice, or black rice
A big handful or two of mixed baby greens, shredded lettuce, baby arugula,
    or baby spinach
1 medium ripe fresh tomato, thinly sliced
1/2 medium firm ripe avocado, peeled and sliced
Strips of sun-dried tomato, as desired, optional

1. Place one wrap on a plate. Spread with about 1/4 cup hummus and sprinkle with hemp seeds, if desired.

2. Arrange half the quinoa down the center of the wrap. Put a big handful of leafy greens next to it on one side and half the tomato slices on the other. Sprinkle half the avocado strips here and there, followed by a few strips of sun-dried tomatoes, if desired.

3. Tuck two ends over the fillings; then, starting from one end, roll tightly, making sure that the ends are kept tucked in and that everything remains snugly inside. Repeat with the second wrap. Cut each wrap in half and eat out of hand.

PER WRAP: Calories: 400; Total fat: 13g; Protein: 15g; Carbohydrates: 65g; Fiber: 13g; Sodium: 500mg

Complete the Meal

- Serve with a simple potato dish (such as Sautéed Paprika Potatoes, page 302), salsa and chips, and/or fresh corn—these wraps go with most anything!
- Pair with a soup. This goes with most any kind of soup other than bean soup—as hummus is, after all, made with beans. See the photo of this wrap paired with Cream of Broccoli Soup on page 133.

Cucumber *and* Avocado Wraps *with* Bean Spread *or* Hummus

This easy hummus wrap is as good for dinner as it is for lunch (or even breakfast). You can use homemade hummus or store-bought; either way, the wrap is ready in minutes. This recipe also doubles easily.

MAKES 2 WRAPS

Two 10-inch wraps, at room temperature
½ to ¾ cup Chunky Bean Spread (page 269) or hummus
    (homemade, page 272, or store-bought), or as needed
12 to 16 thin cucumber slices
1 medium ripe fresh tomato, thinly sliced
½ medium firm ripe avocado, thinly sliced
¼ cup chopped black olives
A big handful or two of finely shredded romaine lettuce, mixed baby greens,
    baby spinach, baby arugula, or a combination

1. Place one wrap on a plate. Spread with about ¼ cup bean spread or hummus.

2. Arrange a row of about 6 to 8 cucumber slices down the center, followed by about half the tomato slices and half the avocado slices. Sprinkle with half of the black olives. Cover with a big handful of the leafy greens of your choice.

3. Tuck two ends over the fillings; then, starting from one end, roll tightly, making sure that the ends are kept tucked in and that everything remains snugly inside. Repeat with the second wrap. Cut each wrap in half and eat out of hand.

PER WRAP: Calories: 340; Total fat: 13g; Protein: 13g; Carbohydrates: 54g; Fiber: 14g; Sodium: 745mg

Complete the Meal

- With the hummus option, this goes well with Lentil Soup, page 124.
- Serve this wrap with another substantial cold dish, such as Quinoa Tabbouleh (page 315) or Classic Potato Salad (page 312). If you'd like more green on the plate, add some steamed broccoli, green beans, or asparagus. Or, if you have some greens in the fridge you'd like to use, consider Garlicky Hardy Greens (page 287).

Tossed Salad Wraps

As mentioned in the introduction to this chapter, if you or those you live with aren't big salad eaters, take most any sort of salad and wrap it up. Suddenly it's transformed into a sandwich with a yumminess factor that makes it a tasty companion to soups, stews, and the like. I enjoy this recipe (which doubles easily) with French Dressing (page 329) or Thousand Island-ish Dressing (page 283), but choose whatever homemade or prepared dressing you like best.

MAKES 2 WRAPS

1 medium ripe fresh tomato, finely diced
1/2 medium red bell pepper, cut into short, narrow strips
1/4 medium cucumber, quartered and thinly sliced
1/2 cup shredded carrots or very thinly sliced red cabbage
1/4 cup sliced sun-dried tomatoes or chopped pitted black or green olives
1/4 cup salad dressing of your choice (see pages 327–31, or use your favorite prepared dressing)
A big handful or two of finely shredded lettuce or mixed baby greens, as desired
Salt and freshly ground pepper to taste
Two 10- to 12-inch wraps or burrito-size flour tortillas

1. Combine all ingredients except the wraps in a mixing bowl and toss together.

2. Divide the salad between the two wraps, distributing it evenly over the entire surface, leaving approximately 2 inches clear at one side of each wrap.

3. Tuck two ends over the fillings; then, starting from one end, roll tightly, making sure that the ends are kept tucked in and that everything remains snugly inside. Repeat with the second wrap. Cut each wrap in half and eat out of hand.

PER WRAP: Calories: 308; Total fat: 12g; Protein: 9g; Carbohydrates: 50g; Fiber: 9g; Sodium: 600mg

Complete the Meal

- This wrap can be paired with several soup recipes in this book:

    Lentil Soup with Tasty Variations (page 124)
    Quick Black Bean Soup (page 126)
    Long-Simmering Bean Soup (page 128)
    Tomato-Vegetable Soup with Variations (page 138; see the photo on page 139)

- With added chickpeas, beans, or chunks of baked tofu, these wraps would also pair nicely with any of the smashed potatoes on pages 303–5 for a light meal.

Thai-Flavored Salad Wraps

This is fairly similar to Tossed Salad Wraps (page 259)—and, like that recipe, it doubles easily—but strips of baked tofu and a delectable peanut dressing make it more of a main event than a "side sandwich."

MAKES 2 WRAPS

½ medium red bell pepper, cut into short, narrow strips

¼ medium cucumber, quartered and thinly sliced

½ cup shredded carrots or very thinly sliced green or napa cabbage

1 medium ripe fresh tomato, finely diced

Two 10-inch wraps or burrito-size flour tortillas

2 tablespoons Coconut-Peanut Dressing (page 330) or store-bought Thai peanut satay sauce, plus more to taste

4 ounces baked tofu, cut into narrow strips

A big handful or two of finely shredded lettuce to taste (romaine is perfect for this)

2 tablespoons crushed peanuts (optional)

Sriracha or other hot sauce (optional)

1. Combine the first four ingredients in a mixing bowl and toss together.

2. Spread the surface of one wrap with half the dressing. Arrange half the veggie mixture down the center.

3. Arrange half the tofu strips alongside the veggies, then top with a big handful of shredded lettuce. Sprinkle with half the crushed peanuts, a drizzle of sriracha, and extra peanut sauce, if desired.

4. Tuck two ends over the fillings; then, starting from one end, roll tightly, making sure that the ends are kept tucked in and that everything remains snugly inside. Repeat with the second wrap. Cut each wrap in half and eat out of hand.

PER WRAP: Calories: 438; Total fat: 20g; Protein: 22g; Carbohydrates: 52g; Fiber: 10g; Sodium: 822mg

Variations

Add additional thinly sliced or grated salad vegetables (such as carrots, turnips, and radishes) and chopped fresh herbs as desired.

Complete the Meal

Serve these wraps with Gingery Miso Soup (page 215) for a delectable pairing. Do include some of the suggested additions from the soup recipe—I recommend mushrooms and fine Asian rice noodles.

Make Your Own Creative Wraps

Here's where I encourage you to break free of the habit of following a recipe and get creative with your wraps. Following is a handy guide that will help you do just that.

Aside from the wraps themselves, there are only two must haves, as far as I'm concerned. First is some sort of tasty spread, which not only adds flavor but also helps the whole shebang stay together, and second is some variety of light leafy greens to give your wraps volume and crunch. All you have to add are two to three more ingredients. Note that the first five spreads listed below are also good protein sources, so adding protein and/or grain fillings is optional. But keep in mind that cold leftover grains are ideal for using in wraps.

Here are the basics steps:

1. Lay the wrap on a large plate or cutting board.

2. Spread the surface evenly with any one of the spreads listed below. Cover nearly the entire surface. Be generous yet judicious; you don't want the spread to ooze out.

3. Place all other fillings down the center of the wrap, leaving about an inch on either end. To get an idea of this arrangement, see the photo on page 256.

4. Tuck two ends over the fillings, then, starting from one end, roll tightly, making sure that the ends are kept tucked in and that everything remains snugly inside.

5. Arrange on plates, seam side down, and cut in half to serve.

SPREADS

Hummus—homemade, page 272, or prepared

Refried beans—homemade, page 250, or prepared

Peanut, cashew, or almond butter (at room temperature for easier spreading)

Guacamole—homemade, page 248, or prepared

Salsa—homemade, page 246, or prepared

Thousand Island-ish Dressing—page 283

Quick Tartar Sauce—page 282

Vegan mayonnaise

LEAFY GREENS

Mixed baby greens

Baby spinach

Baby arugula

Thinly sliced romaine or other lettuce

PROTEIN AND GRAIN FILLINGS

Baked tofu, cut into strips—homemade, page 271, or prepared

Bite-size chunks of seitan (cook in a little soy or teriyaki sauce)

Cooked quinoa

Cooked whole-grain rice, brown or exotic varieties

Chickpea and Kale Sandwich Spread—page 267

Chunky Bean Spread—page 269

Ultimate Eggless Egg Salad—page 270

Smoky Tempeh Strips—page 268

SALAD VEGETABLES

Green sprouts, such as broccoli sprouts or pea shoots

Thinly sliced cucumber

Thinly sliced tomatoes

Narrow strips of bell pepper

Grated carrots

Thinly sliced radishes

CONDIMENTS AND FLAVOR ENHANCEMENTS

Sriracha or other hot sauce

Chutney

Mustard—yellow, spicy, or Dijon-style

Sun-dried tomatoes, preferably not oil-cured

Jarred roasted red peppers

Artichoke hearts (marinated or not)

Chopped black or green olives

Sandwiches *and* Sandwich Fillings

Barbecue-Flavored Chickpea Sandwiches

Cool romaine lettuce and barbecue-flavored chickpeas combine to create great flavor and texture in this hearty pita sandwich. This pairs well with many simple companions—potatoes or sweet potatoes, fresh corn, a simple quinoa salad or pilaf, or a light soup. And steamed green veggies are always welcome, too.

MAKES 2 PITA SANDWICHES OR 4 OPEN-FACED SANDWICHES (2 TO 4 SERVINGS)

1 tablespoon extra-virgin olive oil or 2 tablespoons vegetable broth or water
1 medium onion, quartered and sliced
1 medium red bell pepper, cut into short, narrow strips
2/3 cup barbecue sauce, homemade (page 86) or store-bought
2 teaspoons good-quality chili powder
1½ to 2 cups cooked or canned (drained and rinsed) chickpeas
Two large fresh pitas, preferably whole wheat
Finely shredded romaine lettuce to taste
Fresh green sprouts, such as broccoli sprouts or pea shoots, to taste (optional)
2 medium ripe fresh tomatoes, thinly sliced

1. Heat the oil, broth, or water in a medium skillet. Add the onion and sauté until golden. Add the bell pepper, barbecue sauce, and chili powder, then stir in the chickpeas. Cook over medium heat until the sauce is reduced and envelops the chickpeas and veggies nicely, about 8 minutes.

2. Place whole or half pitas on each serving plate, depending on appetites and what else is being served. Insert a generous amount of lettuce and sprouts and a few slices of tomato into each pita, followed by the chickpea mixture. Eat at once, out of hand.

PER HALF PITA: Calories: 258 with oil, 239 without oil; Total fat: 5g with oil, 3g without oil; Protein: 10g; Carbohydrates: 47g; Fiber: 9g; Sodium: 280mg

continued

Variations

- Substitute 8 ounces of well-drained, well-blotted extra-firm tofu or tempeh, cut into ½-inch dice, for the chickpeas.
- Add half a medium ripe avocado, peeled and thinly sliced, to the sandwiches with the lettuce and tomato.

Complete the Meal

- Since the sandwich already includes salad vegetables, serve with baked potatoes or sweet potatoes and steamed broccoli, Broccolini, or broccoli rabe.
- Instead of baked potatoes or sweet potatoes, try Sautéed Paprika Potatoes or Potato or Sweet Potato Oven Fries or Wedges, both on page 302.

Barbecue-Flavored Chickpea Sandwiches (page 263)

Smoky Tempeh *and* Avocado Reuben Sandwiches

This classic deli sandwich can be made meatless as well as dairy-free. It's great for a quick at-home lunch or for a soup-and-sandwich dinner. The ingredients given here can be easily multiplied for additional servings or halved for a single serving.

SERVES 2 (4 OPEN-FACED SANDWICH HALVES)

4 slices fresh whole-grain rye bread
Thousand Island-ish Dressing (page 283) or yellow mustard to taste
½ recipe Smoky Tempeh Strips (page 268), or to taste (see Note)
½ cup well-drained sauerkraut, or to taste
½ ripe avocado, peeled and thinly sliced
½ cup grated nondairy cheese (mozzarella-style works well for this)

1. Preheat the oven or toaster oven to 375ºF.

2. Spread each slice of bread with a small amount of dressing or mustard. Distribute the tempeh strips, sauerkraut, avocado slices, and grated cheese, in that order. Transfer to a baking sheet.

3. Heat the open-face sandwiches in the oven for 8 minutes, or until the cheese melts. Serve at once.

note: Although this requires only half a recipe of the Smoky Tempeh Strips, you may as well make the entire recipe—you can have them for breakfast or use them to top salads.

PER SERVING (2 OPEN-FACED HALVES): Calories: 470; Total fat: 21g; Protein: 17g; Carbohydrates: 53g; Fiber: 11g; Sodium: 1,062mg

Variation

Step up the flavor and heat by using a spicy cabbage kimchi in place of sauerkraut.

Complete the Meal

- These sandwiches make for hearty soup-and-sandwich meals, and are recommended with White Bean and Corn Chowder (page 130) and Cream of Broccoli Soup (page 132).
- Classic Potato Salad (page 312), dill pickle spears, and a platter of sliced tomatoes and bell peppers make a delish deli-style meal.

Chickpea and Kale Sandwich Spread

Chickpea *and* Kale Sandwich Spread

Chickpeas and kale are a tasty team, and this combination makes a great spread for bread, a filling for a pita or wrap (along with some tender lettuce and sliced tomatoes), or layered on a sturdy flatbread and served open-faced. It also might be a great choice for teens who are on board with healthful food options—pack some in their take-along school lunches.

SERVES 4 TO 6 (MAKES 2 TO 2½ CUPS)

2 medium kale leaves (any variety), rinsed well
1 medium carrot, peeled and cut into chunks
2 cups cooked or one 15- to 16-ounce can (drained and rinsed) chickpeas
2 tablespoons nutritional yeast (optional but highly recommended)
⅓ cup vegan mayonnaise or tahini
2 teaspoons yellow mustard
¼ cup fresh parsley leaves or 1 to 2 tablespoons fresh dill leaves
1 to 2 scallions, green parts only, cut into large pieces (optional)
1 to 2 tablespoons freshly squeezed or bottled lemon juice, or to taste
½ teaspoon good-quality curry powder, or more to taste
½ teaspoon ground cumin, or more to taste
Freshly ground pepper to taste
Fresh green sprouts (optional)

1. Combine the kale and carrot in a food processor; pulse until finely chopped.

2. Add the remaining ingredients and pulse until the chickpeas are evenly chopped and everything is nicely blended—don't overprocess; leave the mixture a bit chunky.

3. Transfer to a serving container and serve at once, or cover and refrigerate until needed.

PER ½-CUP SERVING: Calories: 220; Total fat: 7g; Protein: 13g; Carbohydrates: 29g; Fiber: 9g; Sodium: 208mg

Variation

Use a good handful of baby spinach or arugula in place of the kale.

Complete the Meal

For a light warm-weather meal, serve this with Classic Potato Salad, page 312 (I recommend preparing it with sweet potatoes), and a fruit salad of your choice—see the photo on the facing page.

Smoky Tempeh Strips

It's easy to make your own "fake bacon," similar to the kind sold at natural foods stores. But let's not call it that, as it's nothing like its animal counterpart. Savory, slightly sweet, and as spicy as you choose to make them (rather than just incredibly salty, like the store-bought kind), these strips are delicious in wraps and sandwiches. Or just enjoy them on their own, to bolster meals—tempeh is a great source of protein.

SERVES 4

One 8-ounce package tempeh
2 tablespoons reduced-sodium natural soy sauce or tamari
2 tablespoons good-quality ketchup
2 tablespoons maple syrup
1 tablespoon extra-virgin olive oil or 2 tablespoons water
Sriracha or other hot sauce to taste
1 teaspoon liquid smoke, mesquite seasoning, or smoked paprika, or to taste

1. Cut the block of tempeh crosswise into strips no thicker than 1/4 inch.

2. Combine the remaining ingredients in a small bowl and whisk together.

3. Heat the mixture in a wide skillet. Arrange the tempeh strips over the sauce. Cook, covered, over medium-low heat, turning once halfway through cooking time, until the sauce is absorbed and the tempeh starts to brown lightly and turn crisp on both sides, about 8 minutes per side.

4. Serve warm or at room temperature, either as a sandwich filling or as a side dish.

PER SERVING: Calories: 187 with oil, 158 without oil; Total fat: 9g with oil, 6g without oil; Protein: 11g; Carbohydrates: 17g; Fiber: 5g; Sodium: 380mg

Other Ways to Serve

- Use the strips in wraps (see ideas on pages 257–61).
- Serve with whole-grain toast and fruit for breakfast.
- Mix with Easy Hash Brown Potatoes (page 300).
- Serve as a side dish with Quinoa Pilaf with Vegetable Variations (page 100) or Grits 'n' Greens (page 117).

Chunky Bean Spread

Here's a simple sandwich spread that really satisfies. To serve, let everyone at the table prepare individual wraps or sandwiches with the ingredients listed in Complete the Meal, below. Sandwiches can be served open-faced if you like.

MAKES ABOUT 2 CUPS

½ medium green or red bell pepper, cut into 1-inch chunks
¼ cup pimiento-stuffed green olives
1 to 2 scallions, green part only, coarsely chopped
2 cups cooked or one 15- to 16-ounce can (drained and rinsed) pinto or pink beans
2 tablespoons vegan mayonnaise or tahini, or more to taste
1 tablespoon freshly squeezed or bottled lemon juice
1 teaspoon sweet or smoked paprika
1 teaspoon ground cumin
Salt and freshly ground pepper to taste

1. Combine the bell pepper, olives, and scallions in a food processor. Pulse several times, until everything is coarsely and evenly chopped into approximately ¼-inch pieces.

2. Add the beans, mayonnaise, lemon juice, paprika, and cumin. Pulse until everything is evenly chopped but still chunky. Taste for seasonings and add salt and pepper to taste (salt will likely not be needed if canned beans are used). Transfer to a serving container.

PER SERVING: Calories: 162; Total fat: 4g; Protein: 8g; Carbohydrates: 24g; Fiber: 8g; Sodium: 300mg

Variation

Substitute white beans for the pinto or pink beans and add about ¼ cup sliced sun-dried tomatoes. For a lovely pâté, process to a slightly smoother consistency.

Complete the Meal

Set out fresh whole-grain bread or pitas; sliced tomatoes; thinly sliced romaine lettuce, baby spinach, arugula, or watercress; fresh green sprouts; and yellow or spicy brown mustard. Let everyone prepare his or her own sandwich. There's something about pairing this with potato salad that makes the meal feel like a picnic, even when served indoors. If you have your potatoes baked or microwaved ahead of time, making Classic Potato Salad (page 312) will be a breeze. For a large meal, add fresh corn on the cob and/or any of the simple slaws on pages 322–25.

Ultimate Eggless Egg Salad

Tofu can be quite the chameleon, taking on many forms and flavors. This has the feel, if not the flavor, of regular egg salad. But knockoff or not, it's delicious in its own right. As a brown-bag or at-home lunch, serve it in fresh pitas with sprouts or shredded lettuce. Or serve it on fresh bread with tender lettuce leaves, such as Boston or Bibb, or even baby kale. Any way you serve it, dill pickles on the side make it even better.

SERVES 4 TO 6

One 14- to 16-ounce tub firm tofu
1 large stalk celery, finely diced
1 scallion, finely chopped
1/3 cup vegan mayonnaise, Vegan Sour Cream (page 248),
    or Cashew Cream (page 249), or to taste
1 to 2 teaspoons prepared yellow mustard, or to taste
1 teaspoon good-quality curry powder, or more to taste
2 to 3 tablespoons nutritional yeast (optional but highly recommended)
1 tablespoon sweet pickle relish (optional)
Salt and freshly ground pepper to taste

1. Drain the tofu and cut into 6 slabs crosswise. Blot well between paper towels or clean kitchen towels (or use a tofu press). Place the tofu in a mixing bowl and mash well with a large fork or potato masher. Add the celery and scallion.

2. In a small bowl, combine the mayonnaise, mustard, curry powder, and yeast and relish, if desired. Mix well. Pour the mayonnaise mixture over the tofu mixture, stir well to combine, and season to taste with salt and pepper.

PER SERVING: Calories: 148; Total fat: 9g; Protein: 14g; Carbohydrates: 6g; Fiber: 3g; Sodium: 193mg

Complete the Meal

I prefer this as lunch fare, but there's no reason that it can't be dinner—it's easy and fast, either served in pitas or on fresh bread accompanied by soup. Try it with Cream of Broccoli Soup (page 132) or any of the Tomato-Vegetable Soup variations, pages 138–39. Add a simple green salad.

Homemade Baked Tofu

Packaged baked tofu is tasty and not all that expensive, but homemade baked tofu is even better. The trick to this chewy, savory transformation of bland white tofu is to make sure it's well pressed and to let it marinate for plenty of time. These baked tofu slices are so flavorful that you can serve them as a side dish, add them to the dinner plate for extra protein, or use them to make sandwiches on toast or rolls along with vegan mayonnaise and/or mustard and sprouts or dark green lettuce. They also make a fantastic addition to wraps.

SERVES 3 TO 4

One 14- to 16-ounce tub firm or extra-firm tofu (see Note)
¼ cup reduced-sodium natural soy sauce
¼ cup white wine, cooking sherry, vegetable broth, or water
1 tablespoon dark sesame oil
1 tablespoon agave nectar or other liquid sweetener
2 tablespoons rice vinegar or white wine vinegar
1 to 2 cloves garlic, crushed or minced (optional)
1 teaspoon grated fresh or jarred ginger, or more to taste
Fresh or dried thyme leaves (either regular or lemon thyme) or fresh or
    dried oregano leaves to taste (optional)

1. Drain the tofu and cut into 8 slabs crosswise. Blot well between paper towels or clean kitchen towels (or use a tofu press). Cut each slab into strips.

2. Combine the remaining ingredients in a small bowl and whisk together. Arrange the tofu slices in a single layer in a shallow container or baking dish and pour enough marinade over them to cover. Let stand for an hour or two—the longer the better.

3. Shortly before you'd like to bake the tofu, preheat the oven to 400ºF. If this is the only thing you're making, use a toaster oven—it's the perfect size. Remove the tofu slices from the marinade and transfer to a parchment-lined baking pan in a single layer. If you're using the full-size oven, roast some veggies at the same time (I like to use the excess marinade to roast eggplant or green beans).

4. Bake for 20 minutes, then turn the strips and bake for 15 to 20 minutes longer, or until the tofu is firm and starting to turn light brown along the edges.

note: If you want your baked tofu strips to be extra firm, you can place a cutting board over them and top it with some sort of weight. Then let the strips rest for 20 to 30 minutes or so. Or,

continued

although it's entirely optional, I particularly like to use my TofuXpress or EZ Tofu Press for this dish—it makes the tofu superfirm.

PER SERVING: Calories: 182; Total fat: 10g; Protein: 13g; Carbohydrates: 11g; Fiber: 1g; Sodium: 818mg

Variations

- Add 1 teaspoon liquid smoke (or more to taste) to the marinade for a subtle smoky flavor.
- Instead of baking, cook these tofu slices on a grill. About 5 minutes per side should do—make sure there are nice grill marks on each side.

Basic Hummus *with* Variations

Does the world need another recipe for hummus? Not really. This is a classic, not unlike many recipes you've already seen. But it's useful, and you'll find it in several other recipes and meal suggestions in this book. Besides, I don't want you to have to scurry off to another source mid-recipe to find a formula for hummus. And I've provided some variations below to lift this recipe out of the realm of the ordinary. A fantastic ingredient in wraps or pita sandwiches, hummus can be the centerpiece of your portable lunch as well—just pack some in a Thermos or insulated container and go.

MAKES ABOUT 2 CUPS

One 15- to 16-ounce can chickpeas, drained and rinsed
¼ cup tahini (sesame paste)
1 to 2 cloves garlic, crushed (optional)
Juice of ½ to 1 lemon, or to taste
½ teaspoon ground cumin
Salt and freshly ground pepper to taste
Paprika for garnish

Combine all ingredients except the paprika in a food processor. Add ⅓ cup water and process until smoothly pureed. Transfer to a serving container and sprinkle with paprika. Serve immediately or transfer to a storage container and refrigerate.

PER ½-CUP SERVING: Calories: 164; Total fat: 7g; Protein: 7g; Carbohydrates: 18g; Fiber: 6g; Sodium: 115mg

Variations

- This is nice made with white beans as well (use an equivalent amount). White bean hummus is milder and creamier than chickpea hummus, and once it's pureed, you can whirl in a small amount of pitted black or green olives and a bit of fresh dill or parsley for extra flavor.

- Add a modest amount of any one or two of the following ingredients for some fun and flavorful variations. Either chop finely and stir in by hand or add to the food processor once the hummus is smooth and pulse a few times to blend:

  Green or black pitted cured olives
  Wilted spinach
  Fresh dill
  Fresh parsley
  Roasted red bell pepper
  Artichoke hearts (marinated or non-marinated)
  Toasted pine nuts

Serving Suggestions

- Aside from its use in some of the wraps in this chapter, hummus, along with Quinoa Tabbouleh, is an important part of the Middle Eastern–inspired menu pictured on page 316.

- As lunchtime fare, or as an appetizer, team with triangles of fresh pita (or whole-grain pita chips) and carrots and/or celery sticks.

Leafy Greens Instead of Bread

If you're on a gluten-free diet or prefer a less bready way to enjoy sandwich-style meals, consider using a leafy receptacle for chunky cold spreads, such as those on pages 267 and 269.

Lettuce cups: Use lettuce leaves that have a natural bowl shape. Simply place a scoop of sandwich filling in the center; pick up, and eat as daintily as you can!

Cabbage cups: Bowl-shaped leaves of green cabbage work well, too—they're firmer and crunchier than lettuce leaves.

Collard leaves: Raw-food enthusiasts have discovered how useful collard leaves can be as wrappers. Not everyone will like the flavor, but those who do will love it. Rinse the leaves well. Cut the stem off close to the leaf. Lay the leaf on a surface with the rib side up and pare down the rib with a sharp knife or vegetable peeler so that the stem's depth is as close to the leaf's as possible. Arrange the filling down the center as you would on any other wrapper, and roll up snugly.

Burgers and Sloppy Joes

Quinoa *and* Red Lentil Burgers

Quinoa and red lentils cook in the same amount of time, right in the same saucepan, making these burgers superconvenient. See the photo on page 276 to view these burgers on their way to becoming picture-perfect!

MAKES 8 BURGERS

1 cup uncooked quinoa, rinsed in a fine sieve
1/2 cup dried red lentils
1 tablespoon salt-free all-purpose seasoning blend
1/4 cup quick-cooking oats or quinoa flakes
3 scallions, white and green parts, thinly sliced
2 teaspoons good-quality curry powder
1 teaspoon ground cumin
1 teaspoon sweet or smoked paprika
1/4 to 1/2 cup minced fresh cilantro or parsley
Crushed red pepper flakes or sriracha to taste
Salt and freshly ground pepper to taste
1 tablespoon extra-virgin olive oil (optional)
Whole-grain buns, pitas, or English muffins (optional)

1. Preheat the oven to 425ºF.

2. Combine the quinoa, lentils, seasoning blend, and oats in a medium saucepan with 3½ cups water. Bring to a rapid simmer; then add the scallions, curry powder, cumin, and paprika as the water is heating up.

3. Simmer gently until the water is absorbed and the quinoa and lentils are done, about 15 minutes. Stir in the cilantro, then season with red pepper flakes, salt, and pepper. Stir in the olive oil if desired for a little added richness.

4. Line a baking sheet with parchment paper. Coat the inside of a round 1/2-cup measuring cup (like the one in the photo on the facing page) with a little olive oil. Grab a level scoop of the quinoa mixture; invert it onto the parchment, and give the bottom a sharp tap to release it. Using the bottom of the measuring cup, flatten the quinoa mixture into a 1/2-inch-thick patty. Repeat with the remaining quinoa mixture; you should wind up with 8 patties.

5. If you don't have a round ½-cup measuring cup, you can improvise by using any sort of ½-cup measure and shaping the mounds into burgers once they're on the parchment paper.

6. Bake for 15 minutes, then carefully flip each burger and bake an additional 15 minutes, or until golden and firm on each side. Remove from the oven and serve the burgers on their own or with the bread of your choice.

PER BURGER: Calories: 130; Total fat: 1g; Protein: 6g; Carbohydrates: 24g; Fiber: 3g; Sodium: 20mg

Serving Suggestions

These burgers are tasty enough to stand on their own, but consider any two or three of the following embellishments—whether or not you're serving them on bread:

> Lettuce leaves, baby spinach or arugula, or baby kale (raw or barely wilted)
> Roasted red peppers
> Sliced tomatoes
> Sliced red onions
> Green sprouts
> Peeled and sliced avocado
> Quick Tartar Sauce (page 282) or ketchup and mustard

Complete the Meal

- Consider making one of the roasted vegetable recipes on pages 288–97 and baking it alongside the burgers as they cook in the oven. Add a green salad, one of the simple slaws (pages 322–25), or Creamy Kale and Cabbage Slaw (page 324).
- Serve with Sautéed Paprika Potatoes, as shown in the photo on page 276, or any of the other simple potato dishes on page 302. Any of the simple slaws (pages 322–25) will round this plate out nicely, too.

Quinoa and Red Lentil Burgers (page 274)

Beans *and* Greens Burgers

What better to make plant-powered burgers with than beans and greens? Their flavors, textures, and colors synergize beautifully and add up to one really tasty burger.

MAKES 8 OR 9 BURGERS

1 tablespoon extra-virgin olive oil or 2 tablespoons vegetable broth or water
1 medium onion, finely chopped
2 cloves garlic, minced
½ green or red bell pepper, finely chopped
2 cups cooked or one 15- to 16-ounce can (drained and rinsed) beans of your choice,
    such as black, white, red, pinto, or chickpeas
2 cups or so washed and finely chopped greens, such as regular or baby spinach,
    arugula, kale, chard, collards, or a combination
2 teaspoons good-quality chili powder, or to taste
1 teaspoon mesquite seasoning (optional but highly recommended)
Generous pinch of crushed red pepper flakes
¼ cup wheat germ or hemp seeds
Salt and freshly ground pepper to taste
Whole-grain buns, pitas, or English muffins (optional)

1. Preheat the oven to 425ºF.

2. Heat the oil, broth, or water in a large skillet. Add the onion and sauté over medium heat until translucent. Add the garlic and bell pepper and continue to sauté until the onion is golden.

3. Add the beans. Once heated, mash coarsely with a potato masher or large fork. Add the greens and a very small amount of water, cover, and steam until the greens are wilted and bright green.

4. Add the chili powder, mesquite seasoning (if desired), red pepper flakes, and wheat germ. Then season with salt and pepper.

5. Line a baking sheet with parchment paper. Coat the inside of a round ½-cup measuring cup (see photo on page 275) with a little olive oil. Grab a level scoop of the bean mixture; invert it onto the parchment, and give the bottom a sharp tap to release it. Using the bottom of the measuring cup, flatten the bean mixture into a ½-inch-thick patty. Repeat with the remaining bean mixture; you should wind up with 8 patties.

continued

6. If you don't have a round 1/2-cup measuring cup, you can improvise by using any sort of 1/2-cup measure and shaping the mounds into burgers once they're on the parchment paper.

7. Bake for 15 minutes, then carefully flip each burger and bake an additional 15 minutes, or until golden and firm on each side. Remove from the oven and serve the burgers on their own or with the bread of your choice.

PER BURGER: Calories: 95 with oil, 80 without oil; Total fat: 2g with oil, 1g without oil; Protein: 6g; Carbohydrates: 14g; Fiber: 5g; Sodium: 13mg

Variation

In place of the chili seasonings, take the flavor in the direction of curry. Use 2 teaspoons of good-quality curry powder and 1 teaspoon ground cumin to start, then step them up from there. Curry goes well with white beans and chickpeas; chili goes well with red and black beans. Either way, you can also make these spicier by adding 1 to 2 fresh hot chili peppers, seeded and minced.

Complete the Meal

Follow the serving suggestions following Quinoa and Red Lentil Burgers (page 274).

Pinto Bean *and* Quinoa Sloppy Joes

Seriously—who needs fake meat when you can make hearty, beautifully textured dishes using grains and beans? This serves up deliciously on rolls, but if you're not a bread person, you can serve the mixture in a lettuce-leaf cup or atop a corn tortilla.

SERVES 4 TO 6

½ cup uncooked quinoa, rinsed in a fine sieve
1 tablespoon extra-virgin olive oil or 3 tablespoons vegetable broth or water
1 medium onion, minced
½ medium green bell pepper, finely diced
1½ cups cooked or one 15- to 16-ounce can (drained and rinsed) pinto or
    red beans, coarsely mashed
One 15- to 16-ounce can tomato sauce or crushed tomatoes
1 tablespoon reduced-sodium natural soy sauce or tamari, or to taste
1 teaspoon agave nectar or maple syrup, or to taste
2 teaspoons good-quality chili powder, or more to taste
2 teaspoons sweet paprika
½ teaspoon dried oregano
4 to 6 whole-grain rolls or English muffins

1. Combine the quinoa with 1 cup water in a small saucepan. Bring to a slow boil, then lower the heat, cover, and simmer until the water is absorbed, about 15 minutes.

2. Meanwhile, heat the oil, broth, or water in a medium skillet. Add the onion and sauté until translucent. Add the bell pepper and sauté until both are golden.

3. Add the remaining ingredients except the bread of choice and bring to a gentle simmer. Cook over medium-low heat, loosely covered, for 5 to 7 minutes, stirring occasionally. Let the skillet stand off the heat for 5 minutes to allow the flavors to mingle further and the quinoa to absorb the tomato flavors.

4. Evenly spoon the filling over the bottoms of whole-grain rolls, cover with the tops, or serve open-faced.

PER SERVING: Calories: 252 with oil, 223 without oil; Total fat: 5g with oil, 2g without oil; Protein: 11g; Carbohydrates: 44g; Fiber: 9g; Sodium: 400mg

continued

Complete the Meal

- As shown in the photo below, this is delectable with Apple Slaw with Leafy Greens (page 325) and baked sweet potatoes.
- Keep this supersimple with stone-ground tortilla chips and salsa and a platter of raw veggies.

Pinto Bean and Quinoa Sloppy Joes

Smoky Lentil *and* Mushroom Sloppy Joes

Just as satisfying as the pinto bean and quinoa sloppy joe filling, this filling is ready in minutes if you have your lentils cooked ahead of time or if you use canned lentils. Smoky, spicy barbecue flavors add up to irresistible results.

SERVES 6

1 teaspoon extra-virgin olive oil or 1 tablespoon vegetable broth or water

2 cloves garlic, minced

6 to 8 ounces cremini (baby bella) mushrooms, chopped

3½ to 4 cups cooked or two 15- to 16-ounce cans (drained and rinsed) lentils

1 to 2 tablespoons reduced-sodium natural soy sauce or tamari

1 cup tomato sauce

2 tablespoons molasses or maple syrup

1 to 2 teaspoons smoked paprika or mesquite seasoning (see Note)

2 teaspoons sweet paprika

½ teaspoon dried thyme or oregano

2 to 3 scallions, white and green parts, thinly sliced

Freshly ground pepper to taste

6 whole-grain rolls or English muffins

1. Heat the oil, broth, or water in a large skillet. Add the garlic and sauté over low heat until golden.

2. Add the mushrooms, cover, and cook over medium heat until wilted, about 3 to 4 minutes.

3. Add the remaining ingredients except the rolls. Bring to a simmer, then cook over low heat, uncovered, for 10 to 15 minutes, or until everything is piping hot, the flavors melded, and the liquid thick enough to envelop the lentils and mushrooms nicely.

4. Evenly spoon the filling over the bottoms of whole-grain rolls, cover with the tops, or serve open-faced.

note: Neither smoked paprika nor mesquite seasoning is exotic any longer. You'll find them both in the spice aisle of your supermarket. Try the mesquite seasoning—it adds an intriguing flavor and aroma to hearty dishes.

PER SERVING: Calories: 211 with oil, 205 without oil; Total fat: 1g with oil, 1g without oil; Protein: 15g; Carbohydrates: 38g; Fiber: 12g; Sodium: 154mg

continued

Variation

I like to add some leafy greens toward the end of cooking time. Add narrow ribbons of stemmed lacinato kale, collards, or chard. Or just toss in some baby spinach or arugula. For good measure, I also like to add a tablespoon or two of nutritional yeast.

Complete the Meal

- As with the Pinto Bean and Quinoa Sloppy Joes, Apple Slaw with Leafy Greens (page 325) provides a refreshing note. Yukon gold or other yellow potatoes complement this nicely as well; you can simply serve them baked or microwaved in their jackets or make Sautéed Paprika Potatoes (page 302).
- Unless you're adding greens to the filling itself, any of the kale salads (pages 320–22) would be a welcome addition to this meal.

Simple Sandwich Spreads

Quick Tartar Sauce

This supereasy cold sauce is great as a spread for wraps or veggie burgers. It also makes an excellent dip for raw vegetable platters.

MAKES ABOUT 2/3 CUP

½ cup vegan mayonnaise, Vegan Sour Cream (page 248), or Cashew Cream (page 249)
1 tablespoon sweet pickle relish
2 teaspoons prepared yellow mustard, or to taste

Combine all ingredients in a small bowl and stir together until well blended. Store any leftovers in the refrigerator in a tightly covered container. This keeps well for a week or more.

PER TABLESPOON: Calories: 34; Total fat: 3g; Protein: 1g; Carbohydrates: 1g; Fiber: 0g; Sodium: 115mg

Thousand Island-ish Dressing

This basic dressing is almost embarrassingly simple, but it goes extremely well with veggie burgers and other sandwiches and is a must for the Smoky Tempeh and Avocado Reuben Sandwiches on page 265. I also remember it fondly as the first dressing that inspired my kids to take a few bites of salad from time to time.

MAKES ABOUT ¾ CUP

½ cup vegan mayonnaise, Vegan Sour Cream (page 248),
    or Cashew Cream (page 249)
¼ cup good-quality ketchup
1 tablespoon sweet pickle relish, or more to taste

Combine all ingredients in a small bowl and whisk together until smooth. Store any leftovers in the refrigerator in a tightly covered container. This keeps well for a week or more.

PER TABLESPOON: Calories: 33; Total fat: 2g; Protein: 1g; Carbohydrates: 2g; Fiber: 0g; Sodium: 135mg

More VEGGIE LOVE

SALAD AND VEGETABLE ENTRÉES AND SIDES

This chapter is a bit of a catchall, but it's an important one, because the subtext is "Eat more vegetables." And if that sounds a bit too stern, let's say, "Enjoy more veggies." As you've seen in the chapters leading up to this one, I'm a big believer in serving an array of vegetables as part of the evening meal—a great shift from the old paradigm of protein, starch, and one veg on the dinner plate. This paradigm shift can be accomplished with simple yet gorgeous raw kale salads, salads that combine raw and cooked ingredients (such as potato salads and quinoa salads), or vegetable dishes that might be called sides but that don't exactly sit demurely on the edge of the plate.

Vegan Niçoise-Style Salad (page 306)

As far as I know, there's no such thing as eating too many vegetables. No matter what your culinary persuasion is, chances are good that you can increase your intake of vegetables. Arguably more than any other food group, vegetables—especially if you count leafy greens—offer the greatest nutritional bonanza of vitamins, minerals, and antioxidants for the fewest calories. There aren't many other foods that you can practically binge on and feel quite virtuous as you're doing so!

This chapter doesn't aim to be a comprehensive guide to vegetable dishes, because there are lots more nearly recipe-free ideas for salads and sides throughout the book. Rather, this chapter presents recipes that can either serve as main dishes or side-by-side dishes—that is, when put together on the table, they make a nice centerpiece for a meal. This chapter also contains recipes for vegetable dishes that are frequently suggested as accompaniments in other chapters.

Finally, if you and your family aren't big salad fans, this chapter might help change that. Emerging salad eaters as well as died-in-the-wool salad aficionados will find much to love here, from composed salad platters to quinoa salads; from simple slaws to massaged kale. Though I don't specify it in the recipes, I do encourage the use of organic vegetables, fruits, and other salad ingredients as much as possible. If you can't buy organic 100 percent of the time, consult the list of the Dirty Dozen and the Clean Fifteen on pages 58–59 to learn where to draw the line.

Glorious Greens: A Few Simple Ways to Prepare Them

Leafy greens are used throughout every chapter of this book, in practically every category. You'll find even more recipes later in this chapter, particularly in the way of massaged kale salads (pages 320–22) and two variations of tasty kale slaws (pages 324–25). But if you've brought home a big bunch of kale from your farm market or CSA farm—or if you grow it in your own garden—and you want to cook it down and use it simply, garlicky greens are about as classic a preparation as you'll find.

Garlicky Hardy Greens: You'll want to serve this basic preparation with all sorts of meals. Use a large bunch—12 to 16 ounces—of any kind of hardy greens. The ones you'll likely reach for most often are kale, collards, and chard. But consider other worthy contenders in this category, all of which might be described as pleasantly bitter: escarole, mustard greens, and broccoli rabe. Here are the steps:

1. Wash the greens of your choice well and cut the leaves away from the stems. Then cut the leaves into ribbons or bite-size pieces. Note that kale and chard stems can be thinly sliced and used in the sauté if you like; collard stems are tough and should be discarded. If you're preparing escarole or mustard greens, cut through the soft middle ribs as you're cutting the leaves into ribbons—the ribs are edible.

2. Heat a tablespoon of extra-virgin olive oil (or 2 to 3 tablespoons of vegetable broth or water) in a large pan. Sauté a few cloves of minced garlic until golden. Add the greens and just a little broth or water—just enough to keep the bottom of the pan moist. Cover and cook for 2 to 3 minutes, at which point the greens should be wilted.

3. Uncover and sprinkle in a little salt, which will help the greens retain their color. Cook until tender, but don't overdo it—the greens should still stay nice and bright. Press down on the greens to extract any excess liquid, then drain the liquid from the pan.

4. Season to taste with more salt, if necessary, then add freshly ground pepper and/or crushed red pepper flakes to taste. If you like, you can brighten up the flavor a bit more with any of the following:

   Freshly squeezed or bottled lemon or lime juice
   Apple cider vinegar
   Chopped briny black olives
   Sun-dried tomatoes, cut into strips
   Toasted slivered almonds
   Sesame seeds

Consider dressing up this simple formula in any of the following ways:

Creamed Greens: Puree a 12.3-ounce box of silken tofu in a food processor. Add the finished garlicky greens and pulse and until they're finely chopped and completely integrated with the tofu—but not pureed. Return to a gentle heat and stir in a small amount of minced fresh dill if desired.

Tahini-Lemon Greens: This is one of my favorite ways to dress up simply cooked greens. I just love what the flavor of tahini does for greens. To dress 12 to 16 ounces of greens, combine the following in a small mixing bowl: ⅓ cup tahini, juice of 1 lemon, 2 tablespoons each reduced-sodium natural soy sauce or tamari and agave nectar or other liquid sweetener. Add ¼ to ½ cup water—this will vary greatly depending on the consistency of the tahini. More water will be needed if the tahini is dense and dry. Whisk together. You want the consistency to be fluid but not thin. Stir into finished garlicky greens.

Greens in Nut Butter Sauce: This definitely steps up the yum factor when it comes to greens. Stir about half a recipe of Peanut or Cashew Butter Sauce (page 219) into finished garlicky greens. You want the greens to be nicely enveloped in the sauce but not drowning in it.

Roasted Vegetable Dishes: A Few Tips and Easy Ideas

Roasting vegetables in a hot oven brings their natural sugars to the surface while maintaining their nutrients. If you and yours aren't that keen on steamed or uncooked veggies in the cool months, you may find that roasted veggies are more tempting.

Root vegetables are ideal for roasting due to their natural sugars, but lots of other vegetables fare well with this technique. I've found 425°F to be the ideal temperature for my oven, but 400°F works as well, too. If I have anything else in the oven at either of those temperatures, I try to toss in some vegetables to roast at the same time. Once vegetables are roasted, they're good warm or at room temperature. Leftover roasted vegetables can be used to make wraps or to top pizza. Here are a few tips for coming up with your own combinations.

1. Use vegetables of similar density together, or at least add soft vegetables halfway through the baking time. For example, sweet potato would be good to roast with winter squash, but if you combine sweet potato with zucchini, the latter will be mushy before the sweet potato is done. Broccoli and cauliflower are good to roast together. So are zucchini or yellow squash and sections of asparagus.

2. Cut vegetables into somewhat-larger-than-bite-size pieces.

3. Toss vegetables with a tablespoon or two of olive oil, just enough to coat the surfaces lightly.

4. Scatter onto a lightly oiled or parchment-lined roasting pan in a single layer.

5. Bake at 400ºF to 425ºF, stirring every 10 minutes or so and keeping an eye on them as they're roasting, until slightly crisp and touched with brown on the outside and tender on the inside.

Maple-Roasted Baby Carrots: This is one of the easiest and most delightful things you can do with carrots—and it's a good bet that kids will love this. Combine a 16-ounce bag of baby carrots with about a quarter cup of maple syrup. Add a tablespoon or so of safflower or sesame oil or melted Earth Balance (a vegan buttery spread) for a little richer flavor. Sprinkle in some cinnamon, toss well to coat, and roast in a 400ºF to 425ºF oven for about 20 minutes, or until the carrots are tender. Once the carrots are out of the oven, you can add some chopped walnuts or pecans and/or sliced dried fruit, such as Turkish apricots.

Cauliflower with Bread Crumbs: Even those who think they don't like cauliflower might fall in love with this roasted rendition. Cut a medium head of cauliflower into bite-size pieces and florets. Place in a large bowl and drizzle with a small amount of olive oil. Sprinkle with salt and pepper and toss together. Arrange in a roasting pan (parchment-lined, if you wish). Roast in a 400ºF to 425ºF oven for 15 minutes. Meanwhile, whirl two medium slices of whole-grain bread in a food processor (or use one slice of bread and a half cup of walnuts or pecans) until the mixture is reduced to fine crumbs. Stir the cauliflower and sprinkle it evenly with the crumbs. Continue to roast until the cauliflower is tender-crisp and touched with brown spots, about 10 to 15 minutes longer.

Cruciferous Combo: Cut about half a medium head of cauliflower and a broccoli crown or two into bite-size florets. Cut the broccoli a little larger than the cauliflower to equalize the baking time. Place in a large bowl and drizzle with a small amount of olive oil. Sprinkle with salt and pepper and toss together. Arrange in a roasting pan (parchment-lined, if you wish). Roast in a 400ºF to 425ºF oven for 25 to 30 minutes, stirring once or twice during that time, or until lightly browned. Season with salt and freshly ground pepper.

Roasted Brussels Sprouts: Roasting these tiny cabbages has converted many a brussels sprouts naysayer. Trim the stem ends of about a pound of brussels sprouts. Cut them in half and toss with a small amount of olive oil. Roast in a 400ºF to 425ºF oven for about 20 to 25 minutes, stirring once or twice, or until lightly browned. To vary this, add a cup or two of baby carrots for a colorful medley. Season with salt and freshly ground pepper.

Roasted Sesame Asparagus: Trim off about an inch from the bottoms of medium-thick asparagus spears; peel the bottom halves of the spears if the skin looks thick. Arrange on a lightly oiled baking pan and drizzle with sesame oil. Sprinkle with sesame seeds. Roast in a preheated 400°F to 425°F oven or toaster oven until tender and lightly browned, stirring occasionally, about 15 to 20 minutes.

Garlic and Rosemary Roasted Potatoes: Scrub a few medium yellow potatoes or peel three or four medium sweet potatoes. Or use some of each. Cut into quarter-inch-thick slices, thick wedges, or bite-size chunks. In a mixing bowl, toss with about a tablespoon of olive oil. Transfer to a roasting pan. Roast in a preheated 400°F to 425°F oven for 15 minutes. Stir in a few cloves of chopped garlic and the leaves from two to three sprigs fresh rosemary. Roast for 10 minutes longer, or until the potatoes are golden and crisp. Season with salt and pepper and serve.

Roasted Sweet Potatoes or Butternut Squash with Apples or Pears: Roasting naturally sweet orange vegetables with apples or pears is a cool-weather treat. Peel three or four medium sweet potatoes, then cut into quarter-inch-thick slices, thick wedges, or bite-size chunks. If you're using butternut squash, follow the directions for prebaking on page 298, then cut into bite-size chunks. Arrange vegetables in a parchment-lined roasting pan; roast in a preheated 400°F to 425°F oven for 15 minutes.

Add two to four medium crisp apples or firm pears (depending on how many you're serving and how much you like roasted fruit), cut to match the sweet potatoes or squash. You can peel them or not, as you like. Drizzle in two to three tablespoons maple syrup or blackstrap molasses, sprinkle in some cinnamon and nutmeg, and give the mixture a good stir. Bake for 15 minutes longer, or until everything is tender and lightly browned in spots. This is delicious served with the Brown and Wild Rice Pilaf on page 109.

Roasted Butternut Squash with Greens: Prebake a butternut squash as directed on page 298. Cut into chunks and arrange in a parchment-lined roasting pan. Drizzle with a tablespoon or so of olive oil and roast in a preheated 400°F to 425°F oven for 20 minutes. Stir in a generous portion of thinly sliced collard greens or kale and continue to roast for 10 minutes longer, or until the squash is tender and lightly browned in spots. Season to taste with savory or sweet herbs and spices.

Roasted Beets: Even those who say they don't like beets might change their minds when they taste the vegetables served this way; those who like beets will love this dish. Peeling and cutting raw beets is a bit of a mess, so I like to partially cook or microwave them ahead of time, which makes it a breeze (see the Note on page 293). Place prepped beets (allow one medium beet per serving) in a parchment-lined baking dish and drizzle with a bit of olive oil. Bake at 400°F or 425°F for 20 to 30 minutes, or until tender to your liking. Stir once or twice during that time. Beets are nice roasted with other root vegetables, including carrots and sweet potatoes, as in the recipe for Roasted Root Vegetables (page 293).

Roasted Butternut Squash with Greens (page 290)

Roasted Root Vegetables on a bed of lentils

Roasted Root Vegetables

Oven-roasting brings out the natural sweetness of many vegetables, and this is particularly true in the case of root vegetables. You can vary the vegetables suggested here as well as the quantities. And do explore the variations and ways to serve this, both as a main dish and salad. As you're slicing and cutting the vegetables, make sure everything is a uniform thickness—about half an inch—to ensure even roasting.

SERVES 4 TO 6

1 large sweet potato, peeled, cut in half lengthwise, and sliced
2 medium beets (red or golden), peeled and cut into bite-size chunks (see Note)
3 to 4 medium carrots, peeled and cut into ½-inch-thick slices, or about 1 cup baby carrots
2 to 3 medium parsnips, peeled and cut into ½-inch-thick slices
1 large or 2 medium turnips, peeled and cut into large chunks
1 tablespoon extra-virgin olive oil
2 tablespoons maple syrup, blackstrap molasses, or agave nectar
Pinch each of ground cinnamon and nutmeg
Fresh rosemary leaves to taste (optional)
Salt and freshly ground pepper to taste

1. Preheat the oven to 425ºF.

2. Combine all the vegetables in a large mixing bowl.

3. Drizzle in the oil and maple syrup, then sprinkle in the cinnamon and nutmeg. Stir together.

4. Transfer the mixture to a lightly oiled large roasting pan (lined with parchment if you like). Bake for 30 minutes, more or less, stirring every 10 minutes or so. The vegetables should be tender on the inside and touched with golden brown on the outside.

5. Toward the end of the cooking time, sprinkle on some fresh rosemary leaves, if desired. Season with salt and pepper; then transfer to a covered serving container. Serve immediately or keep warm until mealtime.

note: Peeling raw beets is challenging. Partially cooking them, either in a saucepan with just enough water to cover or in the microwave (about 2 minutes per raw beet), really helps. Cook just until you can poke through about a quarter inch into the beet with a knife. Let the beets cool to room temperature (if you need to expedite this, plunge them into a bowl of ice water). To minimize the mess when cutting, peel the beets over the trash or compost container, then slice or chop them on a cutting board covered with wax paper.

PER SERVING: Calories: 196; Total fat: 4g; Protein: 3g; Carbohydrates: 40g; Fiber: 8g; Sodium: 133mg

continued

Variations

- Though they break the root veggie theme, brussels sprouts and/or thinly sliced red onions are terrific additions, lending a nice contrasting flavor and color.

- Stir in ribbons of collards or lacinato kale about 10 minutes before the vegetables are done.

- Experiment with other root veggies, including ordinary white or yellow potatoes, Jerusalem artichokes, Chioggia beets, rutabagas, and daikon.

Complete the Meal

- To make this a main dish, serve on a bed of cooked brown or green lentils, as shown in the photo on page 292, or on a bed of quinoa mixed with black or small red beans. This meal is delicious served with the Middle Eastern (Fattouche) variation in "Tossed Salads Go Global," page 318.

- Like Roasted Ratatouille (page 296), this can be transformed into a delicious salad. Let the vegetables cool, then toss them with a splash of extra-virgin olive oil and balsamic or wine vinegar or any of the variations of Basic Vinaigrette, page 327. Give the salad a little crunch with sliced red bell peppers. Serve with Sweet and Smoky Beans and Greens (page 92) or Lemon and Garlic Beans or Lentils (page 94).

- Serve with any of the baked versions in "Simple Preparations for Tofu, Tempeh, and Seitan" (pages 79–80), which you can have in the oven at the same time.

Barbecue-Flavored Roasted Vegetables
with Protein Options

This dish is bold and flavorful yet somehow also comforting. If advance planning is possible, make the barbecue sauce and have the vegetables prepped ahead of time. Then, when ready to bake, just prepare your protein option, toss everything together, and bake.

SERVES 4 TO 6

One of the following protein options:

> One 14- to 16-ounce tub extra-firm tofu
> Two 8-ounce packages tempeh (any variety), diced
> 16 ounces seitan, cut into bite-size chunks
> 2 cups cooked or canned (drained and rinsed) chickpeas or white beans

1 large broccoli crown or ½ medium cauliflower, cut into bite-size florets
1 large red bell pepper, cut into wide strips
1 cup baby carrots
1 medium red or yellow onion, halved and thinly sliced
4 to 6 ounces small whole baby bella (cremini) mushrooms
1 cup No-Cook Barbecue Sauce (page 86) or store-bought natural barbecue sauce, plus more to finish, if desired

1. Preheat the oven to 425ºF. If using tofu, drain the tofu and cut into 6 slabs crosswise. Blot well between paper towels or clean kitchen towels (or use a tofu press), then cut each slab into dice. Combine with remaining ingredients in a mixing bowl. If using tempeh, seitan, or beans, stir all the ingredients together in a mixing bowl.

2. Transfer the mixture to a foil-lined, parchment-lined, or lightly oiled roasting pan. Bake for 15 minutes, then stir. Bake for 10 to 15 minutes longer, or until the vegetables are tender but not overdone. Transfer to a covered serving container. If you'd like this a bit saucier, add a little more barbecue sauce, then serve.

PER SERVING WITH TOFU: Calories: 190; Total fat: 7g; Protein: 15g; Carbohydrates: 24g; Fiber: 6g; Sodium: 220mg

PER SERVING WITH TEMPEH: Calories: 334; Total fat: 11g; Protein: 25g; Carbohydrates: 38g; Fiber: 15g; Sodium: 220mg

PER SERVING WITH SEITAN: Calories: 254; Total fat: 3g; Protein: 32g; Carbohydrates: 28g; Fiber: 7g; Sodium: 640mg

PER SERVING WITH BEANS: Calories: 228; Total fat: 3g; Protein: 12g; Carbohydrates: 45g; Fiber: 12g; Sodium: 220mg

continued

Variations

- Use other vegetables in place of the ones listed above. Consider potatoes, sweet potatoes, and winter squash, all about halfway cooked or baked, then peeled and cut into bite-size chunks.

- Sliced zucchini or yellow squash work, too, though I suggest adding them halfway through, when you do the stirring, as they take less time to bake than the other vegetables.

Complete the Meal

- If you aren't using potatoes or sweet potatoes, this goes well with Garlic and Rosemary Roasted Potatoes, page 290. They and the other vegetables can—conveniently—be in the oven at the same time. Apple Slaw with Leafy Greens (page 325) is a good salad to serve with this.

- This can be served over quinoa, brown rice, or other grains. One of the cool-season variations in "Fruity, Nutty Mixed Greens Salads" (see page 326) is a nice way to round out the meal.

Roasted Ratatouille

The veggies that make the classic famous French stew called ratatouille so delicious are transported to a hot oven for similarly delectable results. This flexible dish can be enjoyed in a number of ways, either warm or at room temperature. Leftovers make delicious wraps—spread the wraps with vegan mayonnaise, hummus, or pesto, then add plenty of leafy salad greens.

SERVES 4 TO 6

2 Japanese eggplants or 1 medium eggplant

1 medium onion, preferably red, halved and thinly sliced

2 to 3 cloves garlic, minced

1 medium red bell pepper, cut into ½-inch-thick slices

¼ cup vinaigrette, homemade (page 327) or store-bought, plus more to finish

1 medium zucchini, sliced ½ inch thick

2 medium ripe fresh tomatoes, diced

¼ to ½ cup sliced pitted briny black olives (such as kalamata)

Salt and freshly ground pepper to taste

¼ to ½ cup thinly sliced fresh basil leaves, minced fresh parsley, or a combination

1. Preheat the oven to 425ºF.

2. If using Japanese eggplants, stem them and slice ½ inch thick. If using regular eggplant, stem and cut into ½-inch-thick slices. Cut each slice into large dice.

3. Combine the eggplant in a mixing bowl with the onion, garlic, and bell pepper. Drizzle in the vinaigrette and stir together.

4. Transfer to a lightly oiled or parchment-lined roasting pan. Bake for 10 minutes, then stir in the zucchini. Bake for 15 to 20 minutes longer, stirring occasionally, or until the vegetables are tender but still firm and just beginning to brown.

5. Transfer back to the mixing bowl. Stir in the tomatoes and olives, then season with salt and pepper. Stir in the fresh herbs. Serve warm or at room temperature.

PER SERVING: Calories: 120; Total fat: 8g; Protein: 2g; Carbohydrates: 13g; Fiber: 4g; Sodium: 100mg

Complete the Meal

- Combine with about 8 ounces cooked pasta, as shown in the middle photo, for a warm or cold dish. Use additional vinaigrette as needed. Serve with Marinated Bean Salad, page 313.

- Serve over soft polenta. Round the meal out with a simple bean dish such as Marinated Bean Salad (page 313) or Lemon and Garlic Beans or Lentils, page 94. If you go with the latter, add a simple salad.

- Serve atop salad greens; stir some chickpeas into the veggies to make a substantial warm salad, as shown in the bottom photo. Make Garlic and Rosemary Roasted Potatoes (page 290) at the same time as an accompaniment.

How to Tame Winter Squashes

I'm a bit embarrassed to admit this, but until just a few years ago, winter squashes in my house were more likely to be used as kitchen decor (a job for which they're well suited during the late fall and winter) than as standard dinner fare. That's because when a recipe instructed me to "peel and dice a butternut squash" (or any other hard winter variety), I'd feel quite inadequate. My knives are pretty good, but I always felt like I needed to borrow my husband's chain saw to do the job.

Then, as I started to give more talks about recipes and food, I found that a lot of cooks shared my little secret. So I developed a completely lazy way to tackle the winter squash dilemma. I've demonstrated this in the photos on the facing page with a butternut squash, but it works for any kind of hard squash.

A proliferation of squash varieties seems to have emerged over the past few years. Previously, butternut, acorn, and sugar pumpkin were the primary choices, but now you're likely to encounter golden acorn (a sweeter, smoother cousin of the dark green acorn squash), banana squash, delicata, turban, Hubbard, and more.

Winter squashes are nutrient-dense as well as delicious and versatile. Their cheery color and smooth texture bring great comfort to cool-weather meals. Now that I know how to tame them, they're a frequent part of my fall and winter repertoire, instead of just sitting on the table looking pretty.

Here is the secret to avoiding the squash struggle:

1. Wrap the entire squash in aluminum foil and place in a casserole dish.

2. Bake at 375°F. Small squashes will take about 30 minutes; large squashes, such as butternut and sugar pumpkin, will take 45 minutes or slightly more. You should be able to just pierce through the skin and flesh with a knife—a couple of inches for large squashes, about an inch for small ones.

3. Once the squash is cool enough to handle, cut it in half and scoop out the seeds and fibers.

4. Cut the squash into thick slices, then peel and cut into large dice or chunks—whatever is called for in the recipe. Use as directed, or continue to roast in combination with other vegetables. If you're using small squashes like acorn, one way to prepare them is to leave the halves intact and stuff the cavities with grain or bean dishes (see Chili-Stuffed Winter Squash, page 143). The photo on page 291 shows Roasted Butternut Squash with Greens (page 290).

The Potato Chronicles

Many recipes in cookbooks and articles (including my own, alas!) simply call for potatoes in a generic way—e.g., "4 medium potatoes"—without specifying any particular variety. While it's true that potatoes are fairly interchangeable, each variety has unique characteristics.

Russet potatoes are usually fairly large and oval in shape, with thick brown skin and ivory-colored flesh. Because of their soft, mealy texture (indicating a high starch content), these are best for baking, mashing, or smashing. They work well in soups, especially those in which you want the potato to break down and thicken the stock. But they don't hold their shape well in other dishes, such as potato salad, hash browns, and other sautéed skillet dishes.

Yellow-fleshed potatoes such as Yukon gold and yellow Finn have firm flesh, sometimes referred to as "waxy." In other words, they're lower in starch than russet and white potatoes. These work well when you want the potatoes to hold their shape, as in potato salads, oven fries, and other roasted vegetable and skillet dishes. They work well in soups and stews, and if cooked or baked thoroughly, they work just as well as russets for baking, smashing, and mashing. These are my favorite all-purpose potatoes; they're a little more flavorful than red-skinned or all-purpose white potatoes, and the golden hue of the flesh is appealing.

Red-skinned potatoes, like yellow-fleshed potatoes, also fall into the category of waxy, low-starch potatoes. Use them for the same purposes.

White all-purpose potatoes such as white rose fall somewhere between mealy and waxy and often have a thin skin. While these really do work for most purposes, they're on the bland side.

Fingerling, blue, tiny new potatoes, and other specialty varieties are fun as a change of pace. Fingerlings are, as the name implies, small, finger-shaped potatoes, and blue potatoes have dramatic purplish-blue flesh that adds visual flair to your potato dishes. New potatoes are tiny young potatoes that are anywhere from one to two inches in diameter. Not surprisingly, these unusual varieties are more expensive than their common counterparts.

Potatoes on the Side

Easy Hash Brown Potatoes

This versatile, variable dish has been a favorite in my family for eons. We especially like it for Sunday brunch, made with the tofu variation below and served with a simple Israeli-style salad of tomatoes, cucumbers, and peppers. Without the tofu, this is a perfect companion to many of the variations of Tofu and Veggie Scrambles, page 82.

SERVES 6

5 to 6 medium-large yellow-fleshed or red-skinned potatoes, baked or
    microwaved and cooled to room temperature
2 tablespoons extra-virgin olive oil
1 medium onion, finely chopped
1 medium red bell pepper, finely diced
1 teaspoon sweet or smoked paprika, or more to taste
Salt and freshly ground pepper to taste

1. Peel and dice the potatoes. You can do a medium or fine dice, depending on how you like your hash browns.

2. Heat the oil in a large skillet. Add the onion and sauté over medium heat until translucent. Add the bell pepper and continue to sauté until the onion is golden.

3. Add the potatoes and sauté, stirring frequently, until the mixture is hot and golden brown. If it seems dry, add a small amount of water to the skillet. Season with paprika, salt, and pepper. Serve from the skillet.

PER SERVING: Calories: 197; Total fat: 5g; Protein: 3g; Carbohydrates: 37g; Fiber: 3g; Sodium: 9mg

Variations

- **Make it with sweet potatoes:** Replace any or all of the potatoes with sweet potatoes. Like yellow-fleshed or red-skinned potatoes, sweet potatoes should be baked or microwaved until done but still nice and firm. Mushy sweet potatoes don't hold their shape too well in hash browns, so watch them carefully!

- **Use a different kind of onion:** Instead of onion, add a medium chopped and well-washed leek (white and palest green parts only) along with the bell pepper; or add 2 or 3 thinly sliced scallions (white and palest green parts only) once the potatoes start turning golden and crisp.

- **Tofu and potato hash browns:** Dice 8 to 16 ounces drained and very well blotted (or pressed) extra-firm tofu and add it at the same time as the potatoes.

- **Add leafy greens:** Greens are great in this dish. Add well-rinsed, stemmed, and thinly sliced kale or collards at the same time as the potatoes. Or use a couple of big handfuls of baby spinach or arugula—up to 4 ounces. Add the greens once everything is done; place them over the potato mixture in the skillet, a bit at a time if need be, cover, and allow them to wilt down. Then stir in.

- **Make it "meaty":** Add half a recipe of Smoky Tempeh Strips (page 268), cut into small pieces, toward the end of cooking time. Or add 1 to 2 links good-quality vegan sausage, such as Tofurky or Field Roast (cut into small dice), once the onion is translucent.

Three Easy Potato Side Dishes

Sautéed Paprika Potatoes*:* This is one of my favorite easy potato side dishes. Red-skinned or yellow-fleshed potatoes work best for this. Cook, bake, or microwave as many potatoes as you like (allowing one good-size potato per average eater) until done but still firm. Plunge into a bowl of ice water. When cool enough to handle, peel and slice the potatoes about half an inch thick. Sauté in a skillet that holds them comfortably with a small amount of olive oil over medium-high heat. When the potatoes begin to turn golden, add lots of sliced scallions and a generous sprinkling of sweet or smoked paprika. Continue to sauté, stirring occasionally, until the potatoes brown lightly.

Barbecue-Flavored Potato Skillet: Cook, bake, or microwave as many potatoes as you like (allowing one good-size potato per average eater) until done but still firm. Plunge into a bowl of ice water. When cool enough to handle, peel and slice the potatoes about half an inch thick or cut into bite-size chunks. Heat a small amount of olive oil in a large skillet. Sauté a quartered and thinly sliced large onion over medium heat until golden. Add the potatoes. Cook over medium-high heat, stirring often, until the potatoes start turning golden. Add one-half to one cup No-Cook Barbecue Sauce from page 86 (or your favorite natural prepared brand), depending on how many potatoes you're using. Cook for four to five minutes longer over medium heat.

Potato or Sweet Potato Oven Fries or Wedges: Use one large or two medium potatoes or sweet potatoes per person (preferably red-skinned, Yukon gold, or another firm-fleshed variety), or allow one large sweet potato for every two servings. Peel the potatoes or sweet potatoes and cut them into long, fry-shaped strips about half an inch thick, or cut small potatoes into wedges (quarter them, then cut each quarter in half). Combine the cut potatoes in a large mixing bowl with a modest amount of olive oil and toss well to coat. Transfer to a nonstick baking sheet and sprinkle with a little salt. Bake in a preheated 425°F oven, stirring gently every 10 minutes, until the potatoes are crisp and lightly browned, about 20 to 30 minutes. Serve at once. Note that this is also an excellent way to prepare sweet potatoes.

Sweet Potatoes

Let's set the record straight first, as the confusion over the difference between sweet potatoes and yams seems ever-present. Sweet potatoes are potatoes that have smooth, bright orange flesh. Yams are starchy tubers that have mealy yellow flesh and are actually much less commonly available. Often they'll be longer and narrower than sweet potatoes, with deep-red skin. They're not bad if you like mealy potatoes, but if you buy them with the expectation that they're sweet potatoes, as I've done a few times, you may be disappointed.

Sometimes sweet potatoes are sold as "southern yams" and recommended for use in classic recipes (e.g., candied yams), but "yams" is a misnomer. Adding to the confusion is that there are many varieties of sweet potatoes whose name includes the word "yam." Garnet yams, for example, actually are sweet potatoes (if you ever see them at the market, get some and try them—they're really good and extra sweet!).

The bright orange flesh of sweet potatoes heralds their rich nutritional content—they're a good source of vitamin C, beta-carotene (an antioxidant that converts into vitamin A), and several minerals, notably, potassium. They're also a good source of fiber. Sweet potatoes have so much going for them that I recommend using them often as a side dish, just as they are. A modest dab of vegan buttery spread is often embellishment enough.

Did you know that sweet potatoes are actually quite good raw, too? You can peel them, thinly slice them, and use the slices as a tool for scooping up dip, or you can grate them or finely dice them and add them to salads. The flavor is like that of a sweet, slightly creamy carrot.

Smashed Potatoes

Twice-baked potatoes, also known as stuffed potatoes, seem like they'd be an easy thing to prepare for quick meals. They look so enticing and have "comfort food" written all over them. But if you're preparing them for several people, the process can be tedious. Let's say you start with four big baked potatoes. You have to neatly scoop out eight centers just so, leaving not too thin or thick a shell. Then you need to mash and combine the scooped-out flesh with other ingredients that have been prepped and cooked. The resulting mixture must then be stuffed neatly back into the potato shells (with the hope that you didn't add in too many or too few additional ingredients). And finally, it all needs to be heated up in some way—hence, "twice baked."

Smashed potatoes, on the other hand, are far easier to prepare. The nooks and crannies created by smashing will readily accommodate all manner of toppings. There's no need for measuring or mixing or to be particularly neat. And sweet potatoes are just as good for smashing as white or yellow-fleshed potatoes—perhaps even better.

Smashed potatoes can be the main event of a light meal if you serve them with a hearty salad. Any of the variations of Marinated Bean Salad (page 313) work beautifully; another fun pairing is with the Taco Salad variation in "Tossed Salads Go Global" (page 319). As part of a larger meal, you can serve smashed potatoes with one of the simple skillet bean dishes on pages 92–97 or any of the simple preparations for tofu, tempeh, and seitan on pages 79–80. A simple salad or slaw would complete those pairings.

Here are the basic steps:

1. Use large potatoes (yellow-fleshed potatoes are my favorite for this, though russets work, too) or sweet potatoes, allowing one-half to one whole potato per person, depending on what else is being served. Scrub the potatoes well, because you'll be serving them with their skins on. Of course, you can eat the skins if the potatoes are organic and you can get the skins really clean.

2. Bake or microwave the potatoes until they can be easily pierced with a fork. Cut the potatoes in half lengthwise. Arrange cut side up on a platter or in a baking dish, depending on whether you'll be reheating them in the microwave or in the oven. Or, if you're making this just for one person, simply arrange the potato on a heatproof dinner plate.

3. Smash each potato half with a potato masher. Press the masher nearly all the way through the potato. Some large potatoes, such as russets, are a bit mealy, so drizzling a bit of rice milk over their surfaces before adding the toppings can improve the consistency. You can add extra richness by working some vegan buttery spread into the nooks (about half a teaspoon per potato half is sufficient).

4. Now the fun begins—arrange toppings generously on each potato or sweet potato half. Finally, if need be, reheat in the microwave or in a 350ºF oven before serving.

Here are some topping ideas—in the form of what I call semirecipes—to get you started, whether you're making a meal for one person or several people. And remember that having your potatoes or sweet potatoes prebaked means you can make a nearly instant meal just when you need it.

Broccoli and Cheddar: Sprinkle grated vegan Cheddar cheese over the surfaces of the smashed potatoes, followed by finely chopped and steamed broccoli florets. For a nice flavor boost, top with a sprinkling of scallions, chopped black olives, or sun-dried tomatoes.

Mushroom and Wilted Spinach: Clean and slice a few brown mushrooms (such as shiitake or baby bella) and place in a skillet with a small amount of water—just enough to coat the surface. Cover and cook until done to your liking. Depending on how many potatoes you'd like to top, add baby spinach (or baby arugula) to the skillet in batches, then cover and cook each time until just wilted. Season gently with salt and pepper. Use a little of the liquid that has formed in the skillet to moisten the potatoes' surfaces, then top with the mushroom-and-spinach mixture. If you like, add a zigzag of sriracha as a final flourish.

Mushroom Gravy and Parsley: Ladle the mushroom variation of Basic Gravy (page 87) over your smashed potatoes and top with a generous sprinkling of minced fresh parsley. Mmm . . . such comfort!

Chili-Topped: Smother your potatoes with leftover chili (any that you have on hand, or see the recipes on pages 140–41). Have it just as it is or top with minced cilantro, a dollop of salsa, and/or a sprinkling of vegan Cheddar cheese. This is excellent on sweet potatoes as well as on white or yellow-fleshed potatoes.

Pizza-Flavored: Using potatoes instead of a bread-based crust can become a family-style tradition. Simply spoon some marinara sauce over the surface of the potatoes, followed by a sprinkling of mozzarella-style grated vegan cheese. Then pile on your favorite pizza-compatible veggies (finely chopped and lightly steamed)—any combination of broccoli florets, mushrooms, bell peppers, eggplant, zucchini, and olives. Finish with a dusting of dried oregano.

Onion and Peppers: Follow the simple formula for making Caramelized Onions with Bell Peppers on page 88. This is wonderful on yellow-fleshed or sweet potatoes, topped with a sprinkling of chopped briny black olives.

Nut Butter and Veggie: Top smashed sweet potatoes with Peanut or Cashew Butter Sauce (page 219) and any kind of steamed leafy greens you have on hand—this is particularly good with spinach, baby kale, or any chard variety. For extra excitement, top with finely diced avocado and/or minced fresh hot chilies. This is a favorite of mine!

Main Dish Salads

Vegan Niçoise-Style Salad

Salade niçoise is a beautifully composed salad of French origin that looks fancy but is incredibly easy to make. The traditional version is often made with tuna, but here the fish is replaced with baked tofu, which makes a great stand-in. And the array of ingredients—white beans or chickpeas, slender green beans, tomatoes, and olives—makes it a splendid main dish salad for a summer meal, either on busy weeknights or festive occasions.

SERVES 4 TO 6

8 to 10 ounces fresh slender green beans, trimmed (see Note)
1 large head Boston or Bibb lettuce, torn, or mixed baby greens
Sliced fresh basil or chopped fresh parsley to taste
One 8-ounce package baked tofu, diced, 1 recipe Homemade Baked Tofu (page 271),
    or 8 ounces combined baked tofu and dense herbed tofu (see Note)
1 heaping cup whole fresh grape or cherry tomatoes or diced ripe fresh tomatoes
One 15- to 16-ounce can cannellini or chickpeas, drained and rinsed
Pitted green or black olives, or a combination, to taste
Marinated artichoke hearts to taste (optional)
Sliced red onion to taste (optional)
Vinaigrette, homemade (page 327) or prepared, to taste

1. Steam the green beans just until bright green and tender-crisp. Err on the side of undercooking rather than overcooking. Drain and rinse with cool water until they're at room temperature.

2. On a large serving platter or large shallow serving bowl, arrange the lettuce or greens. Scatter the basil or parsley over it. Arrange the green beans, tofu, tomatoes, beans, olives, and artichoke hearts, if desired, in separate mounds over the lettuce or greens. Top everything with a few thinly sliced rings of red onion if you like.

3. Drizzle a little vinaigrette over the salad, then serve at once, passing the remainder of the vinaigrette at the table.

note: If fresh slender green beans are unavailable, use organic frozen whole green beans, thawed and steamed just until tender-crisp.

Some natural foods markets carry a type of tofu that's very dense (with a texture similar to that of a very dry feta cheese) and prepared with herbs. Unlike tub tofu, it doesn't need to be drained and pressed. Try it for a change of pace!

PER SERVING WITHOUT DRESSING: Calories: 233; Total fat: 8g; Protein: 17g; Carbohydrates: 26g; Fiber: 9g; Sodium: 655mg

Complete the Meal

- As an easy summer meal, serve with any combination of fresh corn on the cob, a crusty bread, cold soup, or grilled vegetables. Add a little heft by pairing this with Sautéed Paprika Potatoes, page 302.
- For a more filling soup-and-salad meal, serve this with Vegetable-Barley Soup (page 136) or Tomato-Vegetable Soup (page 138)—either the basic recipe or the Tomato-Rice or Tomato-Quinoa variation.
- This also goes well with Pasta with Leafy Greens and Basil Pesto, page 172.

Composed Asian-Flavored
Salad Platter

Composed Asian-Flavored Salad Platter

Color, flavor, texture, protein—this main dish salad has it all. It's one of my favorites because it's so flexible. After you follow this recipe for the first time, I encourage you to experiment with other varieties of crisp raw veggies and to serve the salad alongside grains or noodles, so that each time you make it it's a deliciously different experience.

SERVES 4

2 teaspoons dark sesame oil
1 tablespoon reduced-sodium natural soy sauce or tamari
One 8-ounce package tempeh, cut into ½-inch-thick strips
3 to 4 ounces baby spinach or arugula, or a combination
1 cup thinly sliced red cabbage
¼ to ½ cup chopped fresh cilantro
1 cup baby carrots, halved or quartered lengthwise until skinny
A few radishes, sliced, or a 6-inch or so segment of daikon, sliced
1 red or yellow bell pepper, cut into long, narrow strips
2 to 3 stalks bok choy, with greens, thinly sliced, or 1 baby bok choy, thinly sliced
2 to 3 scallions, white and green parts, thinly sliced
¼ to ½ cup crushed peanuts, walnuts, or cashews (optional)
1 recipe Coconut-Peanut Dressing (page 330), Japanese-Style Carrot-Ginger Dressing (page 331), or Sesame-Ginger Dressing (page 328)

1. Heat the oil and soy sauce in a medium skillet. Add the tempeh strips and sauté over medium-high heat, stirring frequently, until golden brown on most sides.

2. Meanwhile, combine the spinach, cabbage, and cilantro in a mixing bowl and toss together. Spread on a large serving platter.

3. Arrange the salad as artfully as you like. Consider mounding the carrots in the center, then surrounding them with neat piles of the sautéed tempeh, radishes, bell peppers, and bok choy.

4. Sprinkle the scallions over the top, followed by the crushed nuts, if desired. Or pass around the nuts to top individual portions.

5. Use salad tongs to grab a little of each part of the salad and place it on individual plates. Pass around the dressing at the table.

PER SERVING WITHOUT DRESSING: Calories: 170; Total fat: 7g; Protein: 13g; Carbohydrates: 17g; Fiber: 7g; Sodium: 208mg

continued

Variations

- Vary the veggies as you like. Use celery, turnip, raw or lightly steamed broccoli, and/or cucumber in place of any of the veggies recommended above.

- To make this even easier, use an 8-ounce package of baked tofu instead of tempeh. Simply cut the tofu into narrow strips and off you go—no need to sauté the strips, so omit the oil and soy sauce.

- To make this even easier yet, use a store-bought natural sesame-ginger or Thai peanut dressing.

- Increase the protein content of the meal by doubling the quantity of tempeh.

Complete the Meal

- As shown in the photo on page 310, this is practically a meal in itself when served with the Asian noodles of your choice. My favorite is brown rice vermicelli, but soba work well, too. Or you can go domestic and choose a whole-grain spaghetti. Brown basmati and black rice are both compatible with this also. Serve the grains or noodles separately from the salad platter lest it become too crowded; flavor the noodles or rice with the same dressing. If you want to add a simple cooked vegetable to the meal, choose Wilted Sesame Greens (page 222) or the basic recipe for Garlicky Hardy Greens (page 287).

- If you want to keep things simple and don't want to follow another recipe, serve this hearty salad with baked or microwaved sweet potatoes. The Coconut-Peanut Dressing (page 330) suits them as well.

Cold Peanut Butter–Sesame Noodles
with Crisp Veggies

Here's an easy rendition of peanut butter noodles that includes a dollop of tahini and a dash of spice. Double this recipe when you bring it to a potluck, and you'll be a very popular guest! But these are welcome anytime and need not be worked into any sort of Asian-themed menu—they go with many other dishes as well.

SERVES 4 TO 6

8 ounces long Asian noodles, such as soba, udon, or rice vermicelli
⅓ cup smooth natural peanut butter
2 to 3 tablespoons tahini, or to taste
½ cup water
¼ cup freshly squeezed or bottled lime juice
2 to 3 tablespoons agave nectar, or to taste
3 tablespoons reduced-sodium natural soy sauce, or to taste
Sriracha or other hot sauce or crushed red pepper flakes to taste (optional)
3 to 4 cups finely chopped fresh vegetables of your choice, such as broccoli, zucchini,
    bell peppers, celery, bok choy, leafy greens, cucumbers, carrots, and turnips
2 to 3 scallions, white and green parts, thinly sliced
Chopped fresh cilantro to taste

1. Cook the noodles according to package directions until al dente, then drain and rinse under cool running water until they're at room temperature. Drain well again.

2. Meanwhile, combine the next seven ingredients in a mixing bowl and whisk together. Go easy on the hot stuff—you can always pass around extra for those who like more heat. Pour the sauce over the cooked and drained noodles and toss together.

3. Combine the cooked noodles, sauce, and chopped vegetables in a serving container and toss together. Sprinkle the scallions and cilantro over the top and serve.

PER SERVING: Calories: 424; Total fat: 15g; Protein: 16g; Carbohydrates: 65g; Fiber: 2g; Sodium: 923mg

Complete the Meal

This is delicious as a warm-weather dinner served with an easy tofu dish such as the Sweet and Savory variation in "Simple Preparations for Tofu, Tempeh, and Seitan" (pages 79–80) or Double Fruit-Glazed Tofu (page 193) and a bowl of red or golden cherry or grape tomatoes.

Classic Potato Salad *with* Variations

It's a rare eater who doesn't love a good potato salad. It's warmly welcomed in the plant-based repertoire as an accompaniment to sandwiches, veggie burgers, and as part of warm-weather meals along with grilled veggies and corn on the cob. This basic template for potato salad can be varied a number of ways, from the choice of veggies to the choice of dressings.

SERVES 6

5 medium-large red-skinned or Yukon gold potatoes; alternatively, replace
    2 of the potatoes with 1 large or 2 medium sweet potatoes or garnet yams
½ cup vegan mayonnaise or about ½ cup vinaigrette, homemade (page 327) or
    store-bought
2 teaspoons yellow mustard
1 large celery stalk, finely diced
1 cup frozen green peas, thawed
2 to 3 scallions, white and green parts, thinly sliced
Salt and freshly ground pepper to taste

ADDITIONS AND VARIATIONS

1 medium red bell pepper, finely diced
½ bulb fennel, thinly sliced
¼ cup finely chopped red onion
Toasted sunflower or pumpkin seeds to taste
Minced fresh dill to taste
Chopped fresh parsley to taste

1. Microwave or bake the potatoes in their skins until done but still firm. When cool enough to handle, peel and cut into ½-inch to ¾-inch dice.

2. Transfer the diced potatoes to a serving container and add the remaining ingredients. Stir together gently.

3. Stir in as many or as few of the additions and variations as you like. Cover and refrigerate until needed or serve at once.

PER SERVING WITHOUT ADDITIONS: Calories: 180; Total fat: 5g; Protein: 2g; Carbohydrates: 30g; Fiber: 4g; Sodium: 165mg

Complete the Meal

- This is the perfect companion to many of the sandwich meals you'll find in chapter 6; for one example, see this paired with Chickpea and Kale Sandwich Spread in the photo on page 266.
- For a nice warm-weather meal of hearty side-by-side salads, serve this with the Taco variation in "Tossed Salads Go Global" (page 319) and corn on the cob.

Marinated Bean Salad

For meals that need a protein boost, this quick bean salad offers an easy solution. For a larger quantity, this recipe doubles easily. You can dress this up a bit, as suggested in the variations following the recipe.

SERVES 4

2 cups cooked or one 15- to 16-ounce can (drained and rinsed) beans or lentils (see Note)
1 medium red bell pepper, cut into narrow strips
2 to 3 scallions, white and green parts, thinly sliced or minced
1/4 to 1/2 cup minced fresh parsley, or to taste
1 tablespoon minced fresh dill or 1 teaspoon dried dill
1 tablespoon extra-virgin olive oil
3 to 4 tablespoons freshly squeezed or bottled lemon or lime juice, or more to taste
1 tablespoon agave nectar or maple syrup
Salt and freshly ground pepper to taste

Combine all the ingredients in a serving bowl and stir together. If time allows, cover and let stand at room temperature for an hour or two before serving, stirring occasionally.

note: This works well with most any kind of beans—black beans, chickpeas, and any of the white or red varieties. It's also terrific with black-eyed peas; don't forget to make it with lentils from time to time.

PER SERVING: Calories: 173; Total fat: 4g; Protein: 8g; Carbohydrates: 28g; Fiber: 8g; Sodium: 5mg

continued

Variations

- To feed a large group, double the recipe and use two contrasting varieties of beans. Try combining small red beans with edamame, black beans with black-eyed peas, chickpeas with kidney beans—or use whatever you happen to have on hand!

- Substitute vinaigrette (homemade, page 327, or prepared) for the olive oil and lemon juice.

- Make this more "salady" by stirring in some fresh whole cherry or grape tomatoes and serving atop mixed greens.

- Prepare the recipe with chickpeas and add about ½ cup grated carrots and/or chopped green olives for a delicious variation.

- Peeled and diced ripe avocado or mango—or some of each—make this extra yummy. For this recipe, I'd go with a whole medium avocado; half a good-size mango will suffice. This variation is especially good with black beans.

Complete the Meal

- This is delicious with any of the tasty grits variations on page 117—especially if you make the black bean, avocado, and mango variation of the salad, described above. Add some slices of flavorful ripe fresh tomato as well.

- Pair this bean salad with another abundant salad. Some excellent side-by-sides include Quinoa Tabbouleh (page 315), Southwestern Quinoa Salad (page 317—but omit the beans), and Classic Potato Salad (page 312).

Quinoa Tabbouleh

Here's a simple, standard tabbouleh recipe with a couple of twists. Bulgur (presteamed cracked wheat) is the grain traditionally used, but quinoa makes it fluffier and lighter, not to mention even more nutritious and higher in protein. It's gluten-free as well. But if you want to return to this recipe's roots, prepare it with bulgur for a change of pace.

SERVES 4 AS A MAIN DISH, 6 OR MORE AS A SIDE DISH

1 cup quinoa, rinsed in a fine sieve

2 to 3 medium ripe fresh tomatoes, diced, or about 1 cup halved fresh cherry
   or grape tomatoes

3 scallions, green parts only, thinly sliced

1/2 cup minced fresh parsley, or more to taste

Juice of 1 lemon, or more to taste

1 tablespoon extra-virgin olive oil, or more to taste

Salt and freshly ground pepper to taste

1/4 to 1/2 cup chopped pitted black olives (optional)

2 to 3 tablespoons toasted sunflower seeds or 1/4 cup toasted pumpkin seeds
   for topping (optional)

1. Combine the quinoa with 2 cups water in a small saucepan. Bring to a simmer, then lower the heat. Cover and simmer gently for 15 minutes, or until the water is absorbed.

2. Transfer the quinoa to a serving container and allow to cool to room temperature.

3. Add the next seven ingredients and toss gently until well combined. Sprinkle sunflower or pumpkin seeds over the top, if desired. Serve at room temperature.

PER SERVING: Calories: 173; Total fat: 4g; Protein: 8g; Carbohydrates: 28g; Fiber: 8g; Sodium: 5mg

Variations

- If you won't be serving this with a bean-based dish such as hummus, toss in 1 to 1 1/2 cups cooked or canned (drained and rinsed) chickpeas or black beans. Served this way, it becomes more of a main dish salad.

- Serve on a bed of mixed baby greens, baby spinach, arugula, or a combination.

- Leftovers of this salad are delicious in wraps. Spread the wraps with hummus, mound a bit of the tabbouleh down the center with any of the greens listed above, and roll tightly.

continued

Complete the Meal

- My favorite way to complete this meal is to make a practically instant Mediterranean platter, as shown in the photo below. Serve with any of the variations of Basic Hummus, page 272, plus fresh pita bread, stuffed grape leaves, and olives. If you're pressed for time, you can use prepared hummus. If you make the hummus and cook the quinoa ahead of time, and if you pick up the rest of the goodies on the way home from work, you won't believe how quickly this meal comes together!

- Another fantastic accompaniment is Hummus Wraps with Grains and Greens. See the recipe on page 257.

Quinoa Tabbouleh

Southwestern Quinoa Salad

High-protein quinoa joins forces with avocado in a sturdy salad with southwestern flavors. It's a perfect main dish salad when paired with simple soups or quesadillas, as described in the meal plans following the recipe. Omit the beans if you'd like to serve this with a bean dish.

SERVES 6

¾ cup uncooked quinoa, rinsed in a fine sieve
1 cup halved yellow or red fresh cherry tomatoes
1 cup lightly cooked or thawed frozen corn kernels
1 medium firm, ripe avocado, peeled and diced
½ medium orange or yellow bell pepper, diced
2 cups cooked or one 15- to 16-ounce can (drained and rinsed) black, pinto, pink, or small red beans (optional; see Note)
2 scallions, green parts only, thinly sliced
½ cup Fresh Tomato Salsa (page 246) or your favorite prepared salsa
¼ to ½ cup chopped pitted black or green olives (optional)
2 tablespoons extra-virgin olive oil (optional)
Juice of ½ to 1 lime, or to taste
1 teaspoon ground cumin
¼ to ½ cup chopped fresh cilantro or parsley
Salt and crushed red pepper flakes to taste

1. Combine the quinoa with 1½ cups water in a small saucepan and bring to a rapid simmer, then lower the heat. Cover and simmer gently for 15 minutes, or until the water is absorbed. Transfer the quinoa to a large serving bowl to cool. If need be, speed up the cooling process by refrigerating for a while.

2. Once the quinoa is just warm, combine it with the remaining ingredients in the mixing bowl and stir together. Serve at room temperature.

PER SERVING: Calories: 232; Total fat: 6g; Protein: 10g; Carbohydrates: 39g; Fiber: 10g; Sodium: 45mg

Complete the Meal

- This is such an abundant meal-in-a-bowl that you can embellish it with recipe-free accompaniments. Baked sweet potatoes and or simply prepared broccoli, leafy greens, or green beans are good companions.
- This is delicious with the Tortilla Soup variation of Tomato-Vegetable Soup (page 138).

Tossed Salads Go Global

An ordinary salad using a few standard ingredients goes international with a few add-ins, and takes salad from so-so to lots of fun. See the photo of the Greek salad variation with Quick Black Bean Soup on page 127.

BASIC INGREDIENTS

Start with the basic ingredients listed below, then add the additional ingredients specified under whichever global variation you'd like to try.

4 ounces or so mixed baby greens (mesclun) or dark green lettuce leaves, or more to taste
3 to 4 medium flavorful ripe fresh tomatoes, diced
1/3 to 1/2 medium cucumber, thinly sliced
1 medium green or red bell pepper, sliced

Greek Salad

1/3 to 1/2 cup chopped pitted briny black olives (such as kalamata)
1 to 2 tablespoons extra-virgin olive oil
Red wine vinegar to taste
6 to 8 stuffed grape leaves, halved (optional)
4 to 8 ounces well-blotted (or pressed) extra-firm tofu, cut into cubes and tossed
    with 1 to 2 tablespoons lemon juice and dried oregano (optional—the vegan
    version of feta cheese)

Thai Salad

1 cup or so small broccoli florets, raw or lightly steamed
1 large stalk celery or bok choy, thinly sliced on the diagonal
1 cup mung bean sprouts or 1/2 cup fresh green sprouts, such as pea shoots
1 cup or so small pineapple chunks (optional)
3/4 cup Coconut-Peanut Dressing (page 330), or to taste

Middle Eastern Salad (Fattouche)

2 large pitas, cut into approximately 1-inch pieces and baked at 350ºF until crisp
2 to 3 scallions, white and green parts, thinly sliced
1/4 to 1/2 cup chopped fresh parsley, or to taste
A few thinly sliced fresh mint leaves
Olive oil and lemon juice for dressing

Taco Salad

1 medium avocado, peeled and diced

¼ cup pitted black or green olives, sliced

2 scallions, white and green parts, thinly sliced

1 cup grated Cheddar-style nondairy cheese (optional)

1 to 2 cups cooked pinto or kidney beans (omit beans if this is to accompany a bean dish)

2 good handfuls of natural, stone-ground tortilla chips, lightly crushed

¾ cup French Dressing (page 329) or Vegan Ranch-Style Dressing (Cilantro-Lime variation, pages 328–29), or to taste

Italian Salad

1 or 2 jarred roasted red peppers, drained and sliced

⅓ to ½ cup chopped pitted briny black olives (such as kalamata)

½ cup or so quartered artichoke hearts (marinated or not)

½ cup or so thinly sliced radicchio or red cabbage

Vinaigrette, homemade (page 327) or store-bought, as needed to moisten

How to Massage Kale, and a Few Raw Kale Salad Ideas

If you're at all on top of food trends, you know what a big deal kale has become over the past few years. And for good reason (see page 60). If you're already a kale fan, step it up a notch by discovering how to make delicious raw kale salads—sometimes referred to as massaged kale salads. By literally massaging this hardy green, you'll see it soften, become brighter green, and feel it become more tender right in your (lightly oiled) hands. Most important, it will have a more pleasant mouth feel and flavor, making it a fantastic ingredient for a wide variety of salads.

My favorite kind of kale for raw salads is the common curly green kale. Lacinato kale works well, too, as long as it isn't too large and tough to begin with. Here's how to massage kale:

1. **Strip the kale leaves from the stems.** If you want to use the stems, slice them very thinly and set aside; if not, discard them.

2. **Cut the kale into ribbons or bite-size pieces.**

3. **Give the kale a good rinse, then dry it thoroughly.** You can let the kale air-dry on a clean kitchen towel, blot between layers of paper towel, or twirl in a salad spinner.

4. **Transfer to a serving bowl.**

5. **Rub a small amount of olive oil onto your palms and massage the kale leaves for thirty to sixty seconds.** Massage the ribbons until they turn bright green and soften. You can also use salad dressing to do this; some people even enjoy massaging their kale with mashed avocado. Any of these will work.

Once kale is prepared in this way, you can create an amazing array of salads. Even when kale isn't the main leafy green in a salad, use this technique to prepare just a few leaves for adding to any kind of green salad, grain salad, or pasta salad. Try the easy ideas below or refer to the recipes for kale slaws that follow. Then use your creativity to create your own.

For each of these salads, start with a medium bunch of kale (about 8 ounces), though you can use more or less to taste. Finish each salad with salt and freshly ground pepper, though this is optional.

Southwestern-Flavored Kale Salad (shown on the facing page, bottom-right photo): To the massaged kale, add two or three medium ripe fresh tomatoes, a peeled and diced avocado, one to two cups cooked or raw fresh corn kernels, some strips of red bell pepper, and, if you like, some chopped green or black olives. Flavor with freshly squeezed or bottled lime juice and a little olive oil (or creamy Cilantro-Lime Dressing, pages 328–29) and some chopped cilantro. For extra protein, and to make this a main dish salad, add some cooked or canned (drained and rinsed) black or pinto beans and sprinkle some pumpkin seeds over the top.

Mediterranean Kale Salad: To the massaged kale, add two or three medium chopped ripe fresh tomatoes, strips of sun-dried tomato, plenty of bell pepper strips, and chopped or whole cured black olives. If you're looking to bolster the protein content of the meal, add a cup or two of cooked or canned (drained and rinsed) chickpeas. Top the salad with thinly sliced fresh basil leaves.

Colorful and Luscious Kale and Avocado Salad: Add a peeled and diced avocado, plus thinly sliced red cabbage to taste, sliced carrots, diced yellow squash, halved red and/or yellow fresh grape tomatoes, and sunflower or pumpkin seeds. Add a little more olive oil in addition to what you used for massaging, if you like, and some freshly squeezed or bottled lemon or lime juice.

Asian-Flavored Kale Salad: Massage the kale with dark sesame oil instead of olive oil, though this isn't mandatory. Add a medium red bell pepper, cut into narrow slices, three stalks bok choy with leaves, sliced (or one sliced baby bok choy), and one or two thinly sliced scallions. Dress with a sesame-ginger dressing (homemade, page 328, or prepared). Nice optional additions include some crushed toasted peanuts or cashews, a drained can of baby corn, and 4 ounces or so of baked tofu, cut into narrow strips. This is a sensational accompaniment for many of the meals in chapter 4 and is suggested for several of the menus.

Simple Slaws

A simple coleslaw is a versatile choice that goes well with many types of meals. While it's really not a big deal to shred a quarter or half a cabbage by hand, there are some days when having to do so means the difference between having at least some kind of salad and forgoing it altogether.

So although I'm not usually drawn to buying precut or prepped vegetables, other than baby carrots, I do indulge in precut coleslaw cabbage, which is available in 8- or 16-ounce bags. I appreciate its convenience and versatility—and besides, cabbage is never part of "most contaminated" vegetables lists, which is good news considering that coleslaw cabbage is generally not organic. I like the kind that includes shredded carrots. Make sure that the cabbage looks crisp and fresh. If it looks wilted, slightly yellowed, or watery, don't buy it.

Coleslaw was one of the first kinds of salads my kids would gladly eat, and I think it's probably appealing to picky eaters of all ages. My favorite dressing for coleslaw is simply vegan mayonnaise, but you can also choose from the following:

- Vegan Sour Cream (page 248)
- Cashew Cream (page 249)
- Sesame-Ginger Dressing (for an Asian spin; page 328)
- Basic Vinaigrette (for a marinated flavor; page 327)
- Vegan Ranch-Style Dressing (any variation; page 328)

I also like to dress up plain coleslaw cabbage with other ingredients that are easy to toss in and don't require a lot of prep—after all, that's the point of using this convenient prepackaged ingredient. Here are a few add-ins to mix and match.

- Diced tart apple
- Dried cranberries or raisins
- Toasted sunflower seeds
- Toasted slivered or sliced almonds
- Chopped toasted walnuts or pecans
- Lightly cooked fresh or thawed frozen corn kernels
- Thinly sliced scallions
- Thinly sliced green or red bell peppers
- Minced fresh parsley and/or dill

I encourage you to make your own improvisational slaws and to try the two tasty coleslaws that follow. See also the easy semirecipes for Southwestern Slaw (page 251) and Red Cabbage and Carrot Salad (page 223).

Creamy Kale *and* Cabbage Slaw

I find this simple raw kale and slaw combo to be positively addictive. It goes with so many kinds of meals, adding a refreshing note when served with hearty stews like chili or bold-flavored sandwiches and burgers. You'll find it recommended as an accompaniment to a number of recipes throughout this book.

SERVES 6

6 or so large leaves curly green or lacinato kale, rinsed well
3 cups finely shredded green or napa cabbage
1/2 cup vegan mayonnaise, Vegan Sour Cream (page 248),
    or Cashew Cream (page 249), or to taste
Juice of 1/2 lemon (about 2 tablespoons), or to taste
1/2 medium red bell pepper, cut into short, narrow strips, or about a dozen baby carrots,
    quartered lengthwise
2 to 3 tablespoons toasted sunflower seeds
1/4 cup minced fresh herb of your choice, such as parsley, dill, or cilantro
Salt and freshly ground pepper to taste

1. Strip the kale leaves off the stems. Slice the kale into narrow ribbons and place in a serving container.

2. Coat your palms lightly with olive oil and massage the kale until it softens and becomes bright green, about 45 seconds. Add the remaining ingredients to the serving container and mix well to combine. Serve at once.

PER SERVING: Calories: 86; Total fat: 6g; Protein: 3g; Carbohydrates: 6g; Fiber: 2g; Sodium: 167mg

Apple Slaw
with Leafy Greens

You'll feel less guilty about using precut coleslaw (at least I feel less guilty) when you bolster it with leafy greens and apples. Of course you're welcome to shred your own cabbage if you prefer. Crunchy, savory, and sweet, this is a salad I make frequently, and it's one you'll find recommended here and there throughout this book.

SERVES 6

8 ounces shredded coleslaw cabbage (preferably including carrots)
1 medium apple, cored and diced
2 to 3 big handfuls baby spinach or baby arugula, well rinsed
½ cup vegan mayonnaise
Splash of freshly squeezed or bottled lemon or lime juice, or more to taste
2 to 3 tablespoons toasted sunflower seeds
Salt and freshly ground pepper to taste

Combine all ingredients in a serving bowl and stir together until thoroughly mixed. Serve at once or cover and let stand until needed.

PER SERVING: Calories: 94; Total fat: 6g; Protein: 3g; Carbohydrates: 8g; Fiber: 2g; Sodium: 166mg

Variations

- Substitute kale for the spinach or arugula. Use 5 or 6 leaves, stemmed and cut into ribbons. Rub a little olive oil onto your palms and massage the kale until it softens and becomes bright green, about 30 to 60 seconds.

- Feel free to use half a small head of fresh green or savoy cabbage, thinly sliced, instead of precut coleslaw cabbage. Add some grated carrots if you do.

Fruity, Nutty Mixed Greens Salads

Fresh seasonal fruits and a sprinkling of nuts are an easy way to dress up mixed baby greens, spinach, arugula, or a combination of the three. This kind of salad adds a refreshing note to most any kind of meal, but it is especially good with hearty or spicy dishes. There's almost nothing to it; no recipe required!

Choose a green: Baby greens, arugula, baby spinach, or a combination.

Add fresh fruit: Apples, pears, Asian pears, or small seedless oranges are good almost year-round; use whole blueberries or sliced strawberries for summer salads. Mango or pineapple chunks are also splendid, whenever available.

Toss in some nuts: Choose one or two from among toasted walnuts, pecans, slivered almonds, toasted pumpkin seeds, and sunflower seeds.

Welcome additions: Use one or two of the following for added color and flavor: diced peeled avocado, thinly sliced red bell pepper, thinly shredded red cabbage, or sliced radicchio.

Dressing: Use French, papaya-poppyseed, raspberry vinaigrette, or keep it simple with fruity olive oil and a splash of lemon juice.

Salad Dressings

Basic Vinaigrette

Here's a basic, all-purpose dressing for salads, slaws, and marinating. Increase the quantity of vinegar if you prefer a more pungent taste.

MAKES ABOUT 1 CUP

½ cup extra-virgin olive oil
¼ to ⅓ cup white or red wine vinegar, or to taste
1 tablespoon Dijon-style mustard
1 tablespoon natural granulated sugar or agave nectar
1 teaspoon dried Italian seasoning blend

Combine all ingredients in a tightly lidded bottle and shake thoroughly. Shake well before each use.

PER 1-TABLESPOON SERVING: Calories: 63; Total fat: 7g; Protein: 0g; Carbohydrates: 1g; Fiber: 0g; Sodium: 11mg

Variations

- **Balsamic Vinaigrette:** Replace the wine vinegar with balsamic vinegar.
- **Lemon or Lime Vinaigrette:** Use freshly squeezed or bottled lemon or lime juice to replace some or all of the vinegar.

Sesame-Ginger Dressing

Since I love to make homemade Asian-style meals, and since I believe in serving salads with just about everything, this is quite a useful dressing in my kitchen. There are good store-bought versions of this dressing, but it's easy to make with pantry ingredients—so why not?

MAKES ABOUT 1 CUP

⅓ cup neutral vegetable oil, such as safflower oil or sunflower oil
2 tablespoons dark sesame oil
⅓ cup rice vinegar or white wine vinegar
1 tablespoon agave nectar or maple syrup
1 tablespoon reduced-sodium natural soy sauce or tamari
1 to 2 teaspoons grated fresh ginger, or to taste
1 tablespoon sesame seeds

Combine all ingredients in a tightly lidded bottle. Shake well before each use. Refrigerate whatever is not used at once; bring to room temperature before using.

PER 1-TABLESPOON SERVING: Calories: 63; Total fat: 7g; Protein: 0g; Carbohydrates: 2g; Fiber: 0g; Sodium: 38mg

Vegan Ranch-Style Dressing *or* Dip

The well-loved creamy dressing can be made dairy-free by using white beans or softened raw cashews as the base.

MAKES ABOUT 1 CUP

⅔ cup raw cashews, soaked in hot water for 2 to 3 hours, or ⅔ cup cooked or canned (drained and rinsed) large white beans, such as cannellini
¼ cup unsweetened rice milk
¼ cup vegan mayonnaise
Juice of ½ to 1 lemon, or to taste
½ teaspoon salt-free all-purpose seasoning blend (see page 121 for recommended brands)
1 to 2 tablespoons chopped fresh dill or ½ teaspoon dried dill
½ teaspoon salt, or to taste
Freshly ground pepper to taste

1. Combine all ingredients except dill, salt, and pepper in a food processor or blender and process until completely smooth and creamy. Add the dill and pulse a few times.

2. Taste for salt. If you use canned beans, you might not need much or any at all. Add salt to taste, a few grindings of pepper, and pulse a few more times.

3. If you'll be using this as a dip, let it remain thick, but if you'll be using it as a salad dressing, add a bit more rice milk (enough to give it a pourable consistency). Serve immediately from a small bowl or cruet, or transfer to a tightly lidded container and refrigerate. This keeps for up to a week in the refrigerator.

PER 1-TABLESPOON SERVING WITH CASHEWS: Calories: 44; Total fat: 3g; Protein: 1g; Carbohydrates: 3g; Fiber: 0g; Sodium: 104mg

PER 1-TABLESPOON SERVING WITH BEANS: Calories: 22; Total fat: 1g; Protein: 1g; Carbohydrates: 3g; Fiber: 0g; Sodium: 104mg

Variation

Cilantro-Lime: Replace the lemon juice with lime juice to taste and the dill with ¼ to ½ cup chopped cilantro.

French Dressing

I hope you'll agree that this French dressing is just as good, or even better, than the store-bought variety. It certainly is more economical. Plus it's simple to make, and uses ingredients you likely already have on hand.

MAKES ABOUT 1 CUP

¼ cup good-quality ketchup
½ cup vegan mayonnaise
3 tablespoons extra-virgin olive oil
2 tablespoons red wine vinegar
1 tablespoon agave nectar or maple syrup
½ teaspoon sweet paprika, or more to taste

Combine all ingredients in a small mixing bowl and whisk together until smoothly blended. Serve immediately from the bowl, or transfer to a tightly lidded container and refrigerate. This keeps for up to a week in the refrigerator. Shake well before each use.

PER 1-TABLESPOON SERVING: Calories: 50; Total fat: 4g; Protein: 0g; Carbohydrates: 2g; Fiber: 0g; Sodium: 95mg

Coconut-Peanut Dressing

This delectably rich dressing works well on Asian-influenced salads, cold noodles, and steamed green veggies. You'll see this pop up in recipes throughout the book.

MAKES ABOUT 1¹/₂ CUPS

---

¹/₂ cup smooth or chunky natural peanut butter, at room temperature
³/₄ cup light coconut milk
Juice of 1 lime
2 tablespoons low-sodium natural soy sauce or tamari
¹/₂ teaspoon sriracha, hot sauce, or cayenne pepper, or to taste
2 teaspoons agave nectar

1. Combine all ingredients in a small mixing bowl and whisk together until completely blended. If the peanut butter is very dense, you might need to use a food processor or blender.

2. Serve immediately from a small bowl or transfer to a tightly lidded container and refrigerate. This keeps for up to a week in the refrigerator.

PER 2-TABLESPOON SERVING: Calories: 156; Total fat: 12g; Protein: 5g; Carbohydrates: 9g; Fiber: 1g; Sodium: 210mg

Japanese-Style Carrot-Ginger Dressing

Whenever I go out for veggie sushi, I enjoy the gingery carrot dressing that comes atop the accompanying simple salad of tender greens. It turns out that this dressing is easy to duplicate at home. Serve it with leafy salads as part of Asian-style meals. See the photo on page 194 for one such delectable repast, featuring Skillet Tofu Teriyaki and store-bought vegetable sushi.

MAKES ABOUT 1 CUP (4 SERVINGS)

3 medium carrots, peeled and cut into chunks, or 1 cup baby carrots
1- to 2-inch piece peeled fresh ginger, or to taste
3 tablespoons rice vinegar, white wine vinegar, or apple cider vinegar
Pinch of salt
Pinch of natural granulated sugar
2 teaspoons dark sesame oil (optional)

1. Combine all the ingredients in a food processor. Pulse until the carrots and ginger are finely chopped.

2. Add 2 tablespoons water and let the machine run until the mixture turns into a coarse puree. Scrape down the sides of the work bowl from time to time. If you'd like a thinner consistency, add a little more water and let the machine run again. This is meant to be fairly thick, so don't overdo it with water.

3. Transfer to a small bowl and serve by spooning about ¼ cup over the top of each salad. Store any leftovers in a tightly lidded container in the refrigerator, where this will keep for 3 or 4 days. Stir before each use.

PER 4-TABLESPOON SERVING: Calories: 9; Total fat: 0g; Protein: 0g; Carbohydrates: 2g; Fiber: 0g; Sodium: 42mg

CHAPTER 8

BREAKFAST, LUNCH, SNACKS, *and* HEALTHFUL SWEETS

Those of us of the plant-powered persuasion look forward to the evening meal just as much as everyone else does, but there are two other meals as well as between-meal grazings to consider when you're making the effort to add more plants to your daily fare. Breakfast, lunch, and snacks in the standard American diet have traditionally been bready and starchy, so read on to learn how to get more whole and fresh plant-based foods into these meals and snacks.

(From left to right) Banana-Blueberry Smoothie (page 338), Green Smoothie with
Banana and Apple (page 339), and Pineapple-Mango Smoothie (page 338)

Sustaining Breakfasts

It's been said countless times—a nutritious breakfast is the best way to start the day. But that's a challenge for those of us who are rushed, tired, and not all that hungry first thing in the morning.

Unlike dinner, in which most people crave a certain amount of variety, breakfast is often limited to only a handful of choices—or fewer. Here are some possibilities to help you break out of the mold:

Smoothies: For many people, fruity smoothies are a great way to get the day started. See some basic ideas on pages 337–39.

Good-quality cold breakfast cereals: Choose organic, whole-grain varieties.

Granola: This is tasty on its own or mixed with other cold cereals.

Hot cereals and cooked whole grains: Even leftover brown rice, millet, or quinoa can serve the same purpose as oatmeal or other traditional grains in a breakfast bowl. See a multitude of possibilities on pages 335–37.

Fresh fruit in season: Bananas are welcome year-round, berries are good for summer, and oranges and mangoes are delicious in winter. Eat them out of hand or use them to make juices, smoothies, or to top cereals.

Whole-grain pancakes and waffles: If making pancakes or waffles is a possibility during the week, keep a good-quality whole-grain pancake and waffle mix on hand for those mornings when starting completely from scratch isn't practical.

Fresh whole-grain breads, rolls, bagels, and English muffins: Mix and match for variety; keep some in the freezer.

Spreads for breads: My family and I enjoy all-fruit preserves, vegan buttery spread, and nut butters. Some people do enjoy hummus in the morning, though its flavor is a bit too distinct for many morning appetites.

Nondairy milk: Almond, rice, hemp, soy, or other nondairy milks are useful to have on hand in plain, vanilla, and/or chocolate flavors.

Avocado, plain and simple: I know a number of people—and I count myself among them—who enjoy avocado in the morning. Spread on toast or just eaten out of its shell with a spoon, avocado provides good fats and fiber and is heavenly to those of us who love it.

Hearty breakfasts: If you have a good appetite in the morning, you might enjoy the following recipes for breakfast. Though most of these are quick—a good thing, since time is almost always at a premium in the morning—consider making them the evening before you'd like to have them. Or you can make them for dinner and plan on leftovers for breakfast (or lunch, if you prefer).

- Tofu and Veggie Scrambles (page 82)
- Easy Hash Brown Potatoes (page 300)—try the tofu and tempeh variations
- Smoky Tempeh Strips (page 268)
- Ultimate Eggless Egg Salad—delicious on toast or in a pita (page 270)
- Easy, flexible quesadillas (pages 240–43)
- Make your own creative wraps—mix and match combinations to appeal to your morning palate (pages 261–62)
- Give grits a chance—many breakfast-worthy possibilities (page 117)

WHOLE-GRAIN HOT CEREALS AND WAYS TO SERVE THEM

Though cream of wheat and oatmeal make fine hot cereals, there are myriad other grains to explore for breakfast—from tiny whole grains to cracked, rolled, and ground grains. Explore the hot cereals section of your natural foods store. If any of the grains are new to you, buy them in packaged form so you can follow specific instructions for cooking. Once they're familiar, you have the option of purchasing them in bulk. Here are a few to explore:

Rolled grains: These are made from whole grains that have been steamed then flattened with steel rollers. Barley, rye, kamut, and spelt are available this way.

Whole grains: Nutritious whole grains that be served cooked for breakfast include quinoa, millet, amaranth, and teff. You'll likely find these shelved with the whole-grain products or in bulk rather than with the regular boxed hot cereals.

Cracked grains: Many (but not all) cracked grains have been presteamed, so they cook more quickly. Among these are bulgur (wheat), couscous (semolina wheat), and barley.

Cornmeal and grits: Cooked cornmeal is often referred to as polenta, in the Italian tradition, but cooked cornmeal also has a long and illustrious background in American cuisine, in which it is referred to as cornmeal mush. Grits, or hominy grits, are a traditional breakfast staple of the American South. You'll find quick-cooking grits in most any supermarket, but whole-grain stone-ground grits (available in natural foods stores) are more flavorful and nutritious. Read more about cornmeal and grits on pages 115–17.

Oats: Many forms of cooked oats have traditionally graced the breakfast table. Rolled oats and quick-cooking oats are perhaps the most common; the quick-cooking version is simply a finely ground form of rolled oats—which also cook relatively quickly. Steel-cut oats, sometimes called Scottish or Irish oatmeal, are simply sliced whole oat groats; they make for a hearty cereal.

"Cream of" cereals: In this category is farina, the most familiar brands of which are Cream of Wheat and Cream of Rice. These are generally made from refined grains with vitamins and sometimes iron added back in. Their smooth, light textures make them especially appealing to very young children. If hearty hot cereals don't appeal to your kids, "cream of" cereals may be good for getting them into the hot cereal habit. Stir in a little wheat germ for extra flavor and nutrition, and gradually mix them with small portions of heartier hot cereals. Look for organic versions in natural foods stores.

EMBELLISHMENTS FOR HOT CEREALS

Start with any of the cooked grains listed above, then add a bit of sweetening, spice, fresh fruit, and nuts or seeds for a nourishing breakfast that will sustain you until lunchtime. (Leftover unseasoned quinoa is ideal for this—less to do in the morning!)

Nondairy milk: Once hot cereals are cooked, you can add a little nondairy milk to the saucepan and continue cooking until the milk is absorbed to give the grain a creamier texture. Or, for added richness and protein, use a combination of water and nondairy milk to cook the grain from the start.

Dried fruits: Regular or golden raisins, cranberries, cherries, and currants; chopped apricots, dates, and Turkish figs; and diced dried tropical fruits are all worth a try.

Fresh fruits: Sliced bananas, sliced strawberries, and whole blueberries are naturals with hot (as well as cold) cereals. In the winter, lightly cooked sliced apples and pears are also wonderful with hot cereals.

Nuts and seeds: Toasted slivered or sliced almonds, chopped walnuts or pecans, and sesame and sunflower seeds are all good for sprinkling on hot cereals.

Wheat germ, ground flaxseeds, hemp seeds, and chia seeds: All of these additions provide concentrated nutrition. Wheat germ is an excellent source of vitamin E and the B vitamins; the seeds are also good plant sources of valuable omega fatty acids.

Spices: Ground cinnamon gives a lively flavor boost to sweetened hot cereals; ground nutmeg works, too, in small doses.

Natural sweetener: If you like your hot cereal slightly sweet, add a judicious amount of maple syrup, agave nectar, or any natural granulated sugar—coconut sugar is a good choice.

Vegan buttery spreads and/or nondairy cheeses: Some people like their hot cereals with a sweet theme; others prefer a savory theme. Daiya and Vegan Gourmet are two good nondairy cheese brands. For added richness, you can also melt a bit of nonhydrogenated vegan buttery spread (such as Earth Balance) into the hot cereal.

THE SEASONAL SMOOTHIE

Smoothies are all the rage these days, and with good reason. They're an excellent source of nutrients and a perfect way to wake up sluggish appetites in the morning. They're also a great way to get a few servings of fruit in each day if you don't think to do so otherwise. And they provide yet another way to entice kids and teens who are picky eaters to the plant-powered table.

Since this book covers so much ground, there's not enough space to discuss smoothies in depth. But there are many books entirely devoted to the subject of smoothies, from the ordinary (but still delicious) fruit-based smoothies to green smoothies to those featuring superfoods such as chia seeds and maca powder. You'll find much inspiration once you begin to look if you wish to delve more deeply into the subject.

If you want to use seeds, raw cashews, or hardy greens (such as kale and collards) in your smoothies, you need a high-speed blender. Otherwise, regular blenders suffice. If your smoothies focus mainly on bananas, berries, apples, and other relatively soft fruits, even using an immersion blender (see page 44) will be fine. Following are three simple smoothies that demonstrate the beautiful hues that can be achieved with certain combinations of ingredients. And if you want to create your own combinations, here's a basic formula for two to three servings:

1. **Combine in the container of a blender:** 2 cups coarsely chopped fresh fruit or 1 cup coarsely chopped fresh fruit and 1 cup berries—a banana can be among these; peel and freeze chunks of banana for this purpose.

2. **Then add:** 1½ to 2 cups liquid (unsweetened fruit juice, vanilla nondairy milk, coconut water, or even plain filtered water).

3. **Add any of these optional ingredients:** Ice, hemp seeds, chia seeds, superfoods or other nutritional supplements (avoid soy protein isolate), and coconut-milk or soy yogurt.

4. **Blend until smooth** and pour into glasses.

Pineapple-Mango Smoothie

1 cup pineapple chunks, preferably fresh
1 cup mango chunks, fresh or frozen
1 cup orange juice, preferably freshly squeezed
1 cup coconut water, unsweetened rice milk, or unsweetened almond milk
One 6-ounce container vanilla or pineapple coconut-milk yogurt (optional; see Note)

Combine all ingredients in a blender. Blend on high speed until completely smooth. Serve at once in tall glasses or tumblers.

PER SERVING: Calories: 166; Total fat: 1g; Protein: 3g; Carbohydrates: 40g; Fiber: 4g; Sodium: 130mg

note: Using pineapple-flavored yogurt will give this a more pronounced piña colada flavor and a richer texture.

Banana-Blueberry Smoothie

Blueberries are one of the most antioxidant-rich fruits available, making this a supercharged way to start your day.

SERVES 2 TO 3

1 medium banana, peeled and broken into large chunks (pieces may be frozen for 1 hour prior to blending, if desired)
1 to 1½ cups fresh or frozen blueberries
1 cup unsweetened plain or vanilla nondairy milk
1 cup pomegranate juice or other unsweetened berry juice

Combine all ingredients in a blender. Blend on high speed until completely smooth. Serve at once in tall glasses or tumblers.

PER SERVING: Calories: 218; Total fat: 2g; Protein: 2g; Carbohydrates: 52g; Fiber: 4g; Sodium: 60mg

Green Smoothie *with* Banana and Apple

Once you get more deeply into the world of smoothies, this might well become your favorite. The flavor of the greens is extremely subtle, but it looks and tastes so healthful! If you're making it with kale or collards, a high-speed blender will do a better job of pureeing the greens than a regular blender. But a regular blender can handle spinach quite well.

SERVES 2 TO 3

2 medium curly kale or collard leaves, rinsed well and torn, or 2 handfuls of baby spinach
    leaves
1 medium banana, peeled and broken into large chunks (pieces may be frozen for 1 hour
    prior to blending, if desired)
1 medium apple, cored and cut into chunks
2 cups unsweetened plain or vanilla nondairy milk (see Note)
2 tablespoons hemp seeds (optional but highly recommended)
Agave nectar to taste (optional)

Combine the greens, banana, apple, nondairy milk, and hemp seeds (if desired) in a blender. Blend on high speed until completely smooth. Taste to see if you'd like a bit more sweetness; if so, add just a little agave nectar. Serve at once in tall glasses or tumblers.

PER SERVING: Calories: 157; Total fat: 2g; Protein: 2g; Carbohydrates: 37g; Fiber: 4g; Sodium: 55mg

(From left to right)
Banana-Blueberry
Smoothie, Green
Smoothie with
Banana and Apple,
and Pineapple-
Mango Smoothie

Portable Lunches for School and Office

There are many topics in this book that warrant their own separate volume, and plant-based portable lunches is certainly one of them. I wrote a lot about the topic of healthful vegetarian and vegan school lunches over the years when my kids were growing up. Packing lunch was a daily reality for me for some fourteen years, and admittedly it wasn't always fun. To keep from going stark raving mad, I tried to infuse my school lunches with new ideas, but it was I who was bored, not the kids. They were perfectly content with the same half dozen of their favorite lunches, repeated ad infinitum, because it spared them from standing in line every day for a selection of food that wasn't all that appealing and that was limited in range—after all, not many kids were vegetarians.

One thing I know is that, being the visual cook that I am, I would have adored making bento box lunches for them. It would have taken the routine from humdrum to lots of fun. Jennifer McCann really sparked a movement when she popularized bento lunches in her blog, *Vegan Lunch Box*, and in her subsequent books. Right around the same time, two California moms noticed how much waste portable school lunches create—from the disposable containers to the juice boxes to the lunch bags themselves. So they founded Laptop Lunches, a company that sells PVC-free plastic bento lunch boxes in styles appropriate for kids and adults alike. Now there's a kind of "bento mom" movement worldwide: moms (as well as dads) are making appealing lunches and showing them off in their blogs.

While the new generation of bento boxes would have made my job as chief lunch packer more interesting, there are lots of other nifty kinds of containers that can make this pursuit fulfilling, whether for yourself or your kids.

We don't have a lot of room to spare for this section on portable lunches, so I'll break lunch possibilities into three categories for simplicity's sake. The latter two categories can consist entirely of leftovers from the previous night's dinner—either hot soups, packed in a Thermos and accompanied by fresh bread and fruit, or hearty salads, packed in a container alongside fresh bread and fruit or stuffed in a pita and accompanied by fresh fruit.

PORTABLE SANDWICHES AND WRAPS

Hummus Wraps with Grains and Greens (page 257)

Cucumber and Avocado Wraps with Bean Spread or Hummus (page 258)

Thai-Flavored Salad Wraps (page 260)

Smoky Tempeh and Avocado Reuben Sandwiches (page 265)

Chickpea and Kale Sandwich Spread (page 267)

Chunky Bean Spread (page 269)

Ultimate Eggless Egg Salad (page 270)

HOT SOUPS

Lentil Soup with Tasty Variations (page 124)

Quick Black Bean Soup (page 126)

White Bean and Corn Chowder (page 130)

Cream of Broccoli Soup (page 132)

Coconut Cream of Orange Vegetables Soup (page 134)

Vegetable-Barley Soup with Mushroom Variation (page 136)

Tomato-Vegetable Soup with Variations (page 138)

Classic Veggie Chili (page 140)

Curried Chickpea, Eggplant, and Green Bean Stew (page 149)

Southeast Asian–Style Vegetable and Nut Butter Stew (page 150)

HEARTY SALADS

Classic Potato Salad (page 312)

Marinated Bean Salad (page 313)

Quinoa Tabbouleh (page 315)

Southwestern Quinoa Salad (page 317)

Any of the kale salads (pages 321–22)

Greek Salad (page 318)

Thai Salad (page 318)

SCHOOL LUNCH TIPS AND IDEAS FOR KIDS AND TEENS

Here are a dozen tried-and-true tips that kept me sane over many years of lunch making:

1. Vary the types of bread used for sandwiches. Bagels, rolls, pita pockets, English muffins, raisin bread, and even fresh flour tortillas or wraps can add interest to standard sandwich fillings. Get your children accustomed to whole-grain breads!

2. Dishes that taste good at room temperature are more successful Thermos fare than dishes that need to stay hot (because they usually don't). But if your child's school has a microwave available, your Thermos offerings can include macaroni and cheese, soups, and other leftovers.

3. I always packed fruit with my kids' lunches, but it often came home uneaten until I resorted to some simple tricks. Small chunks of fruit, such as strawberries, grapes, melons, and tiny seedless orange sections served on a skewer were always eaten

(long cocktail toothpicks are perfect); similarly, apple slices are more likely to be eaten if you supply a tiny container of peanut butter to dip them into.

4. Raw vegetables, too, become more of a draw when you supply a dip. When packing carrot sticks, baby carrots, celery, or bell pepper strips, add a tiny container of hummus (homemade, page 272, or purchased) or Thousand Island-ish Dressing (page 283).

5. Cereal is standard fare for breakfast but is an unexpected treat when served for lunch. Pack some nutritious cereal in a lidded bowl-shaped container, and your child can add his or her favorite nondairy milk to it when it's time to eat (vanilla almond milk is particularly good with cereal). Teamed with a banana, this makes a filling meal.

6. Salads in pita bread appeal to kids with more adventurous palates. Augment simple lettuce, tomato, and carrot salads with chickpeas, chunks of baked marinated tofu, or grated nondairy cheese. Keep pita sandwiches fresh by wrapping first in foil, then in sandwich bags.

7. Expand your child's PBJ horizons (especially since many schools are now peanut-free zones) by offering other nut butters (such as cashew and almond) and no-sugar-added fruit spreads or apple butter. Or try nut-butter-and-banana sandwiches.

8. A warmed veggie burger (either homemade, pages 274–78, or one of the excellent prepared varieties) on a whole-grain roll or English muffin spread with favorite condiments makes an easy and hearty lunch. If packed up while warm, it will still be slightly warm or at least at room temperature by lunchtime, and will taste good either way.

9. Pasta salad is a perennial kid-friendly favorite. Use fun shapes such as wagon wheels, small shells, or tiny tubes. Small shapes pack best into containers. Add a couple of your child's favorite veggies, such as lightly steamed broccoli, carrots, green peas, and corn. Add an appealing dressing, such as Quick Tartar Sauce (page 282), Vegan Ranch-Style Dressing (page 328), or a favorite prepared dressing.

10. Put some extra love in the lunch box with Homemade Chocolate Energy Bars (page 345) or, if you're a baker, your favorite kind of wholesome homemade baked goods. Muffins are always welcome, and they can even replace sandwiches and wraps.

A Sampling of Healthful Snacks

Here's a rundown of easy snack ideas that add to the day's nourishment rather than provide empty calories. These snacks aren't just for kids! They're all made from whole grains, legumes, vegetables, and fruits. Sometimes it's all about presentation and having items prepped ahead of time. The last three suggestions in the following list, for example, are seen in this photo *(left)*, which shows how easy it is to make fruits and vegetables look enticing to kids of all ages.

- **Fully Loaded Emergency Nachos** (page 239)
- **Fresh Tomato Salsa** (page 246) or store-bought salsa: Serve with stone-ground tortilla chips.
- **Basic Hummus** (page 272) or store-bought hummus: Serve with whole-grain pita wedges, stone-ground tortilla chips, and/or baby carrots.
- **Vegan Ranch-Style Dressing** (page 328): Use as a dip for raw vegetables.
- **Crisp fruit and nut butter:** Serve apple, crisp pear, and/or Asian pear slices with small bowls of peanut or cashew butter for dipping.
- **Fruit on skewers:** Simply thread chunks of fruit onto short bamboo or wooden skewers.
- **Fruity parfaits** (page 353)
- **Chocolate Nut-Butter Truffles** (page 349)
- **Homemade Chocolate Energy Bars** (page 345)
- **Popcorn:** Preferably organic, popped either in an air popper or on the stove top.
- **Edamame (fresh green soybeans):** Cook fresh or frozen edamame in the shell—kids love opening them, and it makes the snack that much more fun.

- **Baby carrots with pimiento-stuffed green olives:** Somehow briny pimiento-stuffed green olives make a nice flavor counterpoint to sweet carrots—and the duo looks good together, too.

- **Multicolored bell pepper strips:** Serve as is or gently flavored with apple cider vinegar and agave nectar or maple syrup.

- **Pineapple chunks or rings with raisins or cranberries**: Use fresh pineapple whenever possible, though the canned mini rings are irresistible.

A Trio of Healthful Chocolate Treats

A few years ago, the media burst forth with reports of studies claiming that chocolate in its pure form is actually a healthful food. Chocolate's caffeine contributes to quick energy bursts, perfect for athletic and intellectual effort. These studies even presented evidence that dark chocolate is good for heart health and contains cancer-fighting antioxidants.

It's encouraging to learn about the virtues of chocolate, but it's still wise to be choosy about what kind of chocolate you consume. Dairy-free dark chocolate is the way to go, whether in bars for snacking or as chips and cocoa powder (or raw cacao) for baked or unbaked treats. It's important to choose fair trade chocolate in any form. Many major chocolate manufacturers will not confirm that they comply with fair trade laws. These laws protect against unethical growing and harvesting practices, the exploitation of child labor, and even child slave labor (which has been documented in Ivory Coast, a major exporter of cocoa). Pleasing your palate should not come at the cost of human suffering.

Homemade Chocolate Energy Bars

Tired of overpriced energy bars that taste like cardboard? You can make your own in minutes using nourishing seeds, pureed dates, and dark chocolate—no baking required!

MAKES 9 SQUARES

6 pitted dried dates, preferably Medjool
½ cup hemp seeds
¼ cup chia seeds
¼ cup sunflower seeds (see Note)
¾ cup dairy-free semisweet chocolate chips
Generous pinch of ground cinnamon

1. Line the bottom of an 8 × 8 or 9 × 9-inch baking pan with parchment paper or wax paper.

2. Soak the dates in enough hot water to cover for 10 to 15 minutes, then drain and transfer to a food processor. Process until pureed.

3. Transfer the date puree to a small saucepan and add the remaining ingredients. Heat gently until the chocolate is melted, stirring often.

4. Pour the mixture into the prepared pan and smooth out until even. Refrigerate for 2 to 3 hours. Cut into 9 more or less equal squares. Cover and store any leftovers in the refrigerator.

note: I think toasted and salted sunflower seeds add the most flavor to these bars, but you can use toasted, untoasted, salted, or unsalted seeds, as you prefer.

PER SQUARE: Calories: 216; Total fat: 15g; Protein: 8g; Carbohydrates: 17g; Fiber: 4g; Sodium: 27mg

Unbaked Fudgy Brownies

Unbaked Fudgy Brownies

You won't believe how easy it is to make these unbaked vegan chocolate brownies, enriched with nuts and sweetened with dates—and no added sugar. They're flourless, gluten-free, and altogether rich and yummy.

MAKES 12 SQUARES

1 cup untoasted slivered or sliced almonds
1 cup pitted Medjool dates
3 tablespoons unsweetened cocoa powder
1/2 teaspoon vanilla extract
1/4 teaspoon ground cinnamon
1 cup dairy-free chocolate chips
1/4 cup untoasted walnuts

1. Place the almonds in the container of a food processor and process until ground to a fine powder.

2. Add the dates, cocoa powder, vanilla, cinnamon, and half the chocolate chips. Process until the mixture holds together as a mass—this will take a few minutes.

3. Add the remaining chocolate chips and pulse for about 30 seconds. Add the walnuts and pulse for another 20 to 30 seconds, or until the walnuts are finely chopped but still visible in the mixture.

4. Transfer to an 8 × 8-inch baking pan. Press the mixture into the pan, using the back of a spatula to get it nice and even. Cut the mixture into 12 squares. Refrigerate for at least an hour before serving. Cover any leftovers and store in the refrigerator.

PER SQUARE: Calories: 177; Total fat: 11g; Protein: 4g; Carbohydrates: 21g; Fiber: 3g; Sodium: 0mg

Chocolate Nut-Butter Truffles

These were, and still may be, my kids' favorite homemade snack, even though my kids are quite grown up now! A combination of nut butter, chocolate, raisins, and hemp seeds or wheat germ adds up to a high-protein snack for kids, teens, and adults alike.

MAKES 1 DOZEN TRUFFLES

½ cup natural peanut butter or your favorite nut butter
½ cup dairy-free chocolate chips
½ cup raisins
½ cup wheat germ or hemp seeds
Sesame seeds for rolling (optional)
Unsweetened cocoa powder for rolling (optional)

1. Combine all ingredients except sesame seeds and cocoa powder in a food processor. Process until the mixture is completely smooth. You may have to stop the machine and reach in with a spoon a couple of times to break up clumps.

2. Roll into a dozen 1-inch balls, then roll the balls in sesame seeds and/or cocoa powder if desired.

3. Refrigerate for about an hour, or until the truffles are firm, then serve. Cover and refrigerate any leftovers.

PER TRUFFLE: Calories: 125; Total fat: 7g; Protein: 4g; Carbohydrates: 13g; Fiber: 1g; Sodium: 1mg

‹ Homemade Chocolate Energy Bars (page 345) and Chocolate Nut-Butter Truffles

Eat More Fruit!

Fruit should have a prominent place in any discussion of seasonal fare, even if fruit can't compete with vegetables for sheer variety. And although fruits—because of their natural sugars—are secondary only to vegetables as the kind of produce you should aim to consume most, they often get short shrift. Set an array of whole fruits in a bowl on the table, and the members of your household are more likely to regard it as a still life than as food. I've always found that, whether for my family or guests, fruit needs to be cut up, releasing its subtle scents and showing off its lovely colors. Served like this, even with no further embellishment, fruit is likely to be devoured on the spot.

In some ethnic cuisines, fruit is served with the main part of the meal as well as after it. I've adopted this practice, as my family and I have never been big on fruit eaten alone, much as we enjoy it. Think of fruity pilafs in Indian cuisine, or mango salsa served with Mexican-style meals. Fruits add a refreshing note and a surprising flavor when served with savory fare. I also enjoy serving sliced oranges with Asian or Thai-style stir-fries. And adding small amounts of fruit to otherwise simple green salads is downright delicious—you'll find several informal ideas for doing so in "Fruity, Nutty Mixed Greens Salads," page 326.

Imported fruits have helped expand seasonality and variety, but in general, strawberries are best in June, blueberries in July, and peaches in August. Pears are available most any time of year, but the palate seems to welcome their comforting flavor in the late fall and winter. Fruits, as with vegetables, are best consumed in organic form whenever possible. Some fruits are safer than others if you must buy nonorganic. Consult the lists on pages 58–59.

COOL-SEASON FRUIT TREATS

Orange and Pineapple Ambrosia: This fruit combo can be enjoyed when there's a dearth of other fruits. Combine two cups or so of pineapple chunks (fresh or canned and drained) with three or four small peeled and sectioned oranges. Toss with a few dried cranberries or raisins. If you want to have this for dessert, or even breakfast, stir in a small container of vanilla coconut-milk yogurt and top with a few toasted almonds or a handful of granola. This makes about four servings.

Sautéed Pears with Chocolate Drizzle: Allow a half to one pear per person. Cut firm pears into quarters lengthwise and core them (but don't peel). Then cut each quarter in half lengthwise. Heat a little fruit juice and maple syrup in a medium skillet. Add the pears, cover, and steam until the fruit is tender, about five to seven minutes. Transfer the pears to a serving plate, and sprinkle with cinnamon. Drizzle with melted dairy-free chocolate chips. If you're very lazy, use organic chocolate syrup. Finish with a sprinkling of toasted almonds.

Skillet Cinnamon Apples: Use firm sweet or tart apples—your choice! Figure on one apple per serving; most medium skillets will comfortably hold four or five. Peel apples, then quarter and seed them. Cut each quarter into three or so slices. Heat just enough apple juice to coat the bottom of a medium nonstick skillet. Steam the apple slices over medium heat until just tender, about four to five minutes, stirring occasionally. If you started with tart apples, stir in maple syrup or agave nectar to taste. Sprinkle with cinnamon. Transfer to a serving container. Let cool until just warm or at room temperature and serve alone or with a dollop of nondairy vanilla yogurt or ice cream. Garnish with a sprinkling of granola, if you'd like.

SUMMER FRUIT COMBOS AND COMPOSITIONS

With so few fruit varieties available in the cool months, summer is the time to take full advantage of vitamin-rich fruits. Berries, in particular, are one of the most antioxidant-rich fruits on the planet. Giving just a little thought to their presentation makes all the difference between their languishing in the refrigerator or being devoured—as they should be.

Composed Fruit Platters: When spring and summer roll around, fruit platters are the best kind of dessert. They can also be a showstopping feature of weekend brunches. Quantity isn't as important as arrangement: the fruit should be ripe and luscious. Vary the kind of fruit used according to what's available. Alongside this kind of platter, you can serve small bowls of toasted sliced or slivered almonds and nondairy yogurt for dressing up individual portions, as shown in the photo below. Here are some fruits to choose from:

Melon Cup with Strawberries and Blueberries >

- Blueberries or blackberries

- Strawberries, hulled and halved

- Melons—cantaloupe, honeydew, and/or watermelon, peeled and cut into wedges

- Mango or papaya, peeled and sliced

- Peaches or nectarines, sliced

- Grapes—green and/or red, cut into small bunches

- Kiwifruits, peeled and sliced

Melon Cups with Strawberries and Blueberries: The presentation of this medley of common summer fruits is incredibly appealing. Again, no need to follow an exact recipe. Use small cantaloupes if you can find them; each half cantaloupe makes a generous serving. Scoop the flesh out of them using the small end of a melon baller, leaving a shell about a quarter inch thick. You can cut a nice zigzag pattern around the perimeter of the cantaloupe as shown in the facing photo, but that's entirely optional. Cut a thin slice from the bottom of each melon so that it will stand more securely.

Combine the melon balls with halved strawberries and whole blueberries (or other berries) and stir together. Divide the fruit mixture among the shells. Garnish with mint leaves if you like.

Fruity Parfaits: Parfaits might look fancy, but they're so simple that a formal recipe is really not required! Layering nondairy yogurt with seasonal fruits takes almost no effort, creating a treat that looks as appealing as it tastes. For each serving, use a 6- to 8-ounce container of vanilla, lemon, or pineapple nondairy yogurt (coconut-milk or soy) and a half to one cup of fruit (see suggestions below). In medium-size glass tumblers, layer half the yogurt, then half the fruit; then repeat. For a breakfast parfait, top with a little granola; if the parfait is served as a dessert, top with dairy-free semisweet chocolate chips and/or toasted sliced almonds. To make it even more of a dessert, use vanilla nondairy ice cream instead of yogurt. Here are some ideas for fruits to combine:

- Sliced strawberries and blueberries

- Sliced peaches or nectarines with any type of berries

- Diced mango and berries

- Berries and sliced banana

Summer Fruit Duos: Often a simple pairing of two contrasting fruits makes them far more interesting than serving single fruits alone. Honestly, you don't need a formal recipe or even quantities, but I give some as a guideline in the ideas that follow:

Fruity Parfaits (page 353)

- **Mango and blueberries:** Depending on how many you're serving, combine one or two peeled and diced mangos (large chunks are fine) with one to two cups blueberries.

- **Strawberries and blueberries or blackberries:** Hull about one pint of sweet, ripe strawberries. Cut them in half and combine with one cup or so of blueberries or blackberries.

- **Honeydew and raspberries:** The pretty red of raspberries adds a decorative touch to the pale green of honeydew. Cut up half a large, lush honeydew into bite-size chunks and combine with about a cup of raspberries—or more if you like.

- **Peaches or nectarines and berries:** If the fruit is perfectly ripe, this is heavenly. Use late-summer peaches or nectarines from a farm market, not those that arrive at the supermarket as hard as stones. Use about four to six peaches or nectarines, pitted and diced, and a cup or two of whatever late-summer berry you can find, such as blueberries or blackberries.

- **Cantaloupe and black plums:** Combine a lush cantaloupe, cut into bite-size chunks, with a few pitted and diced black plums—the kind that are supersweet and deep red inside.

- **Cantaloupe or watermelon and blueberries:** Here's a classic duo for midsummer. For ease, I like to use seedless watermelon. Use about half a cantaloupe or a quarter of a good-size watermelon, both cut into large, bite-size chunks, and a cup or so of blueberries. Of course, if you'd like to use both cantaloupe and watermelon, feel free to do so.

ACKNOWLEDGMENTS

First, I'd like to acknowledge my editor, Gideon Weil, who not only came up with the concept and title for this book, but then quite flatteringly chose me to execute his initial vision. It has been quite a pleasure to work together.

Lisa Ekus and Sally Ekus are not only my agents, but dear friends. If I ever accidentally fall off a cliff, I'd be confident that they'd be standing underneath, waiting to catch me. Thank you for always being there for me, my dear literary ladies.

This book wouldn't be what it is without Hannah Kaminsky's colorful and appetizing photography. Though we got to work together in person several times, Hannah didn't *really* need me, since she handled the food preparation, prop and food styling, shooting, and digital processing with amazing ease and grace.

I always appreciate a good copy editor, and Barbara Clark applied a very skillful eye to this large task. Thank you so much, Barbara, for making sure that I said what I meant and meant what I said, consistently and thoroughly, throughout the pages.

Nikki Goldbeck supplied the nutritional analyses for this book, a set of data that readers always seem to appreciate. And I appreciated the fact that this experienced nutrition expert and author in her own right was able to work with me once again on this project.

My assistant, Rachael Braun, helped me with research and other details. She has also been invaluable in helping me run my overstuffed life and massive VegKitchen website, which helps me tackle intensive projects like this one.

To my friends and extended family who had to withstand rigorous guinea pig sessions, I say thank you for sacrificing your valuable weekend time, allowing me to test out my experimentations with plant-powered pizzas, tacos, kale salads, and other fare on you (often washed down with mojitos).

Thanks to Progressive International, who provided some of the kitchenware shown in the photos throughout this book.

My family of four (my husband, Chaim Tabak, and young adult offspring, Alice and Evan) may be last on this list, but they are first in my heart. Thanks to all of you for truly being there for me, as hackneyed a phrase as that may be, and for (almost) always eating everything I've ever made for you. Those who are parents will understand just how big a deal that is, and for a plant-based family, it means everything to have been on the same plate all these years.

Thanks also to friends and family who contributed tips for living or leaning in to the plant-based life: Leslie Cerier, Heidi Efner, Rachel Evans, Kevin Fort, Ricki Heller, Kathy Hester, Lee Iden, Ellen Kanner, Colette Martin, and Sharon Nazarian.

OVEN TEMPERATURE EQUIVALENTS

250°F = 120°C
275°F = 135°C
300°F = 150°C
325°F = 160°C
350°F = 180°C
375°F = 190°C
400°F = 200°C
425°F = 220°C
450°F = 230°C
475°F = 240°C
500°F = 260°C

MEASUREMENT EQUIVALENTS

Measurements should always be level unless directed otherwise.

⅛ teaspoon = 0.5 ml
¼ teaspoon = 1 ml
½ teaspoon = 2 ml
1 teaspoon = 5 ml
1 tablespoon = 3 teaspoons = ½ fluid ounce = 15 ml
2 tablespoons = ⅛ cup = 1 fluid ounce = 30 ml
4 tablespoons = ¼ cup = 2 fluid ounces = 60 ml
5⅓ tablespoons = ⅓ cup = 3 fluid ounces = 80 ml
8 tablespoons = ½ cup = 4 fluid ounces = 120 ml
10⅔ tablespoons = ⅔ cup = 5 fluid ounces = 160 ml
12 tablespoons = ¾ cup = 6 fluid ounces = 180 ml
16 tablespoons = 1 cup = 8 fluid ounces = 240 ml

RECIPE INDEX

Page numbers of photographs appear in italics.

agave nectar
    Cold Peanut Butter–Sesame
        Noodles with Crisp Veggies,
        311
    Peanut or Cashew Butter Sauce,
        219
    Sweet and Savory Tofu, 80
    Sweet and Smoky Beans and
        Greens, 92–93, *93*
    Sweet-and-Sour Sauce, 221
    Tahini-Lemon Greens, 288
    Teriyaki Sauce, 220–21
almonds
    Basmati Rice Pilaf with Fresh
        Fruit or Cauliflower, 110–11
    Brown and Wild Rice Pilaf with
        Mushrooms and Nuts, 109–10
    "Fruity, Nutty Mixed Greens
        Salads," 326
    Simple Dried Fruit and Nut
        Couscous, 147
    Unbaked Fudgy Brownies, 346
apples
    Apple Slaw with Leafy Greens,
        325
    Basmati Rice Pilaf with Fresh
        Fruit or Cauliflower, 110–11
    Green Smoothie with Banana
        and Apple, *333, 339,* 339
    Roasted Sweet Potatoes or
        Butternut Squash with Apples
        or Pears, 290
    Skillet Cinnamon Apples, 351
Arrabbiata Sauce, 157
artichokes
    easy salads, 155
    Italian Salad, 319
    Red Pizza with Bell Peppers and
        Artichokes, *46, 182,* 183
arugula
    Apple Slaw with Leafy Greens,
        325
    Beans and Greens Burgers, *276,*
        277–78

    Composed Asian-Flavored Salad
        Platter, 308–9, *310*
    "Fruity, Nutty Mixed Greens
        Salads," 326
    Hummus Wraps with Grains and
        Greens, *256,* 257
    Leafy Greens and Basil Pesto,
        172–73
    Lemon and Garlic Beans or
        Lentils, 94
    Lentil and Greens Soup, 125
    Potato or Sweet Potato and
        Arugula Pizza, 189
    Quinoa Pilaf with Vegetable
        Variations, *98,* 100–101
Asian-style dishes. *See also* stir-
    fries
    Asian-Flavored Kale Salad, 322
    Asian Noodle Bowls, *191,* 218–19
    Asian-Style Tofu and Vegetable
        Soup, 217
    Asian Succotash, 222
    Baby Carrots, Broccoli, and Baby
        Corn, 222–23
    Basic Chinese Sauce, 220
    Bok Choy, Spinach, and Romaine
        Salad, 223
    Chinese-Style Vegetable Fried
        Rice, 208–9
    Cold Peanut Butter–Sesame
        Noodles with Crisp Veggies,
        311
    Composed Asian-Flavored Salad
        Platter, *308,* 309–10
    Double Fruit-Glazed Tofu, 193
    Gingery Miso Soup, 215–16
    Japanese-Style Carrot-Ginger
        Dressing, 331
    Peanut or Cashew Butter Sauce,
        219
    Plant-Powered Pepper Steak, 206
    Red Cabbage and Carrot Salad,
        223
    Skillet Tofu Teriyaki, *194,* 195
    Southeast Asian–Style Vegetable
        and Nut Butter Stew, 150–51
    Spicy Eggplant in Garlic Sauce,
        201–3

    Spicy or Gingered Broccoli,
        Asparagus, or Green Beans,
        222
    Stir-Fried Tofu with Leafy
        Greens, *202,* 204–5
    Sweet-and-Sour Sauce, 221
    Sweet-and-Sour Stir-Fried
        Vegetables with Seitan or
        Tempeh, *70–71, 198,* 199–200
    Teriyaki Sauce, 220–21
    Thai-Flavored Salad Wraps,
        260–61
    Thai Salad, 318
    Thai-Style Pineapple-Coconut
        Rice, *7,* 210–11
    Veggie Lo Mein, *212,* 213–14
    Wilted Sesame Greens, 222
asparagus
    Asparagus and Spinach Pizza,
        189
    Roasted Sesame Asparagus,
        289–90
    Spicy or Gingered Broccoli,
        Asparagus, or Green Beans,
        222
avocado
    Colorful and Luscious Kale and
        Avocado Salad, 322
    Cucumber and Avocado
        Wraps with Bean Spread or
        Hummus, 258
    Fresh Tomato Guacamole, 248
    Hummus Wraps with Grains and
        Greens, *256,* 257
    Smoky Tempeh and Avocado
        Reuben Sandwiches, 265
    Southwestern Quinoa Salad, 317
    Taco Salad, 319
    Tomato, Corn, and Avocado
        Salad, 250

Balsamic Vinaigrette, 327
banana
    Banana-Blueberry Smoothie,
        338, *339*
    Green Smoothie with Banana
        and Apple, *333, 339,* 339
Barbecue Sauce, No-Cook, 86

barley
  how to cook, 112
  Lentil and Grain Soup, 125
  Vegetable-Barley Soup with
    Mushroom Variation, 137–38
basil
  Eggplant Pizza with Green
    Olives and Basil, 189
  Leafy Greens and Basil Pesto,
    172–73
  Pesto and Heirloom Tomato
    Pizza, *188*, 189
  Pesto Pizza, 178
  Pesto Pizza with Roasted Mixed
    Vegetables, 186
beans
  Barbecue-Flavored Roasted
    Vegetables with Protein
    Options, 295–96
  Beans and Greens Burgers,
    277–78
  Beer-Stewed Pinto or Pink
    Beans, 250
  Black Bean Tostadas, *226*, 228–
    29
  Chunky Bean Spread, 269
  cooking from scratch, 89–90
  Cream of Broccoli Soup, 132–33,
    133
  Cucumber and Avocado
    Wraps with Bean Spread or
    Hummus, 258
  Latin American–Style Black
    Beans and Rice, 108
  Lemon and Garlic Beans or
    Lentils, 94
  Long-Simmering Bean Soup,
    128–29
  Marinated Bean Salad, 313–14
  Pasta with Beans and Greens
    with Variations, 164–65, *166*
  Pinto Bean and Quinoa Sloppy
    Joes, 279–80, *280*
  Pinto Bean and Quinoa Soft
    Tacos, 246
  pressure-cooking, 90
  Quick Black Bean Soup, *119*,
    126–27, *127*
  Quinoa and Red Lentil Burgers,
    274–75, *276*
  Refried Pinto Beans (Frijoles
    Refritos), 250

  Skillet Barbecue-Flavored Beans,
    95
  slow-cooker, 90
  Southwestern Quinoa Salad, 317
  Spanish-Style Rice with Red
    Beans and Olives, 106–7, *107*
  Sweet and Smoky Beans and
    Greens, 92–93, *93*
  Taco Salad, 319
  Tofu and Black Bean Rancheros,
    234–35
  Vegan Niçoise-Style Salad, 306–7
  Vegan Ranch-Style Dressing or
    Dip, 328–29
  White Bean and Corn Chowder,
    130–31
beets
  Roasted Beets, 290
  Roasted Root Vegetables, *292*,
    293–94
  tips for peeling, 293
blackberries
  Peaches or Nectarines and
    Berries, 355
  Strawberries and Blackberries,
    355
blueberries
  Banana-Blueberry Smoothie,
    333, 338, *339*
  cantaloupe or watermelon and
    blueberries, 355
  mango and blueberries, 355
  melon cups with strawberries
    and blueberries, *352*, 353
  peaches or nectarines and
    berries, 355
  strawberries and blueberries,
    355
bok choy
  Bok Choy, Spinach, and Romaine
    Salad, 223
  Stir-Fried Tofu with Leafy
    Greens, 203–5, *204*
  Thai Salad, 318
  Wilted Sesame Greens, 222
broccoli
  Baby Carrots, Broccoli, and Baby
    Corn, 222–23
  Broccoli and Cheddar Topping,
    304
  Cream of Broccoli Soup, 132–33,
    133

  Cruciferous Combo, 289
  Quinoa Pilaf with Vegetable
    Variations, *98*, 100–101
  Spicy or Gingered Broccoli,
    Asparagus, or Green Beans,
    222
  Steamed Broccoli and Yellow
    Squash, *226*, 251
  Thai Salad, 318
  Tofu and Veggie Scrambles,
    82–83, *85*
broccoli rabe
  basic preparation, 61
  Garlicky Hardy Greens, 287
  Pasta with Beans and Greens
    with Variations, 164–65, *166*
Brownies, Unbaked Fudgy, *346*, 347
Brussels Sprouts, Roasted, 289
bulgur
  how to cook, 112
  Tabbouleh, 315–16, *316*
burgers
  Beans and Greens Burgers,
    277–78
  Quinoa and Red Lentil Burgers,
    274–75, *276*
Burritos, Veggie, 236–37
butternut squash
  Chili-Stuffed Winter Squash, 143
  Quinoa Pilaf with Vegetable
    Variations, *98*, 100–101
  Roasted Butternut Squash with
    Apples or Pears, 290
  Roasted Butternut Squash with
    Greens, 290, *291*
  secrets of how to prepare, 298,
    299
  White Bean and Corn Chowder,
    130–31

cabbage
  Apple Slaw with Leafy Greens,
    325
  Composed Asian-Flavored Salad
    Platter, 308–9, *310*
  Creamy Kale and Cabbage Slaw,
    324
  Italian Salad, 319
  Red Cabbage and Carrot Salad,
    223
  simple slaws, 322–23
  Southwestern Slaw, 251

cantaloupe
 Cantaloupe and Black Plums, 355
 Cantaloupe and Blueberries, 355
 melon cups with strawberries
  and blueberries, *352, 353*
carrots
 Baby Carrots, Broccoli, and Baby
  Corn, 222–23
 Coconut Cream of Orange
  Vegetables Soup, 134–35
 Japanese-Style Carrot-Ginger
  Dressing, 331
 Maple-Roasted Baby Carrots,
  289
 Red Cabbage and Carrot Salad,
  223
 Roasted Root Vegetables, *292,*
  293–94
cashews
 Basmati Rice Pilaf with Fresh
  Fruit or Cauliflower, 110–11
 Cashew Butter Sauce, 219
 Cashew Cream, 249
 Greens in Nut Butter Sauce, 288
 Nut Butter and Veggie Topped
  Smashed Sweet Potatoes, 305
 Vegan Parmesan-Style Cheez,
  173
 Vegan Ranch-Style Dressing or
  Dip, 328–29
cauliflower
 Basmati Rice Pilaf with Fresh
  Fruit or Cauliflower, 110–11
 Cauliflower with Bread Crumbs,
  289
 Cruciferous Combo, 289
 Quinoa Pilaf with Vegetable
  Variations, *98,* 100–101
chard
 Beans and Greens Burgers, *276,*
  277–78
 Creamed Greens, 288
 Garlicky Hardy Greens, 287
 Greens in Nut Butter Sauce, 288
 Grits 'n' Greens, *116,* 117
 Lentil and Greens Soup, 125
 Nut Butter and Veggie Topped
  Smashed Sweet Potatoes, 305
 Pasta with Beans and Greens
  with Variations, 164–65, *166*
 Stir-Fried Tofu with Leafy
  Greens, 203–5, *204*

 Tahini-Lemon Greens, 288
 Tofu and Veggie Scrambles,
  82–83
 Wilted Sesame Greens, 222
cheese, nondairy
 Baked Macaroni and Cheez with
  Crisp Bread Crumbs, 175
 Broccoli and Cheddar Topping,
  304
 Easy, Flexible Quesadillas, 240–
  43, *242*
 Fresh Tomato Pizza with Mixed
  Mushrooms and Fresh Herbs,
  187
 Mixed Vegetable Lasagna, 162–63
 Pesto Pizza with Roasted Mixed
  Vegetables, 186
 Potato or Sweet Potato and
  Arugula Pizza, 189
 Taco Salad, 319
 Vegan Cheez and Corn Grits, 117
 Vegan Macaroni and Cheez, *174,*
  175
 Vegan Parmesan-Style Cheez,
  173
chia seeds
 Homemade Chocolate Energy
  Bars, 345, *348*
chickpeas
 Barbecue-Flavored Chickpea
  Sandwiches, *253,* 263–64, *264*
 Barbecue-Flavored Roasted
  Vegetables with Protein
  Options, 295–96
 Basic Hummus with Variations,
  272–73
 Chickpea and Kale Sandwich
  Spread, *266,* 267
 Curried Chickpea, Eggplant, and
  Green Bean Stew, 149–50
 Curried Chickpeas or Lentils
  with Spinach, 96–97
 Minestrone, 139
 Vegan Niçoise-Style Salad, 306–7
chili
 Chili-Stuffed Winter Squash,
  143, *143*
 Chili-Topped Smashed Potatoes,
  305
 Chili-Topped Smashed Sweet
  Potatoes, 143
 Cincinnati Chili Mac, *143,* 143

 Classic Veggie Chili, *4,* 140–41,
  142
chili peppers (jalapeño or serrano)
 Fresh Tomato Salsa, 246–47
 Nut Butter and Veggie Topped
  Smashed Sweet Potatoes, 305
 Tofu and Veggie Scrambles, 82, 84
 Tomato and Chili Pepper Grits,
  117
chocolate
 Chocolate Nut-Butter Truffles,
  348, 349
 Homemade Chocolate Energy
  Bars, 345, *348*
 Sautéed Pears with Chocolate
  Drizzle, 350
 Unbaked Fudgy Brownies, *346,*
  347
Chowder, White Bean and Corn,
  130–31
cilantro
 Cilantro-Lime Dressing, 329
 Composed Asian-Flavored Salad
  Platter, 308–9, *310*
 Southwestern Quinoa Salad, 317
cinnamon
 Cincinnati Chili Mac, *143,* 143
 Skillet Cinnamon Apples, 351
coconut
 Coconut Cream of Orange
  Vegetables Soup, 134–35
 Coconut-Peanut Dressing, 330
 Curried Vegetable Stew, 146–47,
  148
 Thai-Style Pineapple-Coconut
  Rice, *7,* 210–11
collards
 Beans and Greens Burgers, *276,*
  277–78
 Creamed Greens, 288
 Garlicky Hardy Greens, 287
 Greens in Nut Butter Sauce, 288
 Green Smoothie with Banana
  and Apple, 339, *339*
 Grits 'n' Greens, *116,* 117
 Lentil and Greens Soup, 125
 Quinoa Pilaf with Vegetable
  Variations, *98,* 100–101
 Roasted Butternut Squash with
  Greens, 290, *291*
 Stir-Fried Tofu with Leafy
  Greens, 203–5, *204*

Sweet and Smoky Beans and Greens, 92–93, *93*
Tahini-Lemon Greens, 288
Tofu and Veggie Scrambles, 82–83
Wilted Sesame Greens, 222
corn
Asian Succotash, 222
Baby Carrots, Broccoli, and Baby Corn, 222–23
Corn-Kernel Cornbread or Muffins, *4*, 144
Quinoa Pilaf with Vegetable Variations, *98*, 100–101
Sautéed Zucchini, Corn, and Bell Pepper, 251
Southwestern Quinoa Salad, 317
Southwestern Slaw, 251
Tomato, Corn, and Avocado Salad, 250
Vegan Cheez and Corn Grits, 117
White Bean and Corn Chowder, 130–31
cornbread
Corn-Kernel, *4*, 144
Leftover Cornbread Skillet Stuffing, 145
cornmeal. *See also* grits
Corn-Kernel Cornbread or Muffins, *4*, 144
Cornmeal-Crusted Tofu, Tempeh, or Seitan, 80
grits, various ways, 115
polenta, basic cooked, 115
polenta, using prepared, 115
couscous
how to cook, 113
Lentil and Pasta Soup, 125
Simple Dried Fruit and Nut Couscous, 147
cucumber
Cucumber and Avocado Wraps with Bean Spread or Hummus, 258
Easy Cucumber Raita, 147
curries
Coconut Cream of Orange Vegetables Soup, 134–35
Coconut Curried Vegetable Stew, 146–47, *148*

Curried Chickpea, Eggplant, and Green Bean Stew, 149–50
Curried Chickpeas or Lentils with Spinach, 96–97
Curried Split Pea or Red Lentil Soup, 122–23
dates
Homemade Chocolate Energy Bars, 345, *348*
Unbaked Fudgy Brownies, *346*, 347
desserts
Chocolate Nut-Butter Truffles, *348*, 349
composed fruit platters, *351*, 351–52
fruity parfaits, 353, *354*
melon cups with strawberries and blueberries, *352*, 353
orange and pineapple ambrosia, 350
sautéed pears with chocolate drizzle, 350
skillet cinnamon apples, 351
summer fruit duos, 353, 355
Unbaked Fudgy Brownies, *346*, 347

edamame
Asian Succotash, 222
as snack, 343
Tomato-Rice (or Tomato-Quinoa) Soup, 139, *139*
eggplant
Curried Chickpea, Eggplant, and Green Bean Stew, 149–50
Eggplant and Peppers Sauce, 158
Eggplant Pizza with Green Olives and Basil, 189
Roasted Ratatouille, 296–97, *297*
Spicy Eggplant in Garlic Sauce, 201–3
Energy Bars, Homemade Chocolate, 345, *348*
escarole
basic preparation, 61
Garlicky Hardy Greens, 287
Pasta with Beans and Greens with Variations, 164–65, *166*

Fajitas, Sizzling Tempeh or Tofu, *7*, 230–31, *232*

Fattouche, 318
French Dressing, 329
Frijoles Borrachos (drunken beans), 250
Soft Tacos, 246
Frijoles Refritos (refried beans), 250
fruits, dried
Basmati Rice Pilaf with Fresh Fruit or Cauliflower, 110–11
Simple Dried Fruit and Nut Couscous, 147
fruits, fresh. *See also specific fruits*
Basmati Rice Pilaf with Fresh Fruit or Cauliflower, 110–11
composed fruit platters, *351*, 351–53
"Fruity, Nutty Mixed Greens Salads," 326
fruity parfaits, 353, *354*
summer fruit duos, 353, 355

garlic
Garlic and Rosemary Roasted Potatoes, 290
Garlicky Hardy Greens, 287
Lemon and Garlic Beans or Lentils, 94
Spicy Eggplant in Garlic Sauce, 201–3
ginger
Coconut Cream of Orange Vegetables Soup, 134–35
Gingery Miso Soup, 215–16
Japanese-Style Carrot-Ginger Dressing, 331
Sesame-Ginger Dressing, 328
Spicy or Gingered Broccoli, Asparagus, or Green Beans, 222
grains, whole. *See also* quinoa; rice
basics, 112–14
easy ways to dress up, 114
Lentil and Grain Soup, 125
Whole-Wheat Pizza Crust, 180
Gravy, Basic, with Mushroom and Miso Variations, 87
Greek Salad, *119*, 318
green beans
Curried Chickpea, Eggplant, and Green Bean Stew, 149–50
Spicy or Gingered Broccoli, Asparagus, or Green Beans, 222
Vegan Niçoise-Style Salad, 306–7

greens, bitter. *See also* escarole;
    mustard greens
  basic cooking of, 61
  Garlicky Hardy Greens, 287
  traditional additions, 61
greens, tender or baby
  "Fruity, Nutty Mixed Greens
    Salads," 326
  Hummus Wraps with Grains
    and Greens, *256, 257*
  Tofu and Veggie Scrambles,
    82–83
grits, 115
  basic cooked, 117
  Grits 'n' Greens, *116,* 117
  Tomato and Chili Pepper Grits,
    117
  Vegan Cheez and Corn Grits, 117
Guacamole, Fresh Tomato, 248

hemp seeds
  Homemade Chocolate Energy
    Bars, 345, *348*
  Vegan Parmesan-Style Cheez,
    173
herbs, fresh
  Fresh Tomato Pizza with Mixed
    Mushrooms and Fresh Herbs,
    187
  Tofu and Veggie Scrambles,
    82–83
Honeydew and Raspberries, 355
hummus
  Basic Hummus with Variations,
    272–73
  Cucumber and Avocado
    Wraps with Bean Spread or
    Hummus, 258
  Hummus Wraps with Grains
    and Greens, *256,* 257

kale
  Asian-Flavored Kale Salad, 322
  Beans and Greens Burgers, *276,*
    277–78
  Chickpea and Kale Sandwich
    Spread, *266,* 267
  Colorful and Luscious Kale and
    Avocado Salad, 322
  Creamed Greens, 288
  Creamy Kale and Cabbage Slaw,
    324

Garlicky Hardy Greens, 287
Greens in Nut Butter Sauce, 288
Green Smoothie with Banana
  and Apple, 339, *339*
Grits 'n' Greens, *116,* 117
Kale, Mushroom, and Red Onion
  Pizza, 189
Lentil and Greens Soup, 125
massaged, 60–61, 321
Mediterranean Kale Salad, 322
Nut Butter and Veggie Topped
  Smashed Sweet Potatoes, 305
Pasta with Beans and Greens
  with Variations, 164–65, *166*
Quinoa Pilaf with Vegetable
  Variations, *99,* 100–101
Roasted Butternut Squash with
  Greens, 290, *291*
Southwestern-Flavored Kale
  Salad, *320,* 321
Stir-Fried Tofu with Leafy
  Greens, 203–5, *204*
Sweet and Smoky Beans and
  Greens, 92–93, *93*
Tahini-Lemon Greens, 288
Tofu and Veggie Scrambles,
  82–83
Wilted Sesame Greens, 222

lasagna
  Mixed Vegetable Lasagna,
    162–63
  no-boil noodles, note, 163
lemon
  Lemon and Garlic Beans or
    Lentils, 94
  Lemon or Lime Vinaigrette, 327
  Tahini-Lemon Greens, 288
lentils
  cooking, 91, 160
  Curried Chickpeas or Lentils
    with Spinach, 96–97
  Curried Split Pea or Red Lentil
    Soup, 122–23
  Lemon and Garlic Beans or
    Lentils, 94
  Lentil and Grain Soup, 125
  Lentil and Greens Soup, 125
  Lentil and Pasta Soup, 125
  Pasta with Hearty Lentil and
    Spinach Sauce, *153,* 159, *160,*
    161

Quinoa and Red Lentil Burgers,
  274–75, *276*
Soup with Tasty Variations,
  122–23
lime
  Cilantro-Lime Dressing, 329
  Lemon or Lime Vinaigrette, 327

macaroni and cheese
  Baked, with Crisp Bread
    Crumbs, 175
  Macaroni and Almost-Raw
    Cheez Sauce, 176
  Vegan, *174,* 175
  Veggie Toppings for, 177
mango
  mango and blueberries, 355
  Pineapple-Mango Smoothie,
    333, 338, 339
maple syrup
  Maple-Roasted Baby Carrots,
    289
  No-Cook Barbecue Sauce, 86
  Peanut or Cashew Butter Sauce,
    219
  Roasted Sweet Potatoes or
    Butternut Squash with
    Apples or Pears, 290
  Smoky Tempeh Strips, 268
  Sweet and Savory Tofu, 80
  Sweet and Smoky Beans and
    Greens, 92–93, *93*
Marinara Sauce, 157
  Red Pizza, 178
mesquite seasoning, 281
  Smoky Lentil and Mushroom
    Sloppy Joes, 281–82
  Smoky Tempeh Strips, 268
  Sweet and Smoky Beans and
    Greens, 92–93, *93*
millet, how to cook, 113
Minestrone, 139
miso
  Gingery Miso Soup, 215–16
  Miso Gravy, 87
Muffins, Corn-Kernel, 144
mung bean sprouts
  Thai Salad, 318
mushrooms
  Brown and Wild Rice Pilaf
    with Mushrooms and Nuts,
    109–10

Classic Marinara Sauce, 157–58
Fresh Tomato Pizza with Mixed
    Mushrooms and Fresh Herbs,
    187
Kale, Mushroom, and Red Onion
    Pizza, 189
Mushroom and Wilted Spinach
    Topping, 304
Mushroom Gravy, 87
Mushroom Gravy and Parsley
    Topping, 304
Mushroom-Seitan Stroganoff,
    169
Mushroom Stroganoff, 169
Pasta with Hearty Lentil and
    Spinach Sauce, 159–60, *161*
Quinoa Pilaf with Vegetable
    Variations, *99*, 100–101
Tofu and Veggie Scrambles,
    82–83
Vegetable-Barley Soup with
    Mushroom Variation, 137–38
mustard greens
    basic preparation, 61
    Garlicky Hardy Greens, 287

Nachos, Fully Loaded Emergency,
    225, *238*, 239–40
nectarines and berries, 355
nutritional yeast, 82
    Basic Gravy, 87
    Vegan Parmesan-Style Cheez,
    173

olives
    Eggplant Pizza with Green Olives
        and Basil, 189
    Greek Salad, *119*, 318
    Italian Salad, 319
    Puttanesca Sauce, 157
    Spanish-Style Rice with Red
        Beans and Olives, 106–7, *107*
    Taco Salad, 319
    Vegan Niçoise-Style Salad, 306–7
    White Pizza with Caramelized
        Onions and Olives, 184–85
onions
    Caramelized Onion-Smothered
        Tofu, Tempeh, or Seitan, 80
    Caramelized Onions with or
        without Bell Peppers, 88
    Kale, Mushroom, and Red Onion
        Pizza, 189

Onion and Peppers Topped
    Smashed Sweet Potatoes, 305
Tofu and Veggie Scrambles,
    82–83
White Pizza with Caramelized
    Onions and Olives, 184–85
Orange and Pineapple Ambrosia,
    350

Paella, Quick Quinoa, *77*, 102–3, *103*
Paprika Potatoes, Sautéed, 302
parsley
    Middle Eastern Salad
        (Fattouche), 318
    Mushroom Gravy and Parsley
        Topping, 304
    Quinoa Tabbouleh, 315–16, *316*
parsnips
    Roasted Root Vegetables, *292*,
        293–94
pasta. *See also* sauces and toppings
    Asian Noodle Bowls, *191*, 218–19
    Cincinnati Chili Mac, 143, *143*
    Cold Peanut Butter–Sesame
        Noodles with Crisp Veggies,
        311
    Easy Salads to Go with, 155
    Lentil and Pasta Soup, 125
    Macaroni and Almost-Raw
        Cheez Sauce, 176
    Mixed Vegetable Lasagna, 162–63
    Pasta with Beans and Greens
        with Variations, 164–65, *166*
    Pasta with Hearty Lentil and
        Spinach Sauce, *153*, 159, *160*,
        161
    Pasta with Leafy Greens and
        Basil Pesto, 172–73
    Primavera, 170–71
    Vegan Macaroni and Cheez with
        Variations, *174*, 175
    Vegan Pasta Alfredo with Two
        Stroganoff Variations, 167–69,
        168
    Veggie Lo Mein, *212*, 213–14
peaches and berries, 355
peanut butter
    Chocolate Nut-Butter Truffles,
        348, 349
    Coconut-Peanut Dressing, 330
    Cold Peanut Butter–Sesame
        Noodles with Crisp Veggies,
        311

Greens in Nut Butter Sauce, 288
Nut Butter and Veggie Topped
    Smashed Sweet Potatoes, 305
Peanut Butter Sauce, 219
Southeast Asian–Style Vegetable
    and Nut Butter Stew, 150–51
pears
    Basmati Rice Pilaf with Fresh
        Fruit or Cauliflower, 110–11
    Roasted Sweet Potatoes or
        Butternut Squash with Apples
        or Pears, 290
    Sautéed Pears with Chocolate
        Drizzle, 350
peas (green)
    Asian Noodle Bowls, 218
    Chinese-Style Vegetable Fried
        Rice, 208–9
    Cream of Broccoli Soup, 132–33,
        133
    Minestrone, 139
    Quick Quinoa Paella, 102
pecans
    "Fruity, Nutty Mixed Greens
        Salads," 326
peppers, bell
    Caramelized Onions with or
        without Bell Peppers, 88
    Eggplant and Peppers Sauce, 158
    Onion and Peppers Topped
        Smashed Sweet Potatoes, 305
    Plant-Powered Pepper Steak,
        206–7
    Puttanesca Sauce, 157
    Red Pizza with Bell Peppers and
        Artichokes, *46*, *182*, 183
    Sautéed Zucchini, Corn, and Bell
        Pepper, 251
    Sizzling Tempeh or Tofu Fajitas,
        230–31, *232*
    Tofu and Veggie Scrambles,
        82–83
peppers, roasted red
    Italian Salad, 319
pesto
    Leafy Greens and Basil Pesto,
        172–73
    Pesto Pizza, 178
pineapple
    Orange and Pineapple Ambrosia,
        350
    Pineapple-Mango Smoothie, *333*,
        338, *339*

Thai-Style Pineapple-Coconut Rice, *7*, 210–11
pine nuts
Leafy Greens and Basil Pesto, 172–73
pistachio
Leafy Greens and Basil Pesto, 172–73
pitas
Barbecue-Flavored Chickpea Sandwiches, *253*, 263–64, *264*
Basic Hummus, 272
Chickpea and Kale Sandwich Spread, 267
for pizza, 64, 179
pizza
Asparagus and Spinach Pizza, 189
complete your pizza meals, 179
crust options, 179
Easy Salads to Go with, 155
Eggplant Pizza with Green Olives and Basil, 189
Fresh Tomato Pizza, 178–79
Fresh Tomato Pizza with Mixed Mushrooms and Fresh Herbs, 187
Gluten-Free Poured Crust, 181
Kale, Mushroom, and Red Onion Pizza, 189
Pesto and Heirloom Tomato Pizza, *188*, 189
Pesto Pizza, 178
Pesto Pizza with Roasted Mixed Vegetables, 186
Pizza-Flavored Smashed Potatoes, 305
Potato or Sweet Potato and Arugula Pizza, 189
Ratatouille Pizza, 189
Red Pizza, 178
Red Pizza with Bell Peppers and Artichokes, *46*, *182*, 183
vegan cheese for, 179
Veg-Centric Pizzas, 178–79
White Pizza, 178
White Pizza with Caramelized Onions and Olives, 184–85
Whole-Wheat Crust, 180
Plums, Black, and Cantaloupe, 355
Polenta, 115
potatoes
Barbecue-Flavored Potato Skillet, 302

Classic Potato Salad with Variations, 312–13
Easy Hash Brown Potatoes, 300–301
Garlic and Rosemary Roasted Potatoes, 290
Oven Fries or Wedges, 302
Potato or Sweet Potato and Arugula Pizza, 189
Sautéed Paprika Potatoes, 302
smashed potatoes, 303–4
Tofu and Potato Hash Browns, 301
White Bean and Corn Chowder, 130–31
pumpkin seeds
"Fruity, Nutty Mixed Greens Salads," 326
Puttanesca Sauce, 157

quesadillas, easy, flexible, 240–43, *242*
quinoa
basic cooked, 99
Hummus Wraps with Grains and Greens, *256*, 257
Lentil and Grain Soup, 125
Pilafs with Vegetable Variations, *98*, 100–101
Pinto Bean and Quinoa Sloppy Joes, 279–80, *280*
Pinto Bean and Quinoa Soft Tacos, 246
Quick Quinoa Paella, *77*, 102–3, *103*
Quinoa and Red Lentil Burgers, 274–75, *276*
Quinoa Tabbouleh, 315–16, *316*
Southwestern Quinoa Salad, 317
Tomato-Quinoa Soup, 139, *139*

radicchio
easy salads, 155
"Fruity, Nutty Mixed Greens Salads," 326
Italian Salad, 319
Raita, Easy Cucumber, 147
Rancheros, Tofu and Black Bean, 234–35
Ranch-Style Dressing or Dip, Vegan, 328–29
raspberries and honeydew, 355
ratatouille

Ratatouille Pizza, 189
Roasted Ratatouille, 296–97, *297*
rice
basic cooked brown rice, 105
Basmati Rice Pilaf with Fresh Fruit or Cauliflower, 110–11
Brown and Wild Rice Pilaf with Mushrooms and Nuts, 109–10
Chinese-Style Vegetable Fried Rice, 208–9
Hummus Wraps with Grains and Greens, *256*, 257
Latin American–Style Black Beans and Rice, 108
Lentil and Grain Soup, 125
Spanish-Style Rice with Red Beans and Olives, 106–7, *107*
Thai-Style Pineapple-Coconut Rice, *7*, 210–11
Tomato-Rice Soup, 139, *139*
romaine lettuce
Barbecue-Flavored Chickpea Sandwiches, 263
Bok Choy, Spinach, and Romaine Salad, 223
Cucumber and Avocado Wraps with Bean Spread or Hummus, 258
Sizzling Tempeh or Tofu Fajitas, 230–31
Thai-Flavored Salad Wraps, 260
Rosemary Roasted Potatoes, Garlic and, 290

salad dressings
Balsamic Vinaigrette, 327
Basic Vinaigrette, 327
Cilantro-Lime Dressing, 329
Coconut-Peanut Dressing, 330
French Dressing, 329
Japanese-Style Carrot-Ginger Dressing, 331
Lemon or Lime Vinaigrette, 327
Sesame-Ginger Dressing, 328
Thousand Island-ish Dressing, 283
Vegan Ranch-Style Dressing or Dip, 328–29
salads. *See also* slaw
Asian-Flavored Kale Salad, 322
basic ingredients, 318
Bok Choy, Spinach, and Romaine Salad, 223

Classic Potato Salad with
Variations, 312–13
Cold Peanut Butter–Sesame
Noodles with Crisp Veggies,
311
Colorful and Luscious Kale and
Avocado Salad, 322
Composed Asian-Flavored Salad
Platter, *308*, 309–10
Easy Salads to Go with Pasta and
Pizza, 155
"Fruity, Nutty Mixed Greens
Salads," *326*, 326
Greek Salad, *119*, 318
Italian Salad, 319
Marinated Bean Salad, 313–14
Mediterranean Kale Salad, 322
Middle Eastern Salad
(Fattouche), 318
Quinoa Tabbouleh, 315–16, *316*
Red Cabbage and Carrot Salad,
223
Southwestern-Flavored Kale
Salad, *320*, 321
Southwestern Quinoa Salad, 317
Taco Salad, 319
Thai-Flavored Salad Wraps,
260–61
Thai Salad, 318
Tomato, Corn, and Avocado
Salad, 250
Tossed Salad Wraps, 259
Ultimate Eggless Egg Salad, 270
Vegan Niçoise-Style Salad, *285*,
306–7
Salsa, Fresh Tomato, 246–47
sandwiches. *See also* wraps
Barbecue-Flavored Chickpea
Sandwiches, *253*, 263–64, *264*
Homemade Baked Tofu, 270–71
"Leafy Greens Instead of Bread,"
273
Smoky Tempeh and Avocado
Reuben Sandwiches, 265
Ultimate Eggless Egg Salad, 270
sandwich spreads
Basic Hummus with Variations,
272–73
Chickpea and Kale Sandwich
Spread, *266*, 267
Chunky Bean Spread, 269
Quick Tartar Sauce, 282

Thousand Island-ish Dressing,
283
sauces and toppings
Almost-Raw Cheez Sauce, 176
Arrabbiata Sauce, 157
Basic Chinese Sauce, 220
Basic Gravy with Mushroom
and Miso Variations, 87
Caramelized Onions with or
without Bell Peppers, 88
Cashew Cream, 249
Classic Marinara Sauce with
Variations, 157–58
Eggplant and Peppers Sauce, 158
Fresh Tomato Guacamole, 248
Fresh Tomato Salsa, 246–47
Garden Vegetable Sauce, 158
Garlic Sauce, 201–3
Leafy Greens and Basil Pesto,
172–73
No-Cook Barbecue Sauce, 86
Peanut or Cashew Butter Sauce,
219
Puttanesca Sauce, 157
Quick Tartar Sauce, 282
for stir-fries, 196
Sweet-and-Sour Sauce, 221
Teriyaki Sauce, 220–21
Vegan Sour Cream, 248–49
Veggie Toppings for Macaroni
and Cheez, 177
Scrambles, Tofu and Veggie, *82*,
83–85
seitan
Barbecue-Flavored, 80
Barbecue-Flavored or Gravy-
Smothered Protein Skillet, 81
Barbecue-Flavored Roasted
Vegetables with Protein
Options, 295–96
Caramelized Onion-Smothered,
80
Cornmeal-Crusted, 80
Mushroom-Seitan Stroganoff,
169
Plant-Powered Pepper Steak,
206–7
simple preparations for, 79–80
Sweet-and-Sour Stir-Fried
Vegetables with Seitan or
Tempeh, *70–71*, *198*, 199–
200

sesame
Roasted Sesame Asparagus,
289–90
Sesame-Ginger Dressing, 328
Vegan Parmesan-Style Cheez,
173
Wilted Sesame Greens, 222
slaw
add-in ingredients for, 323
Apple Slaw with Leafy Greens,
325
Creamy Kale and Cabbage Slaw,
324
dressings for, 322
Southwestern Slaw, 251
sloppy joes
Pinto Bean and Quinoa Sloppy
Joes, 279–80
Smoky Lentil and Mushroom
Sloppy Joes, 281–82
smashed potatoes, 303–4
topping suggestions, 304–5
smoothies
Banana-Blueberry Smoothie,
338, *339*
basic formula, 337
Green Smoothie with Banana
and Apple, 339, *339*
Pineapple-Mango Smoothie,
338, *339*
soups
Asian Noodle Bowls, *191*, 218–19
Asian-Style Tofu and Vegetable
Soup, 217
Coconut Cream of Orange
Vegetables Soup, 134–35
Cream of Broccoli Soup, 132–33,
133
Curried Split Pea or Red Lentil
Soup, 122–23
Gingery Miso Soup, 215–16
Lentil Soup with Tasty
Variations, 122–23
Long-Simmering Bean Soup,
128–29
Minestrone, 139
Miso Soup, 214
Quick Black Bean Soup, *119*,
126–27, *127*
seasoning tips for, 120–21
Tomato-Rice (or Tomato-
Quinoa) Soup, 139, *139*

Tomato-Vegetable Soup with
Variations, 138–39
Vegetable-Barley Soup with
Mushroom Variation, 137–38
White Bean and Corn Chowder,
130–31
Sour Cream, Vegan, 248–49
soy sauce
Basic Gravy, 87
Sweet and Savory Tofu, 80
Tahini-Lemon Greens, 288
spinach
Apple Slaw with Leafy Greens,
325
Asparagus and Spinach Pizza, 189
Beans and Greens Burgers, *276,*
277–78
Bok Choy, Spinach, and Romaine
Salad, 223
Composed Asian-Flavored Salad
Platter, 308–9, *310*
Curried Chickpeas or Lentils
with Spinach, 96–97
"Fruity, Nutty Mixed Greens
Salads," 326
Grits 'n' Greens, *116,* 117
Hummus Wraps with Grains
and Greens, *256, 257*
Leafy Greens and Basil Pesto,
172–73
Lemon and Garlic Beans or
Lentils, 94
Lentil and Greens Soup, 125
Mushroom and Wilted Spinach
Topping, 304
Nut Butter and Veggie Topped
Smashed Sweet Potatoes, 305
Pasta with Beans and Greens
with Variations, 164–65, *166*
Pasta with Hearty Lentil and
Spinach Sauce, *153,* 159, *160,*
161
Quinoa Pilaf with Vegetable
Variations, *98,* 100–101
Wilted Sesame Greens, 222
Split Pea Soup, Curried 122–23
squash, winter. *See also* butternut
squash
Chili-Stuffed Winter Squash,
143, *143*
Coconut Cream of Orange
Vegetables Soup, 134–35

secrets of how to prepare, 298,
299
squash, yellow
Quinoa Pilaf with Vegetable
Variations, *98,* 100–101
Steamed Broccoli and Yellow
Squash, *226,* 251
stews
Classic Veggie Chili and Ideas
for Leftovers, 140–41, *142*
Coconut Curried Vegetable
Stew, 146–47, *148*
Curried Chickpea, Eggplant, and
Green Bean Stew, 149–50
seasoning tips for, 120–21
Southeast Asian–Style Vegetable
and Nut Butter Stew, 150–51
stir-fries
Baby Carrots, Broccoli, and Baby
Corn, 222–23
basics of, 196–97
sauces for, 196
Stir-Fried Tofu with Leafy
Greens, 204–5
Sweet-and-Sour Stir-Fried
Vegetables with Seitan or
Tempeh, *70–71, 198,* 199–
200
strawberries
melon cups with strawberries
and blueberries, *352,* 353
strawberries and blueberries or
blackberries, 355
Stroganoff
Mushroom-Seitan, 169
Mushroom, 169
Stuffing, Leftover Cornbread
Skillet, 145
sunflower seeds
"Fruity, Nutty Mixed Greens
Salads," 326
Homemade Chocolate Energy
Bars, 345, *348*
Sweet-and-Sour Sauce, 221
sweet potatoes
Chili-Topped Smashed Sweet
Potatoes, 143
Coconut Cream of Orange
Vegetables Soup, 134–35
Easy Hash Brown Potatoes, 301
Nut Butter and Veggie Topped
Smashed Sweet Potatoes, 305

Onion and Peppers Topped
Smashed Sweet Potatoes, 305
Oven Fries or Wedges, 302
Potato or Sweet Potato and
Arugula Pizza, 189
Quinoa Pilaf with Vegetable
Variations, *98,* 100–101
Roasted Root Vegetables, *292,*
293–94
Roasted Sweet Potatoes with
Apples or Pears, 290
White Bean and Corn Chowder,
130–31

Tabbouleh, Quinoa, 315–16, *316*
tacos
Beer-Stewed Pinto or Pink Beans
Soft Taco, 250
Frijoles Borrachos Soft Tacos,
246
Pinto Bean and Quinoa Soft
Tacos, 246
Soft Tacos, 243, *244*
Steamed Broccoli and Yellow
Squash Soft Taco, 251
Taco Salad, 319
Tempeh and Walnut Soft Taco
Filling, 245–46
Veggie Soft Tacos, 246
tahini
Basic Hummus with Variations,
272–73
Cold Peanut Butter–Sesame
Noodles with Crisp Veggies,
311
Tahini-Lemon Greens, 288
Tartar Sauce, Quick, 282
tempeh
Barbecue-Flavored, 80
Barbecue-Flavored or Gravy-
Smothered Protein Skillet, 81
Barbecue-Flavored Roasted
Vegetables with Protein
Options, 295–96
Caramelized Onion-Smothered,
80
Composed Asian-Flavored Salad
Platter, 308–9, *310*
Cornmeal-Crusted, 80
simple preparations for, 79–80
Sizzling Tempeh or Tofu Fajitas,
7, 230–31, *232*

Smoky Tempeh and Avocado
Reuben Sandwiches, 265
Smoky Tempeh Strips, 268
Sweet-and-Sour Stir-Fried
Vegetables with Seitan or
Tempeh, *70–71*, *198*, 199–
200
Tempeh and Walnut Soft Taco
Filling, 245–46
Teriyaki Sauce, 220–21
Thousand Island-ish Dressing, 283
tofu
Asian-Style Tofu and Vegetable
Soup, 217
Barbecue-Flavored, 80
Barbecue-Flavored or Gravy-
Smothered Protein Skillet, 81
Barbecue-Flavored Roasted
Vegetables with Protein
Options, 295–96
Caramelized Onion-Smothered,
80
Cornmeal-Crusted, 80
Creamed Greens, 288
Cream of Broccoli Soup, 132–33,
133
Double Fruit-Glazed Tofu, 193
Greek Salad, *119*, 318
Homemade Baked Tofu, 270–71
prep basics, 79
simple preparations for, 79–80
Sizzling Tempeh or Tofu Fajitas,
7, 230–31, *232*
Skillet Tofu Teriyaki, *194*, 195
Stir-Fried Tofu with Leafy
Greens, 203–5, *204*
in stir-fries, 197
Sweet and Savory Tofu, 80
Thai-Flavored Salad Wraps,
260–61
Tofu and Black Bean Rancheros,
234–35
Tofu and Potato Hash Browns,
301
Tofu and Veggie Scrambles, *82*,
83–85
Ultimate Eggless Egg Salad, 270
Vegan Macaroni and Cheez with
Variations, 175
Vegan Niçoise-Style Salad,
306–7

Vegan Pasta Alfredo with Two
Stroganoff Variations, 167–
69, *168*
White Pizza, 178
White Pizza with Caramelized
Onions and Olives, 184–85
tomato
Classic Marinara Sauce with
Variations, 157–58
Curried Chickpea, Eggplant, and
Green Bean Stew, 149–50
Fresh Tomato Guacamole, 248
Fresh Tomato Pizza, 178–79
Fresh Tomato Pizza with Mixed
Mushrooms and Fresh Herbs,
187
Fresh Tomato Salsa, 246–47
Pesto and Heirloom Tomato
Pizza, *188*, 189
Quinoa Pilaf with Vegetable
Variations, *98*, 100–101
Quinoa Tabbouleh, 315–16, *316*
Roasted Ratatouille, 296–97, *297*
Southwestern Quinoa Salad, 317
Tofu and Veggie Scrambles,
82–83
Tomato, Corn, and Avocado
Salad, 250
Tomato and Chili Pepper Grits,
117
Tomato-Rice (or Tomato-
Quinoa) Soup, 139, *139*
Tomato-Vegetable Soup with
Variations, 138–39
Vegan Niçoise-Style Salad,
306–7
Vegetable-Barley Soup with
Mushroom Variation, 137–39
tomato sauce (premade)
Fresh Tomato Pizza with Mixed
Mushrooms and Fresh Herbs
(variation), 187
Mixed Vegetable Lasagna, 162–
63
No-Cook Barbecue Sauce, 86
Pasta with Hearty Lentil and
Spinach Sauce, 159–60
Red Pizza, 178
tortillas
accompaniments for, 250–51
Black Bean Tostadas, *226*, 228–29

"Easy, Flexible Quesadillas,"
240–43, *242*
Frijoles Borrachos Soft Tacos, 246
Fully Loaded Emergency
Nachos, *225*, *238*, 239–40
Pinto Bean and Quinoa Soft
Tacos, 246
Sizzling Tempeh or Tofu Fajitas,
230–31, *232*
Soft Tacos, 243, *244*
Taco Salad, 319
Tempeh and Walnut Soft Taco
Filling, 245–46
Tofu and Black Bean Rancheros,
234–35
topping suggestions, 246–49
Veggie Burritos, 236–37
Veggie Soft Tacos, 246
Tostadas, Black Bean, 228–29
turmeric
Quick Quinoa Paella, 102–3
turnips
Roasted Root Vegetables, *292*,
293–94

vegetable medley dishes. *See also
specific vegetables*
Asian-Style Tofu and Vegetable
Soup, 217
Barbecue-Flavored Roasted
Vegetables with Protein
Options, 295–96
Chinese-Style Vegetable Fried
Rice, 208–9
Coconut Curried Vegetable
Stew, 146–47, *148*
Cold Peanut Butter–Sesame
Noodles with Crisp Veggies,
311
Garden Vegetable Sauce, 158
hard, soft, and quick-cooking,
for stir-fries, 196
Mixed Vegetable Lasagna, 162–
63
Pasta Primavera, 170–71
Pesto Pizza with Roasted Mixed
Vegetables, 186
Quick Quinoa Paella, *77*, 102–3,
103
Quinoa Pilaf with Vegetable
Variations, *98*, 100–101

Roasted Ratatouille, 296–97, *297*
Roasted Root Vegetables, *292,* 293–94
"Roasted Vegetable Dishes: A Few Tips and Easy Ideas," 288–89
soups, 132–36
Southeast Asian–Style Vegetable and Nut Butter Stew, 150–51
Sweet-and-Sour Stir-Fried Vegetables with Seitan or Tempeh, *70–71,* 197–98, *198*
Tofu and Veggie Scrambles, *82,* 83–85
Tossed Salad Wraps, 259
Vegetable-Barley Soup with Mushroom Variation, 137–38
Veggie Burritos, 236–37
Veggie Lo Mein, *212,* 213–14
Veggie Soft Tacos, 246
Veggie Toppings for Macaroni and Cheez, 177

vinaigrettes
    Balsamic, 327
    Basic, 327
    Lemon or Lime, 327

walnuts
    Brown and Wild Rice Pilaf with Mushrooms and Nuts, 109–10
    "Fruity, Nutty Mixed Greens Salads," 326
    Leafy Greens and Basil Pesto, 172–73
    Tempeh and Walnut Soft Taco Filling, 245–46
watercress
    Leafy Greens and Basil Pesto, 172–73
    Lemon and Garlic Beans or Lentils, 94
    Lentil and Greens Soup, 125
watermelon and blueberries, 355
wraps, 254–55
    basics of creating, 261–62

Chickpea and Kale Sandwich Spread, 267
Cucumber and Avocado Wraps with Bean Spread or Hummus, 258
Hummus Wraps with Grains and Greens, *256,* 257
Thai-Flavored Salad Wraps, 260–61
Tossed Salad Wraps, 259

yogurt, nondairy
    fruity parfaits, 353, *354*
    orange and pineapple ambrosia, 350

zucchini
    Roasted Ratatouille, 296–97, *297*
    Sautéed Zucchini, Corn, and Bell Pepper, 251
    Tofu and Veggie Scrambles, 82, 84

agave nectar, 27–28
Asian noodles: a mini lexicon,
    207
athletes and a plant-based diet, 10

barbecue sauce, 34
barley, 112
beans and legumes
    basics, 89–91
    beans for your pantry, 19
    bean threads, 207
    beluga or French lentils, 20
    BPA caution in canned, 91
    brown or green lentils, 20
    canned versus home-cooked, 91
    cooking dried beans and lentils,
        19, 89–90
    green and yellow split peas, 21
    lentils and split peas for your
        pantry, 20–21
    protein in, 15
    red lentils, 20
    shopping for, 53
Becoming Vegan (Davis and
    Melina), 10, 12
BPA (bisphenol A), 91
breads, 43
    Ezekiel 4:9, 68
breakfast
    hot cereals, embellishments for,
        336–37
    hot cereals, whole-grain, and
        ways to serve them, 335–36
    sustaining breakfasts, choices
        for, 334–35
buckwheat noodles (soba), 207
bulgur, 112
buttery spread, vegan (Earth
    Balance), 39, 289, 337

calcium, 12–13
    best sources, 13
Campbell, T. Colin, 12
Campbell, Thomas M., 12
"carboholics," 10
cheese, nondairy, 11, 13, 42–43
    for hot cereal, 337

for pizza, 64, 179
shopping for, 53
storing, 40
children and plant-powered meals,
    62–65
    being persistent but not pushy
        with, 64–65
    "clean your plate" rule caution,
        64–65
    giving choices and teaching
        good decisions to, 62
    guideline: don't bargain, don't
        force, 63
    kid-friendly meals even adults
        can enjoy, 64
    letting them help with meal
        planning and preparation, 63
    not keeping foods in the house
        you don't want them to eat, 63
    taking to natural foods store or
        farm market with you, 62–63
    using subterfuge to hide foods
        for, 63–64
China Study, The (Campbell and
    Campbell), 12
chocolate, 344
coconut milk, 34
*Complete Idiot's Guide to Plant-
    Based Nutrition, The* (Hever),
    12
couscous, 113
CSA (community-supported
    agriculture) farms and farm
    markets, 4
    advantages of joining, 56–57
    website, 57

Davis, Brenda, 10, 12

Earthlings (film), 9
E. coli, 7
Efner, Heidi Rettig, 68–69
environmental issues and food
    animal agriculture and
        greenhouse gasses, 10
    animal waste problems, 9
    deforestation, 10

food security, 9
    GMO issues, 9
    pesticide use, 9
    toll of raising livestock, 10
Environmental Working Group
    (EWG), 58
    Clean Fifteen, 59
    Dirty Dozen Plus, 58
    Shopper's Guide to Pesticides,
        58
    website, 58
Evans, Rachel, 68

families or couples and main-
    taining a plant-powered diet
    finding common ground in, 66
    ground rules for at-home
        meals, 65
    having the courage of your
        convictions, 67
    plant-based eating as an
        opportunity to improve the
        family diet, 66–67
    respecting one another's
        choices, 65
farina, 336
farm markets, 55, 56
    CSA, 4, 56–57
    taking children with you, 62–63
fiber, dietary, 12
Food and Agriculture Organization
    (FAO) report, 10
Forks Over Knives (ed. Stone), 12
Fort, Kevin and Cindy, 49, 64
freezer staples, 43
fruits, dried, 25, 27
    for hot cereal, 336
    making a liquid sweetener
        from, 27
    nutritional content, 25
    preservative used in (sulfur
        dioxide), 25, 27
    types, 27
    uses of, 27
fruits, fresh, 37
    for countertop, 39
    farm markets, buying tips, 56

frozen, 43
for hot cereal, 336
for kids, versus vegetables, 65
organic, 57–58, 350
seasonal, 350

gluten-free foods
bean threads, 207
corn tortillas for lasagna, 163
cross-contamination issues, 156
pasta/pasta brands, 154, 156
pizza crust, 179, 181
rice vermicelli, 207
tortillas, 233, 240
wraps, 255
GMOs, 9
sweet corn, 59
grains, 39
calories per cup, 112
easy ways to dress up whole
grains, 114
list of staple grains, 21
nutritional content, 21, 112
protein in, 16
storing, 21, 23, 39
types to explore, 112–13
whole-grain hot cereals and
ways to serve them, 335–36
for your pantry, 21, 23
greens
bitter greens, 61
five easy ways to eat more,
60–61
kale, massaged, 60–61, 321
leafy spring, in salads, 61
nutritional content, 60
in smoothies and juices, 60
in stir-fries, 61
grits, 117, 336

health benefits (of a plant-based
diet), 3, 6–7
antibiotic resistance avoided, 7
cancer risk reduced, 6, 11
cholesterol levels lowered, 6
food-borne diseases reduced, 7
heart disease risk reduced, 6
longevity increased, 7
obesity and obesity-related
diseases reduced, 6–7
Heller, Ricki, 65

herbs, fresh, 29
herbs and spices, dried, 29–30
buying tips, 29
common, to keep on hand, 30
seasoning blends, 30
shopping for, 55
storing, 29
Hester, Kathy, 65
Hever, Julieanna, 12
honey, 28
Humane Society of the United
States website, 10

ice cream, nondairy, 43
Iden, Lee, Bruce, and family,
66–67
iron, 13
vitamin C with, 13

"junk-food vegans," 10

kale, massaged, 60–61, 321
Kaminsky, Hannah, 3, 29, 66, 73
Kanner, Ellen, 66
kitchen tools, 44–45
appliances for singles, 68–69
blender, high-speed, 60, 69
food processor, 44
immersion blender, 44
kitchen shears, 44
nut chopper or grinder, 45
pizza pan or pizza stone, 44
rice cooker, 68–69
salad spinner, 44–45
stir-fry pan, 44
tofu press, 45, 79
wire whisk or coated wire
whisk, 44

Laptop Lunches company, 340
Learning to Bake Allergen-Free
(Martin), 181
lemon or lime juice, 34–35
storing, 40
Listeria, 7
lunches, portable, for school and
office, 340–42
hearty salads, 341
hot soups, 341
portable sandwiches and
wraps, 340

school lunch tips and ideas for
kids and teens, 341–42

Main Street Vegan (Moran and
Moran), 12
make-ahead meals, top ten, 51–52
maple syrup, 28
marinara sauce, 35
Martin, Colette, 181
McCann, Jennifer, 340
meal planning basics and
strategies, 45–50
creating a seasonal repertoire,
50
developing a weekly repertoire,
49–50
keeping things simple, 50
make-ahead meals, top ten,
51–52
planning meals after going
shopping, 48–49
planning meals before going
shopping, 48
planning three full meals for
each week, 47–48
preparing a big one-pot or one-
pan meal, 49
preparing basics for the week
ahead, 48–49
stocking your refrigerator,
pantry, and freezer with basic
ingredients, 47
meat substitutes, 3, 78
tempeh bacon, 40
vegan sausages, 40
Melina, Vesanto, 10, 12
Messina, Virginia, 12
milks, nondairy, 11, 13, 42–43
almond, 42
coconut (canned), 34
hemp, 42
less common, 43
rice, 42
soy, 43
storing in the refrigerator, 39
millet, 113
miso, 207
molasses, 28
blackstrap or Barbados, 28
nutritional content, 28
Moran, Victoria and Adair, 12

MSG
 in bouillon and seasoning bases,
  120
 secret code words for, including
  "hydrolized," 120
myths about plant-based diets,
 10–12

natural foods store, 53–55
 taking children with you, 62–63
Nazarian, Sharon, 67, 68
New Becoming Vegetarian, The
 (Melina and Davis), 12
Norris, Jack, 12
nutritional analyses of recipes, 75
 note on cholesterol, 75
nutritional yeast, 13, 17, 40, 82
nuts and nut butters, 52
 calories per cup, 23
 for hot cereal, 336
 milks, 42
 nut chopper or grinder, 45
 nutritional content, 23, 25
 nuts to keep on hand, 23
 for occasional use, 25
 protein in, 16
 shopping for, 53–55
 storing, 23
 types of butters, 25
 for your pantry, 23–25

oats, 336
oils, 30–31
 canola, pros and cons, 31
 coconut oil, 31
 dark (or toasted) sesame oil, 31
 extra-virgin olive oil, 31
 peanut oil, 31
 safflower, 31
 sunflower, 31
 types good for stir-fries, 31
organic products
 cornmeal, 117
 EWG's Clean Fifteen, 59
 EWG's Dirty Dozen Plus, 58
 farm markets and, 56, 58
 produce, 57–58, 350
 USDA Organic designation, 56

pantry guide (staples to have on
 hand), 17–35

beans, canned and dried, 19
convenient foods versus
 convenience foods, 18
fruits, dried, 25
grains, 21, 23
herbs and spices, dried, 29–30
nuts, seeds, and their butters,
 23–25
oils, 30–31
optional items, 34–35
pastas and noodles, 33
produce for, 35, 37
for singles, 67
soy sauce, 32
sweeteners, natural, 27–29
tofu, silken, 33
tomato products, canned, 33
vinegars, 34
pasta, 33
 Asian noodles: a mini lexicon,
  207
 gluten-free, 156
 nutrition notes, 155
 protein in, 16
 types, 155–56
Peaceable Kingdom (film), 9
Physicians Committee for
 Responsible Medicine
 (PCRM), 11
 website, 11
pizza
 kid-friendly, 64
 pan or stone, 44
 vegan cheese for, 179
 Veg-Centric, 178–79
 whole-grain crust, frozen,
  43, 179
plant-based diet
 environmental considerations,
  8, 10
 ethics, 9
 health benefits, 3, 6–7
 hunger vs. feeling of fullness,
  10–11
 myths about, 10–12
 nutrition basics, 12–17
plant-powered table
 families and couples with mixed
  dietary preferences, 65–67
 getting kids on board, 62–65
 singles and, 67–69

polenta, 115, 336
Pollan, Michael, 4
potatoes, varieties, 299–300
produce: stocking up and storing,
 35–39
 countertop produce, 39
 extending the life of your
  refrigerated produce, 37
 in the pantry, 37
 in the refrigerator, 35, 37
 for singles, 68
protein, 10, 14–17
 in beans and legumes, 15
 in grains, 16
 miscellaneous sources, 17
 in nut butters, 16
 in nuts, 16
 in pastas, 16
 in quinoa, 21
 recommended RDA, 14
 in seeds, 16
 in soy milk, 43
 in tofu, tempeh, and seitan,
  15
 in vegetables, 17

quinoa
 basics, 98
 gluten-free pasta, 156
 protein in, 21
 for your pantry, 21

refrigerator staples (to have on
 hand)
 freezer staples, 43, 67
 nondairy milks, 42–43
 non-produce staples in deli
  drawer, 40–41
 non-produce staples in
  doors, 40
 non-produce staples on the
  shelves, 38
 produce for, 35, 37
rice
 basmati/basmati brands, 106,
  111
 brown rice basics, 104
 brown rice varieties, 104–5
 gluten-free pasta, 156
 nutrition notes, 104
 rice cooker, 68–69

vermicelli (mei fun or rice sticks), 207
rice milk, 42

Salmonella, 7
salsa, 35
storing opened, 39
seeds
for hot cereal, 336
milks, 42
most useful, 25
protein in, 16
shopping for, 53–55
storing, 23
storing perishable, 39
trio of superseeds, 25
for your pantry, 23–25
seitan, 15, 41, 200
Seventh-day Adventists, 7
shopping, 4, 52–59
CSA, advantages of joining, 56–57
farm markets, 55, 56
natural foods store, 53–55
organic produce, 57–58
tips, tried and true, 52
singles and a plant-based diet, 67–69
appliances for, 68–69
focusing on favorite fresh produce staples, 68
meal sharing, 68
stocking the pantry, 67
smoothies
greens in, 60
hiding ingredients in (for kids), 64
high-speed blender for, 60, 69
seasonal, 337
snacks
sampling of healthy, 343–44
trio of healthful chocolate treats, 344
sofrito, 108

soy and soy-products, 11
milk, 43
protein content, 15, 43
seitan, 15, 41, 200
soy protein isolate, 11, 52
soy sauce, 33
tempeh, 15, 41, 52, 200
tofu, 15, 33, 40–41, 52, 271–72, 307
standard American diet, 10
stir-fries
basics of, 196–97
stir-fry pan, 44
supplements
vegan multivitamin, 13
vitamin D, 13–14
sweeteners, natural, 27–29
agave nectar, 27–28
honey, 28
for hot cereal, 337
liquid, from dried fruit, 27
maple syrup, 28
molasses, 28
natural granulated sugar, 29
sweet potatoes, 302–3
nutritional content, 303
yams vs., 302

tempeh, 15, 41, 52, 200
Thai peanut satay sauce, 35
tofu, 52
baked, 41
extra-firm, 41, 271–72
shopping for, 53, 307
soft and firm, 40–41
storing, 40
tofu press, 45, 79
very dense, 307
tomato products, canned, 33
tortillas, choosing good, 233

vegan diet, 2, 3
agave nectar in, 27–28

author's family adoption of, 5
dairy milk eliminated from, 42
defined, 6
ethical vegans, 6
protein and, 14
vitamin D supplement awareness, 14
Vegan for Life (Norris and Messina), 12
Vegan Lunch Box (blog), 340
Vegan Soups and Hearty Stews for All Seasons (Atlas), 120
vegetables
for countertop, 39
farm markets, buying tips, 56
frozen, 43, 52
must-have, in refrigerator, 35
organic, 57–58
protein in, 16
seasonal and occasional veggies, 35
tips for roasted vegetable dishes, 288–89
Vegetariana (Atlas), 5
vegetarian diet, 3
author's adoption of, 4–5
defined, 6
lacto-ovo, 10
Vegucated (film), 9
vinegars, 34
vitamin B$_{12}$, 13, 17
vitamin C, 13
vitamin D, 13–14

wheat germ, 336
wraps
basics, 254–55
creating, 261–62
gluten-free, 255
lavash for, 255

yeast, nutritional, 13, 17, 40, 82